"Careful exegetical study and refined theological reflection ought always to be wedded by biblical scholar and theologian alike. Sadly, this union is less common than one might expect. But in Brian Vickers's *Jesus' Blood and Righteousness*, we see a careful and clear biblical exegesis joined to a richly refined theological reformulation displayed with beauty and grace. Vickers's work is sure to be one of the most significant contributions to the ongoing discussion of the nature both of the imputation of Christ's righteousness and of God's justification of the believer in Christ. The reader will be informed of the broad range of scholarly proposals on these issues and will be served well by the judicious judgments Vickers offers. While upholding a fully reformational understanding of imputation, his defense is altogether fresh, at times surprising, and everywhere filled with insight. For the sake of one's own soul, and for richer biblical and theological understanding, I commend to Christians that they read with care this excellent work."

    —BRUCE A. WARE

       Professor of Christian Theology,

       The Southern Baptist Theological Seminary

"The historic reformational doctrine of imputation is under serious duress in our day. Interestingly, it is often evangelical, Protestant, biblical studies scholars who have the doctrine in their sights. The critiques come from different angles, but almost all suggest that we've read imputation back into Paul, and that it's high time we understood and articulated Paul's theology more biblically. In order to do so, they say, we must reject the Protestant confessional formulations of imputation. Brian Vickers comes to our aid in this important discussion. He gives us a helpful survey of the trajectory of the doctrine in history—from Luther to N. T. Wright—and then engages in a vigorous exegetical and biblical theological defense of imputation. Arguing that imputation is not merely possible but a necessary synthesis of Paul's teaching, Vickers thoroughly analyzes the key passages of Romans 4:1-8; 5:12-21; and 2 Corinthians 5:21. He counters a reductionist/ minimalist reading of those texts and articulates instead a strong Pauline, biblical, theological argument for what we would call the traditional view of the imputation of Christ's righteousness. The book is accessible to any intelligent reader with an interest in theology, exegesis, and doctrine, but especially helpful to pastors, teachers, and seminarians. For all of us who are servants of the Word, we can ill afford indifference to this debate. If our evangelical forebears were right in their understanding of the Bible's teaching on the gracious and just divine salvation of sinners, it is the very stuff of the gospel. Vickers says they were right, and does a yeoman's service in this volume showing why."

    —J. LIGON DUNCAN III

       Chancellor and CEO,

       Reformed Theological Seminary, Jackson, Mississippi

D1478792

"Unfortunately, the Reformation doctrine of the imputation of Christ's righteousness is today a matter of debate, even among evangelicals. Brian Vickers, therefore, has performed a valuable service for the church by affirming imputation in *Jesus' Blood and Righteousness*. With great clarity Dr. Vickers bases his theological conclusions on careful, contextual study of the Scriptures. (This is so important today, when theology and exegesis often go their separate ways.) He correctly situates justification as a subset of union with Christ. Wisely, he does not overreach the evidence but makes a cumulative case for imputation based on a synthesis of the teaching of three passages—Romans 4:3; 5:19; and 2 Corinthians 5:21. In my judgment, his case succeeds. And he does all of this with a gentle spirit that refuses to demonize those who disagree with him. I heartily commend this volume as a needed, constructive, and helpful piece of theological exegesis."

> —ROBERT A. PETERSON
> Professor of Systematic Theology,
> Covenant Theological Seminary

"Integral to the Pauline understanding of salvation is the idea of imputation—not only of that of human sin to Christ, but also that of his righteousness to sinners. Yet, this doctrine has been somewhat neglected in recent years and in a number of evangelical quarters it is even being seriously questioned. Brian Vickers's study of what our evangelical forbears regarded as vital to the gospel is therefore a welcome study. He clearly demonstrates how it fits within the contours of Pauline theology and masterfully exegetes the pertinent texts on which the doctrine is founded. Highly recommended!"

> —MICHAEL A. G. HAYKIN
> Professor of Church History and Biblical Spirituality,
> The Southern Baptist Theological Seminary

"One rarely finds books today that display knowledge of church history, systematic theology, and biblical exegesis. Brian Vickers's contribution on imputation is a sterling exception, showing that the best biblical exegesis is informed by, but never captive to, historical and systematic theology. Too often discussions on imputation produce quarrels rather than understanding, but here we have a work that furnishes an exegetical basis for the Pauline teaching."

> —THOMAS R. SCHREINER
> James Buchanan Harrison Professor of New Testament,
> The Southern Baptist Theological Seminary

JESUS' BLOOD *AND* RIGHTEOUSNESS

JESUS' BLOOD *AND* RIGHTEOUSNESS

PAUL'S THEOLOGY OF IMPUTATION

BRIAN VICKERS

WHEATON, ILLINOIS

Cover design: Jon McGrath

Cover illustration: Getty Images

First printing 2006

Printed in the United States of America

ISBN-13: 978-1-58134-754-8
ISBN-10: 1-58134-754-5
ePub ISBN: 978-1-4335-1838-6
PDF ISBN: 978-1-4335-1520-0
Mobipocket ISBN: 978-1-4335-0828-8

Library of Congress Cataloging-in-Publication Data

Vickers, Brian J., 1966–
    Jesus' Blood and Righteousness: Paul's theology of Imputation /
Brian J. Vickers.
      p. cm.
    Includes bibliographical references and index.
    ISBN 13: 978-1-58134-754-8
    ISBN 10: 1-58134-754-5
    1. Righteousness. 2. Bible. N.T. Epistles of Paul—Theology.
3. Paul, the Apostle, Saint. I. Title.
BT764.3.V53   2006
234'.7—dc22   2006019337

Crossway is a publishing ministry of Good News Publishers.

LS   25   24   23   22   21   20   19   18   17   16   15

For Lloyd (1922-2004)
and Virginia Vickers

My son, keep thy father's commandment,
and forsake not the law of thy mother:
Bind them continually upon thine heart,
and tie them about thy neck.
When thou goest, it shall lead thee;
when thou sleepest, it shall keep thee;
and when thou awakest, it shall talk with thee.

Proverbs 6:20-22 (kjv)

Contents

Partial List of Abbreviations

2 Bar.	*2 Baruch (Syriac Apocalypse)*
AB	Anchor Bible
ABD	*Anchor Bible Dictionary*
AV	Authorized Version
BDAG	Danker, F. W., W. Bauer, W. F. Arndt, and F. W. Gingrich. *Greek-English Lexicon of the New Testament and Other Early Christian Literature.* 3rd ed.
BDB	Brown F., S. R. Driver, and C. A. Briggs. *A Hebrew and English Lexicon of the Old Testament*
BDF	Blass F., A. Debrunner, and R. W. Funk. *A Greek Grammar of the New Testament and Other Early Christian Literature*
BECNT	Baker Exegetical Commentary on the New Testament
CBQ	*Catholic Biblical Quarterly*
EvT	*Evangelische Theologie*
ICC	International Critical Commentary
JBL	*Journal of Biblical Literature*
JSNT	*Journal for the Study of the New Testament*
Jub.	*Jubilees*
LSJ	Liddell, H. G., R. Scott, H. S. Jones. *A Greek-English Lexicon.* 9th ed.
MeyerK	Meyer H. A. W., Kritischexegetischer Kommentar über das Neue Testament
NCB	New Century Bible
NICNT	New International Commentary on the New Testament
NICOT	New International Commentary on the Old Testament
NTS	*New Testament Studies*

NTTS	New Testament Tools and Studies
Odes Sol.	*Odes of Solomon*
Pss. Sol.	*Psalms of Solomon*
WBC	Word Biblical Commentary
WTJ	*Westminster Theological Journal*
ZAW	*Zeitschrift für die alttestamentliche Wissenschaft*

PREFACE

SOMETIMES A PHONE CALL can change your life. I was a Ph.D. student working happily away in preparation for a dissertation on the letter to the Hebrews when one day I pressed the button on our answering machine. A familiar voice said, "I want to tell you something that will change your life"—a dramatic message to say the least. Ultimately it took three days to get the life-changing message. One can think a lot of things in three days, though admittedly as more time went by I began to doubt just how radical this life change could really be if the delivery of the message could be postponed indefinitely. Finally, after several missed phone calls and a twenty-four hour virus, I was home when the phone rang. There was a pause, no hello, and then I heard, "You should work on imputation." It was my then supervisor and now colleague, Tom Schreiner. To make a long story short, that phone call resulted in a dissertation, and that dissertation later resulted in this book. It was, at least on one level, a phone call that changed my life.

Though I was working on Hebrews, I had been studying justification and related topics in Paul and tracking with the ongoing debates since my days as a graduate student at Wheaton College. In my own thinking, however, there were lots of loose ends. I needed some time to work on the issues. Writing a dissertation provided the time I needed. It also led to the writing of this book, something I doubt I would have done were it not for that phone call.

Maybe the phrase "changed my life" is a bit too dramatic, but the months and years spent writing the dissertation were formative in my own thinking and experience. The dissertation informed my thinking because my thoughts had time to solidify as I studied and restudied the relevant texts, and as I read and often reread (at least some of) the mountains of secondary literature. It shaped my experience because in the final months of writing, my father, Lloyd Vickers, was diagnosed with cancer, and as I wrote, he fought. Yet he did not fight in desperation, even though the prognosis never got better than a hope of a slight prolonging of weeks, perhaps months. After the initial shock, he faced cancer with confidence—not confidence that he would "beat it," but confidence that came from resting, as he put it, "only in Jesus and all he has done for me." My dad was resting in the imputation of Christ's righteousness in the face of a disease that was quickly ending his life. He lived to see me finish a dissertation and watch me be hooded. Just under four months later, right after finding out that I was hired to teach New Testament, he died, clinging more than ever to Jesus and his righteousness. It dawned on me later how my thesis topic and my Dad's battle with cancer had dovetailed. I was working on the topic that sustained him and gave him hope and confidence in the face of the last enemy; the defeated enemy. In my dad's life and in his death I witnessed the doctrine of imputation in action.

Like all books, this book could not have been written without the encouragement and assistance of many people. First of all, heart-felt thanks to my friend and colleague Tom Schreiner. Tom was always quick to give his insights, suggestions, corrections, and encouragements. Tom not only read the dissertation, he has gladly read parts of this book, whether new, old, or revised. Bruce Ware and Shawn Wright also deserve a special note of appreciation. Both were an encouragement to me as I pursued the possibility of publishing this work and helpful to me because of their keen theological and historical insights. Thanks also to Jim Hamilton for his friendship and for his remarkable ability to rejoice in the Lord at all times and to give thanks in all things.

Special thanks go to Matthew Anderson, who converted all the Greek fonts in my manuscript, and to John Meade who helped with reading the manuscript in its final stages.

My mother, Virginia, though living with the loss of her companion of sixty-one years, continues on with a resilience that flows from her indomitable view of life under the sovereignty of God. Her wit and wisdom are untarnished as she turns eighty this year. Her ability to tell her son what he needs to hear, even if he does not want to hear it, is invaluable.

Finally, no one can compare to my lovely wife, Denise. She is a gift from God and a constant source of strength and joy in all things. Jamie, our daughter, could not have a better model of faith, hope, and love.

INTRODUCTION

"I'M SO THANKFUL FOR the active obedience of Christ; no hope without it."[1] One day before his death, J. Gresham Machen sent this message to John Murray. This one short phrase is theologically loaded. "The active obedience of Christ" means the obedience that Jesus rendered to the Father during his incarnation, and which, along with the forgiveness that flows from his sacrifice on the cross, is imputed to the believer by faith. When we sing "My hope is built on nothing less than Jesus' blood *and* righteousness," we are singing about the same thing that Machen wrote to Murray. In theology, a conjunction can be extraordinarily important.

The "active obedience of Christ," just like the short phrase *"and* righteousness," is a statement about what it means to be justified. In much of both the Calvinist and Lutheran traditions, the active obedience of Christ is a vital component in the doctrine of justification.[2] Specifically, the doctrine of justification is formulated so as to include both the non-imputation of sin (forgiveness) and the imputation of Christ's righteousness (his active obedience). The latter aspect, namely that justification must necessarily include the imputation of Christ's righteousness, draws the lion's share of controversy.

The debate over imputation is not a mere academic debate. The discussion strikes at the heart of what it means to be right with God. Core biblical themes like forgiveness, sacrifice, and union with Christ

---

[1] J. Gresham Machen, *God Transcendent*, ed. Ned B. Stonehouse, (Edinburgh; Carlisle, PA: Banner of Truth), 14. The quotation appears in Stonehouse's introduction. In this collection of Machen's essays there is a chapter entitled "The Active Obedience of Christ" that summarizes the essential content of the traditional view of imputation in simple terms (ibid., 187-96). Readers not familiar with the topic may want to consult Machen's essay for a brief, pastoral introduction.

[2] I recognize that there is a great deal of debate over whether there is continuity or discontinuity between Calvin and Luther and the traditions that bear their names. That is not the issue here. This investigation is not concerned primarily with how doctrine has developed within these traditions (though that issue does surface in the section on historical background below) but with how representative theologians have dealt with the imputation of Christ's righteousness.

are woven into the doctrine of imputation. There is more at stake than merely continuing a debate. What is the connection between Adam and the human race? How did Christ fulfill the role of the second or new Adam? How can the "ungodly" stand before a righteous God? Is faith itself, or the object of faith, the foundation for righteousness? These are but a few of the questions related to the topic of imputation. At the center of the debate over the imputation of Christ's righteousness is the interpretation of key Pauline texts.

"KEY" TEXTS

The main goal of this book is to investigate Pauline texts linked histori-cally to the topic of imputation.[3] The bulk of this investigation is driven by a consideration of three general questions: (1) In Romans 4 when Paul quotes Genesis 15:6, "Abraham believed God and it was reckoned to him as righteousness" (v. 3), and shortly thereafter quotes Psalm 32:2, "blessed is the man against whom the Lord does not reckon sin" (v. 8), what is the implication for the doctrine of imputation? More to the point, does Romans 4 create a tension for the traditional view of imputation since the emphasis there seems to be primarily on forgive-ness? (2) Does the parallel and antithesis between Adam and Christ in Romans 5:12-21 imply that Paul understands that Christ not only pro-vided pardon for Adam's (and his posterity's) sin *but also*, in contrast to Adam, fulfilled God's commands thus providing a positive status for "the many who will be made righteous"? (3) Does Paul's statement in 2 Corinthians 5:21, "God made him who knew no sin to be sin for us that in him we might become the righteousness of God" (which, according to Paul, includes the non-imputation of sin, "God was reconciling the world to himself in Christ, not reckoning their trespasses against them" [5:19]), also include the imputation of righteousness? In the history of the debate these are the primary issues discussed in these texts.

Once these three texts are identified as the central texts in the debate, a rather common-sense observation arises: In these three "impu-tation" texts, Paul deals with different, albeit related, issues. Romans

---

[3] The terms *imputation, impute, reckon,* and *count* are used interchangeably throughout this work. This decision is not driven by any particular theological bias or presupposition. Although the word *impute* may appear theologically loaded to some, it is treated here as synonymous with *reckon* and *count.*

5:19 is not simply another way of putting Romans 4:3, and 2 Corinthians 5:21 is not a restatement of either Romans 4:3 or 5:19. In other words, the three imputation texts do not appear to be about the exact same thing. In each text Paul discusses similar ideas (e.g., righteousness, sin, God, and/or Christ) but the texts are not the same. There are different subjects, actors, actions, and concepts. For instance, there is an emphasis on "faith" in Romans 4:3 but no explicit mention of it in either Romans 5:19 or 2 Corinthians 5:21. In Romans 5:19 obedience is at the core of Paul's discussion, but obedience is not at all the emphasis in Romans 4:3 and even if "knew no sin" in 2 Corinthians 5:21 implies Christ's obedience, it is still not the primary focus as it is in Romans 5:19. This observation regarding the differences between the key texts plays a major role throughout this book.

Secondly, there are other texts that have both textual and conceptual links to the "key" texts and have also played a role in the historical debates. These other texts (i.e., 1 Cor. 1:30; Phil. 3:9; and Rom. 9:30–10:4) are presented along with the "key" texts in an attempt to develop a Pauline synthesis regarding the doctrine of imputation. These texts are essential for understanding Paul's theology of imputation. The goal here is to focus as narrowly as possible on the issues in these texts that link them with the doctrine of imputation and present a kind of "synoptic" reading of these texts along with the "key" texts.

Finally, part of the goal of this work is to try to avoid the two extremes that too often characterize the debate. On one hand defenders of imputation, because of a healthy desire to know and understand the whole counsel of God, sometimes ignore the differences between, and subsequently the unique contribution of, the texts typically associated with the doctrine. When this happens the biblical texts are flattened out and become mere springboards for lectures and sermons on the doctrine of imputation.

On the other hand, critics of the doctrine, rightly concerned about eisegesis (reading into rather than from a text), often miss the connections not only between the major texts but between the texts and a larger biblical-theological framework. Ironically, critics often end up doing the very thing that defenders of imputation often do—they expect too much from a single text, and when they find (as they inevitably will) that the entire doctrine of imputation in the traditional sense is not in Romans

4:1-8 or 2 Corinthians 5:16-21, they pass the doctrine off as just so much "systematic theology" and pronounce imputation dead on arrival.

The truth, as someone once said, is somewhere in the middle. The traditional doctrine of imputation is not theology apart from exegesis, nor does one have to subscribe to one particular theological presupposition before accepting imputation. At the same time, no historical doctrine was ever established, or denied, on the basis of one text alone. Though a great deal of time will be spent on the particulars of each text, one eye will be kept on the broader biblical horizon. Imputation, like other doctrines of Scripture, must be investigated exegetically and synthetically. The contention of this book is that the imputation of Christ's righteousness is a legitimate and necessary synthesis of Paul's teaching. While no single text contains or develops all the "ingredients" of imputation, the doctrine stands as a component of Paul's soteriology.

THEOLOGY AND HISTORY

Although this work deals primarily with the New Testament, specifically, New Testament theology, the nature of the topic demands inquiry into areas typically associated with historical and systematic theology. The reason for this is twofold: (1) the doctrine of imputation formally arose in Protestant confessional settings; and (2) the most comprehensive treatments of the doctrine appear in works written by Protestant systematic theologians. Contrary to the opinion of some biblical scholars, the fact that "imputation" is closely associated with confessional and systematic theology does not make it off limits, or illegitimate, for biblical scholarship. In addition, it should be kept in mind that confessional statements and systematic theologies are usually based on the reading of biblical texts.[4]

While some readers may think that this book belongs in the realm of systematic rather than biblical theology, a clear distinction remains between true systematics and the type of work found here. The clearest differences are in method and arrangement. Rather than moving along and organizing on synthetic lines, the pattern will be to move along

---

[4] I hope, as a corollary goal, to confirm that contrary to some modern caricatures, Protestant theology, particularly the Reformed tradition, has not been dominated only by systematicians who cared little for exegesis.

through the exegesis and interpretation of a selected number of biblical texts, then weighing the evidence. Even if systematic theology provides a jumping off point, the majority of the work is exegetical. After the work is done, then we will move on to a synthesis of Paul's teaching on imputation.

Although I have included a fair amount of historical and systematic theology, I have tried, for the most part, to stay above the historical debates, choosing rather to include, usually in notes, the main ideas that have characterized the historical discussion and the various presuppositions that lie behind it. Not the least of my reasons is that I make no claim to be an expert in a large part of the history discussed in the first chapter. I am not setting forth a comprehensive study of imputation in the theology of, say, Luther or Calvin, but rather focusing on places where their work helps build historical-theological trajectories that aid in presenting a streamlined view of the history of the doctrine. It is my hope that others will perhaps follow some of these trajectories and do what I am not able to do in the scope of this work. In sum, the historical chapter is intended to (1) frame my discussion by providing a way to move back and forth between history and the exegesis that comprises the bulk of this book, and to (2) provide readers, especially those not familiar with the historical aspect of the question, with a context for understanding the breadth of the topic of imputation.[5]

DRAWING BOUNDARIES

The subject of imputation lends itself to the discussion of a variety of exegetical, biblical, theological, linguistic, and historical issues and questions. The intention is to proceed with as narrow a focus as such a broad topic will allow. If we paused all along the way for thorough discussions or definitive answers to every question or explorations of every connection, the book would not only exceed the allotted page limit, but also

---

[5] I have obviously biased my historical interaction toward the Reformed tradition. There are two reasons for this. The first is that imputation, as it is typically formulated, is a consistent and vital tenet of Reformed theology, so it only makes sense to interact with sources from that tradition. The second reason is that my own background and relative level of expertise lie in the Reformed traditions. Since this is not a book on historical-theology, I thought it best to stay as close as possible to the tradition with which I am most familiar. For those interested in the type of work that has influenced the method and goal of this book, see Richard B. Gaffin, Jr, "Systematic and Biblical Theology," *WTJ* 38 (1976): 281-99.

try the patience of even the most determined reader. For instance, even though this work focuses on the imputation of righteousness, it does not present a thorough linguistic discussion of the biblical language of righteousness. Rather than retrace the disputed question of "righteousness" in Paul, the discussion of righteous/righteousness in the relevant texts is determined by their immediate contexts, with particular attention given to the pivotal phrases, "reckoned as righteous," "made righteous," and "become . . . righteous." To take but one other example, the theme of union with Christ plays an important role later in this study, but that theme is not presented in anything like an exhaustive treatment. Rather, it is limited to how it functions in texts associated with imputation. Secondly, this topic has vast amounts of historical background not only in the areas of historical and systematic theology, but also in the history of both Old Testament and New Testament interpretation, and all of the "key texts" are accompanied by extensive secondary literature on any number of exegetical topics and debates. Care has been taken to consider only those aspects of exegesis that have direct bearing on imputation. The goal is primarily to investigate the texts in Paul most closely associated with imputation, keeping an eye on the history of interpretation and sticking as close as possible to those issues in the texts that directly speak to the topic. Finally, there is no section in this book devoted to a study of the "New Perspective" on Paul. There are many studies on the New Perspective, so rather than simply repeat what can be easily read in various other sources, the scholars associated (to various degrees) with the New Perspective are dealt with when appropriate in the course of interpreting biblical texts.[6]

---

[6] Works on or about the New Perspective abound increasingly. For readers already possessing knowledge of the debate and who want to pursue both the background and the technical aspects of the central issues, the clear choice is the set of volumes edited by D.A. Carson, Peter T. O'Brien, and Mark A. Seifrid: *Justification and Variegated Nomism*, vol. 1, *The Complexities of Second Temple Judaism* (Grand Rapids: Baker, 2001), and *Justification and Variegated Nomism*, vol. 2, *The Paradoxes of Paul* (Grand Rapids: Baker, 2004). These volumes stand out because the debate over the New Perspective is essentially a debate that begins with the reading of Second Temple Jewish literature. For analysis and engagement of the various streams of the New Perspective, and an exegetical/theological study of Paul's theology of justification, one cannot do better than to read Stephen Westerholm, *Perspectives Old and New on Paul: The "Lutheran" Paul and his Critics* (Grand Rapids: Eerdmans, 2004). For an overall introduction to the New Perspective that does not assume prior knowledge and that carefully and fairly sets forth the various proponents of the New Perspective and responds to them accordingly, see Guy Prentiss Waters, *Justification and the New Perspectives on Paul: A Review and Response* (Phillipsburg, NJ: Presbyterian and Reformed, 2004).

A NOTE TO THE READER

There is in places a fair amount of Greek and Hebrew. I have not transliterated the languages. The reason is simple: I know few, if any people, who actually find transliterations helpful, much less people who can read them. Moreover, people who do not read Hebrew or Greek are not made to do so by transliterations. Essentially all it does is introduce two additional foreign languages into the text. It may *look* a bit more like English, but in reality it is not English nor is it Greek or Hebrew. I have provided translations and I have tried to keep the languages in the text only when I thought it was helpful for readers who might want to see the text, phrase, or word for themselves.

ONE

Tracing Trajectories: The History of Imputation

THE DOCTRINE OF IMPUTATION is not, historically speaking, cut and dry. This may come as a surprise to some readers since lately we are used to hearing that someone either affirms or denies imputation. Like most things, it all has to do with how we define our terms. The term "imputation," is a fairly specific, almost technical term for the traditional Reformed view of justification consisting of the forgiveness of sins and the counting of Christ's active obedience (his positive righteousness) to the believer. We cannot, however, limit ourselves historically only to those authors who use the word "imputation." For this reason, if we want to do justice to the historical background, the best way to approach the subject is to focus as much as possible on the interpretation of the texts commonly associated with imputation. When we come at imputation from this angle, we can interact not only with those who hold explicitly to the traditional doctrine, but also with theologians who hold a more-or-less traditional view but do not use the word "imputation." We can also interact with those who seem to avoid the term because they want to discuss the texts apart from "systematic" categories, and with those who do not so much deny imputation as seem not to have it on their horizon at all, and also with those who reject the doctrine outright. The best way to get started in the discussion is to follow loose trajectories through theological traditions. Along the way we will hear not only from well-known theologians, but also at times from some lesser-known scholars whose work sheds light on the various debates in our own day.

REFORMATION TRAJECTORIES

Luther

There is considerable debate over Luther's teaching on imputation, or whether he held to anything like the later Reformed and Lutheran understanding of the doctrine.[1] Though such a discussion runs the risk of asking anachronistic questions, it is essential that we consider Luther in the debate. While it is difficult to see in Luther a developed idea of both the negative and positive elements of imputation, as spelled out so precisely in later Lutheran and Reformed theology, the selections included here contain some of the necessary elements of the later formulation.

Imputation language is prevalent in Luther's treatment of Romans 4:1-8. This is hardly surprising, since Paul's argument hinges on the quotation from Genesis 15:6, "Abraham believed God and God reckoned it to him as righteousness." For instance, Luther asserts that people "are righteous only when God imputes righteousness to them."[2] Believers are righteous "outwardly" (i.e., in the eyes of God), "solely by the imputation of God and not of ourselves or of our own works."[3] A central element of Luther's view of righteousness is his understanding of believers being equally righ-

---

[1] Imputation, like nearly everything else in Luther, is subject to a debate characterized by diametrically opposite conclusions. For instance, Alistair McGrath states that "The origins of the concept of 'imputed righteousness,' so characteristic of Protestant theologies of justification after the year 1530, may . . . be considered to lie with Luther" (*Iustitia Dei: A History of the Christian Doctrine of Justification*, 2nd ed., [Cambridge: Cambridge University Press, 1998], 201). Conversely, Stephen Strehle argues that "Luther and his theology cannot be considered its [imputation] primary inspiration, even if the doctrine comes to be interpreted within his thought. Luther, in fact, considered it most improper to so accentuate divine *imputatio*—a term which he also connects with nominalism—as to turn God's work into 'eyn lautter spiegelfechten und tauckelspiell'" (Strehle, "Imputatio Iustitiae: Its Origin in Melanchthon, its Opposition in Osiander," *Theologische Zeitschrift* 50 [1994], 205). Luther's phrase is translated, "mere mockery and deception." This translation is from Martin Luther's sermon "New Year's Day," in *Luther's Epistle Sermons: Advent and Christmas Season*, vol. 1, in *Luther's Complete Works*, vol. 7, trans. John Nicholas Lenker (Minneapolis: Luther Press, 1908), 283. While this debate is interesting, and important, it is not within the purpose of this work, nor the expertise of the writer, to delve into it in detail. Certain specific issues will be noted, but this section will follow the general method, as stated above, of showing representative selections from Luther's writings in which he discusses imputation or from the texts that are most commonly connected to the doctrine.

[2] Martin Luther, *Epistola beati Pauli apostoli ad Romanos incipit*, WA 56 (1938), 268, trans. Walter G. Tillmanns (chaps. 1–2) and Jacob A. O. Preus (chaps. 3–16) under the title *Lectures on Romans*, in Luther's Works [*LW*], vol. 25, ed. Hilton C. Oswald (St. Louis: Concordia, 1972), 256. Unless otherwise indicated, translations are taken from *LW*.

[3] Martin Luther, *Epistola beati Pauli apostoli ad Romanos incipit*, WA 56: 268-69, trans. Tillmanns and Preus, *LW* 25: 257. Here Luther uses the term *reputare*, following the Vulgate in Romans 4:3, 5. In 4:4, 8 the Vulgate has *imputare*. Bernhard Lohse notes the debate that has taken place in regard to Luther's use of these terms, and the influence of both Occam and Augustine. Without diminishing these influences, Lohse maintains that Luther's main influence was the text itself (*Martin Luther's Theology: Its Historical and Systematic Developments* Minneapolis: Fortress, 1999), 261.

teous (before God) and unrighteous (in their own eyes). He can even say that "in their [believers'] own sight and in truth they are unrighteous, but before God they are righteous because He reckons them so because of their confession of sin."[4] The emphasis here is on the continuance of sin in the lives of believers even though God has imputed righteousness to them.[5]

A second emphasis, and important for the issue at hand, is the central role of forgiveness. Luther's discussion of this text clearly focuses on the connection between the imputation of righteousness and forgiveness. It is indeed the righteousness of Christ that is in view here, but Luther speaks specifically of Christ's righteousness that covers sin.[6] This covering righteousness of Christ does not inhere in the believer but lies outside; it is imputed to the believer.[7] There is no emphasis given to Christ's fulfillment of the law which in turn is imputed to the believer.[8] At least in his interpretation of Romans 4:1-8, Luther does not view the imputation of righteousness and the non-imputation of sin as two distinct

---

[4] Martin Luther, *Epistola beati Pauli apostoli ad Romanos incipit*, WA 56: 269; trans. Tillmanns and Preus, *LW* 25: 258. He continues: "They are actually sinners, but they are righteous by the imputation of a merciful God" (ibid.). Soon after this comes Luther's famous "sick patient" illustration: "It is similar to the case of a sick man who believes the doctor who promises him a sure recovery and in the meantime obeys the doctor's order in the hope of the promised recovery and abstains from those things which have been forbidden him, so that he may in no way hinder the promised return to health or increase his sickness until the doctor can fulfill his promise to him. Now is this sick man well? The fact is that he is both sick and well at the same time. He is sick in fact, but he is well because of the sure promise of the doctor, whom he trusts and who has reckoned him as already cured because he is sure that he will cure him; for he has already begun to cure him and no longer reckons unto him a sickness unto death" (ibid., 260). Similar ideas will later draw the accusation that justification, in the traditional Protestant formulation, amounts to a "legal fiction" (the accusation is used broadly against the traditional idea of justification as chiefly forensic—as summed up succinctly in Luther's formulation, *simul iustus et peccator* ("at once righteous and a sinner"). That is, so the accusation goes, God declares someone "just" who, to use Luther's words, "in truth" is not just. This accusation continues down to this day. As will be discussed later, this accusation cannot be supported in light of the eschatological unfolding of redemptive history in Scripture and because of the believer's union with Christ.

[5] Ibid., 272, trans. Tillmans and Preus, *LW* 25: 260. Interpreting the quote from Psalm 32 (Rom. 4:7-8), Luther says that the "blessed" man is he "who through grace is made free from the burden of his offense, that is, of the sin which he actually committed. But this is not enough, unless at the same time he 'is covered in regard to his sin,' that is, his root evil is not imputed to him as sin" (ibid., 265).

[6] Like Ruth at the feet of Boaz (Ruth 3:7), "the soul lays itself down at Christ's humanity and is covered with His righteousness." Here Luther is speaking of "covered" in relation to Psalm 32:1 "Blessed is the man whose transgressions are forgiven, whose sin is *covered*" (ibid, 267).

[7] It is only through "faith and hope" in Christ that righteousness in any sense belongs to the believer; faith and hope in something outside himself, i.e., the righteousness of Christ. "[T]hey [the saints] know that there is sin in them but that for the sake of Christ it is covered and is not imputed to them, so that they may declare that all their good is outside of them, in Christ, who yet through faith is also in them" (ibid.).

[8] The only mention of fulfilling the law is in regard to the impossibility of fulfilling the law except by grace (ibid., 262). This mention occurs when Luther takes exception at the view of sin and grace held by the "scholastic theologians." Thus in this text, the positive fulfillment of the law is spoken of only in terms of the believer's absolute need of grace to fulfill the law. See also, *LW* 25: 266.

elements but rather as synonymous concepts. Commenting on Psalm 32:1-2, Luther says: "Thus the man to whom these two evils (evil deeds and sin) are forgiven, behold, he is the man whom God regards as righteous. Hence it follows, 'Blessed is the man to whom the LORD imputes no iniquity.'" Luther adds: "It is the same thing, whether we say, "to whom God imputes righteousness' or, 'to whom the LORD does not impute sin,' that is, unrighteousness."[9] Thus God imputing a person as righteous is, in this text, *the same thing* as God forgiving a person's sin.

Commenting on Romans 5:12, Luther emphasizes that sin "enters into men" even though "they do not commit it."[10] Thus while the imputation of Adam's sin to the human race is implied, as Luther continues through the passage the imputation of Christ's righteousness in terms of his active obedience is less obvious. When, however, Luther comes to 5:14, he states that "the likeness of Adam's transgression is in us because we die as if we had sinned in the same way he did. And the likeness of Christ's justification is in us, because we live, as if we had produced the same kind of righteousness that he did."[11]

He goes on to say that the gift, "by the grace of that one Man" (5:15), is "by the personal merit and grace of Christ."[12] Luther's use of the term "merit," and his statement that when we are justified it is "as if" we ourselves had done "the same kind of righteousness," bear similarities with the later Protestant formulations of the imputation of positive righteousness, but we must be careful not to import all the later distinctions back into Luther.

The same tendency to come short of asserting positive imputation explicitly is seen also in Luther's other writings.[13] For instance, in *"Two Kinds of Righteousness,"* Luther states that, "through faith . . . Christ's righteousness becomes our righteousness and all that he has becomes ours, rather he himself becomes ours."[14] Here the emphasis on Christ's

---

[9] Ibid., 272.

[10] Ibid., 301.

[11] Ibid., 305, 317.

[12] Ibid., 306, 318.

[13] This is not to imply that Luther himself failed to formulate adequately his doctrine of justification to include the imputation of positive righteousness. It merely means that Luther, for whatever reason, and regardless of how "close" he comes, does not formulate the idea with the *same* precision that would later be evident in both Lutheran and Reformed Protestantism.

[14] Martin Luther, *Sermo de duplici iustitia*, WA 2 (1884): 146, trans. Lowell J. Satre under the title *Two Kinds of Righteousness*, in *LW* 31, *The Career of the Reformer: I*, ed. Harold J. Grimm (Philadelphia: Mulenberg, 1957), 298.

righteousness becoming ours is thought of more in terms of union than imputation. More accurately, Luther's concept of imputation is tied closely to his understanding of union. Luther goes on to say that "he who trusts in Christ exists in Christ; he is one with Christ, having the same righteousness as he."[15] Again, as in Romans, Luther emphasizes the "alien" nature of this righteousness we have in Christ—it is Christ in us that is our righteousness, not anything that we have, even as gift, that becomes intrinsically our own.[16]

Similarly, in *"The Freedom of the Christian,"* it is union with Christ that Luther emphasizes:

> By the wedding ring of faith he [Christ] shares in the sins, death, and pains of hell which are his bride's. As a matter of fact he makes them his own and acts as if they were his own as if he himself had sinned; he suffered, died, and descended into hell that he might overcome them all. . . . Thus the believing soul by means of the pledge of its faith is free in Christ, its bridegroom, free of all sins, secure against death and hell, and is endowed with the eternal rights, life, and salvation of Christ its bridegroom.[17]

Note that Luther does emphasize the imputation of sins to Christ, but he is more apt to emphasize forgiveness (as evident above) and union with Christ, rather than the imputation of positive righteousness.[18]

---

[15] Ibid. Luther's language here appears somewhat enigmatic in terms of what union with Christ means, but the idea is that we are righteous only "in Christ." He goes on to say, "This righteousness is primary; it is the basis, the cause, the source of all our own actual righteousness. For this is the righteousness given in place of the original righteousness lost in Adam. It accomplishes the same as that original righteousness would have accomplished; rather, it accomplishes more" (ibid., 298-99). One might say that for Luther, Christ's righteousness is imputed in so far as the believer is in union with Christ; thus, the believer is counted righteous in Christ in that he has a real share in Christ's righteousness (though not in terms of his actual person, or essence, as Osiander thought). As Luther says in another place: "Unquestionably Christ is given to us in a way that makes his righteousness, all he is and all he has, stand as our surety; he becomes our own" (Martin Luther, "New Year's Day," 288).

[16] "[T]his alien righteousness, instilled in us without our works by grace alone—while the Father, to be sure, inwardly draws us to Christ—is set opposite original sin, likewise alien, which we acquire without our works by birth alone. Christ daily drives out the old Adam more and more in accordance with the extent to which faith and knowledge of Christ grow. For alien righteousness is not instilled all at once, but it begins, makes progress, and is finally perfected at the end through death" (Luther, *Sermo de duplici iustitia*, 299).

[17] Martin Luther, *De libertate Christiana*, WA 7 (1897): 55, trans. W. A. Lambert and rev. Harold J. Grimm under the title *The Freedom of the Christian*, in *LW* 31, I: 352.

[18] The doctrine of union with Christ in Luther's theology has received renewed interest as a result of the work of Finnish scholars. Referring to the "breakthrough" in Luther studies, pioneered by Tuomo Mannermaa, Braaten and Jenson state: "Mannermaa's key idea is that 'in faith itself Christ is really present," a literal translation of Luther's '*in ipsa fide Christus adestd.*' This idea is played off against a purely forensic concept of justification, in which the *Christus pro nobis* (Christ for us) is separated

In a sermon on Galatians 3 Luther says in regard to imputation that "it is of pure grace that God reckons not to us our sins, yet he would not so forgive were not his Law and his standard of righteousness already completely satisfied."[19] Here the fulfillment of the law and imputation are linked although, again, the emphasis is on the resulting forgiveness. Here, however, the imputation of a positive righteousness is explicit. This is particularly true in regard to the law being fulfilled on our behalf. Luther develops this idea further when he states: "It is impossible for us to purchase forgiveness; God ordained in our stead one who took upon himself all our deserved punishment and fulfilled the Law for us, thus averting from us God's judgment and appeasing his wrath."[20] Here the language is quite similar sounding to later Protestant teaching. Jesus, in our place, bears our sin and obeys the law of God on our behalf, with the result that God's justice is met and we are free from his wrath.

It seems, then, that Luther does indeed understand justification as including both forgiveness and the imputation of Christ's obedience to God's "standard of righteousness." What we see in Luther may not be the same explicit, systematic formulation of imputation that marks later Protestantism, but the raw material, so to speak, is there. We do need to recognize the primary role of forgiveness in Luther's theology of justification, but this emphasis is hardly surprising since Luther was facing

---

from the *Christus in nobis* (Christ within us). . . . Righteousness as an attribute of God in Christ cannot be separated from his divine being. Thus, Luther found it appropriate to say that through faith in Christ a real exchange occurs, the righteousness of God in exchange for the sinfulness of human beings. The righteousness of God that is ours by faith is therefore a real participation in the life of God. This seems to come close to what the Orthodox understand by deification and *theosis*" (Carl Braaten and Philip Jenson, *Union with Christ: The New Finnish Interpretation of Luther* [Grand Rapids: Eerdmans, 1998], viii). Mannermaa himself describes his interpretation in the following: "The indwelling of Christ as grasped in the Lutheran tradition implies a real participation in God, and it corresponds in a special way to the Orthodox doctrine of participation in God, namely, *theosis*. . . . According to Luther, Christ (in both his person and his work) is present in faith and through this presence is identical with the righteousness of faith. Thus the notion that Christ is present in the Christian occupies a much more central place in the theology of Luther than in the Lutheranism subsequent to him. The idea of a divine life in Christ who is really present in faith lies at the very center of the theology of the Reformer." Tuomo Mannermaa, "Why is Luther so Fascinating? Modern Finnish Luther Research" (in Braaten and Jenson, *Union with Christ*, 2).

I include this lengthy citation for three reasons: (1) the "exchange" motif in Luther is usually thought of as arguing for some kind of traditional understanding of imputation; (2) the idea of the believer actually participating in the life of God sounds somewhat similar to the idea set forth by Osiander but disputed by Melanchthon, Chemnitz, Calvin, and others, namely, that justification includes the believer experiencing Christ in his essence in union with him; and (3) as will be readily apparent below, many arguments against the traditional idea of imputation derive from a de-emphasis of the forensic nature of justification.

[19] Martin Luther, "New Year's Day," 284.
[20] Ibid., 294.

issues such as the Roman Catholic view of the propitiation of divine wrath through penance.[21] Perhaps this is the background for Luther's statement that "it is impossible for us to purchase forgiveness." Certainly Luther's statements and emphases must be read ultimately in light of his historical context. In short, Luther's underscoring of forgiveness cannot simply be interpreted as proof that he did not have a conception of the imputation of positive righteousness.[22]

In a final selection from Luther there is a clearer connection with the

---

[21] I am grateful to R. Scott Clark for helping me understand this particular background to Luther's teaching on forgiveness in justification.

[22] In regard to the doctrine of imputation, there seems to be a great deal more coherence between Luther and later Protestant theology, both Lutheran and Calvinistic, than some are willing to allow. For instance, Strehle cites this very sermon as evidence that imputation, as traditionally formulated, is not only absent in Luther but is opposed by Luther. There are statements in this sermon that appear to justify Strehle's claim. For instance, Strehle cites a long section from this sermon in which Luther says: "Some there are, particularly among our modern high school men, who say: 'Forgiveness of sins and justification depend altogether on the divine imputation of grace; God's imputation is sufficient. He to whom God does not reckon sin, is justified; to whom God reckons sin, is not justified.' They imagine their position is verified in the testimony of Psalm 32:2 quoted in Romans 4:8" ("Imputatio Iustitiae," 205-6). Luther's next words (which were cited, in part, above [see n. 1]) are yet stronger: "Were their theory true, the entire New Testament would be of no significance. Christ would have labored foolishly and to no purpose in suffering for sin. God would have unnecessarily wrought mere mockery and deception; for he might easily, without Christ's sufferings, have forgiven sins—have not imputed them. Then, too, a faith other than faith in Christ might have justified and saved—a faith relying on God's gracious mercy not to impute sin" (Luther, "New Year's Day," 283). This may seem to be an invective against what became the traditional doctrine, but it is not. Luther's "modern high school men" (*den newen hohen schullerern*) are nominalists, not Protestants. Strehle recognizes this fact and freely associates the Protestant doctrine of imputation with nominalist teaching. Note, however, that Luther criticizes those who teach a "divine imputation of grace" (*der gnaden . . . gottlichen imputation*). This is not the same thing as imputation in the traditional formulation. Moreover, Luther himself (as seen above), freely talks about imputation in this same sermon, albeit with an emphasis on forgiveness. While there may be similarities between Luther's criticism of the nominalists, and later criticism of the traditional doctrine of imputation, they cannot be equated. Heiko Oberman points to the "widespread misunderstanding according to which the nominalistic doctrine of justification would be essentially forensic" (*The Harvest of Medieval Theology: Gabriel Biel and Late Medieval Nominalism* [Durham, NC: The Labyrinth Press, 1983], 356). This "misunderstanding" is based on the word "*acceptation*" employed not only by Biel, Occam, and Scotus, but also by Melanchthon (Strehle's thesis that the traditional doctrine of imputation stems from debates with Osiander will be discussed shortly). Oberman, showing the distinction between forensic justification and nominalist teaching, particularly in regard to grace as "a created gift of the Holy Spirit which links the converted sinner in a bond of love with Jesus Christ," states: "This interpretation [that justification is forensic in the nominalist scheme] is probably due to the term 'acceptation' itself. In connection with the theology of Duns Scotus, for whom this term received a new importance, it has often been alleged that justification would not refer to an internal enrichment of the sinner but only to a changed relation with God." Oberman continues: "One can easily understand that the Scotistic and nominalistic doctrine of sin with its relational emphasis on the obligation to punishment could facilitate a parallel relational understanding of their doctrine of justification. . . . The acceptation by God, however, is not the exterior declaration or *favor dei* of later Protestant orthodoxy; it is the coming of the Holy Spirit himself. In justification, therefore, two gifts are granted: (1) created grace, necessary according to God's revealed will as the *ratio meriti*; (2) the Holy Spirit, necessary in an absolute sense, as the *ratio acceptationis*" (ibid.). Later Oberman, now speaking specifically of Biel's theology, concludes that it is "beyond doubt that this doctrine of acceptation can in no sense of the word be characterized as forensic" (ibid., 357). Oberman would thus disagree with Strehle, who begins his essay with a discussion of "*acceptilatio*" in the nominalist and Franciscan (particularly evident in Erasmus) traditions ("Imputatio Iustitiae," 201-4).

traditional formulation. In *"Adversus armatum virum Cokleum"* (1523), Luther asserts: "God does everything to justify us. Christ has merited our justification, and the Holy Spirit implements the merit of Christ, so that we are justified."[23] Without entering into the discussion of the various meanings of "merit," this statement sounds closer to the traditional doctrine than what was seen in some of the earlier examples. From this brief overview, including recognition of Luther's emphasis on union with Christ, and the primary place of forgiveness in our justification, Luther's understanding is not incompatible with what followed in Melanchthon, Calvin, et al. As we shall see later, both union and forgiveness are central to understanding a full-orbed doctrine of imputation. At the end of the day, Luther's interpretation neither proves nor disproves the validity of the traditional formulation. Even if it were true that Luther opposes the later formulation of the doctrine (granted, an anachronistic idea) that would not be grounds to reject it as false. Whatever one concludes about Luther, he is, nevertheless, the beginning of a trajectory. We now turn to his immediate successor, Philip Melanchthon.

Melanchthon

In the writings of Luther's companion and successor, Philip Melanchthon, we see a clearer formulation of imputation that includes forgiveness and the imputation of Christ's righteousness.[24] Commenting

---

[23] Martin Luther, *Adverses armatum virum Cokleum*, WA 11 (1899): 132. Luther's text reads: "Deus enim omnia facit, ut iustificemur, Christus meruit, ut iustificemur, Spiritus sanctus exequitur meritum Christi, ut iustificemur." I am grateful to Michael Horton for bringing this text to my attention.

[24] Melanchthon is often credited with developing Luther's understanding of the alien righteousness of Christ into the traditional doctrine of imputation. Some, like Strehle, see Melanchthon as corrupting, not following, Luther's theology ("Imputatio Iustitiae," 201). As seen above, Strehle links imputation to medieval nominalism, and Melanchthon is chiefly to blame for forging this link that continues down to this day. According to Strehle, "it was not until the 1530s that the doctrine began to emerge in the writings of Philip Melanchthon, and its initial inspiration was not so much engendered by the seminal ideas of Protestantism, but, if anything, by the exegetical and theological analysis of Catholic scholars" (ibid.). Strehle sees more continuity regarding justification between Andreas Osiander and Luther than between Melanchthon and Luther. Strehle himself opts for a position which is quite close to Osiander's. For Osiander, as Jaroslav Pelikan points out, justification rests on the participation of the believer with the divine essence of Jesus (Pelikan, *Reformation of Church and Dogma*, vol. 4 in *The Christian Tradition: A History of the Development of Doctrine* [Chicago: University of Chicago Press, 1983], 151). Osiander, in the articles of agreement published after the Marburg Colloquy (1529), writes, "Faith is our righteousness before God, for the sake of which God accounts and regards us as righteous, faithful, and holy." He then adds that this takes place "for the sake of his Son, in whom we believe and thereby receive and participate in the righteousness, life and all blessings of his Son" (ibid., 151). Osiander believed he was following in Luther's steps. In this scheme, justification is made possible by faith in Christ's death on the cross as a sacrifice for sins. "Through such faith," Carl J. Lawrenz writes, "justification is, however, not yet appropriated to us. Rather, through such faith Christ the eternal Word, who is God himself, now is able to come and

on Romans 5:12, Melanchthon sounds quite similar to Luther when he asserts that the guilt of sin comes to those who follow Adam not because of "actual transgressions" (which they do commit), but because "all are guilty on account of one, Adam."[25] As he comes to verse 15, however, the parallel between Adam and Christ is more finely tuned and developed than in Luther:

> Here Paul joins together two things: grace and gift through grace. Grace signifies gratuitous acceptance because of Christ, that is, gratuitous remission of sins, and gratuitous imputation of righteousness because of Christ.[26]

There are two things to note in this passage. First, Melanchthon's distinction between remission and imputation is significant because the traditional formulation rests on a division of imputation to include forgiveness and the imputation of positive righteousness; this is true whether the distinction between active and passive obedience is pressed or not. Furthermore, Melanchthon's insertion of "imputation," commenting on a text in which the word does not appear, may suggest that he understood the parallel and antithesis between Adam and Christ and their connection with humanity in terms of Adam's disobedience and Christ's obedience, best explained in terms of imputation.[27]

Statements in Melanchthon's *Loci* are clearer than what we see in *Romans*.[28] In the 1543 edition Melanchthon equates justification with

---

dwell in the believers' hearts with his perfect divine righteousness and thereby makes them righteous. It is this then, according to Osiander, that we are justified by faith" (Lawrenz, "On Justification: Osiander's Doctrine of the Indwelling Christ," in *No Other Gospel: Essays in Commemoration of the 400th Anniversary of the Formula of Concord 1580–1980*, ed. Arnold J. Koelpin [Milwaukee: Northwestern Publishing House, 1980], 155). Osiander's position drew sharp criticism from many opponents, not the least of whom, as we shall see, was Calvin.

[25] Philip Melanchthon, *Commentary on Romans*, trans. Fred Kramer (St. Louis: Concordia, 1992), 134.

[26] Ibid., 137.

[27] In Romans 5:12-21, λογίζομαι does not appear. The closest word, semantically, to it is ἐλλογέω, which appears in verse 13. In that verse it refers to sin not being reckoned "when there is no law," not to the imputation of righteousness.

[28] The *Loci* went through several editions, and there were many changes, including additions in regard to imputation, made along the way. It seems to me, however, that it reveals relatively little to show that a doctrine is more developed in a later edition of a work than in an earlier edition—unless one has a direct statement, or at least an intimation, from the author himself. There is no inherent reason to borrow the romantic notion that what is earlier is somehow better, or more pure, than what comes later. Any number of reasons could explain the differences between editions. Furthermore, one would have to study *all* the differences, not just one doctrine or idea in isolation, before a reliable hypothesis could be drawn. Nevertheless, conclusions would still rest to some degree on speculation.

the "remission of sins, reconciliation, or the acceptance of a person unto eternal life."[29] That justification means more than forgiveness, or that there are aspects of justification that accompany forgiveness, is evident in his definition of the gospel: "This is the definition of the Gospel in which we lay hold on three Gospel blessings: that for the sake of Christ our sins are freely remitted; that we are freely pronounced righteous, that is, reconciled or accepted by God; that we are made heirs of eternal life."[30] On the one hand it could be argued that Melanchthon is simply restating what it means to have sins "freely remitted," or the results of that remission, when he uses the words "freely pronounced righteous," and "made heirs of eternal life." On the other hand, however, Melanchthon's definition of the gospel centers on "three Gospel blessings," making it seem unlikely that he is merely saying the same thing, i.e., the gospel is forgiveness, in three different ways. In that case there would be only one gospel blessing.

In the 1555 edition of the *Loci* there are no longer ambiguities in Melanchthon's statements. In the section entitled "How Man Obtains Forgiveness of Sin and Is Justified before God," he states that as believers we "have forgiveness of sins, and *Christ's* righteousness is imputed to us, so that we are justified and are pleasing to God for the sake of Christ."[31] He cites Romans 3:24-25 and says:

> Now to be justified is to obtain forgiveness of sins, to please God, to be clothed with the righteousness of Christ, and endowed with the Holy Spirit. This occurs when he [Paul] expressly says, *without merit on our part*, through faith in the Lord Christ, God and Man, because he bore for us the wrath of God. By speaking of blood, he includes the entire obedience and merit of the Lord Christ.[32]

There can be no question that here Melanchthon is describing different aspects of justification, of which forgiveness, though mentioned first, is

---

[29] Philip Melanchthon, *Loci Communes 1543*, trans. J. A. O. Preus (St. Louis: Concordia, 1992), 86. At the end of Locus 8 Melanchthon makes it clear that forgiveness is central to his understanding of justification. "I have set forth the doctrine of the gospel concerning the remission of sins and reconciliation, or justification, as correctly and properly as I could" (ibid., 96).
[30] Ibid., 82.
[31] *Melanchthon on Christian Doctrine: Loci Communes 1555*, trans. and ed. Clyde L. Manschreck, A Library of Protestant Thought (New York: Oxford University Press, 1965), 156.
[32] Ibid., 156. Other texts cited here are, in order of appearance, Acts 10:43; John 3:16; Romans 4:3; Romans 5:1; Ephesians 3:12; 2:8; Isaiah 53:11.

but one. There is at least one thing that should be noted here in regard to the development of the doctrine. Melanchthon sees "blood" ("justified freely by faith, in his blood," Rom. 3:25) as Paul's shorthand for Christ's entire work. There is no clear distinction, as made by later Lutheran and Reformed theologians, regarding the so-called "passive" and "active" obedience of Christ. Apparently, Melanchthon understood the cross as a metonymy for Christ's saving work, including his obedience in life and in death. This idea is made explicit later when he says that "the Mediator's entire obedience, from his Incarnation until his Resurrection, is the true justification which is pleasing to God, and is the merit for us."[33]

Melanchthon makes a direct link between righteousness and obedience to the law: "Righteousness is uniformity with, or fulfillment of, the entire law."[34] The sinner, unable to fulfill the law of God perfectly, can through Christ nevertheless "obtain forgiveness, and become pleasing to [God]." Since righteousness is equated with fulfillment of the law, and righteousness is required to approach God, the sinner being unable to fulfill the law must receive, by faith, "an imputed righteousness," which is the righteousness of Christ, i.e., his obedience.[35]

While it may not be eminently clear that Melanchthon speaks of an imputation of positive righteousness in the explicit language of the later Reformers, his insistence on forgiveness *and* imputation—not simply forgiveness *as* imputation—lends itself to the later formulations.

One need not look far to find a figure who saw himself as carrying on this trajectory and who strongly emphasized imputation. Melanchthon's best known student, Martin Chemnitz, commenting on Melanchthon's *Loci* no less, states:

> The free imputation in the article of justification is the grace of God, which for the sake of Christ, does not impute against us the sins inher-

---

[33] Ibid., 161.

[34] Ibid., 167.

[35] Ibid., 168. It is worth noting that Osiander's name is mentioned in this section. It is indeed likely that the debates with Osiander helped Reformers like Melanchthon refine the doctrine of imputation with added precision. As we will see shortly, this was true of Calvin as well. The degree to which Osiander provided the spark for the development of the doctrine is, however, difficult to determine. The desire of the Reformers to understand and interpret Scripture should not be underestimated. Secondly, it should be remembered that even if it is true that "imputation" as classically formulated arose out of debate, this should not immediately cast doubt over the validity of the doctrine as a description of what is taught in the Bible. The history of the church is filled with incidents where the formulation of certain biblical doctrines became more precise as a result of debate. The christological and Trinitarian controversies in the early church, and even the doctrine of justification itself, are examples.

ing in us, 2 Cor 5.19, and imputes to us (as though it actually did inhere in man) the perfect righteousness which does not inhere in us and which is worthy of eternal life.[36]

Chemnitz's insistence on imputation of "perfect righteousness" that is "worthy of eternal life" is perfectly in keeping with the theology of the later Lutheran and Reformed scholars and their followers. The similarities are clearer still when Chemnitz asserts that justification depends on both "satisfaction" for the penalty of the law *and* the fulfillment of the law "by perfect obedience."[37] Both elements of the traditional formulation, forgiveness and positive imputation, are explicit. Thus in little more than one generation, in one tradition, a clear trajectory arises regarding the interpretation of texts, particularly in Paul, that deal with the function of imputation in justification.

Calvin

In his commentaries on the major imputation texts, Calvin speaks of justification explicitly in terms of forgiveness, but this does not mean that the positive imputation of Christ's righteousness is absent in his interpretations. In Romans 4 Calvin interprets Paul's discussion of God reckoning Abraham's faith as righteousness and David's declaring that the blessed man is the one whom "the Lord does not reckon sin" as meaning that "righteousness . . . is nothing other than the remission of sins."[38] Although he also states that justification requires "obedience, perfect and complete in all its parts," and that the believer is "covered by the purity of Christ," the bulk of his discussion centers on forgiveness. On the other hand, when he comes to Romans 5:18-19 he speaks of being "made righteous by the obedience of Christ."[39] Furthermore he states that if we want "to be justified by works, viz., obedience to the law," we

---

[36] Martin Chemnitz, *Justification: The Chief Article of Christian Doctrine as Expounded in Loci Theologici*, trans. J. A. O. Preus (St. Louis: Concordia, 1985). It should be noted that in contrast to the Reformed tradition, the doctrine of imputation in the Lutheran tradition is not based on covenant theology. Thus while the majority of covenant theologians hold to the imputation of positive righteousness and while the covenant framework more or less requires it, the doctrine is not restricted to, nor does it necessarily imply, covenant theology.

[37] Ibid., 150.

[38] John Calvin, *Romans and Thessalonians*, vol. 8, in Calvin's New Testament Commentaries, trans. Ross Mackenzie, ed. David W. Torrence and Thomas F. Torrence (Grand Rapids: Eerdmans; Carlisle, Cumbria: Paternoster, 1960), 86.

[39] Ibid., 118.

must have total obedience to all points of the law. His point, of course, is that we cannot be justified by our works. This observation comes in the context of discussing Christ's obedience as both the "character" of his righteousness and that which makes us righteous, and Christ's righteousness being "imputed" to us. Taken all together, Calvin implies that perfect obedience, which we cannot render but which is required for justification, is rendered by Christ and imputed to us and on this basis we are justified.

Calvin again focuses on forgiveness in his interpretation of 2 Corinthians 5:19-21, saying that "we were made the righteousness of God as a result of Christ's having been made sin."[40] Thus being "the righteousness of God in him" (5:21) means we are righteous just "as Christ became a sinner." Christ was "reckoned a sinner" in our place, bearing our sin so that we "are judged in relation to Christ's righteousness which we have put on by faith."[41] So while Calvin does speak here of the reckoning of our sins to Christ and the imputation of Christ's righteousness to us, he emphasizes Christ's sacrifice for the forgiveness of sins.

When we turn to Calvin's *Institutes,* his connection to the theological tradition that bears his name is clearly evident.[42] While Calvin's language in the passages from his commentaries may be inconclusive, a more developed idea of positive imputation is made explicit in the *Institutes.*[43] Commenting on a series of Pauline texts, particularly 2 Corinthians 3:6, Calvin says that Paul "means that righteousness

---

[40] 2 *Corinthians and Timothy, Titus and Philemon,* vol. 10 in Calvin's New Testament Commentaries, ed. David W. Torrence and Thomas F. Torrence (Grand Rapids: Eerdmans; Carlisle, Cumbria: Paternoster, 1960), 81.

[41] Ibid., 81-82

[42] At least in regard to the subject at hand. Ritschl claimed that the doctrine of imputation of Christ's righteousness "as a formula for justification" does not appear prominently in Luther or Melanchthon, but it does in Calvin. Albrecht Ritschl, *The Christian Doctrine of Justification and Reconciliation,* ed. H. R. Macintosh and A. R. Macaulay, Library of Religious and Philosophical Thought (Clifton, N.J. Reference Book Publishers, 1966), 65. It should be added, however, that imputation is far more "prominent" in Melanchthon than Ritschl claims.

[43] It is entirely legitimate to read Calvin's statements about imputation in the commentaries through the lens of the *Institutes.* Calvin himself intends it. In his Introduction, Calvin states that he has "arranged it [the sum of religion] in such an order, that if anyone rightly grasps it, it will not be difficult for him to determine what he ought especially to seek." He then adds, "If, after this road has, as it were been paved, I shall publish any interpretation of Scripture, I shall always condense them, because I shall have no need to undertake long doctrinal discussions." John Calvin, *Institutes of the Christian Religion,* vol. 1, ed. John T. McNeill, The Library of Christian Classics (Philadelphia: Westminster Press, 1960), 5.

is taught in vain by the commandments until Christ confers it by free imputation."[44] Soon after this he adds: "We cannot gainsay that the reward of eternal salvation awaits complete obedience to the law."[45] Later on, Calvin concludes that "if righteousness consists in the observance of the law, who will deny that Christ merited favor for us?"[46] Though in the context Calvin stresses forgiveness, the basic formulation of positive imputation is evident, as in the following statement:

> He is said to be justified in God's sight who is both reckoned righteous in God's judgment and has been accepted on account of his righteousness. . . . Therefore, we explain justification simply as the acceptance with which God receives us into his favor as righteous men. And we say it consists in the remission of sins and the imputation of Christ's righteousness.[47]

When he sets out to refute Osiander's view regarding union with Christ as meaning union with Christ's essential righteousness as derived from his divinity, Calvin leaves little room to doubt where he stands on the imputation of righteousness. Calvin's fundamental problem with Osiander's view is that it results in righteousness "by the infusion both of his [Christ's] essence and of his quality," rather than a righteousness "that has been acquired for us by Christ's obedience and sacrificial death."[48] Since union with Christ plays such an important role in Osiander's view, Calvin counters with his own understanding of the doctrine. This is particularly significant here because of the connections that will later be drawn between imputation and union. In Calvin we find an example of how it is not a matter of *either* imputation *or* union, but that the two ideas work together. Christ's righteousness is imputed to the believer in the context of the believer's union with Christ. Imputation is not an abstraction but a reality that comes as a result of faith in Christ

---

[44] Ibid., 3.7.2, 351.
[45] Ibid., 3.7.2, 351.
[46] Ibid., 3.17.5, 533.
[47] Ibid., 3.11.2, 726-27.
[48] Ibid., 3.11.5, 730. Calvin provides a helpful summary of Osiander's position, saying that in Osiander's scheme, "to be justified is not only to be reconciled to God through free pardon but also to be made righteous, and righteousness is not a free imputation but the holiness and uprightness that the essence of God, dwelling in us, inspires. Secondly, he [Osiander] sharply states that Christ is himself our righteousness, not in so far as he, by expiating sins as Priest, appeased the Father on our behalf, but as he is eternal God and life" (ibid., 3.11.6, 731-32).

and being "engrafted into his body—in short, because he deigns to make us one with him."[49]

PROTESTANT SYMBOLS[50]

The doctrine of the imputation of Christ's righteousness, as meaning more than the forgiveness of sins, is arguably present in Luther, more pronounced in Melanchthon, and clearer still in Calvin. In much of both the Lutheran and Reformed traditions, justification by the imputation of Christ's righteousness, including his positive obedience, became accepted orthodoxy. The developments and refinements that took place in the generations immediately following the early Reformers are well illustrated in their confessional statements.[51]

THE AUGSBURG CONFESSION (1530), ARTICLE IV

> They [Scriptures] teach that man cannot be justified (obtain forgiveness of sins and righteousness) before God by their own powers, merits, or works; but are justified freely (of grace) for Christ's sake through faith, when they believe that they are received into favor, and their sins forgiven for Christ's sake, who by his death hath satisfied for our sins. This faith doth God impute for righteousness before him.

Though the emphasis is on forgiveness, the parenthetical remark does point to the positive imputation of Christ's righteousness, the rest of

---

[49] Ibid., 3.11.10, 737. The connection between imputation and union will be discussed later. For now it is sufficient to say that much of the modern debate surrounding imputation has already been addressed in the writings of Reformed scholars. Secondly, the link Calvin (and Luther) forges between imputation and union will play a significant role in the conclusions reached in this study.

[50] Unless otherwise noted, all quoted examples are taken from Philip Schaff, *The Creeds of Christendom*, vol. 3, *The Evangelical Protestant Creeds* (New York: Harper and Row, 1931; reprint ed., Grand Rapids: Baker, 1983).

[51] The statements included here are, for the most part, intended to be read as crystallizations of Protestant thought after the Reformation. Most of these symbols will speak for that era. Although the era is often thought of as a time of stale orthodoxy void of true biblical exegesis, it was in reality a time of remarkable creativity and theological insight; the few confessional statements included here bear this out. Even given the abuses and extremes that led to the common stereotypes (for truly every stereotype gets its start in something real), it was the era that refined the early period of discovery typified by the work of Luther and Calvin. However, in order to avoid the debates about "Calvin *v*. Calvinists" or "Luther *v*. Lutherans," and because I do not think I can adequately survey the different nuances and influences that affected the various theologians, following Calvin particularly, I decided not to include the Scholastics in this chapter (apart from the degree to which their thought is contained in the confessional statements). Furthermore, in the following section the theological presuppositions and conclusions reached by the theologians surveyed were highly influenced by the Protestant Scholastics (especially in the Reformed tradition).

the statement affirms that a positive imputation of righteousness is not summed up fully in forgiveness.

When we compare the statements on justification in the 1644 London Confession (Baptist) and the Second London Confession of 1689, there is discernable development.

FIRST LONDON CONFESSION, 1644, ARTICLE XXVIII

> Those which have union with Christ, are justified for all their sins, past, present, and to come, by the blood of Christ; which justification we conceive to be a gracious and free acquittal of a guilty, sinful creature for all sin by God, through the satisfaction that Christ has made by his death; and this applied in the manifestation of it through faith.[52]

SECOND LONDON CONFESSION (1689), ARTICLE XI

> Those whom God Effectually calleth, he also freely justifieth, not by infusing Righteousness into them, but by pardoning their sins, and by accounting, and accepting their Persons as Righteous . . . not by imputing faith itself . . . but by imputing Christ's active obedience unto the whole Law, and passive obedience in his death, for their whole and sole Righteousness.[53]

Clearly the 1689 article on justification is more sharply defined than the 1644 article that speaks of justification exclusively along the lines of the forgiveness of sins. Whether the addition is a clarification or a correction, it does witness to the fact that it is possible for those in the same basic historical trajectory—affirming justification by faith alone through Christ alone—to conceive of justification with or without explicit mention of the imputation of Christ's positive obedience.

For the most part, the major Protestant, particularly Reformed, creeds, confessions, and catechisms affirm both negative and positive imputation:

THE FORMULA OF CONCORD (LUTHERAN) 1584, ARTICLE III, 1 AND 2

> 1. [W]e unanimously believe, teach, and confess that Christ is truly our righteousness . . . in his sole, most absolute obedience which he

---

[52] W.L. Lumpkin. Baptist Confessions of Faith (Valley Forge: Judson Press, 1959), 164.
[53] Ibid., 266.

rendered to the Father even unto death, as God and man, and thereby merited for us the remission of all our sins and eternal life.[54]

2. We believe, therefore, teach, and confess that this very thing is our righteousness before God, namely, that God remits to us our sins of mere grace, without any respect of our works, going before, present, or following, or of our worthiness or merit. For he bestows and imputes to us the righteousness of the obedience of Christ; for the sake of that righteousness we are received by God into favor and accounted righteous.

The French Confession of Faith (1559), Article XVIII

We believe that all our justification rests upon the remission of our sins, in which also is our only blessedness, as with the Psalmist (Ps. 32:2). We therefore reject all other means of justification before God, and without claiming any virtue or merit, we rest simply in the obedience of Jesus Christ, which is imputed to us as much to blot out all our sins as to make us find grace and favor in the sight of God.

The Belgic Confession (1561), Article XXIII

We believe that our salvation consists in the remission of our sins for Jesus Christ's sake, and that therein our righteousness is implied. . . . And therefore we always hold fast this foundation . . . without presuming to trust in any thing in ourselves or in any merit of ours, relying and resting on the obedience of Christ crucified alone, which becomes ours when when we believe in him.

The Heidelberg Catechism (1563)

Question 60: How art thou righteous before God?
Answer: Only by true faith in Jesus Christ; that is, although my conscience accuse me that I have grievously sinned against all the commandments of God, and have never kept any of them, and that I am still prone always to all evil, yet God, without any merit of mine, of mere grace, grants and imputes to me the perfect satisfaction, righteousness, and holiness of Christ, as if I had never committed nor had any sin, and had myself accomplished all the obedience which Christ has fulfilled for me, if only I accept such benefit with a believing heart.

---

[54] The key phrase here is, "*and* eternal life (emphasis mine)."

THE SECOND HELVETIC CONFESSION (1566), CHAPTER 15

> For Christ took upon himself and bare the sins of the world, and did satisfy the justice of God. God, therefore, is merciful unto our sins for Christ alone, that suffered and rose again, and does not impute them unto us. But he imputes the justice of Christ unto us for our own; so that now we are not only cleansed from sin, and purged, and holy, but also endued with the righteousness of Christ. . . . To speak properly, then, it is God alone that justifieth us, and that only for Christ, by not imputing unto us our sins, but imputing Christ's righteousness unto us.

THE WESTMINSTER CONFESSION OF FAITH (1647), VII.V

> The Lord Jesus, by his perfect obedience and sacrifice of himself, which he through the eternal Spirit once offered up unto God, has fully satisfied the justice of the Father, and purchased not only reconciliation, but an everlasting inheritance in the kingdom of heaven, for all those whom the Father hath given unto him.[55]

There were, historically, voices within Protestantism that did not assert a positive imputation of righteousness; nevertheless, the doctrine of the imputation of Christ's active obedience—positive righteousness— became firmly established as a point of orthodoxy for a large number of Protestants.

THE ANGLO-AMERICAN TRAJECTORY

The theologians included in this section are representative of the Reformed theological tradition that took hold with the English Puritans and later crossed the Atlantic and settled in New England.[56] In America,

---

[55] While some may think that this statement appears somewhat vague regarding the imputation of Christ's active obedience, the theological framework of the Confession, which is made clear in the Confession itself, and specific statements made in earlier sections affirm the doctrine. First, in the framework of covenant theology justification rests on the active and passive obedience of Christ. Thus his submission to the Father in his life and death and his active fulfillment of the law are required for the forgiveness for the guilt due to Adam's sin and for a positive righteousness which Adam never attained because of the fall. Forgiveness brings the believer up to "level," so to speak, but he also needs the imputation of Christ's active obedience to bring him to that place Adam would have attained had he not fallen. This is the presupposition that lies behind the statement, "[Christ] purchased not only reconciliation, but an everlasting inheritance in the kingdom of heaven." Secondly, the statements found in VIII.IV that "the Lord Jesus . . . was made under the law, and did perfectly fulfill it," and in VII.I, "The first covenant made with man was a covenant of works, wherein life was promised to Adam, and in him to his posterity, upon condition of perfect and personal obedience" confirm that the Westminster divines did indeed hold to the necessity of the imputation of Christ's active obedience.
[56] While John Owen is the only English Puritan in this section, many others could be included. Owen is perhaps the primary, and probably best known, example of the developed Calvinistic theological

this tradition comes down to us (not exclusively) through Jonathan
Edwards and the early Princeton theologians. The imputation of Christ's
righteousness is a prominent aspect of this theological trajectory.

Theological Presuppositions[57]

John Owen provides a classic statement, in the Reformed tradition, for
the doctrine of imputation. Commenting on Paul's teaching, Owen states,

> The doctrine of justification was fully declared, stated and vindicated
> by the Apostle Paul, in a peculiar manner. And he doth it especially
> by affirming and proving that we have the righteousness whereby and
> wherewith we are justified by imputation; or that our justification con-
> sists in the non-imputation of sin, and the imputation of righteousness.[58]

The important thing to note is that for Owen, as for a majority of
Reformed theologians, the act of justification requires imputation. That
is, a positive imputation of Christ's obedience must be imputed to the
believer beyond the forgiveness of sins in order for him to be justified.
Justification, therefore, is viewed as a twofold act: forgiveness and the
imputation of positive righteousness. Jonathan Edwards, in the context of
discussing Romans 4, makes a statement similar to Owen's, commenting
that in the justifying act God accepts "a person as having both a negative,
and a positive righteousness belonging to him."[59] It is important to note
that Edwards does not mean a believer actually becomes, in a subjective

---

tradition in England. Owen's work was influential for many early American theologians (aside
from Owen, James Buchanan, a Scot, is the only other non-American theologian in this "Anglo-
American" group, though technically Edwards was a (colonial) Englishman). There is a consistent
theological stream (at least regarding imputation) flowing from English Puritanism (one of the
exceptions being Richard Baxter), through New England Congregationalists such as Edwards, and
through the Presbyterian and Reformed theologians discussed in this section. Given the influences
in American Reformed theology, this section could also properly be called, "Anglo-Dutch-American
Trajectories." Recognizing the importance of the Dutch theologians, "Anglo-American" will suffice.
[57] This section is intended to illustrate the typical Reformed view of imputation, including the main
presuppositions that lie behind it. While much of the following may appear abstract, that is, detached
from a careful exegesis of texts, it should be noted that the theologians cited in this section discuss
imputation in the context of many biblical texts. Almost invariably, the texts that I will deal with in
this book (specifically Romans 4–5 and 2 Corinthians 5) are the very texts which Owen, Edwards,
Hodge, Berkhof, Buchanan, et al., discuss in their works. In most cases care was taken to cite only
those sections in which these key Pauline texts appear.
[58] John Owen, *Justification by Faith*, in *Faith and Its Evidences*, vol. 5 in *The Works of John Owen*, ed.
William H. Goold (n.p.: Johnstone & Hunter, n.d.; reprint, Edinburgh: Banner of Truth, 1965), 162-63.
[59] Jonathan Edwards, "Justification by Faith Alone," in *Jonathan Edwards Sermons and Discourses,
1734–1738*, ed. M. X. Lesser, *The Works of Jonathan Edwards*, ed. Harry S. Stout, vol. 19 (New
Haven: Yale, 2001), 150.

sense, righteous, but that he is accepted by God on the grounds of an *imputed* righteousness—a righteousness that properly belongs to Christ alone.[60] In this view, imputation is always forensic, i.e., a legal verdict.

In the Reformed tradition the doctrine of imputation is bound to the framework of covenant theology. More particularly, imputation is formulated around the concept of federal, or representative, headship.[61] Simply put, federal headship is the idea that Adam and Christ are the representative heads over all humanity. One is either "in" Adam or "in" Christ. In both cases, it is a legal representation. The state of the representative constitutes the state of those they represent.

In the view of most reformed theologians, when Adam was created, he was placed in a probationary period that he had to pass in order to inherit an eternal blessing. This probation period is typically known as the "covenant of works" because Adam, by virtue of his innocent nature, had to gain eternal life by obeying God's command, "You may surely eat of every tree of the garden, but of the tree of the knowledge of good and evil you shall not eat, for in the day that you eat of it you shall surely die" (Gen. 2:16-17). The reward for the inheritance is, presumably, symbolized in the tree of life. In this scheme, before the fall Adam enjoyed the presence of God but he did not enjoy a state of perfection and immortality. That position had to be earned by obeying God. Adam, however, failed to obey God's command, and as a result he and his offspring were cursed with death and thrown out of the garden and thus unable to inherit eternal life.[62] When Christ comes as the second Adam, therefore, he must not only pay the penalty for the guilt of Adam, but he must fulfill

---

[60] As Hodge notes: "Imputation never changes the inward, subjective state of the person to whom the imputation is made. When sin is imputed to a man he is not made sinful; when the zeal of Phinehas was imputed to him, he was not made zealous. When you impute theft to a man, you do not make him a thief. When you impute goodness to a man, you do not make him good. So when righteousness is imputed to the believer, he does not thereby become subjectively righteous" (Charles Hodge, *Systematic Theology* [New York: Scribner's, 1872–1873; reprint, Grand Rapids: Eerdmans, 1973], 3:145).

[61] There is not room, nor is this the place, to present a comprehensive overview of covenant theology. On the other hand, it must be introduced because it is central to understanding the traditional formulation of imputation. For those interested, a classic treatment of covenant theology is, Herman Witsius, *The Economy of the Covenants between God and Man*, 2 vols. (n.p.: 1677; reprint, Kingsburg, CA: den Dulk Christian Foundation, 1990). J. I. Packer's introduction provides an excellent overview of the major themes of covenant theology.

[62] Again, Owen provides a precise summary: "Adam and all his posterity in him were in a state of acceptation with God, and placed in a way of obtaining eternal life and blessedness, wherein God himself would be their reward. In this estate, by the entrance of sin, they lost the favor of God, and incurred the guilt of death or condemnation for the same. But they lost not an immediate right and title unto life and blessedness; for this, they had not, nor could have before the course of obedience prescribed unto them was accomplished" (*Justification by Faith*, 329).

the law of God in order to provide for eternal life. As we shall see, one does not have to characterize the relationship between God and Adam as a "covenant of works" to maintain a doctrine of imputation within a covenantal framework.[63] This basic covenantal structure must be kept in mind when the doctrine of imputation is discussed, for in the Reformed tradition the covenant framework is *the* interpretive presupposition that lies behind the discussion of the relevant Pauline texts.

It is for the reasons given above that Berkhof insists on both a "negative" and a "positive" element in justification. The "negative element" is "the remission of sins on the ground of the atoning work of Christ."[64] He goes on to add, however, that "it is quite evident from Scripture that justification is more than mere pardon." What is needed is the "positive element" of "the active obedience of Christ."[65] The idea that "mere pardon" is not sufficient grounds for justification is an element that comes up often in the discussion in contemporary scholarship. For now, however, it is worth noting that sometimes a distinction is made between the "active" and "passive" obedience of Christ. This distinction may seem unnecessary, and many theologians in the Reformed tradition understand that the distinction is not explicitly made in Scripture, but the concepts are important for understanding the traditional formulation.[66]

---

[63] In the Reformed tradition there have been those who do not hold to a so-called covenant of works in the garden. John Murray, for instance, calls the period of the first man the "Adamic administration" ("Adamic Administration," in *Collected Writings of John Murray*, vol. 2, *Systematic Theology* [Edinburgh: Banner of Truth, 1977]: 47-59). Murray stresses the principle of grace over that of merit. Nevertheless, on account of federal headship, Christ must provide both forgiveness and positive obedience. In short, the doctrine of imputation is still necessary. Moreover, one may reject both "covenant of works" and "Adamic administration" as descriptive of the Edenic economy, and describe it simply as a covenant which, like all covenants, includes stipulations, blessings, and curses.

[64] Louis Berkhof, *Systematic Theology*, 4th ed. (Grand Rapids: Eerdmans, 1941), 514-16. This idea is connected to the foregoing discussion regarding Adam's original state before the fall. He was innocent but had not inherited God's full blessing. Thus Edwards: "Christ by suffering the penalty, and so making atonement for us, only removes the guilt of our sins, and so sets us in the same state that Adam was in the first moment of creation: and it is no more fit, that we should obtain eternal life, only on that account, than that Adam should have the reward of eternal life, or of a confirmed and unalterable state of happiness, the first moment of his existence, without any obedience at all. Adam was not to have the reward merely on the count of being innocent . . . but he was to have the reward on account of active obedience" (Edwards, "Justification by Faith," 187).

[65] Berkhof, *Systematic Theology*, 515.

[66] Berkhof, citing Romans 5:19; 2 Corinthians 5:21; and Philippians 3:9, speaks of the "passive obedience of Christ" as that which serves as "the ground for the forgiveness of sins" and his "active obedience" as that through "which he merited all the gifts of grace, including eternal life, the ground for adoption as children, by which sinners are construed heirs of eternal life" (*Systematic Theology*, 523). James Buchanan asserts that even though the distinction is "legitimate, and, for some purposes . . . useful," it must be remembered that "two things which are distinguishable in idea may be inseparable in fact" (*The Doctrine of Justification* [Edinburgh: T&T Clark, 1867; reprint, Grand Rapids: Baker, 1954], 333).

Christ's passive obedience, while not limited to his death on the cross, is his submission to the Father's will, "even unto death," and his active obedience is his perfect fulfillment of God's law. The former is required for the satisfaction of justice, the latter for the granting of eternal life.[67] Thus we have another "constant" in regard to the doctrine of imputation: perfect fulfillment of the law.

While by no means limited to the Reformed tradition, the traditional formulation holds that God's command (whatever the form—Adam's prohibition, Mosaic law, etc.) requires perfect obedience. This idea is so pervasive that it hardly needs mentioning, but in light of modern assertions to the contrary it is relevant to touch upon it briefly here. According to this perspective, while the law condemns sin, it also demands perfect obedience, since condemnation is really the consequence of a failure to obey. Again, the principle at work is that for a sinner to be justified two things must happen: (1) the penalty for sin (lawbreaking) must be met; and (2) the law must be perfectly obeyed.[68] The former occurs when sin was imputed to Christ, the perfect sacrifice, whose death atoned for sin (and thus the "non-imputation" of sin to the believer), and the latter is, on the basis of Christ's obedience, imputed to the believer for positive righteousness. Perfect obedience is not simply what Jesus had to render to be a perfect sacrifice and thus atone for the sins of God's people; it was what God's law demanded, and what mankind under Adam failed to do, and so what Jesus had to fulfill on behalf of God's people. Whatever particular distinctions are made, active and passive, negative and positive, suffering and obedience, the twofold nature of justification is the prevalent theme in the traditional Protestant formulation.

VARIOUS TRAJECTORIES

The majority of modern New Testament and Pauline theologies generally do not contain detailed discussions of imputation as traditionally formulated. While specific biblical terms such as "reckoned" and

---

[67] Hodge, *Systematic Theology*, 164.
[68] All the above concepts are interconnected. For instance, note Edwards's comments regarding perfect obedience and the covenant of works: "If Adam had finished his course of perfect obedience, he would have been justified and certainly his justification would have implied something more than what is merely negative; he would have been approved of as having fulfilled the righteousness of the law, and accordingly would have been judged to the reward of it" ("Justification by Faith," 150). It is the tight interweaving of these concepts that necessitates the foregoing "theological" discussion.

"constituted" are obviously present, the definitions often differ from the traditional Protestant treatments. This is due to various reasons such as different definitions of justification in general, a reluctance to use the term "imputation" since it is derived from systematic categories, and fundamental differences regarding biblical-theological themes such as covenant, law keeping, and atonement. There are also arguments that the term imputation, traditionally defined, simply does not convey Paul's teaching, but that "forgiveness" rather than "imputation" is sufficient to describe Paul's thought. Although the secondary literature is immense, the following scholars are fair representatives of the various ways the traditions developed.[69]

German Biblical-Theological Variations[70]

Albrecht Ritschl. Ritschl asserts that the idea of imputation does not originate with Paul but is based on the presupposition that God relates to man on essentially legal grounds.[71] For Ritschl, the imputation of Christ's active obedience (positive righteousness) forms a deduction from the presupposed world order. It was assumed that the reciprocal relation between God and man is originally and necessarily bound to the standard of the law and good works.[72] Ritschl concludes that the imputation of Christ's righteousness is "devoid of intrinsic utility; nor has it any real basis in Paul's typical circle of thought."[73] Ritschl himself pre-

---

[69] The following section presents a serious challenge regarding content. An overview of the history of interpretation is impossible (and unnecessary) here. I have purposefully chosen the representative scholars in this section either because they follow in a particular tradition, i.e., Ritschl, Bultmann, Schlatter, Käsemann, Stuhlmacher (Lutheran), Ridderbos, and Murray (Reformed); are widely associated with modern New Testament studies and the challenge to the traditional Protestant position (e.g., Sanders, Dunn, Wright); and those who present recent, specific challenges (e.g., Gundry). The goal here is to present an overview and to show the various trajectories, in order to present a backdrop for the following chapters. Ritschl and Bultmann are included even though they represent significant departures from their Lutheran traditions.

[70] This discussion does not draw on the history of Lutheran dogmatics as it does on the history of Reformed theology. This is due in large part to the background and experience of the writer. Imputation plays a large role in the development of the doctrine of justification in Lutheran dogmatics, but this study cannot include a treatment of that tradition.

[71] I am not implying that Ritschl represents a natural theological flow from Luther. He, like Bultmann, is included here not primarily because of Lutheranism but because of his broad influence in biblical and theological studies. There is obviously quite a difference between the theology of Ritschl and Bultmann compared to that of Peter Stuhlmacher, even though all three stand in the Lutheran tradition. Secondly, Ritschl is included because like Strehle (see above, n. 28 [throughout this book, note references are to footnotes in the same chapter unless otherwise indicated]) he asserts that the emphasis on imputation stems not from Luther but from later Reformers.

[72] Ritschl, *Justification*, 65.

[73] Ibid., 60.

ferred to speak of justification as "synonymous with the forgiveness of sins."[74] His objection that the idea is not derived from Paul, his assertion that justification is essentially the forgiveness of sins, and his rejection of a legal, or forensic, emphasis in justification, makes Ritschl a kind of touchstone figure in the debate over imputation. His objections, articulated essentially by Roman Catholics and Socinians before him, are repeated by scholars from many different traditions and perspectives.

Rudolph Bultmann. Bultmann retains the forensic understanding of justification and the law/gospel contrast that was prevalent in the traditional discussions. Yet in his rather lengthy discussion in *Theology of the New Testament*, the traditional idea of the imputation of Christ's active obedience is absent. Bultmann states that righteousness is a "forensic-eschatological" declaration, which is "imputed to a man in the present," but he does not go on to discuss "imputation" at any length.[75] In his discussion of Christ's obedience, Bultmann emphasizes Christ's obedience "unto death" rather than his perfect obedience to the law that is subsequently "imputed" to the believer.[76] Likewise, commenting on 2 Corinthians 5:21, Bultmann speaks of "negative" and "positive" elements, but the terms are linked to forgiveness of and deliverance from sin rather than aspects of imputation.[77] Imputation language is limited simply to God's "reckoning" sinners as righteous in the same way as Christ was treated as a sinner, without detailed discussion. Bultmann's framework, which emphasizes experience and the need for decision or "faith," does not include a developed idea of imputation in any traditional sense.

Adolph Schlatter. Though often overlooked, Schlatter is a weighty figure in this discussion. His careful and nuanced approach to New Testament theology, particularly in regard to his views on justification,

---

[74] Ibid., 40.

[75] Rudolph Bultmann, *Theology of the New Testament*, vol. 1, trans. Kendrick Grobel (New York: Scribner's, 1951), 274.

[76] Ibid., 289. Indeed, Bultmann's existentialist framework, which emphasizes experience and the need for decision or "faith," and his mystery religions paradigm for understanding Paul make imputation, in any traditional sense, virtually irrelevant. The point here, however, is to observe his language regarding justification/imputation rather than his larger framework.

[77] Rudolph Bultmann, *The Second Letter to the Corinthians*, trans. Roy A. Harrisville (Minneapolis: Augsburg, 1976), 165-66.

bears a closer examination that it usually receives. Schlatter is a prime, and perhaps the most developed, example of the broad understanding of forgiveness seen in Luther, and in some contemporary scholars as well.

When one reads Adolph Schlatter's *The Theology of the Apostles*, one might get the impression that the traditional formulation of the imputation of Christ's righteousness is a vital component of his view of justification. For instance, Schlatter's insistence on (1) Christ's fulfill-ment of "the positive will of the Law"[78] (2) for justification necessarily including forgiveness accompanied by a "positive equivalent" and the "awarding of righteousness"[79] and (3) the importance, when formulat-ing a doctrine of justification, of establishing what type of human con-duct "meets with God's favor"[80] all have a certain ring of the traditional idea. When these comments are scrutinized carefully and put in the context of Schlatter's highly nuanced discussion of justification, how-ever, the connection between his language and that of the traditional formulation is less clear.

When Schlatter speaks of Christ's fulfillment of the law, he does so in the context of the believer receiving, by faith, the reward of Christ's suffering and death, which is freedom from the law and its verdict.[81] Christ fulfilled the law's "designated purpose for righteousness," and as a result the believer is separated from evil and receives life.[82] For Schlatter the law condemns, but it also communicates what God expects of a righ-teous person and what God will do on behalf of that person. Thus, there is a strong positive element concerning what God required through the law and what Christ accomplished in his cross and resurrection.

Yet there is no explicit reference to the imputation of Christ's positive obedience of the law; there is, rather, Christ's gift of the Spirit. Schlatter proceeds immediately to speak of the giving of the Spirit in regard to the believer walking in the Spirit and receiving love and there-

---

[78] Adolph Schlatter, *The Theology of the Apostles: The Development of New Testament Theology*, trans. Andreas Köstenberger (Grand Rapids: Baker, 1999), 242. Chronologically, Schlatter precedes Bultmann. I chose this order because of the connections between Schlatter's view of justification and those of Käsemann and Stuhlmacher. I include a fairly large selection from Schlatter because of his developed idea of the link between justification and forgiveness, and because, unlike many twentieth-century scholars, he uses the term "imputation" quite freely.
[79] Ibid., 232.
[80] Ibid., 230.
[81] Ibid., 242.
[82] Ibid.

fore obtaining "what the Law desires as that which is good before
God."[83] The idea of positive imputation, which, if anywhere, would be
here, is bypassed in order to establish the effective role of the Spirit—
Christ's gift—that comes as a result of Christ's fulfillment of the law on
behalf of believers. There is a closer connection here between Schlatter
and what Käsemann and (especially) Stuhlmacher will develop later,
when they speak of justification as "gift" and "power," than to the
traditional idea of the imputation of Christ's righteousness.

Schlatter denies the validity of concepts that speak of justification
only in negative terms. Conceiving of justification merely in terms
of "the removal of guilt and of the consciousness of guilt, the end of
divine rejection, the liberation from corruption" fails to grasp that such
conceptions must be joined with "their positive equivalent."[84] This
may sound similar to saying that the negative element of justification
(forgiveness) must be united with the positive element (imputation of
active righteousness) for a person to be declared righteous. Such an
interpretation of Schlatter becomes more appealing when shortly after
this he says: "Because he [Christ] is the one who practiced obedience,
through his obedience the justifying verdict is available and has been
established for all."[85] We cannot, however, ultimately equate what
Schlatter says with the traditional formula because he is not arguing
that "mere forgiveness" is insufficient for justification unless accompanied by the imputation of Christ's active obedience of God's law;
rather, he is arguing against a conception of forgiveness based only
on "the removal of negative consequences arising from evil," that is,
conceptions of forgiveness that "suffer from the idea of arbitrariness,
travesty of justice, and the partiality of God."[86]

In other words, Schlatter is denying ideas about forgiveness that fail
to recognize that true, divine forgiveness can take place only "through
the execution of judgment."[87] Justification is an act of God's grace that
must be connected to "the working of justice."[88] He is guarding against

---

[83] Ibid.
[84] Ibid., 232.
[85] Ibid.
[86] Ibid.
[87] Ibid.
[88] Ibid., 231. As Schlatter says: "The judge's act is grounded in justice, and when God judges, no
doubt remains whether his verdict is based on righteousness or not" (ibid., 229).

a conception of grace and forgiveness that disconnects God's pardon of the sinner from the just punishment of sin. The cross of Christ witnesses to the fact that sin, and indeed sinners, have been judged in Christ's death, and in his resurrection believers have life in Christ's life, which manifests that "life issues from death for us and righteousness from condemnation."[89] The "positive equivalent" of forgiveness is not the imputation of Christ's positive fulfillment of the law to believers—it is, rather, his obedience to death on the cross that results in "the justifying verdict."[90] Thus Schlatter is not, based on his interpretation of Paul, going beyond "mere forgiveness," but is making sure that "forgiveness of sins" is understood properly. Paul's use of the term "justification" is itself the explanation of what "divine forgiveness" really means.

There is a strong ethical element in Schlatter's conception of justification. All notions of justification are required to show what standard of behavior God expects from human beings. Schlatter identifies the ethical element in justification, the determination of "the human conduct that is awarded justification," as part of the "new element" of Paul's understanding of justification.[91] What Schlatter has in mind though is not the imputation of perfect obedience but the establishment of the fact that justification is the result of certain behavior that conforms to God's revealed will, i.e., his law. As a result of sin, these qualifications for righteousness in the eyes of God are impossible for human beings to meet. The ethical requirements God demands can only be met in human beings by an act of God's grace, only through divine forgiveness. This forgiveness is established on the basis of Christ's fulfillment "of the positive will of the law . . . because he carries out God's good will through his death and resurrection, effecting our separation from evil through his death and our life for God with his life."[92]

Christ's "commission" (presumably his obedience to God's ethical requirements), says Schlatter, "is directed against sin" and is fulfilled "through his death." Christ's obedience is tied directly to the cross on

---

[89] Ibid., 233.
[90] Ibid., 232. "Because the guilty person can receive justification only by being forgiven, the phrase initially customary for God's attitude toward sinners, 'forgiveness of sin,' retains for Paul its full significance" (ibid.).
[91] Ibid., 230. Schlatter identifies "statements that describe the divine activity by which God justifies us" as the other element (ibid.).
[92] Ibid., 242.

which he died for our sins so we could be declared justified because he secured our forgiveness. Even when Schlatter develops the ethical aspect of justification and the nature of Christ's obedience, the emphasis is again on forgiveness. For instance, in the context of Schlatter's discussion of the ethical aspect of justification, the following appears:

> God did not spare him, so he might forgive us everything; he gave him over, that he might justify us; he made him sin and a curse, in order to bestow righteousness and blessing on us; he condemned him, in order to justify those who believe in him. Through his blood, Jesus provides the community with forgiveness of sins.[93]

Schlatter speaks of imputation and justification being "linked . . . because the pronouncement of a verdict always depends on what is or what is not imputed to a man."[94] But the thing imputed is primarily tied to forgiveness, the verdict upon which God declares a sinner "righteous," without recourse to a discussion of the imputation of positive righteousness. Schlatter emphasizes the believer's union with Christ through faith. A believer attains a "righteous status" when he puts "his confidence in Christ." Since Christ has taken hold of the believer and the believer "clings to him and has been made his possession, the believer is justified."[95] Schlatter's language is rich in biblical imagery, and he continually cites many different Pauline texts in support of his arguments. His imputation language, while not devoid of a positive element, focuses largely on forgiveness and union. At this point he has much in common with Luther.

Ernst Käsemann. In his formulation of God's righteousness as not only "gift" but also "power," Käsemann emphasizes the eschatological nature of justification. Righteousness is not regarded in terms of something imputed in the past or as "simply a property of the divine nature," but as a creative power (God's own power) that "enters the arena" of human existence and transforms that existence.[96] In this way, God's

---

[93] Ibid., 231.
[94] Ibid., 234.
[95] Ibid., 235.
[96] Ernst Käsemann, *New Testament Questions of Today*, trans. W. J. Montague (Philadelphia: Fortress, 1969), 174-76.

righteousness is never separated from God himself. Similarly, the forensic declaration of Romans 4 is not separated from the "state [Rom 5:19]
. . . founded on righteousness."[97] Justification is never separated from
sanctification. In this formulation, which views the righteousness of God
as "the rule of Christ over the world and his people in anticipation of
God's final cosmic triumph,"[98] there is no need to speak of "imputation"
in the traditional sense.

Peter Stuhlmacher. In his commentary on Romans, Stuhlmacher
links Christ's obedience in Romans 5 specifically with forgiveness without the mention of imputation. "Christ's obedience," says Stuhlmacher,
"makes righteousness possible for all people, because the vicarious atoning death of the righteous Son of God frees all sinners from the curse of
the Law."[99] Similarly, in Romans 4, Stuhlmacher discusses the "reckoning" of Abraham's faith as righteousness apart from the categories
found in the traditional formulation. Following Käsemann, Stuhlmacher
emphasizes the eschatological inbreaking of God's righteousness in
Christ in the present age, but with added emphasis on the role of the
Spirit.[100] The traditional concept of justification as the imputation of
Christ's positive righteousness, formulated as primarily an event that
takes place when one believes, is too narrow for Stuhlmacher. Given
Stuhlmacher's influence over scholars in the last third of the twentieth
century (particularly American scholars), and his distinct understanding of concepts such as the "righteousness of God" and justification,
it is worthwhile to summarize his view. Stuhlmacher's position is not
purposefully antagonistic toward the traditional view, but it does render
the traditional formulation insufficient as a description of justification.
He presents a position that is different not only from the traditional
view but also quite different from other views on justification that have

---

[97] Ibid., 171.
[98] Scott J. Hafemann, "Paul and his Interpreters," in *Dictionary of Paul and his Letters*, ed. Gerald
F. Hawthorne and Ralph P. Martin (Downers Grove: InterVarsity, 1993), 676.
[99] Peter Stuhlmacher, *Paul's Letter to the Romans: A Commentary*, trans. Scott J. Hafemann
(Louisville: Westminster/John Knox, 1994), 88.
[100] Hafemann, "Paul and His Interpreters," 677. According to Hafemann, this emphasis "solves the
tension between the theological categories of imputed or effective righteousness by emphasizing that
the ontological bridge which makes possible the Pauline assertions concerning one's real anticipation
in the righteousness of God is the concept of the Spirit" (ibid.).

gained various measures of popularity (e.g., the New Perspective and those influenced by it).

At the heart of Stuhlmacher's view of justification lies his understanding of Paul's use of the phrase "the righteousness of God "(δικαιοσύνη θεοῦ).[101] For Stuhlmacher, God's righteousness cannot be thought of only as his saving righteousness but also must include his creation power that provides the necessary ground and confidence to stand before God's eschatological judgment. In Paul's letters the righteousness of God is "the embodiment of the saving action of God in Christ, which creates new life for believers as they face the judgment."[102] Thus "the righteousness of God" is both "the power and the gift of God."[103] Moreover, the phrase as it appears in 2 Corinthians 5:21 and Philippians 3:21 "cannot be reduced to the formula that it everywhere concerns only the righteousness of faith that is accepted by God, nor again that God's own righteousness is always in view; both aspects belong indissolubly together."[104] As we shall see, Stuhlmacher's *both/and* understanding of "the righteousness of God" (i.e., *both* saving act *and* new creation; *both* gift *and* power; *both* the righteousness of faith *and* God's own righteousness) naturally carries over into his view of justification. Stuhlmacher argues that this understanding of Paul's use of the phrase "the righteousness of God" is supported by a synthesis based on the concept in the Old Testament—the thought-world of the Apostle Paul.[105]

Stuhlmacher views justification in Paul as "both the sharing in God's grace that has already been given by faith and acquittal before God in the last judgment."[106] The link between "the righteousness of God" and justification in Stuhlmacher's view is evident. Justification is God's activ-

---

[101] The following survey of Stuhlmacher's view should be supplemented by reading Scott Hafemann's introduction to Stuhlmacher's *How to Do Biblical Theology* (Allison Park, PA: Pickwick, 1995), xv-xli. I am indebted to him for the conceptual framework, from both the introduction (including not a few references) and from personal conversations, that he provided for my own understanding of Stuhlmacher's thought.

[102] Stuhlmacher, "The Apostle Paul's View of Righteousness," in *Reconciliation, Law, and Righteousness: Essays in Biblical Theology*, trans. Everett Kalin (Philadelphia: Fortress, 1986), 78.

[103] Stuhlmacher, "Das Lexem, Gottesgerechtigkeit' drückt Macht und Gabe Gottes gleichzeitig aus" (Peter Stuhlmacher, *Biblische Theologie des Neuen Testament*, Band 1, *Grundlegung von Jesus zu Paulus* [Göttingen: Vandenhoeck & Ruprecht, 1997], 236).

[104] Stuhlmacher, "The Apostle Paul's View of Righteousness," 81.

[105] Stuhlmacher devotes a great deal of space to support his argument. See especially, *Biblische Theologie des Neuen Testaments*, 326-32. See also "The Apostle Paul's View of Righteousness," 78-80, and *How to Do Biblical Theology*, 36-37.

[106] Stuhlmacher, "The Apostle Paul's View of Righteousness," 72.

ity that the believer receives both in the past and in the eschatological judgment—just as "the righteousness of God" is God's saving activity in Christ and God's creating action that grants power which will ultimately provide the means of the believer's acquittal in the judgment.

Justification has a "forensic base," a "legal ground," in the cross and resurrection of Jesus Christ.[107] This forensic base provides the foundation for reconciliation, "the result of the justification of the ungodly."[108] The "forensic base" of justification, provided by Christ's atoning sacrifice for sin, is only part of the overall picture of salvation. In order to view fully Paul's doctrine of justification, one must understand it as "the eschatological saving act of God on behalf of his people and by his power in which they are freed from the power of sin and incorporated by means of the Spirit into the body of Christ."[109] Being "justified" means that one receives both an eschatological, forensic acceptance before the judgment of God and the present gift of the Holy Spirit—the very power that enables one ultimately to stand in that judgment.[110]

Again, justification is viewed as both gift and power. It has both a past and an ongoing significance, both of which are inherently tied to the eschatological reality. Seen in this way, justification becomes, for Stuhlmacher, an ongoing process empowered by the Spirit, the power of Christ that is leading up to the future verdict at the judgment seat of God.[111] As Stuhlmacher puts it, "the justification of which he [Paul] speaks is a process of becoming new that spans the earthly life of a believer, a path from faith's beginning to its end."[112]

In Stuhlmacher's view of justification there is really no place for a separate category like imputation in the traditional sense; this is especially true if imputation of righteousness is viewed primarily as a decla-

---

[107] Stuhlmacher, *Revisiting Paul's Doctrine of Justification: A Challenge to the New Perspective* (Downers Grove: InterVarsity, 2001), 61; See also Stuhlmacher, *Biblische Theologie des Neuen Testaments*, 297, 334-35.

[108] Stuhlmacher, *Biblische Theologie des Neuen Testaments*, 320. Stuhlmacher views "reconciliation" as a key term in understanding justification in Paul. In Paul, καταλλαγή (when 2 Cor. 5:18–6:2 and Rom. 5:1-11 are read together) is a term inclusive of God's salvation in history in Christ's sacrificial death, and the present experience of the "end-time renewal" by believers, who, though once were condemned sinners, are now in a relationship with God and stand justified before God and part of Christ's church (ibid.).

[109] Hafemann, "Introduction," xxiv.

[110] Ibid., xxiv-xxv.

[111] Stuhlmacher, *Biblische Theologie des Neuen Testaments*, 266-67.

[112] Stuhlmacher, "The Apostle Paul's View of Righteousness," 72.

ration in the past or located with any specific chronological emphasis. While he does use the word *imputation* (which is, after all, a biblical word) it is clear that the meaning is different from that seen in the Reformed tradition. For instance, when Stuhlmacher says that "the goal of life is having your faith in Christ reckoned as righteousness before God at the last judgment," the difference between his language and the traditional language, given the fact that he gives imputation ("reckoned") a decidedly future emphasis, is easy to see.[113]

Similarly, when Stuhlmacher speaks of Jesus as the second Adam obeying and fulfilling God's law and suffering as a vicarious sacrifice, the emphasis is on the resulting forgiveness and redemption from the law's curse; there is no explicit mention of positively fulfilling the law (whether Mosaic or otherwise) and imputing a positive righteousness to believers.[114] Indeed, Stuhlmacher consistently stresses forgiveness in his discussion of justification.[115] Even when he says, "God effects for sinners forgiveness of sins and new life by virtue of Jesus' atoning death," the phrase "and new life" does not carry the content seen above in the Reformed scholars but refers to the effective righteousness of God, both his saving and creating power.[116]

Stuhlmacher makes it clear that in his understanding, the traditional view of imputation becomes rather obsolete. There is no inherent difference in Paul between imputed and effective righteousness. Thus, for Stuhlmacher, the divine act of a new creation means that a person takes part in "the righteousness and glorious existence of Christ," and in Paul's theology this means that there is "no distinction between simply imputed and effective justification."[117]

---

[113] Ibid., 73. This eschatological dimension does, however, receive emphasis in some streams of the traditional view, e.g., Geerhardus Vos and Herman Ridderbos.

[114] Though Stuhlmacher remarks that Jesus was put under the law ("unter das Gestz gestellt"), and obeyed God's will where Adam had disobeyed ("Anders als Adam hat er aber Gottes Willen gehorsam erfüllt"), he emphasizes the redemption from the law's curse through Jesus' sacrificial death (*Biblische Theologie des Neuen*, 265).

[115] This point can be manifestly proven throughout Stuhlmacher's work, but, for example, see *Revisiting Paul's Doctrine of Justification*, 78; and "The Apostle Paul's View of Righteousness," 78.

[116] Stuhlmacher, The Apostle's View of Righteousness, 78. The content referred to in the Reformed scholars is the idea that justification requires forgiveness and eternal life, i.e., forgiveness for the penalty of sin *and* a positive fulfillment of the law's demands.

[117] Stuhlmacher's larger statement, along with Scripture citations, is "Kraft der von Gott aufgrund dieser Fürbitte wirksam zugesprochenen Rechtferigung gewinnen die πιστεύοντες, Anteil an der Gerechtigkeit und Herrlichkeitsexistenz Christi (2 Kor. 5, 21; Röm. 8, 28-30). Da Paulus die Rechtfertigung als göttlichen Neuschöpfungsakt ansieht, macht, *er keinen* Unterschied zwischen nur imputativer oder effektiver Rechtfertigung; durch die δικαιοσύνη ζωῆς (Röm. 5, 18) wird das Sein

While it is possible to reject the traditional view without blurring the distinction between extrinsic and intrinsic righteousness, Stuhmacher's insistence that there is no distinction between the two kinds of righteousness is not compatible with the traditional view. While Stuhlmacher's position presents a challenge to the traditional view from someone who sees himself, though not uncritically, as standing in the Reformation tradition (at least the Lutheran stream), there are more serious challenges from different quarters.

A Covenant of a Different Color

For some scholars, the traditional idea of imputation is rejected because of a larger theological paradigm that renders the doctrine unnecessary. Many scholars who fit this category are explicitly opposed to much of the traditional Lutheran and/or Reformed understanding of justification. For this reason, a slightly more in-depth discussion of specific areas of disagreement and reasons behind the disagreements is necessary. A primary example of this is seen in the work of E. P. Sanders and the New Perspective on Paul associated with his work.

E. P. Sanders. In the "covenantal nomism" paradigm described by Sanders, first-century Jews, like their forefathers, did not think they had to attain God's favor by works or their own righteousness.[118] God had

---

der Gottlosen vor Gott genichtet und neubegründer (vgl. 1 Kor. 1, 26-29; 2 Kor. 5, 17 mit Röm. 4, 5.17)" (*Biblische Theologie des Neuen Testaments*, 335). Stuhlmacher makes a similar statement in *Rediscovering Paul's View of Justification* and adds a dimension that drives home the fact that his view is quite different from the traditional view: "Justification means the establishment of a new being before God (cf. 2 Cor. 5:17, 21). Therefore, the controversial and—between Protestants and Catholics since the sixteenth century—much discussed distinction between 'imputed' righteousness (which is only credited to the sinner) and 'effective' righteousness (which transforms the sinner in his or her being) cannot be maintained from the Pauline texts. Both belong together" (61-62).

[118] Sanders sums up "covenantal nomism" in the following: "Briefly put, covenantal nomism is the view that one's place in God's plan is established on the basis of the covenant and that the covenant requires as the proper response of man his obedience to its commandments, while providing means of atonement for transgression." E. P. Sanders, *Paul and Palestinian Judaism: A Comparison of Patterns of Religion* (Philadelphia: Fortress, 1977), 75. For further discussion, idem, *Paul, the Law, and the Jewish People* (Philadelphia: Fortress, 1983). Sanders bases his views primarily on his readings of literature from Second Temple Judaism and Rabbinic sources. This study is primarily concerned with the results of Sanders's paradigm as they impact the doctrine of imputation and have influenced biblical scholarship. I will have occasion to refer to some of the same works, particularly from the Pseudepigrapha, in the coming chapters, but I do not propose to enter the discussion about Sanders's reading of the various Jewish texts. A large-scale discussion can be found in D. A. Carson, Peter T. O'Brien, and Mark A. Seifrid, eds., *Justification and Variegated Nomism: A Fresh Appraisal of Paul and Second Temple Judaism*, vol. 1, *The Complexities of Second Temple Judaism* (Tübingen: Mohr Siebeck/Grand Rapids: Baker, 2001).

established his covenant with Israel. They were already the covenant people on the basis of God's grace, and thus they did not have to earn God's favor; they only had to keep the stipulations of the covenant (i.e., the law) as a response to God's grace. Additionally, God did not require perfect obedience to his law, as most traditional Protestant teaching asserts, since the covenant made provision for sin through the sacrificial system. Ultimately the issue is not, for Sanders, *getting in*, but *staying in*.

While the bulk of the discussion about Sanders's work revolves around the issue of the law, the implications for the doctrine of imputation are relatively clear. The most significant issue is the fact that the Mosaic covenant, specifically regarding the law, is not inherently lacking anything; indeed, Paul's complaint is not that the old covenant was insufficient, but that it is obsolete now that the Messiah has come. Thus, before the Messiah came, a member of the covenant community lived in a right relationship with God on the basis of the old covenant system itself. The law and the sacrifices, until Christ, were inherently sufficient. As a result, there is little need for the obedience of Christ to be imputed to the believer because there was no serious problem of disobedience to the law to begin with. Trying to keep the law only became problematic, at least in Sanders's interpretation of Paul, once salvation became a matter of faith in Christ instead of obedience to the law.[119]

In this scheme, the condemning function of the law receives little, if any, emphasis, and so the idea of being guilty before the law of God, and God requiring the vindication of his name and justice for the transgression of his law, which receives such particular emphasis in the traditional formulation, is for all practical purposes a non-issue. Closely related to this is Sanders's insistence that Paul did not view righteousness as being connected to keeping the law. This marked a divergence between Paul and the Judaism of his day in light of the coming of the Messiah.[120]

---

[119] "Since salvation is only by Christ, the following of *any* other path is wrong. Paul does say that faith excludes boasting, and he does warn the Jews against boasting (Rom. 2:17), but the warning is not against a self-righteousness which is based on the view that works earn merit before God. The warning is against boasting of the relationship to God which is *evidenced* by *possession* of the law and against being smug about the *knowledge* of God's will while in fact transgressing. Paul regarded zeal for the law itself as a good thing (Rom. 10:2; Phil. 3:9). What is wrong with it is not that it implies petty obedience and minimization of important matters, nor that it results in the tabulation of merit points before God, but *that it is not worth anything in comparison with being in Christ* (Phil 3:4-11)" (E. P. Sanders, *Paul and Palestinian Judaism*, 550; (author's emphases).
[120] Ibid., 545-46.

It is also worth noting that Sanders stresses the "relational" aspect of justification, i.e., the relationship obtained and preserved in the covenant, and downplays, though does not reject, the forensic nature of Paul's use of "righteousness" language.[121] One result is that with all the talk of God's righteousness as his "covenantal faithfulness," there is little said about God's condemning and judging righteousness as part of the δικαιοσύνη θεοῦ. Though more could be said, this brief overview demonstrates that "covenantal nomism" presents a new paradigm in which the traditional doctrine of imputation is simply unneeded. If perfect obedience to the law is unnecessary, and obedience to the law is not primarily connected to forensic righteousness, and God's righteousness is conceived of as "covenantal faithfulness" with little emphasis on his righteousness in regard to rightfully judging transgressions of his law, then the imputation of Christ's righteousness in terms of his obedience to the law is irrelevant.

James D. G. Dunn. Following Sanders, James Dunn emphasizes the "relational" character of righteousness.[122] Over against a Greek "worldview" that views righteousness as "an idea or ideal against which the individual and individual action can be measured," there is the Hebrew idea of righteousness, a "more relational concept" that focuses on duties that arise in the context of relationship. In other words, being "righteous" means fulfilling whatever obligations are attached to a particular relationship.[123]

---

[121] Ibid., 470, 492 n.57. Speaking of forensic elements in Paul's use of righteousness language in regard to the "righteousness of God," Sanders says that the "juridical-forensic overtones are present . . . but not in the foreground. The forensic declaration is more than simply a proclamation; it is at the same time 'effective' declaration: The man who is 'declared righteous' by God stands under his sovereign, creative-redemptive disposal" (ibid., 540).

[122] James D. G. Dunn, *The Theology of the Apostle Paul* (Grand Rapids: Eerdmans, 1998), 341.

[123] Ibid., 341-42. Dunn expresses his conviction that the relational/Hebrew view of righteousness and justification is the way forward in interpreting Paul in the following: "This recognition that the thought world which comes to expression in the English term (justification) is through and through Hebraic/biblical/Jewish in character is a key factor in gaining a secure hold on Paul's teaching on justification" (ibid., 342). Dunn's bifurcation of Hebrew and Greek thought is asserted but not convincingly defended. The idea that somehow the Jews did not really have a legal conception of righteousness is a clear connection to Sanders. This issue, along with many of the main ideological tenets of the New Perspective and those who follow in its wake, can be traced to Krister Stendahl's inordinately influential essay, "Paul and the Introspective Conscience of the West," in *Paul among Jews and Gentiles* (Philadelphia: Fortress, 1976), 78-96. Many of Stendahl's often unsubstantiated assertions about Paul, Luther, Protestant theology, Western thought, and history have been accepted widely in critical scholarship.

The effects of Dunn's relational view of righteousness/justification are seen most clearly in his discussion of "the righteousness of God." The righteousness of God is almost entirely construed as God's action in the world to fulfill his obligations to his creation and most importantly to the elect, i.e., his covenant people. God's righteousness is manifested in God's own fulfillment of his end of the covenantal relationship. God's righteousness is God's "faithfulness" to the elect, "the fulfillment of his covenant obligation as Israel's God in delivering, saving, and vindicating Israel."[124] As seen in Sanders, the result of this view of righteousness is that there is little emphasis on the righteousness of God including his righteous judgment.[125] Again, the effect is that a concept such as the imputation of Christ's righteousness becomes obsolete in this scheme. Dunn says as much when he asserts that the relational view of justification "undercuts" a large part of "the debates of post-Reformation theology."[126]

Chief among the undercut theological disputes is whether δικαιόω refers to being made righteous or being reckoned righteous. For Dunn this is a non-issue because it is not a question of either/or but both/and:

> The covenant God counts the covenant partner as still in partnership despite the latter's continued failure. But the covenant partner could hardly fail to be transformed by a living relationship with the life-giving God.[127]

On one hand it is difficult to tell who Dunn's dialogue partner is at this point, since no one in the Protestant Reformed tradition believes that justification, even on the forensic basis of the imputation of Christ's righteousness, is absolutely isolated from the transformational work of God through the Spirit. Justification and sanctification are held in distinction, but they are ultimately and necessarily linked in redemption.

On the other hand, Dunn is entirely correct to see a difference

---

[124] Dunn, *Paul*, 342.

[125] This is not to imply that Dunn does not discuss God's judgment. To the contrary, see 79-101, 490-92. The point here is that the theme of God's righteous judgment does not receive a great deal of emphasis in Dunn's work, most noticeably in his discussion of the righteousness of God.

[126] What Dunn means by "post-Reformation theology" (ibid., 344) is left to the imagination. Presumably he is referring to the second and third generation Reformers who formulated and systematized the theology of the first-generation Reformers like Luther, Calvin, and Zwingli. Whatever the case, Dunn's position illustrates an explicit refutation of the traditional Reformed understanding of imputation.

[127] Ibid., 344.

between his understanding and that of traditional Reformed theology. Justification, in Reformed theology, is not so much an issue of a preexisting covenant relationship being maintained as it is a matter of a covenant relationship being established. Secondly, in the Reformed view, a distinction is made between the declaration "just" and the transformation of the believer. This is not, however, an ontological distinction, or even properly a chronological distinction in terms of measurable time (though some proponents may make it sound that way)—a point often missed by opponents of the traditional view.[128]

In Romans 4, one of the "key" imputation texts, the traditional emphasis is nowhere on the horizon. According to Dunn, Paul is stating what "needed no discussion," namely, "that to be 'righteous' is to be not so much acceptable to God as accepted by God—righteousness as the status which God accorded to his covenant people and in which he sustained them."[129] Here Dunn understands Paul to be working contrary to much of the teaching about Abraham in Jewish tradition, particularly in regard to Abraham's offering up of Isaac in Genesis 22 as the interpretive key to Genesis 15:6.[130] Paul is showing that Genesis 15 is not the result of Abraham's faithfulness in Genesis 22; Genesis 15 is the

---

[128] It is worth noting another element in Dunn that is likely tied to the absence of imputation in any traditional sense in his work, namely, his view of the atonement. Although Dunn does maintain that "substitution" is at least part of the atonement, his assertion that "Paul's teaching is *not* that Christ dies "in the place of" others so that they *escape* death (as the logic of substitution implies). It is rather that Christ's sharing their death makes it possible for them to share *his* death" (ibid., 223; his emphasis). It seems, however, that both aspects are true. Even though a believer dies with Christ (Rom. 6:3; Gal. 2:19-20), Christ nevertheless died "in the place of others" (Rom. 6:10). In this sense believers do "escape death." It is not clear why both substitution and representation cannot be applied to the atonement. In fact, Dunn is difficult to understand at this point because he acknowledges the place of "substitution" in Paul's teaching but also refutes (as in the quotation above) the typical way "substitution" has been applied to discussions of the atonement. Putting all confusion aside for a moment, the fact remains that once substitutionary atonement is rejected, or relegated to a minor position, there is no longer any, or at least very little practical need for the traditional understanding of imputation. Opponents would likely be happy to agree with that statement. This issue will be discussed further in chapter 5 of this work.
[129] James D. G. Dunn, *Romans 1–8*, Word Biblical Commentary, vol. 38a (Dallas: Word, 1988), 203. Dunn's *Romans* is dealt with only briefly but does receive more attention in later exegetical chapters.
[130] Dunn cites Sirach 44:19-21 and 1 Maccabees 2:52, among others, in particular (ibid., 200-202). Dunn is careful to point out that Paul's use of terms such as *working* and *reward* does not mean that he is arguing against a common view in the Judaism of his day. First-century Judaism did not focus on meriting God's favor. According to Dunn, Paul's "point is simply that in the case of Gen. 15:6 the whole language of 'payment due' is inappropriate" (ibid., 204). Paul is trying to establish that it is not covenantal faithfulness that God is rewarding, but Abraham's faith. The first-century Jews would have seen Abraham as the ultimate paradigm of covenantal faithfulness. Thus, as the children of Abraham they were to keep the works of the law as a sign of their covenantal faithfulness, the "works" being summed up as circumcision, Sabbath, and purity laws (see Dunn, *Paul*, 354-59). Paul is establishing that Abraham was reckoned righteous on the basis of his faith *before* the law was given (see Dunn, *Romans 1–8*, 208).

declaration that God counts Abraham "righteous" not on the basis of "faithfulness" but on the basis of "'faith' as belief, trust."[131] Paul does not want the commercial term "reckon" (λογίζομαι) to be interpreted to mean that Abraham was counted righteous, as his due wage, on the basis of covenantal faithfulness. Paul is not condemning *covenantal nomism*; he is asserting that Abraham's righteousness, like the righteousness that believers in Christ now have, was established by faith.

The Jews of Paul's day were guilty, not of thinking they could merit God's favor, but of being prideful in their own status as the elect people of God. Paul wants to show that the righteousness reckoned by God, through faith, is a gift of grace, not payment due. This summary of Dunn on Romans 4 is included here to illustrate what was said earlier: the traditional formulation of imputation is often missing in modern interpretations of the "key texts," because the larger biblical-theological paradigms are different from the traditional Protestant scheme, and the discussion of imputation along traditional lines simply does not fit.

N. T. Wright.[132] In formulating his scheme of justification, which emphasizes (1) covenant, (2) law-court, and (3) eschatology, N. T. Wright takes exception to the traditional Protestant view of justification in general and, as a result, to imputation. In regard to imputation, Wright repeats the centuries-old argument that the traditional understanding of imputation amounts to a "legal fiction."[133] Rejecting the position that primarily views righteousness and justification as a status conferred on believers by God, Wright asserts that the main issue is faith in the gospel of Jesus Christ—the new badge of covenant membership in the people of God. In this scheme, justification "is the doctrine which insists that all those who have this faith belong as full members of this family [the family of Abraham], on this basis and no other."[134]

In Romans 4 Wright defines righteousness as "the status of being

131 Ibid., 204.
132 I acknowledge the often substantial differences and disagreements between Wright and both Sanders and Dunn. Wright is often wrongly grouped with Sanders and painted with the same generic New Perspective brush as if he holds to all of Sanders's views. He clearly does not. Regardless of their differences, there are affinities between Wright's position and that of both Sanders and Dunn. For that reason, as part of a trajectory, Wright may justifiably be grouped with Sanders and Dunn.
133 N. T. Wright, *What Saint Paul Really Said: Was Paul of Tarsus the Real Founder of Christianity?* (Grand Rapids: Eerdmans/Cincinnati: Forward Movement Publications, 1997), 102.
134 Ibid., 132-33.

a member of the covenant" and faith as "the badge, the sign, that reveals that status."[135] This, rather than any interpretation of this passage that over-emphasizes the bookkeeping metaphor in 4:3—"But Abraham believed God and it was reckoned to him as righteousness"—and developed in 4:4-5, should inform our reading of the text. The bookkeeping metaphor, though important, should not be overemphasized since in all his discussions about justification Paul uses it only here.[136] Thus, any interpretation, i.e., the traditional view (which, like Dunn, Wright identifies nebulously as "post-Reformation"), that places emphasis on the metaphor, focuses merely on a "brief sidelight."[137] If Paul's use of λογίζομαι is simply a handy illustration and not fundamental to Paul's teaching on justification, then the traditional view is highly questionable.[138]

The Adam/Christ parallel and antithesis in Romans 5:12-21 plays a key role in the traditional view of the imputation of Christ's righteousness to the believer—a role that in Wright's opinion is unjustified. Wright directly addresses the traditional view and concludes that "it is almost certainly not what Paul has in mind here."[139] The "obedience of the one" (5:19) is the Messiah, the Isaianic servant, overturning Israel's disobedience of God's command to bring "salvation to the world, rather than his amassing a treasury of merit through Torah obedience."[140]

---

[135] N. T. Wright, *The Letter to the Romans*, in *The New Interpreter's Bible*, vol. 10, ed. Leander Keck (Nashville: Abingdon Press, 2002), 491. Wright develops three metaphors in 4:3 that serve as the framework for his interpretation and are in continuity with his overall interpretive paradigm: (1) bookkeeping (i.e., the commercial language of "reckoning" or counting to someone's ledger; (2) lawcourt (God the judge pronounces Abraham "in the right" on account of his faith); and (3) covenant (the relationship to which Abraham's faith pointed) (ibid.). I will deal more closely with Wright's exegesis in later chapters.

[136] Ibid., 491. Presumably Wright does not count Galatians 3:6 because the Genesis 15:6 quote is not expanded upon there.

[137] Ibid.

[138] In Romans 4 Paul uses λογίζομαι twelve times (including Old Testament quotes), 4:3, 4, 5, 6, 8, 9, 10, 11, 22, 23 (twice), 24. Although simply counting words does not necessarily prove that the bookkeeping metaphor is not merely "a brief sidelight," and while most of the occurrences are a matter of repetition, one might get the impression that Paul does intend to draw special attention to the metaphor. Does Wright's conclusion apply to Genesis 15:6? Moreover, is Paul's quote of Genesis 15:6 in Galatians 3:6 in the midst of a detailed discussion about issues such as the law, the Abrahamic covenant, and faith in Christ, also a "brief sidelight"?

[139] Wright, *Romans*, 529.

[140] Ibid. Wright addresses the traditional interpretation in the following: "What does Paul suppose the Messiah was obedient to? A long tradition within one strand of Reformation thought has supposed that Paul was here referring to Jesus' perfect obedience to the law. In this view, Christ's 'active obedience' and his 'passive obedience' work together." Contrary to this interpretation, Wright sees the obedience to the law as "beside the point" in this text (ibid.). Wright's comment that it is a matter of Christ's "obedience to God's commission . . . rather than his amassing a treasury of merit through Torah obedience" is a caricature of the traditional position.

Wright's rejection of imputation is clear in his interpretation of 1 Corinthians 1:30 and 2 Corinthians 5:21.[141] Wright refutes the traditional reading by asserting that if we read 1 Corinthians 1:30 as teaching the imputation of righteousness, it must also teach the imputation of "wisdom . . . sanctification and redemption," a reading that "will certainly make nonsense of the very specialized and technical senses . . . in the history of theology."[142] If one insists on the traditional reading of 2 Corinthians 5:21, the text "detaches itself from the rest of the chapter and context, as though it were a little floating saying which Paul just threw in there for good measure."[143] Rather than teaching about justification, or giving the content of his message of reconciliation, Paul is further defending the apostolic ministry. The apostles are the living testimony of "the righteousness of God in Christ."[144]

Yes and/or No: Other Modern Voices[145]

Herman Ridderbos stands unambiguously in the (Dutch) Reformed tradition, yet his treatment of justification in Paul, and in regard to imputation in particular, is not simply a defense for Reformed theology. Ridderbos begins with a discussion of the eschatological nature of justification. God's "judicial verdict . . . has already been settled" at the cross of Christ, so that justification and righteousness can be thought of as present realities. Yet, the righteousness of God already revealed in Christ is the same in content as the Spirit-guided hope of future righteousness (Gal. 5:5).[146] The cross and resurrection, by nature, make justification both a present and a future reality—or rather, a single reality in which the future has dawned in the present. "In the present time" God has

---

141 Wright insists that 1 Corinthians 1:30 is the only place "where something called 'the imputed righteousness of Christ' . . . finds any basis in the text" (*What St. Paul Really Said*, 123). This is not an admission of legitimacy, but merely an observation that this text contains language that is somewhat similar to the traditional formulation.

142 Ibid.

143 Ibid.

144 Although Wright treats this text briefly in *What Saint Paul Really Said*, 104-5, his detailed discussion is found in, "On Becoming the Righteousness of God in Christ," in *Pauline Theology*, vol. 2, *1 & 2 Corinthians*, ed. David M. Hay (Minneapolis: Fortress, 1993), 200-208.

145 The work of Geerhardus Vos, which has been a major influence on my own thinking and development, is not included in this section but plays a significant role in later chapters.

146 Herman Ridderbos, *Paul: An Outline of his Theology*, trans. John R. De Witt (Grand Rapids: Eerdmans, 1975), 165-66. For Ridderbos's focused discussion of eschatological justification see *Paul*, 161-66.

revealed his "vindicating righteousness" in the cross of Christ, and this vindicating righteousness is nothing other than God's final judgment breaking into the present. Likewise, Christ's resurrection is the "breaking through of the new creation."[147] God's eschatological judgment was revealed at the cross on which Christ bore the sins of his people who, in turn, "become 'the righteousness of God'"; that is, they may identify themselves with that which is acquitted in the judgment of God."[148]

In historical-redemptive terms, justification is an eschatological reality; God's future judgment and the new creation have broken into the present. God's judgment was passed on Christ who died for sinners (Christ-for-us). The faith that is reckoned as righteousness is that faith which is grounded on the "obedience and righteous act of the One," apart from works.[149] In this sense it is a purely forensic reality. It regards "man the sinner and not . . . his future reality."[150] Yet, justification is specifically justification "in Christ." It is based not only on the past event of cross and resurrection, but also in the "corporate inclusion" of believers in Christ (we-in-Christ). Because they are in Christ by faith, and because Christ has died for them, believers have received the eschatological pardon of God and participate in the new creation; and this justification is on the basis of "the imputative ground" of faith.[151] In this way, imputation is not the whole, but along with the redemptive-historical and forensic aspects, is one of the "various facets" of justification in Paul.

John Murray, commenting on Romans 4, equates imputation with justification, saying that the imputation of righteousness in Paul "is synonymous with justification."[152] That statement hardly needs inter-

---

[147] Ibid., 167.

[148] Ibid., 168. With the preceding eschatological framework established, Ridderbos explains his understanding of the nature of Christ's death and resurrection in terms of the "Christ-for-us" and the "we-in-Christ." On the one hand, Christ's death takes place objectively, apart from the participation of believers. Ridderbos cites Romans 3:25; 4:25; 2 Corinthians 5:21; and Galatians 3:13 for support. On the other hand, Christ died as one of us, taking on our flesh, and as the second Adam his death was explicitly on our behalf, and thus we are made to be in union with him. Here he cites Romans 5:18-19; 8:3; 1 Corinthians 1:30; 2 Corinthians 5:14, 21 (again) (ibid., 169).

[149] Ibid., 178.

[150] Ibid., 175.

[151] Ibid., 177 n. 58.

[152] John Murray, *Romans*, NICNT (Grand Rapids: Eerdmans, 1968), 134. For another concise overview of Murray's discussion in Romans 4:78 see James R. White, *The God Who Justifies* (Bloomington, Minn.: Bethany House, 2001), 215-17. White's work defends the traditional doctrine and allows for the individual texts to speak for themselves.

pretation. Murray writes from a confessional Reformed perspective and his loyalty to that tradition is seen clearly in his view of justification. The judicial element in justification, the relationship between the judge, the law, and the accused, is the fundamental theme for Murray. In the act of justification the judge does not *make* the defendant righteous, he *declares* him to be righteous: "In a word, justification is simply a declaration or pronouncement respecting the relation of the person to the law which he, the judge, is required to administer."[153] This declaration is not fictitious but is based on a presupposed right standing of the defendant in regard to the law.

When, therefore, God justifies the ungodly (Rom. 4:5), he does not simply call the ungodly "just," but he declares them just because he has a legally valid reason for doing so; otherwise the judge himself would be unjust. When God declares a person "righteous" or "just," he does so because he also constitutes the grounds for the verdict.[154] The basis for God's actions is the righteousness of Christ, specifically, "the righteousness of his obedience."[155] It is the imputed righteousness of Christ that provides both the constitutive and declarative elements of justification.

Murray, like others in the Reformed tradition, explains that justification, though bound up with the forgiveness of sins, also requires a "positive judgment on God's part that gives to justification its specific character."[156] Even when Paul formulates "his positive doctrine of justification" in the "formally negative" language of Romans 4:6-7

---

[153] John Murray, *Redemption Accomplished and Applied* (Grand Rapids, Eerdmans 1955; reprint, 1987), 119.

[154] "God justifies the ungodly by causing "the righteous state or declaration which is declared to be" (Murray, *Redemption*, 123; See also, idem, *Romans*, 205).

[155] Murray, *Redemption*, 123-24. Murray later summarizes his argument in the following: "The righteousness of justification is the righteousness and obedience of Christ (Rom. 5:17-19). Here we have the final consideration which confirms all of the foregoing considerations and sets them in clear focus. This is the final reason why we are pointed away from ourselves to Christ and his accomplished work. And this is the reason why the righteousness of justification is the righteousness of God. It is the righteousness of Christ wrought by him in human nature, the righteousness of his obedience unto death, even the death of the cross. But, as such, it is the righteousness of the God-man, a righteousness which measures up to the requirements of our sinful and sin-cursed situation, a righteousness which meets all the demands of a complete and irrevocable justification, and a righteousness fulfilling all these demands because it is a righteousness of divine property and character, a righteousness undefiled and inviolable" (ibid., 128).

[156] Murray, "Justification," in *Collected Writings of John Murray*, 2:218. As in *Redemption* and *Romans*, Murray's discussion of the positive element in justification focuses on Romans 5:12-21. For a detailed treatment of Murray's view of imputation and the importance of federal headship in understanding it, see *The Imputation of Adam's Sin* (Phillipsburg, N.J.: Presbyterian and Reformed, 1959). Since this book deals extensively with Romans 5:12 it will be considered in chapter 3.

(Ps. 32:8), therefore equating justification with forgiveness, there is no reason to think that Paul is defining justification as forgiveness.[157] Justification cannot be thought of solely in terms of forgiveness because it involves not only the removal of guilt but also God's acceptance—an acceptance that requires positive obedience, which in turn, can only come from the imputation of the obedience of Christ.[158]

One element in Murray's discussion of justification, and salvation in general, that should be noted is his strong emphasis on "the central truth of the whole doctrine of salvation," that is, union with Christ.[159] Imputation, as vital as it is for Murray, is nevertheless secondary to union with Christ; indeed, "the concept is richer than that of imputation."[160] It is 2 Corinthians 5:21 that provides the "fullest expression" of the truth contained in Romans 5:17-19.[161] Believers have Christ's righteousness imputed to them, but they are also identified by that righteousness: "Christ is ours, and therefore all that is his is ours in union with him and we cannot think of him in his vicarious capacity or of anything that is his in this capacity except in union and communion with his people."[162]

There are scholars who use the traditional language, but who do so with hesitancy or in language more nuanced and without the same detail found in the writings of some traditional Reformed theologians. Leon Morris states that while it is "impossible" to deny that Paul taught the imputation of righteousness, he goes on to say that "he [Paul] never says in so many words the righteousness *of Christ* was imputed to believers, and it may fairly be doubted whether he had this in mind in his treatment of justification."[163] Similarly, George Ladd admits that "Paul never

---

[157] Murray, *Romans,* 134. Paul's point, according to Murray, in linking justification with forgiveness, particularly in the quote from Psalm 32, is to further emphasize grace through faith over against reward of merit (ibid., 135). Even with his strong theological presuppositions, Murray judiciously recognizes Paul's emphasis on forgiveness in this text.

[158] Murray, "Justification," 213, 218. Murray says that "it is prejudicial to the grace and nature of justification to construe it merely in terms of remission. This is so to such an extent that the bare notion of remission does not express, nor does it of itself imply, the concept of justification" (ibid.).

[159] Murray, *Redemption,* 161. The last chapter of *Redemption* is devoted to union with Christ because "the whole process of salvation has its origin in one phase of union with Christ and salvation has in view the realization of other phases of union with Christ."

[160] Murray, "Justification," 214.

[161] Ibid.

[162] Ibid., 214. Is there an echo of Luther here? Murray's language sounds similar to, "Christ's righteousness becomes our righteousness and all that he has becomes ours, rather he himself becomes ours." See above, 26.

[163] Leon Morris, *The Apostolic Preaching of the Cross,* 3rd rev. ed. (Grand Rapids: Eerdmans, 1965), 282.

expressly states that the righteousness of Christ is imputed to believers."[164] Ladd nevertheless holds to imputation on the grounds that "[i] t is an unavoidable logical conclusion that people are justified because Christ's righteousness is imputed to them."[165]

In Thomas Schreiner's treatment of Paul the emphasis is on the connection between Christ's atoning death and the "reckoning" of righteousness, as well as the eschatological nature of justification, but the discussion focuses on forgiveness rather than imputation of positive righteousness.[166] In his *Romans*, Schreiner, taking the traditional view regarding the corporate solidarity between Adam and Christ with humanity, states that for "those in Christ, God graciously imputes Christ's righteousness" and that "he [God] reversed the baleful results of Adam's sin by imputing the righteousness of Christ to us."[167] As in his comments on Romans 4, Schreiner refrains from further defining the mechanics of imputation.

Likewise, Douglas Moo's comments on Romans 4 focus on the relationship between imputation and forgiveness in connection with Paul's emphasis on justification apart from works, without further recourse to a discussion of the imputation of Christ's righteousness.[168] In Romans 5:19, Moo holds that while Paul may have Christ's "active righteousness" in mind, he is nevertheless emphasizing Christ's obedience to death on the cross.[169] Interpreting καθίστημι (5:19) within Paul's "forensic categories," Moo insists that "to be righteous" means to be "judged acquitted, cleared of all charges, in the heavenly judgment." Once again, the discussion centers on what was referred to above as "mere forgiveness." Moo does, however, add: "It seems fair . . . to speak of 'imputation' here."[170]

Two recent challenges to the traditional view of imputation deserve to be noted since neither scholar is associated with the New Perspective.

[164] George Eldon Ladd, *A Theology of the New Testament*, rev. ed., ed. Donald A. Hagner (Eerdmans: Grand Rapids, 1993), 491.
[165] Ibid., 491.
[166] Thomas R. Schreiner, *Paul, Apostle of God's Glory in Christ: A Pauline Theology*, (Downers Grove: InterVarsity, 2001), 205.
[167] Thomas R. Schreiner, *Romans*, Baker Exegetical Commentary on the New Testament (Grand Rapids: Baker, 1998), 290. As with Cranfield, Moo, and Murray, I will deal more extensively with Schreiner's commentary in the following two chapters.
[168] Douglas Moo, *The Epistle to the Romans*, NICNT (Grand Rapids: Eerdmans, 1996), 266.
[169] Ibid., 345.
[170] Ibid. n.145. Moo, like so many other interpreters, is more nuanced in his discussion of Paul than that found in some systematic treatments.

First are the arguments put forward by Mark Seifrid, who defends a traditional Protestant view of justification against the views of scholars like Sanders, Dunn, and Wright. "It is worth observing" says Seifrid, "that Paul never speaks of Christ's righteousness as imputed to believers as became standard in Protestantism."[171] Seifrid's main objection to the traditional formulation is that it "treats the justifying verdict of God as an immediate and isolated gift." As a result: "The justification of the believer is thereby separated from the justification of God in his wrath against us."[172] There is, moreover, no need to posit imputation in order to understand Paul's doctrine of justification because "forgiveness" for Paul encapsulates all of justification. What is missing in the traditional formula is an understanding of the eschatological nature of Christ's death, burial and resurrection as the "prolepsis of the final judgment and the entrance of the age to come."[173] The formulation of justification, and hence imputation, that focuses on the past event of the cross as part of an order of salvation, rather than an eschatological reality grasped by faith, creates categories that ultimately lead to a disjunction between "justification and obedience."[174]

Another challenge to the traditional view comes from Robert Gundry who, after considering the primary texts, concludes: "The notion [imputation of Christ's righteousness] is passé, neither because of Roman Catholic influence nor because of theological liberalism, but because of fidelity to the relevant biblical texts."[175] Gundry laments that imputation plays such a central role in "The Gospel of Jesus Christ: An Evangelical Celebration" because it renders the document "deeply

---

[171] Mark A. Seifrid, *Christ Our Righteousness: Paul's Theology of Justification* (Apollos: Leichester, UK; Downers Grove: InterVarsity, 2000), 174. It is interesting to note two things: (1) Seifrid understands himself to be following in Luther's tradition regarding justification in general as well as imputation in particular. (As seen above, Luther's discussion of imputation is not the language found in later Reformers; thus, Seifrid has a legitimate claim about Luther's position on imputation); and (2) Seifrid adamantly opposes Sanders, Dunn, and Wright—all of whom are highly critical of the traditional formulation of justification (whether Lutheran or Reformed), and all of whom deny the traditional doctrine of imputation. This illustrates the fact that criticism about imputation does not stem from the New Perspective alone, but also from quarters aligned with reformational theology.
[172] Ibid., 174.
[173] Ibid., 175.
[174] Ibid., 175.
[175] Robert H. Gundry, "Why I Didn't Endorse 'The Gospel of Jesus Christ: An Evangelical Celebration' . . . Even though I Wasn't Asked To," *Books & Culture* (January/February 2001): 9. Thomas Oden's response to Gundry, "A Calm Answer to a Critique of 'The Gospel of Jesus Christ: An Evangelical Celebration," and Gundry's reply, "On Oden's 'Answer,'" both appear in *Books & Culture* (March/April 2001): 1-12, 39 and 14-15, 39, respectively.

flawed."[176] The reason: "That doctrine of imputation is not even biblical. Still less is it 'essential' to the Gospel."[177] Gundry's essay, though brief, is important because it contains interpretations of the "imputation texts" (Rom. 4:1-8, 5:12-21; 2 Cor. 5:21; Gal. 3:6; Phil. 3:9; and others) that directly oppose traditional exegesis. This essay drew a quick response not only from Thomas Oden, but also from John Piper, who answers Gundry's objections while defending the traditional position.[178]

CONCLUSION

This historical overview illustrates that it can be difficult to speak generally of "imputation." Although many theologians may use "imputation" as shorthand to mean the imputation of the active and passive obedience of Christ, with which he gained for us our forgiveness of sins by dying under the curse of God's law and also merited our positive righteous standing before God on the basis of his perfect fulfillment of God's law, it is wrong to think that if one does not hold to this entire formula, one therefore rejects "imputation." Even the phrase employed frequently for convenience in this work, "the traditional view/idea of imputation," could be interpreted to mean there is really only one way to conceive of imputation and that all others are therefore false, and likely heretical. That is certainly not the intention here.

There are "views" of imputation, not a general concept of imputation. Whether imputation is thought of primarily as relating to union with Christ or as forgiveness or as simply a rather minor Pauline metaphor, or is translated as "reckoned" without further comment, or whether "faith" itself is the righteousness imputed, or whether it is defined according to the "traditional view," it is still *a view* of imputation. This does not make every view correct as long as it employs the term "imputation"—far from it. Such a perspective, however, helps

[176] Gundry, "*Why*," 9.
[177] Ibid.
[178] John Piper, *Counted Righteous in Christ: Should we Abandon the Doctrine of the Imputation of Christ's Righteousness?* (Wheaton: Crossway, 2002). Piper's work is a direct response to Gundry concentrating on the exegesis of the texts disputed by Gundry and most closely associated with the traditional view. Not surprisingly, the same basic texts that are the focus of this study are those Piper discusses as well. Gundry has followed up the pieces in *Books and Culture* with, "The Nonimputation of Christ's Righteousness," in *Justification: What's at Stake in the Current Debates*, eds. Mark Husbands and Daniel J. Treier (Downers Grove: InterVarsity, 2004), 17-44.

establish a good frame of reference for the work of exegesis and biblical theology. If we bear in mind that imputation is not a monolithic term even in theological discourse, perhaps we can avoid jumping to extreme conclusions before weighing the evidence found in the text.

Secondly, it is evident in the modern era, especially in the twentieth century, that the texts in Paul that serve as the proofs for the traditional view of imputation are interpreted in ways quite different from the traditional interpretations. There is also a divergence of interpretations among contemporary scholars and theologians. Certainly the differences can be explained in part by the rise of biblical theology. Many biblical theologians eschew language reminiscent of systematic or dogmatic theology, and "imputation" is notoriously thought of as a "systematic category." Also, the inductive and descriptive nature of biblical theology, while providing a guard against unfounded deductions, often (and often purposely) prevents any kind of synthesis. These observations aside, it is worth taking note of the fact that to a large degree the traditional view of imputation does not receive the same degree of emphasis among biblical theologians as it did (and still does) among systematic theologians. Perhaps it is more helpful to say that it receives *a different kind* of emphasis. But for many, imputation does not appear on the horizon at all. That observation alone justifies a reexamination of imputation.

We now turn again to Paul. Taking this historical overview as a point of departure and as the background for the rich, historical discussion into which we have entered, attention from this point on focuses on the "key" texts in Paul traditionally associated with imputation.

TWO

THE RECKONING OF
RIGHTEOUSNESS: ABRAHAM,
FAITH, AND IMPUTATION

OF ALL THE TEXTS associated with imputation, Romans 4 has the best claim as an "imputation text." The reason for this is simple: the word λογίζομαι appears more often in Romans 4 than in any other single text in the Bible. Paul's quotation of Genesis 15:6 brings the subject of imputation to the foreground: "Abraham believed in God and it was reckoned to him for righteousness." The question is not whether Romans 4 teaches imputation. The question is, what does Paul teach about imputation in Romans 4? This question, does not, or at least should not, assume that Romans 4 is "about" imputation in a comprehensive, theological sense of the word. Even Romans 4, the most explicit "imputation text" in the Bible, is not *about* imputation in the sense of the entire doctrine being spelled out in all its historical fullness. Critics often cite texts like Romans 4 and observe that the imputation of Christ's righteousness is not explicit in Paul's teaching.[1] That observation, however, is off the mark. It is not a matter of bringing, much less *finding*, the entire doctrine in any one text. Romans 4 is but a part, albeit a large part, of Paul's theology of imputation.

Paul introduces imputation to support the main idea that justifica-

---

[1] E.g., Robert H. Gundry, "The Nonimputation of Christ's Righteousness," in *Justification: What's at Stake in the Current Debates*, ed. Mark Husbands and Daniel Treier (Downers Grove: InterVarsity, 2004), 17.

tion is, and always has been, by faith rather than works. The reckoning metaphor, "reckoned to him for righteousness," serves the greater point that a person stands in a right relationship with God only by faith. Paul uses the metaphor of reckoning, taken from Genesis 15:6, to argue that there is only one way for anyone, even father Abraham, to stand before God. Righteousness before God is not a matter of remuneration. Righteousness is, rather, something received as a gift; it is reckoned, not earned—in fact, far from being earned, it is something granted to the ungodly. Paul does not develop a new idea here in order to shore up his argument; he employs the metaphor from Genesis to show that to be "justified as a gift by his grace" (Rom. 3:24) means that one is in a right relationship with God by imputation—God imputes righteousness as a gift apart from works.

Romans 4 is located in the context of a larger argument and as such it has both explicit and implicit links to what precedes and follows it. Seeking to show that justification by faith (3:25) has always been the principle that defines God's relationship with his people, that justification is for both Jews and Gentiles equally (3:28), and, therefore, that no one can boast in anything other than the grace of God (3:29), Paul proceeds to quote Genesis 15:6. Paul confirms what he means by the use of another Old Testament quote (Ps. 32:1-2). Paul has shown already that justification is "through faith" (3:25),[2] and reinforces that point in 5:1. Everyone, both Jew and Gentile, may have their sins forgiven and stand accepted before God through the means of faith. This accepted status (righteousness), for both Jew and Gentile is conferred by God's reckoning.

The goal of this chapter is to investigate what Paul means by imputation, the role of faith in regard to imputation, and what Paul primarily emphasizes about imputation in this text.

ABRAHAM'S FAITH: THE BACKDROP OF ROMANS 4

When Paul chooses to include Abraham in Romans, he is not simply using a handy example that just happens to support his argument, nor

---

[2] I could cite 3:22 here as well. I am fully aware of the ongoing argument over whether 3:22 contains an objective genitive ("through faith *in* Jesus Christ") or a subjective genitive ("through the faithfulness *of* Jesus Christ"). Personally I opt for the former.

does he merely use Genesis 15:6 as a proof text.[3] While Genesis 15:6 is not, as we will see, the first time Abraham believed, and subsequently not the time of his conversion,[4] it is a pivotal moment in the biblical narrative. This text is not at all divorced from soteriological issues, for it is a central text in the midst of the account of a vital era in the unfolding of the history of salvation. It is also a programmatic text that establishes a constant principle: the people of God, those with whom God initiates and establishes a relationship (i.e., a covenant), will relate to God by faith. They must believe in God, and their faith, apart from anything else, unites them to God—the very object of their faith. On the basis of this faith, they are reckoned righteous. For Abraham, it was faith in the promises of God; for Paul and his readers, it is faith specifically in Christ—who is the fulfillment of all God's promises.

Genesis 15:6 in Context

Before discussing some of the details of Genesis 15:6, a brief treatment of the general context leading up to it is in order. Abraham's appearance in Genesis comes on the heels of yet another low point in the history of mankind since the fall, recorded in chapter 3. After the incident in Shinar with the building of the tower of Babel (11:1-7), the Lord scattered humanity throughout the earth and confused their language (11:8-9). It is safe to presume that a substantial amount of time passed between that account and what follows, since by the end of chapter 11 distinct regions are already established. In the flow of the narrative, however, just when the plight of humanity as a result of sin seems to be hopeless, the genealogy of the descendents of Shem, the son who received Noah's greatest blessing (9:26), appears. The list ends with Terah, a man living in Ur of the Chaldees (testimony to the events narrated in 11:8-9), and his son "Abram" (11:26-31).

Out of the chaos of Babel God is creating something new, and in doing so he is being faithful to the promises made to Noah and to the

---

[3] The name "Abraham" will be used throughout for the sake of convenience (except when direct quotes and references to specific events require otherwise). I recognize that in most of the cited texts his name was still "Abram."

[4] Although this is similar to comments made by N.T. Wright in *What St. Paul Really Said* (Grand Rapids: Eerdmans, 1997), 118-19, 125, 133, I am not arguing that this text is not about salvation, I am simply saying that neither Moses nor Paul are focusing on when Abraham believed i.e., his conversion. This seems like a simple enough observation.

promise in 3:15. There is a subtle but important point here as well. Terah's genealogy ends with a comment about Abram's wife: "Sarai was barren; she had no child" (11:30). The genealogy that tracks the promise comes to an abrupt and seemingly conclusive end—there is no child to carry on the bloodline. Though often overlooked, this little comment sets the stage for what comes next. Salvation will require a supernatural work: from Sarai's dead womb life will come, and through that life a blessing to all nations. In the next chapter God will make promises that only he, not Abraham, can fulfill.

In chapter 12 God addresses Abraham directly, telling him to leave Haran and travel to a new land (12:1). Following this command are God's promises:

> And I will make you a great nation, and I will bless you, and make your name great, so that you will be a blessing. I will bless those who bless you, and curse the one who curses you; and through you all the nations of the earth will be blessed. (12:2-3)

This call and pronouncement from God to Abraham is significant because it ushers in a new era in redemptive history. Dumbrell captures this idea when he says "we must not lose sight of the fact that the call of Abraham in this passage is a redemptive response to the human dilemma which the spread-of-sin narratives of 3–11 have posed."[5] Secondly, it is clear that well before the narrative reaches chapter 15, a relationship that includes the elements of promise, condition, and response between God and Abraham is firmly established prior to the covenant ceremony (15:7-18).[6]

---

[5] W. J. Dumbrell, *Covenant and Creation* (Carlisle, Scotland: Paternoster, 1997) 47.

[6] In *Covenant and Creation,* Dumbrell stresses this point in regard to Genesis 15 in several places, e.g., 47, 49, 54-56. Dumbrell is concerned to show that covenants are established, not out of the blue, but in the context of pre-existing relationships. Dumbrell's argument that the major biblical covenants stem ultimately from an existing antediluvian covenant with creation is strongly opposed by Paul R. Williamson ("Covenant," in *Dictionary of the Old Testament: Pentateuch,* ed. T. Desmond Alexander and David W. Baker [Downers Grove: InterVarsity, 2003], 141-43). Williamson's main argument is that the text does not say that a covenant is established anytime before the covenant with Noah in Genesis 6:18; 9:8-17. One does not, however, have to accept Dumbrell's conception of an antediluvian covenant to agree that a covenant is based on a relationship that already exists. In regard to the issue of covenant in general, the position taken in this work, though it will not come up until Chapter 3, is that a covenant relationship did indeed exist between God and Adam, and that every subsequent, major covenant is a step in the history of redemption to restore and recreate that original relationship between God and man. Even if one is disinclined toward a covenant in Genesis 1–3, it seems difficult to avoid at least saying that the relationship was "covenant-like." In this sense one

God called Abraham and certain promises accompanied that call. Abraham responded by packing up his wife, family, and possessions and setting out for Canaan (12:4-6). In 12:7, God appends a specific promise of the land to Abraham's descendants, and then on a mountain east of Bethel and west of Ai, Abraham responds to God by building an altar and calling on "the name of the LORD" (12:8). Abraham's obedient actions are those of a man who believes what God promised. If Abraham did not believe God's promises, there is no conceivable explanation for his departure from his homeland or of his personal worship of God. Abraham trusted God to do as he promised, and his trust is evident through his actions.

Several events take place in the narrative between 11:9 and 15:1, including a clear example of Abraham's weakness (12:10-20), the division of the land with Lot (13:1-13), Abraham's defeat of the kings and the rescue of Lot (14:1-16), and the meeting with and subsequent blessing from Melchizedek (14:17-19). The event that takes place after the division of the land with Lot is worth a special note. God again appears to Abraham, telling him to look in all directions as far as he can see, and promises to give him all the land he sees (13:14-15). Building upon the promises of 12:2 and 12:7, God promises to make the number of Abraham's descendants "as the dust of the earth" (13:16). God then commands Abraham to travel through the land which he is giving him (13:17). Abraham moves through the land and after arriving at Hebron he responds to God in worship (13:18). At each point in the narrative when God appears to Abraham and confirms and further defines the original promise given in 12:2-3 (12:7; 13:14-17), Abraham responds positively to God, just as he did in 12:4-6 (12:8-9; 13:18). Thus, from the moment God called him, though not confirmed explicitly in the text, Abraham's faith in God is evident. His obedience is evidence of his faith. "By faith," as the writer to the Hebrews says, "Abraham, when he was called, obeyed by going out to a place which he was to receive as an inheritance, and he went out not knowing where he was going" (Heb. 11:8).

---

might say that covenants are technically redemptive with the instrumental purpose of fulfilling God's will for his creation as first revealed in Genesis 1–3. Williamson, though critical of Dumbrell, nevertheless says that the Noahic covenant contains "clear echoes of the creation narrative . . . [and] suggests merely that God intended, through Noah, to fulfill his original creative intent: they do not necessarily presuppose the existence of a covenant between God and inanimate creation or indicate that the material in Gen[esis] 1–2 must be understood redemptively" ("Covenant," 143).

Genesis 15:6

Genesis 15 begins with another appearance of God to Abraham. God proclaims, "Do not fear, Abram, I am your shield; your reward will be very great" (15:1). This time, however, Abraham's response is not as sure as his earlier responses to God's pronouncements. Abraham, speaking for the first time in the narrative and obviously concerned about the fulfillment of God's previous promises, since fulfillment is dependent on having an heir, asks, "O Lord God, what will you give me, for I am still without child, and the heir of my house is Eliezer of Damascus?" (15:2). He then complains that God has yet to grant him an heir and as a result a servant will become his heir (15:3). God responds by saying that Eliezer will not be the heir, and he shows Abraham the stars in the sky and challenges Abraham to count them, for the number will be like his descendants (15:4-5)—basically a restatement of 13:16, where the metaphor is the dust of the earth. The narrator breaks in and informs us of Abraham's response: "And he believed the Lord; and he reckoned it to him as righteousness" (15:6). The doubt expressed by Abraham in verses 2 and 3 has disappeared (at least for now, cf., 16:1-6); confronted afresh with the promises of God, Abraham stops wavering and believes the promises of God, and God counts Abraham's faith for righteousness.[7]

The nature of Abraham's faith. When the narrator says, "He believed in the Lord," he is telling us that Abraham put his trust in God

---

[7] I am following the traditional translation of this text, which has God as the subject. This interpretation is certainly defensible from the Hebrew; it is the interpretation of the Septuagint translator and was subsequently employed by Paul. Many scholars have noted the interpretation set forth by Omening, and followed by Gaston, that the subject of the phrase is not God but Abraham and consequently it is Abraham not God doing the reckoning. The verse is about Abraham's response to God's promise in that Abraham reckons God's promise to him as a sign of God's righteousness. See Manfred Oemning, "Ist Genesis 15:6 ein Beleg für die Anrechnung des Glaubens zur Gerechtigkeit?," *ZAW* 95 (1983):182-97; and Lloyd Gaston, "Abraham and the Righteousness of God," *Horizons in Biblical Theology* 2 (1980): 39-68. For arguments against this view see, for example, R.W.L. Moberly, "Abraham's Righteousness," in *Studies in the Pentateuch,* ed. J.A. Emerton, Supplements to Vetus Testamentum 41 (Leiden: Brill, 1990), 106-8, (who points out that the roots of this interpretation can be found in Ramban); and, Bo Johnson, "Who Reckoned Righteousness to Whom?" *Svensk Exegetisk Arsbok* 51-52 (1986): 108-15. Part of the argument rests on the assertion that the traditional translation is a result of the Septuagint translator rendering the qal imperfect רשׁחיּו with the aorist passive ἐλογίσθη. Weavers explains the Septuagint translation: "The second clause has been restructured by Gen (the Septuagint translator of Genesis) so as to avoid confusion as to the subject and modifier." John William Weavers, *Notes on the Greek Text of Genesis,* Society of Biblical Literature Septuagint and Cognate Studies Series 35 (Atlanta: Scholars Press, 1993), 206. By rendering the second clause with a passive verb and the dative modifier αὐτῷ, in contrast to the first clause where Abraham is the explicit subject of the active verb ἐπίστευσεν ("Abraham believed God"), the subject of the second clause (God) becomes clear. "The passive transform removes all possible ambiguity from the passage" (Weavers, *Notes,* 206).

to keep his promises, that Abraham deemed having God's promises to be as good as having their fulfillment. Simply put, Abraham is trusting (אמן) in God to be God.[8] Elsewhere in the Pentateuch אמן is exercised—or is lacking and therefore its absence condemned—in relation to God's acts, commands, and promises. In Exodus 14:31 the Israelites believed in the Lord as a result of the events at the Red Sea. Later in Israel's wanderings the Lord asks how long the people will refuse to believe in him "in spite of all the signs that I have done among them?" (Num. 14:11). In Numbers 20:12, God equates Moses' disobedience in hitting the rock twice, rather than once as commanded, with unbelief. In Deuteronomy 1:32 Moses reminds the people that although the same God who delivered them from Egypt also promised to fight for them in the conquest of the Promised Land, they nevertheless refused to believe his word.

In each case the issue is confidence in the reliability of God and his word, i.e., trusting him to do as he says. In the other texts where this construction appears, the idea is the same.[9] This is the sense of Genesis 15:6 as well. Abraham's faith is his belief in God, specifically his trust that the one who promised is also able to do what he promised.[10] This faith is, moreover, oriented toward but not limited to the future.[11]

---

[8] The word אמן appears eight times in the Old Testament in the hiphil stem followed by preposition ב with God as the object of the preposition. Rather than engaging in a study of the entire usage of אמן in the Old Testament, it is better to survey the other places in which the word appears in a similar context to help determine the meaning in Genesis 15. Surveys can be found in Alfred Jepson, "אמן," in TDOT, 1:292; J. J. Scullion, "Righteousness (OT)," in ABD, 5:742; R.W. L. Moberly, "אמן," in NIDOTTE, 1:427.

[9] Cf., 2 Kings 17:14; 2 Chronicles 20:20; Psalm 78:22; Jonah 3:5.

[10] This conclusion, reached by comparing texts with similar constructions, seems more fruitful and reasonable for the purview of this study than doing a full, lexical study of the meaning of אמן or simply repeating some other abstract definition, such as, "make oneself secure in Jahweh." Gerhard von Rad, *Old Testament Theology*, vol. 1, trans. D. M. G. Stalker (New York: Harper & Row, 1962), 171. Another interpretation of this text should be noted. Kline suggests that "Abraham believed" is Abraham's "confession of faith in the promises of God" (Meredith Kline, "Abraham's Amen," *WTJ* 31 [1968]: 8). With reservations, Robertson supports Klines's idea. O. Palmer Robertson, "Genesis 15:6: New Covenant Expositions of an Old Covenant Text," *WTJ* 42 (1980): 263-64. The verb is thus interpreted as having a "delocutive" force. Abraham is declaring his "Amen" (the word "amen" derives from אמן) to God's promise. Robertson believes that by this reading "the text is thus maintained in its integrity." Even though he says that this reading cannot be asserted with "absolute certainty" it nevertheless "captures the flavor of the affirmation of Genesis 15:5" (ibid.). Robertson's reservations about this reading are actually quite strong. He correctly points out that "establishing the possibility of" "a meaning and "establishing" a meaning are two different things. Furthermore, he admits that the texts Kline cites in support of this reading are not "altogether compelling" (ibid., 264 n. 10). This interpretation does not readily commend itself as the most natural reading, and apparently has not garnered a great deal of support.

[11] It seems von Rad wants to emphasize the future aspect of faith almost exclusively. As he states, faith "refers as a rule to God's future saving act. Belief is an act of trust, a consent to God's plans in history" (Gerhard von Rad, *Genesis*, trans. John H. Marks, Old Testament Library [Philadelphia: Westminster, 1961], 180).

The aspect of אמן in Genesis 15:6 is worth attention because the issue of when Abraham believed and why his belief is reported at this point in the narrative is an important consideration in the discussion of this text. The form (*waw* + hiphil perfect) may suggest that this is not only a comment that relates to Abraham's response at that particular time, but is characteristic of Abraham's relationship with God in general. By choosing this construction (the aspect of *waw* + hiphil perfect is imperfective), the narrator could be drawing attention away from a specific temporal aspect to a more undefined, less time-connected action. The narrator is asserting not only that Abraham believed God's promise in 15:4-5, but that believing, or faith, was his "normal response to the Lord's word."[12] It is, moreover, a response based on a prior, established relationship.[13]

Simply put, this is not the first time Abraham believed God. The Septuagint translator's choice of a simple aorist (ἐπίστευσεν) is in keeping with this interpretation (or at least does not argue against it).[14] It is not surprising that the translator chose an aorist since it is the "default" tense, and does not add particular emphasis on the temporal nature of Abraham's belief in Genesis 15:6. The Septuagint captures the imper-

---

[12] Gordon Wenham, *Genesis 1–17*, WBC, vol. 1 (Waco, TX: Word, 1987), 329. Wenham points out that it is unusual to indicate single events in past time with perfect + *waw*. Imperfect + *waw* consecutive is the more likely construction (ibid. 324). For discussion of this construction, see *Gesenius' Hebrew Grammar*, ed. E. Kautzsch, 2nd ed., ed. A. E. Cowley (Oxford: Clarendon Press, 1910), 330-39; Paul Joüon, *A Grammar of Biblical Hebrew*, trans. and ed. T. Muraoka, Subsidia Biblica 14/2 (Rome: Editrice Pontificio Istituto Biblico, 1991; reprint 1996), 404. Both Gesenius and Joüon list Genesis 15:6 as an unusual occurrence. For a more detailed discussion of the imperfective aspect of biblical Hebrew verbs, particularly in narrative literature, see Peter J. Gentry, "The System of the Finite Verb in Classical Biblical Hebrew," *Hebrew Studies* 39 (1998): 13-20.

[13] Perhaps this is the reason that Abraham's faith is not mentioned directly until Genesis 15. Abraham believed God when he left his home in Haran, but in the narrative an explicit statement regarding Abraham's faith is not mentioned until after the relationship between God and Abraham is firmly established in the text.

[14] This observation is based on the idea that the in terms of verbal aspect, the aorist tense carries the least semantic weight. Moberly agrees with the idea that Genesis 15:6 should be read not as a "new" act on Abraham's part or as a "deeper or truer response" than what is seen in Genesis 12 or in Abraham's response to God's promises in 18:14-17 ("Abraham's Righteousness," 118). However, he is incorrect to say that the ongoing sense of the Hebrew of Genesis 15:6 is "lost in the Septuagint" since an aorist rather than an imperfect is selected to translate ויאמן. He also points out that the Septuagint, and presumably its incorrect rendering of ויאמן with ἐπίστευσεν, is cited three times in the New Testament (ibid. 105). Moberley's comments seem to rest on the idea that in this text the aorist is punctilliar in respect to time. That is, the Septuagint translator, by using an aorist, misconstrues the text to mean that only Abraham's faith at that particular point in time is in view. This could be true, but it may here be functioning as a background tense, and thus say little if anything about temporal elements in the text, punctilliar or otherwise. See Stanley Porter, *Verbal Aspect in the Greek of the New Testament with Reference to Tense and Mood*, vol. 1 of *Studies in Biblical Greek*, ed. D. A. Carson (New York: Peter Lang, 1989), 17-65; 163-239; idem, *Idioms of the Greek New Testament*, 2nd ed. (Sheffield: Sheffield Academic Press, 1994), 20-26, 35-49.

fective aspect of the Hebrew text. The temporal point of Abraham's belief, though not tossed aside, is not the main focus of this narrative.

Eichrodt levies a strong objection to the idea that Abraham's response of faith in Genesis 15:6 is indicative of and in keeping with a prior relationship.[15] He says that to understand this text, "this impressive picture of the decision of faith," as "only adherence to and perseverance in" a prior, established relationship is to "manifestly underrate its importance."[16] Eichrodt, seeking to emphasize the element of "decision" in faith, which is described as "*a voluntary surrender of the ego in full awareness of the implications of this decision,*" isolates the text from the preceding narrative.[17] Contrary to most interpreters, he argues that the *waw* + perfect construction of אמן is evidence for a temporally confined event, something happening "for the first time."[18] He cites texts with similar constructions as support, but these texts are not ultimately persuasive.[19]

Though Eichrodt's arguments, particularly from grammar, are not convincing and in spite of his rather existential definition of faith, there

---

[15] Contra Dumbrell (*Covenant and Creation*).

[16] Walter Eichrodt, *Theology of the Old Testament*, Old Testament Library, vol. 1, trans. J.A. Barker (Philadelphia: Westminster, 1967), 278.

[17] Ibid., 278; his emphasis.

[18] Ibid.

[19] Of the texts Eichrodt cites, only Genesis 21:25 has a verb (יכח "reprove") with *waw* + perfect in the hiphil stem. In that text, Abraham "reproves" Abimelech about a well taken by Abimelech's servants. This text does appear to show the use of a construction like that found in 15:6 in the context of a singular event. By itself, however, this text only suggests that this construction can be used in reference to a singular event, or that it is only used *here* in this way, but the imperfective aspect conveyed by the verb can be maintained. Wenham notes the "unusual" grammatical construction in the context of an event in the past, and suggests that it could be indicative of Abraham's complaining more than once, or frequently, to Abimelech in regard to the well. Gordon Wenham, *Genesis 17–50*, WBC, vol. 2 (Waco, TX: Word, 1994), 92. In Joshua 9:12 the verb הָיָה appears as *waw* + qal perfect referring to bread that "has become crumbled." The imperfective aspect is clearer here. Another *waw* + qal perfect appears in Judges 5:26, which speaks of Jael killing Sisera, when she "struck" (הלם) him in the head with a tent peg. The context itself may rule out any notion of "repeated" action, but on the other hand how many hits does it take to nail a head to the floor with a hammer and tent peg? More than one, presumably. However, is the point in time really the issue? Whatever the case, the temporal element is certainly not the focus in this text. In Isaiah 22:14, the Lord reveals (גָּלָה, here as *waw* + niphal perfect) himself to Isaiah in regard to the punishment of the people's sin. Again, the emphasis is not on the punctilliar nature of the event but that the event simply happened. These texts seem to show, to varying degrees, the verbal construction *waw* + perfect used in what might be regarded as "first time" events that "cannot be incorporated into a continuum." On examination, however, the idea of a continuum or a "time" is not emphasized in these texts. Just as imperfective aspect does not argue specifically for "continual" action in regard to time, neither does the construction argue for a "first time" event. The temporal element is not of particular importance in any of the texts cited by Eichrodt. That is, the "when" of the action is not highlighted in the grammar of the text. It is simply a matter that the events described *happened*, without special emphasis on the *specific time* they occurred. Other factors indicate why Abraham's faith is highlighted at this juncture in the narrative.

is still a sense in which his criticism might help temper the view on the opposite extreme. Just as Eichrodt represents an extreme position in his assertion that the exact moment of "decision" is at the forefront in Genesis 15:6, so also there is a danger of going to the other extreme, i.e., de-emphasizing the moment to the extent that it becomes almost irrelevant that Abraham's faith is mentioned in the narrative. Neither the recognition that Abraham clearly "believed" before Genesis 15 nor the form of אמן, should diminish the significance of the pronouncement at this point in the narrative. That "he believed in the Lord, and he reckoned it to him as righteousness" at that specific time should not be diminished. It is not, after all, a matter of no importance that Abraham's faith receives explicit mention at this point in the narrative, coming as it does right before the covenant ceremony. It is precisely this point, this moment in the narrative, that has significance, even though it is clear that Abraham was already "a believer."

Thus, in spite of the importance of recognizing that there is a pre-existing relationship between God and Abraham before Genesis 15:6, it is not the pre-existing relationship itself or Abraham's actions in the course of that relationship that God reckons as righteousness; it is Abraham's *faith* that the Lord reckons as righteousness. It becomes explicit that the covenant which the Lord makes with Abraham is entered into (on Abraham's part) by faith. The Lord's reckoning of Abraham's faith as righteousness is the entranceway into the covenant. So the narrative of Genesis, centuries before Paul, establishes that it is not a matter of anything Abraham did, but it was his faith in God, including God's promises, that God reckoned as righteousness. Justification by faith is not original to Paul.

Faith "reckoned." The meaning of the verb חשׁב in general Old Testament usage is discussed in detail in numerous works. [20] One basic sense of חשׁב can be seen in a text such as Numbers 18:27. The tithe

[20] Ziesler is right to say that since "the meaning of חשׁב and λογίζεσθαι vary as widely as those of 'think,' 'count,' or 'reckon' in English, a linguistic examination yields only very limited results." J. A. Ziesler, *The Meaning of Righteousness in Paul: A Linguistic and Theological Enquiry* (Cambridge: Cambridge University Press, 1972), 180. For general word studies see W. Schottroff, "חשׁב," in *Theological Lexicon of the Old Testament* [TLOT], ed. Ernst Jenni and Clause Westermann, trans. Mark E. Biddle (Peabody, MA: Hendrickson, 1977), 2:479-82; K. Seybold, "חשׁב," in TDOT, 5:228-45; Hans Wolfgang Heidland, "λογίζομαι," in *Theological Dictionary of the New Testament*, ed. Gerhard Kittle, trans. and ed. Geoffrey W. Bromily (Grand Rapids: Eerdmans, 1967), 4:284-92.

given by the Levites, which is a tenth of what they themselves received as tithes, is reckoned or counted as a tithe of their own produce.[21] Dumbrell narrows the word down to two categories.[22] In the first, something is reckoned (Dumbrell uses "impute") to a person or thing when in reality the facts argue to the contrary.[23] If this is the sense in Genesis 15:6, then God "reckons" Abraham's faith as righteousness; faith counts for something else, namely, righteousness.[24] In the second category, something is reckoned to a person or thing and the facts argue that the "something" is indeed true.[25] Thus the "something" is reckoned appropriately. For Abraham this would mean that his faith is reckoned for righteousness because it *really is* the case.

Scholars often note the similarities between Genesis 15:6 and Psalm 106:31.[26] Psalm 106:31 recounts Phinehas's actions in Numbers 25, where he zealously spears an Israelite and a Midianite woman thereby bringing a plague to an end. The psalmist says that Phinehas's act was "reckoned to him as righteousness" (וַתֵּחָשֶׁב לוֹ לִצְדָקָה).[27] The covenantal context of Psalm 106 should not be missed. The psalm supports the idea stated in verse one, that the Lord's "steadfast love endures forever," by

---

Gerhard Von Rad's idea that "reckoned as righteousness" is derivative of later cultic language in which the priest declares whether an offering is acceptable has been enormously influential in Old Testament scholarship (*Genesis*, 179-80); idem, *Old Testament Theology*, 1:269 n.170, 379. Aside from the unsubstantiated documentary reconstruction required to construe the text in this way, the idea that the phrase is derived from a temple setting is irrelevant to this study.

[21] Wenham, *Genesis*, 1: 329.

[22] Dumbrell, *Covenant and Creation*, 53. Dumbrell acknowledges his reliance on Ziesler, *The Meaning of Righteousness in Paul*, 180-85. Ziesler, quite correctly, limits his study to texts that contain חשב followed by preposition ל (twenty-two occurrences). He narrows these down to thirteen by eliminating those texts where what is stated is merely "a matter of opinion which is either true or false, and also places where it is a simple matter of computation." (Ziesler, *Meaning of Righteousness*, 180). This approach, utilized above in the discussion of אמן, avoids dictionary-like surveys yielding results from which the interpreter finally chooses to discuss those texts which most closely resemble, in form and/or function, the text he or she is examining. While this approach would not work for a study focusing on the lexical and semantic features of a word, it serves its purpose here.

[23] Biblical examples cited by Dumbrell (*ergo* Ziesler) are Job 13:24; 19:11; 33:13; 41:27. From the New Testament he cites Hebrews 11:19. Ibid. 53.

[24] The phrase often used for this sense is "as if." Though somewhat unfortunate, but probably unavoidable, this phrase occurs frequently in the writings of those arguing for the traditional formulation of imputation. It is unfortunate because in an attempt to clarify that the believer's righteousness is not his own but is an "alien" righteousness, i.e., Christ's righteousness, "as if" language opens the position to the seemingly valid charge that it amounts to a "legal fiction." Thus definition becomes extremely important.

[25] In this category Dumbrell lists Leviticus 7:18; 17:4; Numbers 18:27; 2 Samuel 19:19; Psalm 32:2; Psalm 106:31; Proverbs 27:14 (*Covenant and Creation*, 53).

[26] Ibid., 54; Wenham, *Genesis*, 1:329; Westermann, *Genesis*, 223; Ziesler, *The Meaning of Righteousness*, 181.

[27] חשב here is a niphal imperfect, whereas in Genesis 15:6 the form is qal imperfect. The difference in form does not affect the comparison of the texts.

recounting the Lord's faithfulness to his covenant people in contrast to their unfaithfulness to him. The reason for the Lord's faithfulness is explicit—he remembered "his covenant" (v. 45). The nation's rebellion is clearly interpreted within a covenantal framework. Against the background of national faithlessness, Phinehas's action stands out as acceptable, pleasing, and even expected—again, interpreted in a covenantal framework. Phinehas's action appears, by way of contrast with covenantal disobedience and rebellion, as covenantal obedience and fidelity. Given this context, Phinehas's act is reckoned appropriately; it is reckoned as righteousness. This is not a matter of reckoning one thing as something else, but of reckoning a thing for what it is. Phinehas's faithfulness to God is reckoned as righteousness, i.e., Phinehas's righteous act is reckoned as righteousness.

In comparison, the Phinehas text is different from Genesis 15:6 in that an established, covenantal setting is absent from the Genesis narrative. Even if one argues that a relationship already exists between God and Abraham (which it does), one cannot say that Abraham was in a covenantal setting comparable to that of Phinehas—not unless the covenant ceremony in Genesis 15:9-21 is somewhat redundant. A second difference seems to lie in the fact that for Abraham it is faith that is reckoned as righteousness, but for Phinehas it is his action in the established parameters of an existing covenant that is reckoned as righteousness. Another way of putting it is to note that the statements are made from two different perspectives. Genesis 15:6 comes *before* a covenant is established, while the statement in Psalm 106:31 (as well as the recognition of the action in Num. 25:10-13) is made on the other side of an established covenant. Phinehas's action is reckoned appropriately, that is, for what it is. Phinehas's righteous action is counted as righteousness. On the other hand, Abraham's faith is reckoned as something else—namely, righteousness. In Genesis 15:6 it is the the priority of faith that is recognized, whereas in Psalm 106:31 it is Phinehas's action which flows from faith that receives attention.[28]

---

[28] As D.A. Carson observes, the difference between these two texts is that "the equivalence in that case (Ps. 106:28) is not between *faith* and righteousness, but between *a righteous deed* and righteousness" (author's emphasis), ("The Vindication of Imputation: On Fields of Discourse and Semantic Fields," in *Justification: What's at Stake in the Current Debates*, ed., Mark Husbands and Daniel J. Treier [Downers Grove: InterVarsity, 2004], 57).

There are important similarities between these texts to which we will return shortly. For now, and in spite of the similarity in wording, the reckoning of Abraham's faith seems to have more in common with those texts where one thing is reckoned as something else than it does with the reckoning of Phinehas's action. For example, when Laban "reckons" his daughters as foreigners (Gen. 31:15), he clearly is not asserting that they *really are* foreign but that for all intents and purposes he views them as such. He is counting one thing (flesh and blood daughters) as something else (foreigners).[29] As we will see shortly, Paul understands clearly the distinctions that can be made between reckonings.

Reckoned "righteousness." The end of the second clause of Genesis 15:6 presents a major difficulty because it opens the door to the manifold discussions surrounding the meaning and use of the צדק word group, words typically translated "righteous," "righteousness," "just," and "justify."[30] Although some have attempted to construct backgrounds for some kind of meta-concept for understanding "righteousness" in the Old Testament, no attempts have proved satisfying.[31] The only consensus regarding the צדק word group is that the words can

---

[29] Other examples include Proverbs 27:14 in which a loud morning blessing spoken to a friend will be "reckoned a curse" to the inconsiderate early-riser; likewise, Shimei asks David not to "reckon" his guilt to him, i.e., to reckon his guilt as innocence (2 Sam. 19:19 [v. 20 Eng.]; cf. 2 Sam. 16:6-8). Like the case of Laban and his daughters, in both of these examples, one thing (a blessing; Shimei's guilt) is counted for another (a curse; innocence). Other texts cited above in n. 23. See also Carson "Vindication of Imputation," 58.

[30] For general discussion see B. Johnson, "צדק," in *Theologisches Wörterbuch zum Alten Testament*, Band 6, ed. G. Johannes Botterweck (Stuttgart: Verlag W. Kohlhammer,1989), 898-923; David Reimer, "צדק," in NIDOTTE, 3: 744-69; J. J. Scullion, "Righteousness: OT," ABD, 5: 724-36.

[31] For instance, H. Schmid proposes that the main referent behind "righteousness" language is the idea of a cosmic world order to which everything should conform (*Gerechtigkeit als Weltordnung*, Beiträge zur evangelischen Theologie 40 [Munich: Kaiser, 1968]). E. Kautzsch set forward the idea that the basic concept means to conform to a norm (*Über die Derivate des Stammes* צדק im Alttestamentlichen Sprachgebrauch [Tübingen, 1881]). Ziesler, and many others, propose that covenant fidelity or covenantal behavior is the main idea behind the root (*Meaning of Righteousness*, e.g., 40-42); Ziesler also provides a nice summary of much of the scholarly discussion surrounding "righteousness" language in the Old Testament, [ibid., 36-43]). Ziesler recognizes that in terms of God's righteousness as "covenant activity" there is a broad range of connotations in different contexts, thus, "mercy in one situation, triumph in another, judgment in another, the establishment of good government and good justice in another" (ibid., 41). In terms of human righteousness, "it is clearly a possibility only within the covenant" (ibid., 42). The view of righteousness as covenantal fidelity is also held by Dumbrell, and he summarizes his view by saying that "righteousness in the Old Testament basically indicates behavior consistent with the nature of a relationship already established" (*Covenant and Creation*, 54). The view that righteousness equals covenant faithfulness will be explored further in chapter 4.

be used in a variety of ways depending on context.[32] This observation is hardly groundbreaking.

The difficulty of determining a single definition or concept of "righteousness" is evident even when comparison is limited to uses of the same form found in Genesis 15:6 (צְדָקָה).[33] For instance, certain actions can be characterized by "righteousness," as in Genesis 18:19 where Abraham's descendents will keep the Lord's way, and inherit the blessing "by doing righteousness and justice." Similarly, in Deuteronomy 24:13 the act of returning a pledged cloak "will be righteousness" to the one returning it. The Lord's future salvation will be achieved by a branch from David who will "execute justice and righteousness in the land" (Jer. 33:15). The Lord can bestow righteousness as a gift: "he has covered me with a robe of righteousness" (Isa. 61:10), and, "as the earth brings forth its shoots . . . so the Lord God will cause righteousness and praise to spring forth before all the nations" (61:11).

An ideal that characterizes a way of life may be described as "righteousness." An example of this is Proverbs 8:1: "I walk in the way of righteousness." In the same way, Proverbs 11:19 says, "He who is steadfast in righteousness will live" and 12:28, "In the path of righteousness is life." God's own "righteousness," which he manifests in the deliverance of his people, is contrasted with the Israelites "who are far from righteousness" (Isa. 46:12-13). Righteousness may also be a status one has in God: "Only in the LORD, it will be spoken of me, are righteousness and strength" (Isa. 45:24).[34] In Isaiah 51:1 God calls on those "who

---

[32] See Ziesler (*The Meaning of Righteousness*, 23-32), who divides the צדק group between two larger categories, namely, (1) instances where the word group relates to human activity, and (2) where God's activity is in view. These two main categories are then further subdivided. John Reumann provides a summary of Ziesler's categories, along with some of his text references, in *Righteousness in the New Testament: Justification in the United States Lutheran—Roman Catholic Dialogue*, (Philadelphia: Fortress/New York: Paulist, 1982), 14-15. It should be noted that Ziesler has come under heavy fire for falling into "the temptation of imposing modern categories on word usage" (Mark A. Seifrid, "Righteousness Language in the Hebrew Scriptures and Early Judaism," in *Justification and Variegated Nomism*, vol. 1, *The Complexities of Second Temple Judaism*, ed. D. A. Carson, Peter T. O'Brien, and Mark A. Seifrid [Tübingen: Mohr Siebeck; Grand Rapids: Baker, 2001], 422). Seifrid faults Ziesler for "providing his own definition of 'forensic' usage, i.e., righteousness which has to do with 'status' and not activity or behavior." Seifrid's final verdict is, "the resulting statistics in which Ziesler makes a distinction between 'forensic' usage and that having to do with 'activity' . . . are virtually worthless" (ibid.). Seifrid's criticisms noted, Ziesler's two main categories both contain several subdivisions, and even if the two divisions are not satisfactory, his list still illustrates the broad usage of the word group in the Old Testament *even when* an attempt is made to narrow usage down to two basic categories.
[33] The following is a limited number of examples used to illustrate the point.
[34] Verse 25 goes on to say, "In the Lord all the offspring of Israel shall be justified (צדק) and will glory."

pursue righteousness" and tells them to "look to the rock from which you were hewn, and to the quarry from which you were dug." And then, significantly, he directs them to Abraham: "Look to Abraham your father and to Sarah who bore you" (v. 2). What follows is a prophecy concerning God's salvation of his people.[35]

What then shall we say about the meaning of "righteousness" in Genesis 15:6? It is clear from just a few of the approximately 240 occurrences in the Old Testament that צדקה has a wide range of meaning and a great deal of overlap within its range. If we try to establish neat categories between forensic and ethical righteousness based merely on the word itself in the abstract or try to choose from among its various uses we will likely miss the most important point for understanding the nature of righteousness in this text—righteousness in this text is *reckoned* to Abraham. But in general "righteousness" is typically connected to actions that one should do. An exception is Isaiah 61:10 where righteousness is described as a robe surrounding its wearer. In that case, righteousness is more like a granted status than an action one should do.

Reimer observes that whether the subject is lawkeeping (Deut. 6:25), returning a pledge (Deut. 24:13), Phinehas and his spear, or Abraham's belief in God's promises, there is "the notion that an appropriate action has been recognized and approved."[36] Reimer's observation is right, but at the same time it can become problematic to speak of faith's being recognized as "an appropriate action" in the way that defending God's covenant and character, returning a pledge, or keeping the law is an appropriate action—particularly if the result is a declaration of righteousness. That is not to say that faith is somehow "inappropriate," but only to point out that if both faith and what one does are equally accepted or established norms by which one is counted righteous, then we are faced with two ways by which righteousness may be declared. A misunderstanding at this point could lead one to conclude that righteousness could be attained *either* by what one does *or* by faith.

What does it mean for God to declare Abraham's faith as righteousness? Simply put, it means that a declaration that would normally

---

[35] Note that those "who pursue righteousness" are told to consider the one who believed God and was reckoned righteous.

[36] David J. Reimer "צדק," in NIDOTTE, 3: 753.

be declared on the basis of what one does has been granted on the basis of faith. In this way "righteousness" refers to a status declared by God. By faith, Abraham stands before God as one who has fulfilled every standard and condition expected by God. If God declares that Abraham is righteous, it means that God himself views Abraham as a righteous person. The surprising turn in the story is that "righteousness," typically associated with what one does, is here declared on one who believes. We will leave it for Paul to make it more surprising still.

If it is right to view the reckoning in Genesis 15:6 as one thing (faith) being reckoned or counted for something other than what it *actually is* (i.e., "righteousness), then the coupling of חשב and צדקה further establishes the meaning of this text. In the Deuteronomy texts cited above, Moses says explicitly that keeping the law "will be righteousness for you" (6:25), and that returning a poor man's cloak "will be righteousness for you" (24:13). There is no confusion in either text; if a person desires to be righteous, then he must keep the law (which includes returning a cloak). So if an Israelite child were to ask, how can I be righteous? the answer would have been, "keep the law." Keeping the law *is* righteousness, and is the standard by which one will receive either blessing or cursing.[37] This point is reiterated in 8:1: "The whole commandment that I command you this day you shall be careful do do." It is abundantly clear that righteousness is linked to doing the law. Yet in regard to Abraham, his faith is not righteousness to him, but his faith, rather, is *reckoned* to him as righteousness. Faith is not reckoned as belief in the way that keeping the law *is* righteousness; faith is *reckoned* for something it is not, i.e., righteousness.[38]

It is difficult to interpret "righteousness" in this text as referring to some sort of ethical or behavioral norm done by Abraham and then recognized by God. Abraham, in fact, was on the verge of fulfilling God's promise for himself through Eliezer. Nevertheless, "righteousness"

---

[37] As made clear in Deuteronomy 7–8, and especially in chapters 27–29.

[38] Not only does this fit the context of Paul's use of this text in Romans, it fits Paul's use of it in Galatians 3 as well. There Paul contrasts hearing and faith (by which the Spirit is received), supported by Genesis 15:6, with "works of the law." In both Romans and Galatians Paul seems to want to make it clear that a right standing before God is not first a matter of what one must do, but a matter of faith in God, and in both letters he goes to Genesis 15:6 to make his case. This interpretation is, admittedly, open to Reimer's criticism; namely, that it derives from a "Pauline trajectory" (though hopefully it is not too bound by "dogmatic restraints"). Reimer, "צדק," 754-55.

is declared—not on the basis of what Abraham did, but God counts Abraham's faith in him and his promises as righteousness.

It is instructive to note that the narrator chose this time in the narrative to make the statement concerning Abraham's faith. What follows in 15:7-19 is the covenant ratification ceremony. The ceremony indicates that the relationship between God and Abraham is confirmed, because the ceremony presupposes a relationship in good standing, and this is precisely what is affirmed in 15:6. Thus the events narrated in verses 7-19 do not initiate the relationship between God and Abraham—they affirm the relationship through the ratifying of the covenant, and they establish the sure future of that relationship.[39] Genesis 15:6 thus serves to provide the established basis for the ratification ceremony. Abraham's status before God, indicated by the reckoning of "righteousness," is definitely established in the narrative prior to the ratification of the covenant. Just as circumcision presupposes a covenant (Gen. 17; Rom. 4:9-12) as the "sign and seal of the righteousness, which is of faith" (Rom. 4:11b), so too does the ratification ceremony presuppose an established relationship (15:6).

A similar situation exists in Numbers 25. God recognizes Phinehas's zeal "in that he was jealous with my jealousy" and establishes a covenant with Phinehas and his descendants (vv. 10-13). Phinehas's act demonstrates that a prior relationship exists between him and God; otherwise he would not have been "jealous for his God" (v. 13). The ensuing covenant both confirms a prior relationship and, more importantly, establishes the certainty of that relationship in the future. In spite of the different contexts, the accounts of Abraham and Phinehas are quite similar *at this point*. Yet again, the difference is that Phinehas's action is in an *already established covenant* and those actions lead to another covenant between God and Phinehas and his offspring.

Abraham, on the other hand, though already in an existing relationship with God, is not in the same sort of covenantal setting. It is not an action measured against a set of established covenantal standards; it

---

[39] Ronald Youngblood notes that "formalizing a covenant (as in Genesis 15) assumes previous (Genesis 12) as well as present and future relationships." ("The Abrahamic Covenant: Conditional or Unconditional?" in *The Living and Active Word of God: Studies in Honor of Samuel J. Schultz*, ed. Morris Inch and Ronald Youngblood [Winona Lake, Ind.: Eisenbrauns, 1983], 32).

is faith in God that is reckoned as righteousness. And again, it seems to be a matter of the direction from which one views the events.

The antecedent for Paul's argument in Romans is the reckoning of Abraham's faith as righteousness apart from works in general, the law, or circumcision.[40] Though the interpretation might be new to some of Paul's opponents—indeed, it was new to Paul after the Damascus Road—Paul asserts that his message was right there in the Old Testament all along. With this background sketch we now turn to Paul.

FROM ABRAHAM TO THE PRESENT: IMPUTATION AND FAITH IN ROMANS 4

Most scholars agree that Paul's use of Abraham in Romans 4 stands, to different degrees, in opposition to the understanding of the patriarch in contemporary Jewish interpretation.[41] Contrary to some Jewish literature that often focused on Abraham's obedience or his works as the ground for God's acceptance of him—and even the ground that secured the election of Israel—Paul seeks to show that Abraham is rather the "father" of all who are accepted by God on the basis of faith, not on the basis of works.[42] In *Jubilees*, for instance, at a very young age Abraham distances himself from his father and his idols and prays to God to keep him from "the straying of the sons of men" (11:16-17); he lectures his father on the evils of worshiping idols (12:2-5); and at age sixteen he burns down a house of idols (12:12), all of which happens before God appears to him in Haran.[43] In the literature of second temple Judaism,

---

[40] This is precisely Paul's point in the subsequent verses. In verses 9-12 Paul reminds his readers that the reckoning of Abraham as righteous took place prior to his circumcision. Similarly, in verses 13-17 he shows that the promise is through "the righteousness of faith" (v. 13) rather than through the law, thus including Gentiles as well as Jews.

[41] E.g., William Baird, "Abraham in the New Testament: Tradition and the New Identity," *Interpretation* 42 (1988): 375; Michael Cranford, "Abraham in Romans 4: The Father of All Who Believe," *NTS* 41 (1995): 71-88; C. E. B. Cranfield, *Romans*, vol. 1, ICC (Edinburgh: T&T Clark, 1975), 228-30; James D. G. Dunn, *Romans 1–8*, WBC, vol. 38a (Dallas: Word, 1988), 200-201; Douglas Moo, *The Epistle to the Romans*, NICNT (Grand Rapids: Eerdmans, 1996), 256-57; Thomas R. Schreiner, *Romans*, BECNT, vol. 6 (Grand Rapids: Baker, 1998), 215-17.

[42] The list of texts in Jewish literature that stress Abraham's works and/or his testing with Isaac is repeated, and often discussed, in numerous places throughout the literature on Romans 4. Among those texts most frequently cited are: Sirach 44:19-22; Jubilees 17:15-18; 24:11; 23:10; 2 Baruch 57:2; 1 Maccabees 1:52; and, 4 Maccabees 14:20. For various discussions of Abraham in Jewish literature, see Gerhard Mayer, "Aspekte des Abrahambildes in der hellenistisch-jüdischen Literatur," *EvT* 32 (1972): 118-27; Dunn, *Romans 1–8*, 200-201.

[43] Translation of *Jubilees* taken from, James H. Charlesworth, *The Old Testament Peseudepigrapha*, vol. 2 (New York: Doubleday, 1985), 79-80.

as Gathercole points out, Abraham's "justification is presented . . . as God's legitimate pronouncement upon a man who has acted according to the Law and been found faithful in his trials."[44]

It seems likely, at the risk of mirror-reading, that Paul had these sorts of ideas in mind when he wrote this section of Romans, and a grasp of the issues is helpful for a general understanding of the text.[45] For our purposes, however, the important issue to grasp is that Paul cites a text that his Jewish opponents would likely have used against him. Paul names Abraham as *the* support for his argument that justification is not by a mix of faith and works[46] but by faith apart from works. Thus, while Paul's opponents might well point to the *merits*[47] of Abraham's faith, Paul turns and asserts that it is Abraham's faith alone that God counts as righteousness. Paul, contrary to some Jewish literature, asserts that righteousness before God is only a matter of grace, and shockingly, a matter of God's justifying "the ungodly" (v. 5)—the "ungodly," includ-

---

[44] Simon J. Gathercole, "Justified by Faith, Justified by his Blood: The Evidence of Romans 3:21–4:5," in *Justification and Variegated Nomism*, vol. 2, ed. D.A. Carson, Peter T. O'Brien, Mark A Seifrid (Grand Rapids: Baker; Tübingen: Mohr Siebeck, 2004), 156.

[45] In recent years this issue has received more emphasis than anything else in Romans 4, due in large part to the arguments set forth by the people more or less associated with the New Perspective on Paul. The main impetus for the debate centers around whether first-century Jews really believed that Abraham was justified by his "works." There are, of course, many nuances to this debate, and to describe a New Perspective view on Romans 4 is impossible in this context. The issue in Romans 4 is indicative of the debate in general. For both general discussion and also specific discussion on Romans, including chapter 4, see J. D. G. Dunn, "The New Perspective on Paul," in *Jesus, Paul, and the Law*, (London: SCM, 1990), 183-214; idem, *Romans 1–8*, WBC (Dallas: Word, 1988); idem, *Romans 9–16*, WBC (Dallas: Word, 1988); idem, *The Theology of Paul the Apostle* (Grand Rapids: Eerdmans, 1998); E. P. Sanders, *Paul and Palestinian Judaism* (Minneapolis: Fortress, 1977); idem, *Paul the Law and the Jewish People* (Minneapolis: Fortress, 1983); N. T. Wright, "Romans and the Theology of Paul," in *Pauline Theology*, vol. 3, ed. D. M. Hay and E. E. Johnson (Minneapolis: Fortress, 1995); idem, "Romans," in *The New Interpreter's Bible*, vol. 10, ed. Leander Keck (Nashville: Abingdon, 2002). The works of these three scholars are listed because their works (especially Sanders and Dunn) are most closely associated with the New Perspective on Paul. I am aware of the (often dramatic) differences between, say, Sanders, Dunn, and Wright. I am simply citing a general trajectory, not asserting that those scholars cited above represent a unified front called "the New Perspective." For a challenge to the New Perspective, specifically in regard to Romans 1–5, see Simon J. Gathercole, *Where is Boasting?: Early Jewish Soteriology and Paul's Response in Romans 1–5* (Grand Rapids: Eerdmans, 2002). Also, Gathercole's more recent work, cited above ("Justified by Faith"), deals specifically with Romans 3:21–4:5, and like *Where is Boasting?* argues against interpretations associated with the New Perspective.

[46] It is not that first-century Jews believed in salvation by works alone. The literature, rather, points to an admixture of faith and works, so that "the emphasis on the works of Abraham in Jewish literature could easily lead to a synergism that is lacking in Pauline theology" (Schreiner, *Romans*, 216). Schreiner's comments play off those of G. N. Davies, *Faith and Obedience in Romans: A Study in Romans 1–4*, Journal for the Study of the New Testament Supplement Series 39 (Sheffield: JSOT Press, 1990), 155-58. Even given Paul's emphasis on the necessity of works in the life of the believer, it is never a case of "justification by faith *and*. . . ."

[47] Carson cites *Mekhilta* on Exodus 14:15 (35b), and *Mekhilta* 40b, in this regard, "The Vindication of Imputation," 56.

ing Abraham.[48] It is this "crucial component" in Paul's argument that sets his understanding apart from other contemporary perspectives.[49]

One of the more striking examples from Jewish literature is 1 Maccabees 1:52: "Was not Abraham found faithful in testing, and it was reckoned to him for righteousness?" Not only does the author interpret Genesis 15:6 through the events in Genesis 22, but the declaration of 15:6 is appended to Genesis 22.[50]

There seems also to have been at least a strand of Judaism that not only recognized Abraham for his "righteousness" but also for the role Abraham himself played in the events surrounding God's call to him to leave Ur. For instance, the *Apocalypse of Abraham* goes to great lengths to describe Abraham's dissatisfaction with the gods of his father. This dissatisfaction culminates in Abraham's asking the true God to reveal himself (7:12). Though we cannot be sure how representative these texts may be, they do support the notion that at least some Jews viewed Abraham rather heroically, and incorrectly, as an example (*the* example) of how one is righteous before God.[51]

Even a small sampling of Jewish literature suggests that Paul disagreed with much of the typical, contemporary Jewish interpretation of Abraham, and that his understanding of the operative role of faith in the life of Abraham stood in contrast to the views held generally in the Judaism of his day.[52]

---

[48] Thus contra Sirach 44:20-21, in which the promises made to Abraham in Genesis 12 and 15 are practically the inference drawn from Abraham's faithfulness during testing: "Who kept the law of the Most High, and was in covenant with him: he established the covenant in his flesh and when he was proved, he was found faithful. Therefore he assured him by an oath, that he would bless the nations in his seed, and that he would multiply him as the dust of the earth, and exalt his seed as the stars, and cause them to inherit from sea to sea, and from the river unto the utmost part of the land." This text is also cited by Dunn, *Romans 1–8*, 200.

[49] Gathercole, "Justified by Faith," 157. "Paul wants accurately to portray the spiritual condition of Abraham at his justification, that is, that Abraham was not justified on the basis of obedience (Rom. 4:2) but rather on the basis of faith (4:3), of grace (4:4), by the God who justifies the ungodly (4:5), (ibid).

[50] Undoubtedly, James 2:14-26 comes to mind here. In that text James does view Genesis 15 through the lens of later events in Abraham's life. I would argue that James, however, is not following the traditions of Paul's opponents. James does not contrast faith and works, or vaunt works over faith, or make faith and works identical, but comments on the impossibility of a true faith that does not work. James, moreover, argues that Genesis 15:6 was "fulfilled" by Abraham's willingness to sacrifice Isaac (Genesis 22). The declaration made in 15:6 was shown to be true by the events that followed.

[51] These texts also provide more evidence for the assertion that James, like Paul, was not in step with much of the Jewish tradition about Abraham.

[52] Richard Hays ("Have We Found Abraham to Be Our Forefather according to the Flesh? A Reconsideration of Rom 4:1," *NovT* 27 [1985]), and N. T. Wright ("Romans and the Theology of Paul") are correct to discuss the true identity of Abraham's children in this text—but not to the

Abraham, Faith, and Works in Romans 4

In chapter 4 Paul expands and develops one of the main concepts of the letter up to this point, i.e., faith. At the end of chapter 3 Paul declares that rather than abolishing the law, we "establish the law" through faith (3:31). Paul does not, at this point, further take up the subject of the law, but carefully sets forth an extended discussion to show that his argument is supported by the patriarch Abraham, specifically in regard to justifying faith as that which is, and always has been, what characterizes the people of God. The identification of God's people and soteriology go hand in hand.[53] The very presence of Abraham directs attention to matters of soteriology, since Abraham's position vis-à-vis Israel is grounded in redemption, for as Isaiah says, it was "the LORD, who redeemed Abraham" (29:22).

Paul has already established that "faith" means specifically faith in Christ as the propitiatory offering for sin (Rom. 3:21-26), that "faith" is the operating principle in the gospel he preaches (1:17), and that his divinely appointed mission is to "bring about the obedience of faith among the Gentiles" (1:5). Paul continues his argument into chapter 4 by bringing out the "Father" of all who believe, not only to contrast faith with works in justification, but to make it clear that "faith" has always been the basis for the relationship between God and his people, those whom God justifies.

At the risk of over-simplifying, Paul's thought in these five verses

<hr>

exclusion of soteriology. It does not have to be a case of "either/or." Paul not only speaks of "Abraham our forefather according to the flesh," but also of Abraham "the father of all those who believe," Jew and Gentile, all "who also follow in the footsteps of our father Abraham" (4:11-12). Schlatter's comments are appropriate and apprehend the larger argument of the chapter: "'We' is used in the context of the Jewish consciousness, but it does not denote that the instruction about Abraham has significance only for the Jewish component of the community. Jews and Gentiles are made one in the community." Adolph Schlatter, *Romans: The Righteousness of God*, trans. Siegfried S. Schatzmann (Peabody, Mass.: Hendrickson, 1995), 108.

[53] As Schreiner points out: "The theme that binds 3:27-31 and chapter 4 is that all peoples are justified by faith" (*Romans*, 209). If by "soteriology" one means only "conversion," or a detailed discussion of the mechanics of God's salvation, then I agree with Hays and Wright and affirm that this text is not about "how one becomes saved." But saying that the text is not primarily concerned with soteriology is going too far. The presence of Abraham, a former idol-worshipper who became the patriarch of Judaism, argues that soteriology is a central part of this text. The larger context also argues for a concern with soteriology in this text through the uninhibited display of the sinful condition of humanity that has resulted in God's condemnation (1:18–3:20; 3:23), and Paul's linking of forgiveness and justification with the death and resurrection of Christ (4:25). The people of God are identified explicitly as those who believe in Christ who died under the just condemnation of God in their place for their sins (3:25). An absolute separation between covenantal and soteriological themes is unwarranted. The two themes exist in harmony.

can be reduced to the following: righteousness is received by faith, not as wages earned by working. The γάρ in verse 2 focuses the question found in verse 1, "What, therefore, shall we say Abraham, our father according to the flesh, has found?"[54] What about Abraham, one of the most venerated figures in Jewish thought? How does he fit into this discussion about how all people, both Jews and Gentiles, are justified by faith and have no reason to boast in their own works (Rom. 3:21-31)? Paul's answer is simple: Abraham has no reason to boast, because *not even* Abraham was justified by works.

So the life of Abraham, rather than proving an exception to Paul's discussion thus far as the Jewish interpretations of Abraham seem to argue, is the supreme example that verifies exactly what Paul is saying.[55] The boasting Paul excludes in 3:27 is denied to Abraham as well. While

---

[54] Hays's argument that κατὰ σάρκα modifies εὑρηκέναι is noted but is not within the scope of this discussion. R. B. Hays, "Have We Found Abraham to Be Our Forefather according to the Flesh?" 76-98. See also, N. T. Wright, "Romans and the Theology of Paul," 40; idem, "Romans," 489-90; and M. Cranford, "Abraham in Romans 4," 71-88. It must be noted that although Wright and Hays agree on the translation, they, for a time, differed in their reading of the text. While Hays, at least in the article "Have We Found Abraham," understands Paul to mean, "Have we [Jews] found Abraham," Wright reads the text as, "Have we [Christians, both Jews and Gentiles] found Abraham to be our forefather according to the flesh." According to Wright, his reading makes sense of the context of Romans 4 and of Paul's use of the word "found" ("Romans," 490-91). Wright's emphasis is important for understanding the significance of Paul's repeated claim that both Jews and Gentiles have the same standing as the people of God (1:16; 2:10; 3:23, 29; 10:12). Hays has since come to agree with Wright's reading. See Wright, "Adam, Israel, Christ," in *Pauline Theology*, vol. 3, *Romans*, ed. D. M. Hay and E. E. Johnson (Minneapolis: Fortress, 1995), 81. For responses to this interpretation, see Moo, *Romans*, 259-60; Schreiner, *Romans*, 213-14; and, Gathercole, *Where is Boasting?* 234-36. Schreiner remarks that "the immediately succeeding verses answer the question as to whether righteousness is by works; they do not concern the nature of Abraham's paternity. The specific question in verse 1, then, is whether the case of Abraham validates the contention in 3:27-28 that righteousness is by faith rather than works" (*Romans*, 213). Gathercole points out that both Hays and Wright are motivated by a desire to show that the issue here is the identity of the family of Abraham rather than soteriology—a distinction that Gathercole regards as "misleading" (*Where is Boasting?* 234-35). As above, I would suggest that the question regarding the nature of righteousness and the question of who are the true children of Abraham are complementary trajectories in this text. After verse 8 Paul goes on to show that those who follow Abraham in his faith (i.e., his true children) are none other than those who are saved by faith rather than works. I do realize that the position Hays and Wright hold is based on the idea that salvation by "works" is not really at issue here. My point is that Abraham's paternity and soteriology go together in Paul's argument.

[55] Michael Cranford takes exception with interpretations, like this one, that view Abraham as an "example" or as paradigmatic for Christian life or faith. In this text "Abraham is not viewed as an example of Christian faith, but is instead used by Paul to show why Gentiles can be considered members of God's people." He states further: "Abraham provides the reason why Gentiles experience salvation, not the example of how an individual becomes saved" ("Abraham in Romans 4," 73). While I agree with Cranford (as above with Hays and Wright) that this text is not primarily about how someone "becomes saved," in the sense that it is not a treatise on Abraham's, or anyone else's, conversion experience, I do not agree that the text can be reduced to the issue of "Jewish ethnicity and faith as competing boundary markers of God's people." Leaving aside the issue of "boundary markers," it seems that regardless of one's interpretation of Romans 4, the idea of Abraham serving as an "example" in some sense is impossible to avoid. A phrase like "follow in the footsteps" is an indication that an "example" of some sort is established.

acknowledging the difficulties in the conditional sentence,[56] whether Abraham could boast of his works before men is not really the ultimate issue in this verse.[57] The point seems to be that Abraham, the ungodly (v. 5), cannot be justified before God on the basis of works; therefore he has no grounds for boasting. Since Paul's larger aim is to show that justification is on the basis of faith, and since "work(s)" are here contrasted with faith, and, moreover, since God is clearly the one who judges (reckons) a person's status, it is fair to say that whatever respect works gain in the eyes of men is hardly the issue.[58] Paul's concern is the way God views the situation, and the idea of boasting before God is already ruled out (3:27).[59]

Paul grounds his thought about Abraham in Scripture. The distinction between faith and works is solidified in his quotation of Genesis 15:6.[60] The meaning is clear: Abraham's faith was counted by God for righteousness. However this may be explained, there is no other way to read Genesis 15:6: "Abraham believed in God, and it [Abraham's faith] was reckoned to him for righteousness."[61] This of course raises the ques-

---

[56] The protasis, εἰ γὰρ 'Αβραὰμ ἐξ ἔργων ἐδικαιώθη, which would seem to be an "unreal" or "contrary to fact" condition, is followed by καύχημα ἔχει, the verb ἔχει being a present (typical of a "real" condition), rather than the imperfect that one would normally expect in the apodosis of an "unreal" condition. Fitzmyer explains the construction by saying that Paul's "thoughts get ahead of his expression" (Romans, 372-73). Fitzmyer goes on to say that even if Paul means to say that Abraham could boast before men he is "speaking on a theoretical level." Paul will, however, "eventually reject this idea too" (ibid.).

[57] Barth speaks of Abraham's boast before men in terms of the due wages paid to a worker (4:4): "As a worker, Abraham has his reward: if not in the book of life, yet nevertheless in the book of the history of religion, in the record of the achievements of great men and of delicate souls." Yet this reward of recognition "has no bearing upon his righteousness before God." Karl Barth, Romans, trans. Edwyn C. Hoskyns (Oxford: Oxford University Press, 1933; reprint 1968), 122. U. Wilckens argues that Paul does not deny Abraham's boast before men, only before God (Der Brief an die Römer, teilband 1, Röm. 1–5, Evangelisch-Katholischer Kommentar zum Neuen Testament 6.1 [Zurich: Benziger/Neukirchen-Vluyn, 1978], 261).

[58] Calvin comments: "Moses does not relate what men thought of Abraham, but the character which he had before the tribunal of God" (John Calvin, The Epistles of Paul to the Romans and Thessalonians, vol. 8 of Calvin's New Testament Commentaries, trans. Ross MacKenzie, ed. David W Torrance and Thomas F. Torrance [Grand Rapids: Eerdmans, 1960], 84).

[59] As Fitzmyer states: "Thus Paul aligns Abraham with the rejection of boasting in 3:27. In reality, not even Abraham can boast, because his upright status before God comes from divine grace and favor. Paul can so conclude, because his conclusion is based on the premise of 3:27" (Romans, 373). See also Cranfield, Romans, 228; Moo, Romans, 214-15; Schreiner, Romans, 214.

[60] Paul's quotation follows nearly the exact wording of the Septuagint. The differences are (1) in the Septuagint, καί precedes ἐπίστευσεν and Romans reads, ἐπίστευσεν δὲ, and (2) Paul uses the spelling ('Αβραὰμ rather than 'Αβραμ). Neither of these differences is significant. The first may be due simply to a slightly different text (after all, we do not know exactly what text(s) of the Septuagint Paul used); whatever the case, the difference is insignificant. As for spelling, Paul merely uses the form that appears after Abram's name is changed to "Abraham" in Genesis 17.

[61] Murray is entirely right to say that "we must not, for dogmatic reasons, fail to recognize that it is faith that is imputed." (John Murray, The Epistle to the Romans, NICNT [Grand Rapids: Eerdmans, 1965], 132).

tion as to whether faith itself now becomes a work, or more specifically, whether faith itself is being counted as actual righteousness.

On the one hand it seems clear that faith itself cannot be a work of any kind because it is precisely the difference between faith and works that Paul explains in this text. It seems like a case of apples and oranges, i.e., two different things. Faith lays hold of its object (in this case the promises of God) and receives what is freely offered, all the while clinging to its object regardless of circumstances (4:5, 16, 18-21).[62] Works, in contrast, expect to collect payment as what is rightfully due (4:4). On the other hand, if "faith" is counted as righteousness, that is, if "righteousness" consists in faith, then faith does appear to be filling in for a work, or at least functioning in a similar way.[63] In this sense, faith reckoned as righteousness would be similar to "wages reckoned . . . as what is owed" (v. 4). One works, then collects wages; one believes, then is reckoned righteous. Two issues need to be addressed: (1) Paul's contextual discussion of "faith"; and (2) Paul's use of λογίζομαι.

"Faith" in context. In 3:24-26 Paul speaks of faith in specific terms. In verses 24-25 it is "through faith" that one is justified on the basis of Jesus' sacrificial death, and in verse 26 Paul says that God is "the justifier of the one who has faith in Jesus."[64] In these verses faith has a spe-

---

[62] It can be misleading at times to speak of faith as either "active" or "passive." When faith perseveres, as described by Paul in 4:18-21, or by Hebrews (chap. 11), how can one speak of it as "passive"? The distinction between faith and works is likely the cause of the emphasis on faith as something that is only passive. Passive faith, however, can appear oxymoronic. At the same time, it is not "active," if "active" means that faith generates its own initiative or accomplishes its own ends. Thus we can say that faith "receives," but we can also say that faith "acts." Even a "mental" act such as trusting (for one must conclude in one's mind (heart) that an object is trustworthy before "acting" on that trust), has an active element to it. Faith does not require us to build a "passive" hedge around it to protect it from becoming a work.

[63] Robert Gundry notes Paul's contrast between faith and works and argues that the righteousness "consists of faith." He states: "Since faith as distinct from works is credited as righteousness, the righteousness of faith is a righteousness that by God's reckoning consists of faith, even though faith is not itself a work" ("Why I Didn't Endorse 'The Gospel of Jesus Christ: An Evangelical Celebration' . . . Even though I Wasn't Asked To," *Books and Culture*, January/February [2001]: 8). Gundry's interpretation (and to be fair, Gundry's article is not exegetical, so all his arguments are not spelled out in any kind of detail) implies that Abraham's faith was properly reckoned; that is, his faith was reckoned for what it is, i.e., "righteousness." This is in contrast, for example, to Genesis 31:15 where Laban "reckons" his daughters to be "foreigners." There is nothing inherently "foreign" about them, but he counts them as though they are foreigners. For all intents and purposes they become "foreign," but it has nothing to do with any "foreign" quality they possess which Laban recognizes and then reckons to them.

[64] This construction (τὸν ἐκ πίστεως Ἰησοῦ), causes some interpretive problems. Wright, in line with his reading of 3:22, renders this as a subjective genitive, "out of the faithfulness of Jesus" (*Romans*, 474). This is similar to G. E. Howard, "Romans 3:21-31 and the Inclusion of the Gentiles," *Harvard*

cific object (God, Jesus), and justification is through faith in the object. It is important to notice that faith is instrumental in justification.[65] One is not justified on the grounds of faith but by faith. The ground of justification is the propitiatory death of Christ (v. 25).

Paul's readers would have processed this information before coming to chapter 4, so that when 4:3 was read (heard) it would make the most sense to understand that faith is not itself something that is reckoned as righteousness, but that faith unites the believer (Abraham) with an object that serves as the ground for righteousness, just as in 3:24-26.[66] Secondly, in verse 4 Paul says that a worker receives wages because he earns them—the wages are "reckoned according to what is owed"—(λογίζεται . . . κατὰ ὀφείλημα). He makes it clear that the worker/wages scenario is different from when something is "reckoned according to grace" (λογίζεται κατὰ χάριν). There is a difference

---

Theological Review 63 (1970): 230-31. The arguments for the subjective reading for this verse and for verse 22 are not, in my view, ultimately convincing. It is not, moreover, a simple question of grammar. For arguments against the subjective reading, see Schreiner, *Romans*, 185-86 (Schreiner lists four reasons against the subjective reading. These reasons are given at the end of a larger discussion of the issue).

[65] This point is controversial to say the least. However, the instrumentality of faith seems to flow from the context of Romans in which, as Carson points out, "Paul is at pains to stress the instrumental nature of faith" (Vindication of Imputation, 65).

[66] The "it" that is reckoned is vital for understanding the text. It is not λογίζομαι that creates the instrumentality in this text, it is the thing reckoned—faith—that is instrumental. Gundry argues, at least in part, against any kind of instrumental sense in this text by listing several occurrences of λογίζομαι both inside and out of the New Testament (*The Nonimputation of Christ's Righteousness*, 19ff). For instance, he cites Psalm 106:31 and later notes that "it is hard, if not impossible to think that . . . Psalm 105 (106):31 presents Phinehas's zeal as the instrument by which an alien righteousness was received" (ibid., 20-21). Three comments are in order. First, the "counting" done in regard to Phinehas's zeal is, as argued above, a counting of a righteous act for what it in fact is in that context—thus it is different than Genesis 15:6 or Romans 4:3. Second, in the texts he himself cites there are clearly different kinds of reckonings. When an unwalled village is "counted as open fields" (Lev. 25:31), and the excess left over after an offering is "counted for the Levites" (Num. 18:30), the idea is about how these things will be considered. No wall? Then that village goes into the category of an open field. Are there leftovers from the offering? Then those go to the Levites. Again, these seem demonstrably different than faith in God being counted for righteousness. Third, Gundry is in a sense correct to refer to the instrumental readings of the occurrences of λογίζομαι as "gobbledygook" (ibid., 21). They are "gobbledygook" *if* one refused to differentiate between the things reckoned. Things like uncircumcision (Rom. 2:26), and Artemis's temple (Acts 19:27), unlike faith, are not instruments. Gundry of course recognizes that there can be a counting whether or not "what is counted is intrinsically what it is counted to be" (ibid., 22). The question is, what it the object in view here? It is, obviously, "faith," but it is "faith" spoken of in the context of the ungodly being justified, and in a context that seems clearly to assert that justification is "by" faith (Rom. 5:1). The very point seems to be that an extrinsic righteousness is precisely what is needed for the ungodly to be justified (Carson, *The Vindication of Imputation*, 64). Having no righteousness of their own (Rom. 3:18), and having sinned and fallen short of God's glory (Rom. 3:23), they are "justified freely as a gift by his grace, through the redemption that is in Christ Jesus" (3:24). Christ was "set forth as a propitiation in his blood by faith" (Rom. 3:25). The thrust of the overall argument is that God has provided a righteousness that comes from God himself (Rom. 3:21) and that this righteousness is the gift that the ungodly receive by faith—faith in the one who justifies the ungodly. Again, what must be settled here is not only a case of an argument about texts, but one that concerns Paul's (and the NT's) theology.

"between merited and unmerited imputation to be preserved."[67] Taken together with verse 2, which denies that Abraham was justified by works (according to what is owed), the implication is that the reckoning of Abraham's faith as righteousness was not a recognition of faith as the righteousness itself, but rather faith was counted for something that intrinsically it was not, i.e., righteousness.[68] If the "righteousness consists of faith," it is a matter of faith being reckoned properly, a reckoning what is deserved—the very thing that Paul denies. Verse 5 supports this idea by showing that it is not the one "who works" (who, according to v. 4, would receive the reward of his labor), but the one who "believes in the one who justifies the ungodly"; it is that one whose "faith is reckoned as righteousness."

Robertson rightly concludes on the basis of parallel texts that the reckoning of righteousness must mean that Abraham is reckoned with "a righteousness that does not inherently belong to him,"[69] but just the context of Romans alone rules out the idea of an inherent righteousness, whether it be "faith" or otherwise. Not only does Paul declare that there is "no one" righteous (3:10), but he has made it clear that justification comes only on the basis of the righteousness of God in Christ as revealed in the gospel (1:16-17; 3:21-22).

The parallel construction of Genesis 15:6 found in Psalm 106:31 need not be a cause of alarm among those defending the traditional view. Murray's discussion of the differences between Genesis 15:6 and Psalm 106:31 in his interpretation of Romans 4:3 confirms this point. Murray notes that the formula is similar in both texts in that something, (Abraham's faith and Phinehas's act) is counted, imputed, as righteousness.[70] He quickly goes on to point out that Genesis 15:6 involves Abraham's faith, but Psalm 106:31 speaks of Phinehas's zealous act. The former has to do with "justification," while the latter concerns "righteousness in the ethical and religious sense" and "the good works which were the fruit of faith."[71] This is another way of

---

[67] Carson, "The Vindication of Imputation," 60. I find Carson's arguments against Gundry's view of imputation in Romans 4 convincing and they have clarified my own view. See especially, ibid., 64-68.
[68] Ibid., 18.
[69] Robertson, "Gen. 15:6: New Covenant Exposition of an Old Covenant Text," 40. Moo cites this quote from Robertson as well (Moo, *Romans*, 262).
[70] Murray, *The Epistle to the Romans*, 131.
[71] Ibid.

saying, as argued above, that in Phinehas's case, something is reckoned accordingly, whereas with Abraham it is a matter of something (faith) being reckoned as something that it inherently is not.

Paul's use of λογίζομαι. The meaning of λογίζομαι in Romans 4 lies, not surprisingly, at the center of any discussion about the doctrine of imputation in Paul. N. T. Wright significantly downplays the importance of the term in Paul's scheme of justification. Wright asserts that λογίζομαι constitutes "[t]he most obvious metaphorical level" in the text, and he warns that "we should not allow this unique and brief sidelight to become the dominant note.[72] Heiland understands Paul as contrasting a Hebrew sense of "reckoned," in which there is no sense of "recording of merits," with a Greek sense that emphasizes a "statutory reckoning of a reward for those who can produce achievements."[73] The illustration Paul develops in verses 4-5, in which the concept of "reckoning" is connected to "the one who works" and to "wages," argues for a commercial or marketplace background in this text.[74] Here, however, Paul is showing *the difference* between what happens in the marketplace and how the ungodly are justified.

---

[72] The second level is "the law court," and the third, and most important, is "the covenant and membership within it" (Wright, *Romans*, 491). The word appears eleven times in this chapter. Even allowing for simple repetition, it seems to call for a description of something more than a "brief sidelight." Wright's reading of this text is informed by his overall interpretation of Romans, particularly emphasizing the law court and covenant themes. His description of the role of the "book keeping metaphor" is accurate at least within his interpretive framework. At the same time Wright is correct in being cautious not to emphasize imputation at the expense of other issues in Romans 4.
[73] H. W. Heiland, "λογίζομαι," TDNT, 4:291. The "Greek" sense is conveyed in the Septuagint translation of חשב with λογίζομαι. It is this meaning that dominated in the Judaism that Paul opposed. In the text the contrast is between "reckoned according to grace" (Hebrew meaning of חשב in the text of Gen. 15:6), and "reckoned according to what is owed" (Greek sense conveyed by λογίζομαι). Heiland's distinction finds a basis in assertion more than in evidence.
[74] In Louw and Nida's groupings, λογίζομαι and μισθός share a semantic domain (Domain 57, "Possess, Transfer, Exchange"). Johannes P. Louw and Eugene A. Nida, *Greek-English Lexicon of the New Testament Based on Semantic Domains*, 2nd ed. (New York: United Bible Societies, 1989), 1:558-85 (λογίζομαι appears in sub-domain T, "Keep Records," and μισθό" subdomain M, "Hire, Rent Out"). Both words appear in more than one domain. Louw and Nida list Romans 4:3 with λογίζομαι in 57 T (ibid., 583). Dunn states that Paul's use of χάρις would have also been recognized as a business term in this context and cites LSJ as support (*Romans 1–8*, 203). The entry in LSJ (1978-79), however, gives no overtly business or commercial use of the term. Nevertheless, the evidence in Romans 4 supports a marketplace background regardless of the range of meaning of χάρις. Dunn (*Romans*, 203) and Moo (*Romans*, 263, n. 41) both point out the pairing of χάρις and ὀφείλημα in Thucydides 2.40.4, but the significance of the citation is unclear. Dunn merely notes the pairing, and Moo cites the text as an example from "secular commercial language." The text, however, speaks of owing and returning favors in friendships, not business. Thucydides, *History of the Peloponnesian War*, trans. C. Foster Smith, Loeb Classical Library, 108 (G. P. Putnam's Sons: New York, 1919), 326-27.

In verses 4 and 5 Paul unpacks his interpretation of Genesis 15:6.[75] Paul uses two examples of reckoning to show exactly what he means by his example of Abraham. In both cases something is "reckoned," that is, something is laid to an account, but the underlying principles in the two situations are radically different. There is a reckoning based on remuneration and there is a reckoning that is a gift. The structure and content of the verses make the differences clear.

Each verse begins with the object of the reckoning. In verse 4 it is "the one who works," while in verse 5 it is "the one who does not work, but believes." In verse 4 the expressed subject, "wages" (ὁ μισθὸς), comes before the verb, while in verse 5 the expressed subject, "faith" (ἡ πίστις), follows the verb. This could indicate that in verse five Paul is emphasizing the action of reckoning over "faith," thus emphasizing the distinction between what is earned (wages) and reckoned (v. 4), and what is reckoned but not earned (faith, v. 5). In one case what is earned is emphasized, while in the other the focus is on the reckoning of what is not earned. One is reckoned appropriately for what it is, while the other is reckoned as something it inherently is not. In both cases, however, the reckoning is legitimate; the latter is not "fictional." Wages are reckoned for what is owed, not as a gift. Righteousness, on the other hand, is reckoned not as what is owed, but as a gift.

Thus Paul makes it clear that wage earning is not "according to grace," with the implication being that the reckoning of faith as righteousness is according to grace. On one hand, there is a worker who, upon performing his job, can rightly expect to collect his wages. There is no favor or special treatment involved; it is simply a matter of what is proper in that situation. His wages are counted as simply what is owed to him. On the ledger, the worker's column shows that he has been paid his wages. The principle behind Genesis 15:6, on the other hand, is that believing, not working, is the basis for being counted righteous. This is the message of verse 5. This is why Abraham has no boast (v. 2), and why the Scripture says he "believed God and it was reckoned to him as righteousness" (v. 3).

Another element in verse 5 further clarifies Paul's meaning. In verse 5, it is not simply "the one who does not work" in contrast to "the

---

[75] This discussion is somewhat repetitive of the preceding section on "faith." Here, however, there is a more emphasis on the role of "reckoning."

one who works" in verse 4; it is specifically, "the one who does not work, *but believes in the one who justifies the ungodly*," whose faith is reckoned as righteousness. By asserting that Abraham believed in the one who justifies the "ungodly"—thus identifying Abraham himself as "ungodly"—Paul not only runs against the grain of contemporary Jewish thought about Abraham, he makes it clearer that this reckoning was not a matter of Abraham's own righteousness being reckoned as righteousness. In other words, as we saw above, the reckoning here is not counting something for what it is, it is counting it for something that it inherently is not. Here the ungodly are justified, the ungodly are declared to be right before God, not by working and then receiving what is right for their labor, but by believing—by *not working*.

This is precisely the distinction Paul is making. There is a reckoning based on works and there is a reckoning based on faith. Wages, the just payment for work accomplished, are reckoned to those who earn them, but the righteousness of which Paul speaks here is reckoned to the ungodly who believe. The ungodly can have righteousness only as a gift, something they can only "receive" (Rom. 3:24).[76]

Thus, Abraham is no different from the rest of humanity whose "ungodliness" (ἀσέβειαν) is the object of God's wrath (1:18)[77] and no different from other believers, the "ungodly" (ἀσεβῶν) for whom Christ died (5:6). In short, Paul includes Abraham among sinners.[78] This verse simply asserts something about Abraham that Paul has made abundantly clear about the rest of humanity since 1:18. In this sense Paul is not saying anything new; he is merely applying his argument from earlier in the letter to Abraham. The designation, "ungodly" also points to the issue of forgiveness of sins that Paul will address by way of Psalm 32, which will clarify the meaning of "reckon righteous."[79]

As far as God justifying the "ungodly," there is no need to worry

---

[76] Westerholm, *Perspectives Old and New*, 281.

[77] Wright, *Romans*, 492.

[78] Piper sees, correctly, a clear link between "ungodly" and "apart from works" (v. 6) that confirms the externality of the reckoned righteousness, thus ruling out anything internal or subjective, including faith, as the actual righteousness (*Counted Righteous*, 68).

[79] Peter Martyr Vermigli comments that when Paul uses the term "ungodly" he means, "a sinner which is a stranger from God. . . . But he [God] is said to justify the ungodly because he forgives his sins" (*Most Learned and Fruitful Commentaries of Doctor Peter Martir Vermilius*, trans. H. B. Bolton [London: John Daye, 1568], 71). The grammar and spelling of Bolton's translation have been modified slightly to conform to modern style.

whether this violates Old Testament texts that condemn justifying the wicked or acquitting the guilty.[80] Paul's point is to give more evidence that Abraham brought nothing to the table that contributed to his justification. Moreover, we can safely say that the "ungodly" are justified ultimately because Christ died for them (3:25; 5:6); God's just wrath against sin has been met; the guilty did not get off scot-free. In the Old Testament texts, the idea is that justice cannot be suspended or brushed aside, that guilt must be punished, and that right must be upheld. All these criteria are met in the substitutionary death of Christ.[81]

The Blessing of Forgiveness and the Meaning of Imputation in Romans 4

Paul now brings in another text from the Old Testament to support his argument.[82] The purpose of the quote from Psalm 32 is evident in the comparative conjunction καθάπερ "just as."[83] The "just as" tells the reader that a second piece of evidence is coming, evidence that will prove the point. The primary connection between Genesis 15:6 and Psalm 32 is the word λογίζομαι.[84] The two are also connected in that each involves a declaration. Paul introduces the quote by saying: "just as David speaks a blessing on the man whom God reckons righteous apart from works" (Rom. 4:6). Note that God is the explicit subject of λογίζεται.[85] This supports taking God to be the implied agent of the passive ἐλογίσθη in verse 3.[86]

---

[80] For example, in Isaiah 5:23 woe is pronounced on those "who justify the wicked"; Proverbs 17:15 says that "he who justifies the wicked" is "an abomination to the Lord"; and in Exodus 23:7 God says that he "will not acquit the guilty."

[81] Thus, I am hesitant to posit a "new application of justify" (Moo, *Romans*, 264). Do we need a new application of "condemn" to understand, say, the Father's role in the death of the Son? After all, Proverbs 17:15 also says that the one "who condemns the righteous" is "an abomination to the LORD." Even if some understood Paul's gospel as contradicting the Old Testament, Paul has answered the objection by "drawing out the significance of Christ's propitiatory death (3:25, 26)." Andrew T. Lincoln, "From Wrath to Justification: Tradition, Gospel, and Audience in the Theology of Romans 1:18–4:25," in *Pauline Theology*, vol. 3, *Romans*, ed. David M. Hay and E. Elizabeth Johnson (Minneapolis: Fortress, 1995), 151.

[82] gᵉzērāh sāwāh.

[83] As often noted, καθάπερ (seventeen times in the NT) is accompanied with a textual variant, due most likely to the tendency of scribes to change it to the more common καθώς. See A. T. Robertson, *The Grammar of the Greek New Testament in Light of Historical Research* (Nashville: Broadman, 1934), 967; Cranfield, *Romans 1–8*, 182 (commenting on Rom. 3:4); and Schreiner, *Romans*, 221.

[84] Fitzmyer, *Romans*, 376.

[85] Though the form is the same, λογίζεται is surely middle here rather than passive as in verses 4 and 5. The change in voice is due to the quote from Psalm 32: μακάριος ἀνὴρ οὗ οὐ μὴ λογίσηται κύριος ἁμαρτίαν. Moo notes that the change in voice is in anticipation of the quote from Psalm 32 (*Romans*, 265, n. 55).

[86] A so-called "divine passive."

There is another grammatical note, and it is that λογίζομαι is now followed by a direct object, λογίζεται δικαιοσύνην. Rather than being the object of a prepositional phrase, as in verses 3 and 5, "righteousness" is now the object of the verb. It could be that Paul wants to clarify that external "righteousness," rather than faith itself as what is imputed, but it is also possible that Paul simply matches the clause structure of Psalm 32 where λογίζομαι is followed by a direct object (ἁμαρτίαν).[87] Thus Paul links God's reckoning righteousness with God's not reckoning sin, or to state it another way, with forgiveness.

There is also a connection between the prepositional phrase "apart from works" (χωρὶς ἔργων), and the prepositional phrase in verse 2, "by works" (ἐξ ἔργων).[88] As noted above, justification "by works" is ruled out on the basis of Genesis 15:6. In fact, one could turn the conditional clause of verse 2 into the proposition: "Abraham was not justified by works," or to put it positively, "Abraham was justified *apart from* works." It was Abraham's faith, not his works, that God reckoned as righteousness. In verse 6 the phrase "apart from works" modifies "reckons," and in verse 2 "by works" modifies "justified." The parallel between these phrases creates a connection between justification and imputation, with the main idea being that neither is based on works.

There are, then, two important connections formed in this text: (1) God's reckoning righteousness is linked with God's not reckoning sin (forgiveness), and (2) reckoning righteous apart from works is linked to being justified apart from works. These are important elements in the discussion of the traditional view of imputation, because some interpreters assert that forgiveness is, *in this text*, equated with the imputation of righteousness; in other words, faith reckoned as righteousness is practically the same thing as saying that a man's sins are not reckoned to him. This is the majority position in contemporary scholarship.[89] The priority

---

[87] Piper understands this as Paul placing emphasis on the externality of righteousness and the instrumentality of faith by the shift of "righteousness" to the direct object slot (*Counted Righteous*, 58). Even if there is no substantial significance to this grammatical shift, the external, objective nature of righteousness is clear in the text.

[88] Piper sees the essential parallel with "apart from works" as "the ungodly," as well as a parallel with 3:27 (ibid., 58).

[89] It is essential that readers understand that this does not mean that *all* these scholars equate forgiveness and justification absolutely. This note has only to do with Romans 4. Though they may reach their conclusion for very different reasons, the following are examples of scholars who hold this position *specifically in regard to this text*. Note that this list includes some who hold to a traditional view

of forgiveness in Romans 4 was also recognized by both Luther[90] and Calvin, who states, "By these words [the quote from Ps. 32] we also learn that righteousness for Paul is nothing other than the remission of sins. . . . We are therefore left with the glorious statement that he who is cleansed before God by the free remission of sins is justified by faith."[91] Others, however, assert that Paul is not equating forgiveness with imputation, or justification for that matter, because Genesis 15:6 and Psalm

---

of imputation, while others are opponents to the traditional view. That scholars across a broad range on the theological spectrum agree at this point indicates that there is no particular anti-theological bias driving this interpretation. Dunn, *Romans 1–8*, 207; Cranfield, *Romans 1–8*, 233; Daniel P. Fuller, *Unity of the Bible: Unfolding God's Plan for Humanity* (Grand Rapids: Zondervan, 1992), 256; Ernst Käsemann, *Commentary on Romans*, trans. Geoffrey W. Bromiley (Grand Rapids: Eerdmans, 1980), 113; Leon Morris, *The Epistle to the Romans*, Pillar New Testament Commentary, ed. D. A. Carson (Grand Rapids: Eerdmans, 1988), 199; Anders Nygren, *Commentary on Romans*, trans. Carl C. Rasmussen (Philadelphia: Muhlenberg Press, 1949), 171; Schreiner, *Romans*, 219; Schlatter, *Romans*, 111; Mark A. Seifrid, *Christ, Our Righteousness: Paul's Theology of Justification* (Downers Grove: InterVarsity, 2001), 175; Wright, *Romans*, 493.

[90] Luther's extended comments on these verses focus on forgiveness. The following is but an example. Commenting on Psalm 32, Luther states: "Thus the man to whom these two evils [offenses and sins] are forgiven, behold he is the man whom God regards as righteous. . . . For by the use of this word [iniquity] he is trying to prove that righteousness is given through imputation without works, and that this takes place through the nonimputation of unrighteousness. It is the same thing, whether we say, 'to whom God imputes righteousness,' or, 'to whom the Lord does not impute sin," that is, unrighteousness." Martin Luther, *Lectures on Romans*, Luther's Works, vol. 25, ed. Hilton C. Oswald (St. Louis: Concordia), 271-72.

[91] *Romans and Thessalonians*, 86. Calvin makes his comments on the equivalence of justification and forgiveness in Romans 4 shortly after saying that "it is necessary that Christ should be seen to be the one who clothes us with his own righteousness" (ibid., 84). Thus regardless of Calvin's (or Luther's) larger discussion of justification and imputation, it is clear that when focusing on Romans 4 he understands that being clothed in Christ's righteousness means that one's sins are forgiven. Calvin and Luther both show restraint in regard to reading all their theology of justification into this one text. This same kind of restraint is evident in both Moo and Murray, neither one of whom understands justification as equivalent to forgiveness but recognize an emphasis in Romans 4 on forgiveness. Neither Moo nor Murray maintain an essential distinction between the quotes of Psalm 32 and Genesis 15, nor do they merely equate them without qualification. For instance, Moo states that "the forgiveness of sins is a basic component of justification" (ruling out the idea of equating the two) and describes Paul as using "this quotation [Psalm 32] to compare justification to the non-accrediting or not "imputing" of sins to a person" (Moo, *Romans*, 266). It is accurate to say that Moo simply does not limit Paul's meaning to forgiveness based on a broader conception of justification. Even though Murray points out that forgiveness is not all there is to justification, he sees the emphasis on forgiveness in this text, asserting that Paul's "more restricted interest" should be recognized and notes that Paul here teaches "justification as correlative with, if not as defined in terms of, the remission of sins" (Murray, *Romans*, 134). Paul's purpose explains why justification and forgiveness are so closely related here: "The appeal to David and to Psalm 32:1-2, in addition to that said of Abraham, is for the purpose of demonstrating that what the Scripture conceives of as the epitome of blessing and felicity is not the reward of works but the bestowment of grace through faith. Blessedness consists in that which is illustrated by the remission of sins and not by that which falls into the category of reward according to merit. In this passage the correlation of remission and justification and the virtual identification of the one with the other must therefore be understood in the light of the particular interest of the apostle at this point and must not be enlisted as proof that justification and remission are synonymous and reciprocally define each other" (ibid., 135). White notes that Paul's "blessed man" in verse 6 is the one imputed righteous apart from works, and that Paul "defines this in terms of the nonimputation of sin" (James R. White, *The God Who Justifies* [Bloomington, Minn.: Bethany House, 2001], 217 [see also, 215]).

32 present two constituent parts of justification, i.e., the imputation of righteousness and the forgiveness of sins.[92] These ideas should be dealt with before exploring the rest of Romans 4.[93]

"Just as." Paul's inclusion of Psalm 32 seems to have more to do with content than with personalities. In other words, Paul did not choose David but chose David's psalm that contains a textual parallel (λογίζομαι) with Genesis 15:6. Nevertheless, David's sin looms in the background of this psalm. The forgiven lawlessness and the covered and uncounted sin are David's specifically, as Psalm 32 makes clear. Yet the "blessing" is not restricted to David but is spoken on "the man," any man, whom God forgives. Through this psalm David himself becomes paradigmatic of the "blessed" man, the "one to whom the Lord does not reckon sin"; the man who tries to hide his sin but finds God's chastisement too much to bear (32:4-5a); and the man who then turns to God in repentance and finds that *God forgives sin* (v. 5b-c).

In context, this is a man in an established relationship with God, a covenant. In contrast to the covenant man Phinehas, this man has sinned, and God reckons him righteous apart from works, which parallels the justification of the ungodly in verse 5. Like Abraham, this man's faith is reckoned as something that inherently it is not. Thus, being without works, there is no basis for reckoning something inherent to him; the righteousness reckoned to him cannot consist of faith. If he is justified, it is because he has been reckoned righteous according to grace, not according to what is owed. This points to something outside himself as the basis for his righteousness. He finds forgiveness from God and sets

---

[92] Most recently, Gathercole, *Where is Boasting?* 248; Piper, *Counted Righteous*, 116-19. There is, however, a significant distinction between the trajectories of Gathercole's and Piper's interpretations. Gathercole simply posits a positive and negative aspect in the text. If there is a negative reckoning, there is by definition an implied positive reckoning. On the other hand, Piper's book, a defense of the traditional view, argues strongly against the idea that being reckoned righteous is limited to forgiveness, even in Romans 4.

[93] It should also be noted that often a strict distinction between "reckon righteous" and "not reckon sin" is asserted by various scholars in the Reformed tradition, and usually described as the "positive" and "negative" elements of justification. None of these writers, it must be stressed, see either of these elements in isolation or in any way disconnected from the other. A classic example is Turretin, who states: "When Paul argues from the remission of sins to the imputation of righteousness (Rom. 4:5-7), he does not do this on account of their equivalency; as if these two do not differ from each other and signify one and the same thing. Rather he does it on account of the undivided connection between both." Francis Turretin, *Institutes of Elenctic Theology*, trans. George Musgrave Giger, ed. James T. Dennison Jr. (Phillipsburg, N.J.: P&R, 1994), 2:659.

his hope on God and his promises (vv. 8-11, cf., Rom. 4:18-21), and the pronouncement on this man is "blessed."[94] While the formal link may be λογίζομαι, the context of Psalm 32 helps sharpen the focus on Paul's quote of verses 1 and 2.[95]

By quoting Psalm 32, Paul identifies the man "whom God reckons righteous apart from works" (v. 6) as "the man against whom the Lord does not reckon sin" (v. 8). The man reckoned righteous is the forgiven man. Paul's emphasis here is on the non-imputation of sins, i.e., forgiveness. Considering the text, it is easy to see why Calvin can say that "righteousness for Paul is nothing other than the forgiveness of sins."[96] The one on whom David speaks a "blessing" (μακαρισμός) is clearly one of those who is declared "blessed" (μακάριος) because their lawless deeds are forgiven and their sins are covered (v. 7). That man is blessed because God has not reckoned his sin to him (v. 8).[97] This is a description of the same man whom "God reckons righteous apart from works" (v. 6) and who "does not work but believes in the one who justifies the ungodly" (v. 5).[98] In this way Paul's discussion of Abraham, of justification without works, and of imputation of righteousness might be summarized here by one word: forgiveness.[99]

On the other hand, there is the view that Paul is not, even in this text, speaking of the imputation of righteousness only in terms of for-

---

[94] Hays suggests that this "echo" has a particular significance since Paul quoted Psalm 51 earlier. "This pronouncement is fraught with poignancy for the reader who has already heard the echoes of Psalm 51 in Rom. 3:4: David, who confessed his own guilt and God's justice, now speaks blessings in acknowledgement of God's forgiveness." Richard B. Hays, *Echoes of Scripture in the Letters of Paul* (London and New Haven: Yale, 1989), 55.

[95] Melanchthon was also able to hear echoes. In his commentary he includes an exposition of the text of Psalm 32 (Philip Melanchthon, *Commentary on Romans*, trans. Fred Kramer [St. Louis: Concordia, 1992], 111-12).

[96] Calvin, *Romans*, 86. Quoted above, n. 83. Though holding to the imputation of positive righteousness, Calvin did not see everything in this particular text.

[97] Vermigli links "blessed" with justification and speaks of it as both the non-imputation of sin and the forgiveness of sin (*Epistle to the Romans*, 75).

[98] Paul's identification of Abraham as "ungodly" could also have a connection with Psalm 32:5 where David says that in response to his repentance God "ἀφῆκας τὴν ἀσέβειαν τῆς ἁμαρτίας μου ("forgave the ungodliness of my sins"). Paul's use of the noun ἀσεβής is not, however, necessarily influenced by ἀσέβεια in Psalm 32. Hanson's argument that ἀσεβής and cognates do not appear frequently in Paul and therefore may point to Psalm 32:5 as the source provides little evidence to support the idea that Paul is using it here because of ἀσέβεια in Psalm 32. Our linguistic sample from Paul is simply too small to prove that hypothesis. In support of Hansons's view, one could point out that Genesis 15:6 is clearly the source of Paul's use of λογίζομαι (though obviously that is a direct quote, not a cognate). One should go no further than Hanson in saying that Paul "may" have purposely selected a cognate. Anthony Tyrell Hanson, "Abraham the Justified Sinner," in *Studies in Paul's Technique and Theology* (London: SPCK, 1974), 55.

[99] Paul's sermons in Acts clearly show the emphasis he places on forgiveness (see below).

giveness. By using Genesis 15:6 and Psalm 32:1-2, Paul is showing that justification involves both a positive declaration of righteousness and the forgiveness of sins.[100] While this interpretation may rely *a priori* on the idea that forgiveness is not enough because justification requires both forgiveness and positive obedience (active righteousness), it is possible to read Psalm 32 as the blessing that accompanies or is pronounced (simultaneously) upon the one "whom God reckons righteous apart from works," without appealing to a larger theological synthesis.[101] Read in this way Psalm 32 provides more information about what Genesis 15:6 entails.[102] Since so much rides on the connection between Psalm 32 and Genesis 15, a brief consideration of some of Paul's other Old Testament citations should help shed light on this issue.

Paul often cites Scripture with a formula such as καθὼς γέγραπται ("as/just as it is written"). In Romans there are thirteen such citations.[103] For instance, in 1:17 Paul quotes Habakkuk 2:4 to support the statement that "the righteousness of God is revealed from faith to faith" in the gospel. In order to confirm his charge that "both Jews and Greeks are all under sin" (3:10), Paul uses a string of Old Testament quotes to prove his point from Scripture (3:11-18). Similarly, in Romans 11:8-10 Paul cites several Old Testament texts to support his statement about the hardening of Israel. In these texts and in the others where Paul cites

---

[100] For the most part, this is not the emphasis found in exegetical commentaries or in most modern scholarship of any stripe (Some people, no doubt, might take this as the best argument for seeing more than forgiveness in this text.). As stated earlier, Gathercole is a slight exception at this point. He states: "God's declarative act of justification of the sinner (4:5) requires his act of the "nonreckoning" of sin (4:8). However, this is simultaneous with God's *positive* reckoning of righteousness on the other side of the ledger" (*Where Is Boasting?* 248). Gathercole does not go into detail about the mechanics of the "positive reckoning" and the "nonreckoning" of sin.

[101] As Gathercole (*Where Is Boasting?*) apparently does; though this may be a supposition on my part. Piper grounds his argument exegetically (including his understanding of the meaning of David's "blessing" in regard to Abraham in verse 11) but also appeals to Paul's *assumption* that for a person to be justified there must be the forgiveness of sins, which "stand in the way of declaring a person righteous," and a positive pronouncement, a "saving blessing"; i.e., "he must be counted righteous" (Piper, *Counted Righteous*, 117-18; my emphasis).

[102] Again, Piper: "When Paul put Psalm 32:1-2 and Genesis 15:6 together, he saw two essential aspects of justification: forgiveness and imputation—'blotting out' and 'crediting to'" (*Counted Righteous*, 118). Piper understands the bookkeeping metaphor in Romans 4:4 as one of the several texts in all of Paul's letters that point to the need for the imputation of righteousness to mean more than the forgiveness of sins.

[103] 1:17; 2:24; 3:4, 10; 4:17; 8:36; 9:13, 37; 10:15; 11:8, 26; 15:3, 9. Outside of Romans, Paul uses this formula in 1 Corinthians 1:31; 2:9; 2 Corinthians 8:15, 9.9. Technically, γέγραπται by itself constitutes the formula. I include the comparative particle with it here on account of Paul's use of καθάπερ in 4:6.

the Old Testament with the formula "as it is written," the quotations are used to clarify, prove, or confirm what Paul is saying.[104]

One other text in Romans is worth special notice. In Romans 9:10-13 Paul uses the example of Esau and Jacob in his discourse on election, which is at heart based on his interpretation of Old Testament teaching. He quotes Genesis 25:23, "The older will serve the younger," as part of the basis of his interpretation. He then cites another passage of Scripture as the ultimate support for his argument. This second text is linked to Genesis 25:23 with the formula, "as it is written" (καθὼς γέγραπται), "Jacob have I loved but Esau have I hated" (Mal. 1:2-3a). As in Romans 4, Scripture is used to interpret Scripture. Paul uses the quote from Malachi 1:2-3 to clarify the meaning of Genesis 25:23 and the principle of divine election that lies behind it.

The application of these texts to Romans 4 could be met with the objection that unlike the other texts, the citation of Psalm 32 does not begin with the quotation formula "just as it is written." Even if one observes that there is still a Scripture quote introduced by a comparative particle (καθάπερ), there is yet the objection that since the typical formula appears so often in Romans, Paul could have, and indeed probably would have, used the same formula if he had been citing Scripture in the same way. This objection is answered by the fact that there is more than one form of quotation formula in Paul, and that the phrase "David says" (Δαυὶδ λέγει) is one such formula.[105] The phrase "David says" is no different from "Scripture says," and the particle "just as" is possibly used here in place of "just as it is written," in order to place a particular emphasis on the agreement between Psalm 32:1-2 and Genesis 15:6 and its declaration about the imputation of righteousness.[106]

In other words, following his normal practice, Paul quotes an Old Testament text to make his point unmistakably clear; he does not intro-

---

[104] Dunn, *Romans 1–8*, 44. It was Dunn that pointed me in this direction and to Ellis's and Fitzmyer's work.

[105] E. Earl Ellis, *Paul's Use of the Old Testament* (Grand Rapids: Eerdmans, 1957), 92. As Ellis points out, the word λέγει is also used in conjunction with "the Scripture" and "God," and sometimes by itself without an expressed subject.

[106] As Ellis states: "The [introductory clauses] are particularly important in showing Paul's attitude to the Old Testament. Even in the Greek world the formula καθὼς γέγραπται was used with reference to the terms of an unalterable agreement; for the Jew it signified much more—the unalterable Word of God. 'The Scripture says', 'God says', and 'Isaiah says', are for Paul only different ways of expressing the same thing" (ibid., 23).

duce a second element in his argument by citing the Old Testament. Paul, therefore, does not use a quote to raise a further *implication* that may or may not be clear, but rather to make his point *explicit*. That is the vital observation gained by looking at other Old Testament quotations. Paul wants to expel, not add, any notion of ambiguity, the point being that the reckoning of righteousness to Abraham (who was "ungodly") is here explained by the non-reckoning of sin. The blessing of forgiveness interprets the blessing of imputed righteousness in this text. The one to whom God imputes righteousness is the one whose sins are forgiven.

There is one more piece of evidence that supports the argument that Paul intends to stress forgiveness in this text as the main idea behind being "reckoned righteous." After the introductory formula, Paul inserts a quick interpretation of the words he is about to quote from Psalm 32. Paul says that the "blessing" (μακαρισμός is clearly the μακάριος in Psalm 32) is spoken specifically "upon the man whom God reckons righteous apart from works" (v. 6). There is no mention of "works" in Psalm 32, yet Paul says explicitly that the blessed man, the one whose "lawless deeds are forgiven, and whose sins are covered" is the one reckoned righteous "apart from works" (v. 7). This parallels Abraham's not being "justified by works" (4:2). Abraham was not justified by works, but rather his faith was reckoned to him for righteousness (4:2-3).

This is just like David's blessing on the man who is reckoned righteous apart from works, that is, the man who is forgiven. That the phrase, "the blessing upon the man whom God reckons righteousness apart from works" comes after the introductory formula, "just as David also says," could be an indication that Paul is emphasizing that being reckoned righteous apart from works is the blessing of forgiveness.[107] If so, then Paul makes it clear by inserting an interpretive phrase that the quote is supporting what he has said and not providing another element to the structure of his argument.[108]

Moving outside Romans for a moment, this interpretation of Paul's

---

[107] Fitzmyer, *Romans*, 375. Fitzmyer only points out the emphatic position of the added phrase. I drew the possible implication.

[108] Why precisely Paul inserted the phrase after the introductory formula is difficult to say. It will be noted, however, that Paul never inserts phrases between an introductory formula and the following Old Testament quote anywhere else in Romans (cf. 3:4; 9:13; 10:15; 11:8). At any rate, the argument does not stand or fall on this point.

meaning in Romans 4 matches the emphasis in Paul's sermons in Acts.[109] While granting that Luke does not record the sermons in full, it is striking that this one word summarizes Paul's gospel. Of particular interest is Acts 13:38-39, where Paul links "forgiveness" through Jesus with being *"justified* from all things from which you were not able to be justified by the law of Moses." In 26:16-18 Paul recounts the purpose for which Jesus himself appointed him an apostle: "in order that they may receive forgiveness of sins and an inheritance among those who have been sanctified by faith in me."[110] The point here is not to assert that Paul makes "forgiveness" the whole of his soteriology, but that he does not always include every soteriological aspect or detail in his proclamation of the gospel.

Paul's emphasis in Romans 4, the thing which he wants to make explicit by his citation of Psalm 32, is that the imputation of righteousness has primarily to do with the forgiveness of sins. This statement must not be (mis)interpreted, by implication, to mean that justification *is* the forgiveness of sins. *Justification* is not an absolute synonym for forgiveness. That the imputation of righteousness is here explained as the forgiveness of sins simply means that Paul is developing one aspect, one metaphor, of his doctrine of justification, which itself is one aspect of his overall doctrine of salvation.

Secondly, it is biblically sound to think of forgiveness itself as a positive standing before God. The sacrificial texts in the Pentateuch, for instance, consistently refer to a person being forgiven as a result of sacrifices offered.[111] This observation fits the context of Romans up to this point in the text quite well. What is important to note is that the Old Testament does not have a sense of "mere" forgiveness, but often speaks exclusively in terms of forgiveness to describe what people need from God, desire from God, and what God promises to give or warns that he will withhold. Forgiveness is presented as that which is needed for a restored relationship with God. So, whether it is pleading and

---

[109] I am well aware of the scholarly debate concerning the differences between Paul's theology and the theology of Luke-Acts. I am, however, proceeding here on the presupposition that there is compatibility between the theology of Paul and the theology in Luke-Acts.

[110] It is conceivable that "and an inheritance" would be interpreted by some as implying a positive standing beyond forgiveness. Though certainly in the context, Paul is speaking of the full status among the people of God inherited by the Gentiles.

[111] E.g., Lev. 4:20, 26, 31, 35; 5:10, 13, 16, 18; 6:7; 19:22; Num. 14:19; 15:25-26, 28.

seeking forgiveness (Ex. 32:32; Deut. 21:8; 1 Kings 8:30),[112] the denial of forgiveness (Josh. 24:19; Neh. 4:5; 2 Kings 24:4; Isa. 2:9; Jer. 18:23), promised forgiveness (2 Chron. 7:14; Ps. 65:3; Jer. 31:34; 36:3; Hos. 1:6), or describing God as a God of forgiveness (Neh. 9:17; Ps. 86:5; Dan. 9:9), the Old Testament concept of forgiveness encompasses a much broader perspective than is sometimes accorded to it in discussions about imputation.

The Imputation of Righteousness

When the imputation of Christ's righteousness is considered from Romans 4, one first observes that Paul never links explicitly the imputation of righteousness with the righteousness of Christ. There is no explicit mention of Christ in any connection until verses 24 and 25.[113] The content of the imputed righteousness is, however, already spelled out as the righteousness from God that is ours through Christ on the basis of Christ's work on our behalf (3:21ff). It is difficult to see how Paul's readers would not have this referent in mind when they came to Paul's discussion of "reckoned righteous" in chapter 4. That Paul is making an explicit statement about Christ's so-called active obedience as being reckoned to the believer for a positive standing before God is more difficult to discern here. The link with forgiveness, however, is clear, and Paul speaks of forgiveness itself as a positive standing. After cataloging the sins and the hopeless condition of both Jews and Gentiles (1:18–3:9), which concludes with a sweeping indictment on the human race from an array of Old Testament texts (3:10-18), Paul speaks of the new and promised manifestation of God's righteousness in Jesus Christ, which is by faith "for all who believe, for there is no distinction; for all have sinned and have fallen short of the glory of God" (3:22-23). Those who believe, though they are included in the "all who sinned," are "justified freely by his grace through the redemption which is in Christ Jesus" (v. 24).

Thus, the overturning of the sin condition and the wrath of God is applied through justification by faith in Jesus. Paul will then say explicitly that it is Jesus "whom God set forward as a propitiation in his blood" (v. 25), and that faith is the instrument of appropriating Christ's

---

[112] See also, 1 Kings 8:34, 36, 50 (cf. 2 Chr. 6:21, 25, 27, 30, 39); Ps. 25:18; 79:9; Dan. 9:19.

[113] A point made by Gundry and others ("The Nonimputation of Christ's Righteousness," 18, 22, etc.).

sacrifice (v. 26). The justifying act of God in the cross of Christ and the forgiveness that flows from it are inextricably bound together. The pervasive sinfulness of humanity is met with the sacrifice of Christ in the place of sinners, suffering their penalty and obtaining their forgiveness. The conceptual parallels in 3:21-26 and 4:1-8 are as follows.

Romans 3:22-26		Romans 4:1-8
Righteousness through faith in Christ	>	Belief reckoned as righteousness
All have sinned	>	Ungodly; apart from works
Justified as a gift by grace	>	Righteousness reckoned according to grace[114]
Redemption in Christ and propitiation in his blood	>	Lawless deeds forgiven; sins covered; sins not reckoned

The content is thus similar in both sections, with the concept of justification tied most closely to the concepts of sin, grace, and forgiveness. Righteousness is imputed through faith, ultimately in Christ who is himself the manifestation of God's righteousness in both God's just punishment of sin (propitiation—and God himself is justified as well) and his saving righteousness (redemption, forgiveness). The imputation of righteousness and the blessing of forgiveness cannot be neatly separated at this point in Paul's argument. There is no hard distinction made here between negative (forgiveness) and positive (declared right status) aspects of justification. Ungodly sinners who believe are declared by God as "justified apart from works."

At this point in the text, this is the clearest assertion that believers have a positive standing before God. To be forgiven is to stand in a right relation with God on the basis of faith in Christ. Here at least, Jesus' blood and righteousness (3:25) are indistinguishable. Christ's death as an offering for sin is the righteousness that has been revealed, and as our substitute on the cross (3:25) his death counts for us, and thus his righteousness is imputed to our account by faith.[115] Granted, Abraham's faith

---

[114] The other side of wages reckoned according to what is owed.

[115] Paul will further develop the positive side in chapter 5. The forgiveness emphasized thus far in Romans is leading up to Paul's discussion of Christ as the second Adam (5:12-21). It is there that the positive nature of Christ's obedience is developed. I would argue that it is not yet developed in Romans precisely because Paul is working his way back through salvation history to the root problem—the disobedience of Adam, its subsequent effect on humanity, and what was required to overturn it. This, of course, does not mean that there is no hint of positive righteousness yet, but that it awaits chapter 5 to receive fuller development.

was placed in the God who promised him offspring, land, innumerable descendents, etc., but the reader of Romans can scarcely help filling in the meaning of the concepts in Romans 4 with the content flowing from the earlier chapters, particularly from the last part of chapter 3.

CONCLUSION

The actor, action, and result of Romans 4:3-8 can be represented in the following outline.[116]

Actor	Action	Result
Abraham	Faith	Righteousness

There is one element of this text, however, that must be kept in mind regarding this outline. While the action (faith) is Abraham's, the resulting righteousness is mediated, so to speak, through another's action. Abraham believes, but it is God who reckons the righteousness. With that in mind we can say, broadly, that Romans 4:1-8 is about the appropriation of righteousness, and that righteousness, as a status declared by God, is most clearly linked in this text with the non-imputation of sin, i.e., forgiveness. This status is brought about by the reckoning of faith as righteousness. Faith is not itself the righteousness, but as is made clear in the context, faith is the instrument that unites the believer to the object of faith. That object is thus the source of the righteousness that is reckoned to the believer. As we will see in the following chapters, this makes Romans 4 distinct from both Romans 5 and 2 Corinthians 5. What is apparent is that even a text that so clearly speaks of "imputation" does not contain every detail associated with the doctrine. The same will be true in the texts studied in the following chapters.

We now turn our attention to the next step in Paul's argument about what it means to be righteous before God. To do so we must take a step back in the history of salvation. This will take us deeper into the discussion of imputation, for in Romans 5:12-21 Paul deals with the fundamental breach between God and man caused by an act of disobedience and overcome by one gracious act of obedience—an act that does indeed "count."

---

[116] The same categories, with different actors and actions but with the same basic results, will appear in the next two chapters.

THREE

THE FOUNDATION OF
RIGHTEOUSNESS:
ROMANS 5:19

OPENING A BIBLE TO Romans 5:12-21 reveals a vast landscape. In this text one has the unique opportunity of seeing virtually the whole scope of the history of redemption condensed into the space of ten verses. In this way it is arguably the most remarkable passage in the Bible. Contained in this short space is the panorama of salvation from Adam's fall, to the cross, and to the final consummation. Paul takes a step back to the beginning of redemptive history; it is in fact redemptive history at its lowest common denominator.[1] It is, moreover, the place where we understand the human race in its most simplified form. History is boiled down to two figures, and the actions of these two men determine the status of the rest of humanity.

Up to this point in the letter Paul has focused a great deal on the actions of all humanity—whether Jew or Greek. For instance, God's wrath is revealed against ungodliness and unrighteousness (1:18); sinful actions are catalogued and judged (1:19-32); judgment will come upon everyone according to their deeds (2:6 [Ps 62:12]); and all have sinned and fallen short of the glory of God (3:23). On the positive side,

---

[1] Romans 5:12 refers immediately to verses 1-11, but conceptually Paul's theology of corporate representation, as expounded in these verses, functions at a macro level. Here we find an encapsulation of salvation history, starting at the beginning of God's plan of redemption with Adam, and the fulfillment of it in and through Christ. Cranfield is surely incorrect to say that "Adam is only mentioned in order to bring out more clearly the nature of the work of Christ" (*Romans*, 280). It is precisely the order set in place by Adam that Christ had to confront, recapitulate, and overturn. This is a foundational piece of redemptive history, not a mere example.

Paul argues for an individual's faith as the instrument in justification (1:16-17; 3:25; 4:3; 5:1). However, when he comes to the second half of chapter 5, Paul moves beyond his discussion of the sins of humanity *and* his discussion of faith. Perhaps it is better to say that he *gets behind* the issues of both sin and faith to things that explain both the reality of sin and the reality of justification by faith. This text accounts for the presence of sin and condemnation in the world and explains how and why it is possible for "the just to live by faith." What Paul has to say in this text, particularly in verse 19, is the most critical point for understanding the very ground of redemption. Without this there would be no need for discussion of justification, imputation, Abraham, or the Mosaic law. This text is the focal point of the letter, with Paul's argument both leading up to it and flowing from it.

Since everyone is either identified with one man or the other, this text is not primarily about what individual people do, but about what they are as a result of what their representative has done. Here one is either a "sinner" or one is "righteous," and though each status determines what one will, in fact, do, that is not Paul's focus at this point. Thus, Paul is not arguing here for a transformation. What is at issue here is the status one has before God due to the actions of the two men who represent the human race. The status "sinner," established by the disobedience of Adam, is overturned by the obedience of Christ, which makes possible the status "righteous."[2] If Romans 4 is about the appropriation of righteousness, then Romans 5 is about the very foundation of righteousness.[3]

---

[2] "The spheres of Adam and Christ, of death and life, are separated as alternative, exclusive, and ultimate, and this happens in global breadth. An old world and a new world are at issue. In relation to them no one can be neutral. There is no third option" (Ernst Käsemann, *Commentary on Romans*, trans. Geoffrey W. Bromiley [Grand Rapids: Eerdmans, 1980], 147).

[3] The διὰ τοῦτο of 5:12 is most clearly linked to verses 1-11 as a whole. C. E. B. Cranfield, *The Epistle to the Romans*, ICC (Edinburgh: T & T Clark, 1975), 1:271; Adolf Schlatter, *Romans: The Righteousness of God*, trans. Siegfried S. Schatzmann (Peabody, Mass.: Hendrickson, 1995), 126; Leon Morris, *Epistle to the Romans*, Pillar New Testament Commentary (Grand Rapids: Eerdmans, 1988), 228; Joseph A. Fitzmyer, *Romans*, AB (New York: Doubleday, 1992) 410; Brendan Byrne, *Romans*, Sacra Pagina Series, vol. 6 (Collegeville, Minn.: The Liturgical Press, 1996), 182; Douglas J. Moo, *The Epistle to the Romans*, NICNT (Grand Rapids: Eerdmans, 1996), 317; Thomas R. Schreiner, *Romans*, BECNT (Grand Rapids: Baker, 1998), 271 (Schreiner insists that the "thematic" link is "hope"); N. T. Wright, *The Letter to the Romans*, New Interpreter's Bible, vol. 10 (Nashville: Abingdon, 2002), 523. John Murray likewise notes that Paul is referring to what he said previously, but whether it is verses 1-11 or a larger portion, it is "impossible to be dogmatic" (Murray, *The Epistle to the Romans*, NICNT [Grand Rapids: Eerdmans, 1968], 180). James D. G. Dunn sees 5:12-21 as a whole as rounding off everything Paul has said beginning with 1:18 (*Romans 1–8*, WBC 38a [Dallas: Word, 1988], 271-72).

A DIFFERENT METAPHOR

Any reader can recognize that when Paul comes to Romans 5:19 he does not employ the same metaphor in relation to righteousness as he does in chapter 4. There the dominant metaphor is "reckoning": faith is "reckoned" for righteousness. That is clearly not the language of 5:19, where Paul says that "many will be made righteous." In Romans 4 the main word is λογίζομαι ("count" or "reckon") but in 5:19 the word is καθίστημι ("make" or "appoint"). This is quite an important difference and one to which our attention will turn momentarily. There is another, more fundamental difference in these texts, namely, there is a change of both subject and action.[4] In Romans 4 the subject/actor is Abraham/believer and the action is faith, whereas in Romans 5 the subject/actor is Christ and the action is obedience—his obedience. There is a slightly different emphasis in the consequences too. In Romans 4 faith is reckoned for righteousness, whereas in 5:19 the result of Christ's obedience is that "many will be made righteous," which primarily refers to the bare status itself without explicit reference to either faith or the reckoning of righteousness. Having already established the instrumental nature of faith and the reckoning of righteousness, Paul now establishes the righteous status that is counted by God and appropriated by faith. These changes, particularly those in subject and action, account for the change in Paul's language.

Interpretations of these texts must not, therefore, treat them as if they are saying the same thing in different ways. If we ask what "counts" for righteousness in Romans 5, it is not "faith" as in Romans 4, but Christ's obedience. It is hardly surprising that when the text shifts to the most fundamental level of what it means to be righteous before God, all other actions and faith fade into the background. It is Christ and his obedience that take center stage here. Thus, in Romans 4 and 5 Paul is saying two things regarding justification, with the latter moving back and providing the reason why such an event as faith being reckoned as righteousness can exist.

---

[4] "Subject" does not refer to grammatical subject in this case.

Καθίστημι and Domains of Meaning

In Romans 5:19 Paul states: "For just as through the disobedience of the one man the many were made sinners, so also through the obedience of the one [man] the many will be made righteous."[5] The disobedience of one and the obedience of one result in many being either "sinners" or "righteous." The verb Paul employs is καθίστημι, and a study of this word with a particular focus on its semantic domains, i.e., range of meaning, will help determine what Paul means by using it here.[6]

The word καθίστημι occupies two *somewhat* distinct semantic domains.[7] The first domain, following Louw and Nida's lexicon, is "Be, Become, Exist, Happen," which they describe as "a highly generic domain indicating various aspects of states, existence, and events."[8] In this broad domain, καθίστημι refers to a state, as in a state of being."[9] As in the larger domain, this subdomain contains a variety of words that cover a wide range of meaning.[10] In general, καθίστημι and the words associated with it in this subdomain mean, "'to cause to be in a state,' 'to attain a state,' or 'to remain in a state.'"[11] The idea is that something or someone is caused to be in a state or is occupying a status that is somehow different from some previous state or status.[12] In the New Testament, καθίστημι appears infrequently in this domain. Two of the clearer examples are James 4:4, "Whoever wishes to be a friend of the world *makes* [or "causes" καθίσταται][13] himself to be an enemy

---

[5] ὥσπερ γὰρ διὰ τῆς παρακοῆς του ἑνὸς ἀνθρώπου ἁμαρτωλοὶ κατεστάθησαν οἱ πολλοί, οὕτως καὶ διὰ τῆς ὑπακοῆς τοῦ ἑνὸς δίκαιοι κατασταθήσονται οἱ πολλοί.

[6] Semantic domains refers to the range of meaning of a particular word.

[7] As arranged in Johannes P. Louw and Eugene A. Nida, *Greek-English Lexicon of the New Testament Based on Semantic Domains*, 2nd ed. (New York: United Bible Societies, 1989). Louw and Nida's categories are not infallible. Nevertheless, their lexicon is far and away the best tool available at the present for this type of study. The issue here is to try and determine why Paul used καθίστημι.

[8] Domain 13, ibid., 149 n. 1.

[9] Subdomain A, ibid., 150-51.

[10] Καθίστημι appears in the ninth item (13.9) along with, ποιέω τίθημι ἐργάζομαι; κατεργάζομαι; ἐπάγω; and, ἐνεργέω. Like καθίστημι, these words may occupy a number of domains. They are included here to help provide lexical context.

[11] Further, "'to cause to continue in a state,' and . . . 'to be—'to cause to be, to make to be, to make, to result in, to bring upon, to bring about'" (ibid., 150). Louw and Nida point out that the words in 13.9 could be classified under Subdomain B, "Change of State," but note that while "'to cause to be' implies some change in state . . . the focus seems to be primarily upon the changed state rather than upon the process of moving from one state to another" (ibid.).

[12] The previous state is not necessarily made evident or given stress in the various contexts in which καθίστημι and its companion words in this domain appear.

[13] From καταστάνω.

of God;" and, 2 Peter 1:8, "If these [qualities or virtues mentioned in verses 5-7] are yours and are increasing, they render [or "cause" or "make" καθίστησιν] you to be neither useless nor unfruitful." In each of these texts, an action (fellowship with the world or the cultivation and exercise of desired qualities) causes a person to be in some particular state of being (an enemy of God, or being useful and fruitful, respectively). Louw and Nida list Romans 5:19 under this domain as well.[14]

The second domain under which καθίστημι is classified includes words that broadly mean, "Control, Rule."[15] It is further subdivided with words meaning, "Assign to a Role or Function."[16] The general meaning for the word in this domain is "to assign to someone a position of authority over others—'to put in charge of, to appoint, to designate.'"[17] In this sense καθίστημι is used to indicate that a person is set over others in some positional context (e.g., a king), or put in charge of carrying out certain duties, or in a more general sense to indicate something being placed on or in some space or area.[18] The majority of the appearances of καθίστημι in the New Testament fit under this domain.

For example, in Matthew 25 the servants who were faithful "with a few things" will be "put in charge (καταστήσω) of many things" (vv. 21, 23). In Luke 12:14, Jesus asks, "who appointed (κατέστησεν) me judge between you?" Elsewhere, Paul leaves Titus to "appoint (καταστήσῃς) elders in every city" (Titus 1:5); the apostles command that deacons be chosen to be "put in charge" (καταστήσομεν) of serving the church (Acts 6:3); and Hebrews says that "every high priest . . . is appointed (καθίσταται) on behalf of men" (Heb. 5:1).[19] Though listed

---

[14] Ibid., 151.
[15] Domain 37, ibid., 472.
[16] Subdomain E, ibid., 484.
[17] καθίστημι, with καθίζω, is in item 104 (37.104). Ibid., 484.
[18] The last sense appears more often in the Septuagint, referring to some object such as a piece of furniture (2 Chron. 24:11). In the New Testament, καθίστημι may be used in this sense in James 3:6, "the tongue is set (καθίσταται) among our members as that which defiles the entire body," but given the context, specifically the tongue's specific job of defiling, and "setting on fire" our existence, it seems that the appointed role, rather than the mere physical placement of it in the body, is in view. Either way, it fits the basic semantic range.
[19] Other examples of this usage are found in Matthew 24:45, 47 (cf. Luke 12:42, 44; Acts 7:10, 27, 35; Heb. 7:28; 8:3). The participle phrase employed in Acts 17:15, οἱ . . . καθιστάνοντε", though translated as "those who escorted" (NASB), or "those who conducted" (ESV), probably fits under this domain as well, with καθίστημι used here to specify the escorts the Bereans provided for Paul to get him safely to Athens. The translation, "those appointed" (i.e., chosen, picked) is a reasonable rendering of this phrase.

differently by Louw and Nida, this domain could well fit the meaning of the word in Romans 5:19. In any case, rendering καθίστημι as "reckon, count, impute"—i.e., as a synonym for λογίζομαι—is not supported by the use of the word in the New Testament, or by its classification in either of the two domains. This conclusion is further supported by the use of καθίστημι in the Septuagint, including the Apocrypha.

Καθίστημι in the Septuagint. The various Septuagint translators employ καθίστημι to translate over twenty different Hebrew words. The elasticity of καθίστημι in the Septuagint is not surprising given the variety of translation techniques employed by the translators and given the fact that in translation a lack of one-to-one correspondence between words is common. In spite of these observations, and with some exceptions, the majority of uses of καθίστημι in translation in the Septuagint fall broadly within the two domains discussed above. It is evident that καθίστημι was used by a variety of translators because it appears virtually throughout the entire Old Testament canon.

In the Septuagint, καθίστημι is used most often to translate Hebrew words that mean to "appoint; place over; set over; establish; install."[20] The Hebrew words most frequently translated with καθίστημι are, פקד, and שׁום/שׂים, and the consistent meaning is "appoint or place over" (or something quite similar) throughout the Old Testament books.[21] Other Hebrew words translated by καθίστημι in this same sense are משׁל (Ps. 8:6); מלך (2 Chron. 36:1, 4); נסך (Ps. 2:6); צוה (2 Sam. 6:21); and the Aramaic word, שׁלט (Dan. 2:48).[22]

There are some Hebrew words usually translated by καθίστημι

---

[20] In what follows only the basic Hebrew roots are given. The Hebrew words appear in a wide variety of stems, tenses, persons, etc. The same is true in Greek for καθίστημι.

[21] פקד "appoint, set over," is translated by καθίστημι in: Genesis 39:4-5; 41:34; Numbers 3:10, 32; 31:48; Deuteronomy 20:39; Joshua 10:18; 1 Samuel 29:4; 1 Kings 11:28; 2 Kings 7:7; 22:5, 9; 25:22-23; 1 Chronicles 26:32; 2 Chronicles 12:10; 31:13; 34:10; Nehemiah 12:44; Esther 2:3; Psalm 108 (109):6; Isaiah 62:6; Jeremiah 1:10; 20:1; 47 (40):5, 7, 11; 48 (41):2, 18. Note that rather than following the LXX, the divisions of 1 and 2 Samuel, 1 and 2 Kings, and 1 and 2 Chronicles are used throughout. This is done to avoid confusion since the Hebrew texts and English translations are also cited. When chapter number or versification are different, the difference is indicated in parentheses. שׁום/שׂים "put, place (over/on), assign," is translated by καθίστημι in, Genesis 47:5(6); Exodus 2:14 (cf. Acts 7:27); 5:14; 18:21; Numbers 4:19; Deuteronomy 1:13; 17:14-15 (two times. [Note also that נתן is translated by καθίστημι in Deut. 17:15 as well. Again, in the sense of "place over"]); Joshua 8:2 (for "set an ambush"); Judges 11:11; 1 Samuel 8:1, 5; 10:19; 18:5 (LXX = Codex A), 13; 2 Samuel 15:4; 17:25; 18:1; 2 Kings 10:3; 1 Chronicles 11:25; 2 Chronicles 33:14; Esther 8:2; Psalm 17 (18):43; 104 (105):21.

[22] The Aramaic words in Daniel are listed together with Hebrew words throughout.

in the sense of "appoint or place over," but occasionally with some other meaning not immediately associated with the semantic domains of καθίστημι.[23] The first semantic domain noted above for καθίστημι (13.9) meaning to "Be, Become, Exist, Happen," also appears in the Septuagint, but like the New Testament, with less frequency than the second domain (37.104). It is also possible for the domains to overlap when καθίστημι is used for the same Hebrew word. For instance, נתן is translated by καθίστημι for "appoint/set over" in most cases (Gen. 41:41, 43; Deut. 1:15; 16:18; 17:15; Josh. 9:27,[24] 1 Chron. 12:19 [v. 18 Eng.]; 2 Chron. 17:2), but in Deuteronomy 28:13, "the LORD shall *make* you the head and not the tail," the emphasis is on the state of being, or existence (described metaphorically) that results from God's covenant blessings.[25] In the case of other Hebrew words, the reason translators chose καθίστημι is less apparent, and the "meaning" of καθίστημι is clearly influenced by the words it translates.[26]

A brief study of the uses of καθίστημιin the Septuagint reveals that it is not used to mean "count" or "reckon," and this is due not

---

[23] קום is translated by καθίστημι in Deuteronomy 28:36 as "set over," but in 19:16 as "rise up," and in 25:6 "stand upon." Elsewhere, however, the more typical "appoint/set over" is the meaning: Job 16:12; Isaiah 49:8 ("restore [i.e., 'establish'?] the land"); Jeremiah 6:17; 36 (29):15 ("the Lord has raised up [appointed/established] prophets"); Daniel 2:21; 5:11. In Jeremiah 37 (30):24 the translation of קום by καθίστημι in "until he has *accomplished* the intent of his heart" seems unusual but is perhaps a stereotypical use of καθίστημι. נצב ("be stationed, appointed over, set up, erect"), is translated in reference to the position placed in or held, in 1 Samuel 19:20; 22:9; 1 Kings 4:7, 12; 5:30 (5:16, Eng.). In other cases, καθίστημι is also used when the basic meaning of עמד, "take one's stand," is in view: 1 Samuel 1:26 (possibly in 22:9 as well); Isaiah 3:13, "The Lord *arises* to contend" (i.e., "takes his stand").

[24] Although typically translated in English as "made," the idea here seems more about an appointed position (woodcutter), than about the state of being a woodcutter. This does, however, illustrate the overlap that can exist between being "appointed" something and actually "being" that thing.

[25] שים is quite literally translated in Genesis 41:33 with the meaing "set over." But in Psalm 44 (45):17 (v. 16 Eng.), the Septuagint has καθίστημι for "you shall *make* them princes," where a state of being, or a position, is emphasized (again metaphorically). In Psalm 9:21, the Septuagint has "set a lawgiver over them" (κατάστησον, κύριε, νομοθέτην ἐπ᾽ αὐτούς) for the MT, "put them in fear" (שׁיתה יהוה מורה להם). Here it seems that the translator employs a fairly dynamic technique and renders what probably refers to a state of being ("in fear") with the more frequent meaning of καθίστημι ("set, appoint").

[26] יצב, "set station oneself; take one's stand," 1 Samuel 3:10; 10:19, 23; 12:7; 16; Jeremiah 26 (46):4. But note the similarity in meaning with שוב, "turn back, return." In three texts the word refers to returning something to its place: 1 Samuel 5:3; 2 Chronicles 24:11; Jeremiah 23:3. In each text the idea of "set in place" is not too remote. In 1 Samuel 30:12 the choice of καθίστημι is not as clear: "he ate and his spirit was *revived*." The Egyptian's spirit was "returned to him," i.e., put back in it's proper place. בוא "come in, go in," 2 Chronicles 28:15; Jeremiah 51 (44):28. הסר, "gather, remove," 2 Chronicles 29:4. חזק, "be, grow strong," 2 Chronicles 25:3. The use of καθίστημι for this and the two preceding words in 2 Chronicles might be explained by the translation technique(s) employed there. Only a detailed study could answer that question. משׁפט "what is settled, clarified, clear." Ezekiel 34:18. צלל "be, grow dark (evening comes on)," Nehemiah 13:19.

only to the semantics of the word but also to the fact that the Hebrew words considered thus far do not themselves typically mean "count" or "reckon." There is at least one exception. The word מנה often means "count," as in counting or numbering objects like dust, money, stars, days, or people, but in none of these cases do the Septuagint translators choose καθίστημι.[27] Typically the translators choose the words that mean "count" in the sense of numbering (ἀριθμέω and ἐξαριθμέω) since in these texts persons or things are not "counted" or "reckoned" for or as someone or something else, but are merely "counted," i.e., tallied. In other texts מנה is translated by καθίστημι, but with the meaning "appointed" (1 Chron. 9:29; Ezek. 7:25; Dan. 2:24, 49; 3:12).[28]

The more significant point in regard to מנה is that when it means "count" in the sense of "reckon or count" something or someone as something or someone else, the choice for translation is not καθίστημι, but λογίζομαι. The best example of a Septuagint translator faced with a choice of either καθίστημι or λογίζομαι is found in Isaiah. When translating 53:12, "and he was counted with the transgressors" (וְאֶת־פֹּשְׁעִים נִמְנָה), the translator renders מנה with λογίζομαι (καὶ ἐν τοῖς ἀνόμοις ἐλογίσθη). It is also worth noting that λογίζομαι appears two other times in the immediate context, and in both cases it translates its more common Hebrew counterpart חשׁב (53:3, 4 [as in Gen. 15:6]).[29] That the translator had καθίστημι at his disposal is evident since he uses it three times, but never in the sense of "count" or "reckon," and never to translate מנה.[30] When, moreover, he encounters another word in his Hebrew text for which he might choose καθίστημι, he again opts for λογίζομαι (44:19).[31]

The conclusion drawn from this study of καθίστημι in the Septuagint is that the translators did not typically employ καθίστημι to translate words meaning "count, reckon, or impute." In the Septuagint καθίστημι is not a synonym for λογίζομαι. The same tendencies are

---

[27] (e.g., Gen. 13:16; Num. 23:10; 1 Kings 3:8; 2 Kings 12:11; Psalm 90 [89 LXX]:12; 147 [146 LXX]:4).

[28] Theodotion translates מנה with καθίστημι in Daniel 1:11, where Old Greek has ἀναδείκνυμι.

[29] Cf. Genesis 15:6 and Psalm 103:31.

[30] In 3:13 καθίστημι is used for נצב, "the Lord *arises* (takes his stand) to judge;" in 49:8 for קם, "to *restore* (establish) the land;" and in 62:6 for פקד, "I have *appointed* watchmen."

[31] The Hebrew word is שׁוב, "No one *recalls* (returns to his heart)." The choice of λογίζομαι may not be entirely clear, but this text at least shows another example of when he could have chosen καθίστημι.

also seen in the apocryphal literature where καθίστημι appears with relative frequency. As in the New Testament and the Septuagint, it is most commonly used in the sense of "appoint/set over."[32] There are also examples of καθίστημι used to mean "become" or "make" or simply "is" in reference to some state of being.[33] In some texts the domain is not clear.[34] Again, there are no clear examples where the meanings "count" or "reckon" are in apparent view. This must carry at least some weight in an interpretation of Romans 5:12-21. Even if one argues that the counting or reckoning of Christ's righteousness is the conceptual meaning of the text based on Romans 4, or is the instrumental way by which the status "righteous" is conferred, it must be recognized that there is something more fundamental in this text—words after all do mean something—than the accounting metaphor "reckon."

These various examples lead to two observations about the two common semantic domains for καθίστημι. In the first place, the domains are not mutually exclusive. They should not be viewed as static domains of meaning. For instance, if one is "appointed" king or priest, one *really is* a king or a priest. We would not read a text that refers to a person being "appointed" king but disassociate that with the state of being "king." An "appointment" to a position often carries with it the creation of the actual state. On the other hand, though it is often conceptually difficult to separate a state of being from the fact of being placed in that state, either one may receive emphasis over the other. While an appointment to the office of priest means that one actually is a priest, emphasis may fall on either the appointment, or the state of being, or both.

Secondly, in neither domain is the emphasis placed on the actions of the person who holds the office or status.[35] Even if one

---

[32] Domain 37.104. Among the clearer examples are, 1 Maccabees 3:55; 6:14, 17, 55; 7:20; 9:25; 10:20, 22, 32, 37, 69; 11:57, 59; 14:42; 15:9, 38; 16:11; 2 Maccabees 3:4; 5:22; 12:20; 3 Maccabees 3:26; 4 Maccabees 4:16; 5:25 ("established"); Tobit 1:22; Judith 1:3 (5); 5:3; 6:14 ("placed before"); Sirach 17:17; 33:29 ("set to work"); 32:1 ("make," i.e., "appoint").

[33] Domain 13.9. For example, 2 Maccabees 4:50; 15:9; 3 Maccabees 1:7; 2:5, 33; 3:5, 19, 21; 5:51; 4 Maccabees 1:11, 18; 15:4; 17:5; Wisdom of Solomon 10:7. Often a change in state is not noted, but only the existing state.

[34] For example, 2 Maccabees 12:30 ("the Jews *who lived* there"); 3 Maccabees 4:18; 13:23.

[35] Rainbow, however, argues that because of the contrasting ideas of Christ's obedience and Adam's disobedience, "neither of which nouns has the slightest forensic overtone, there can be little doubt that καθίστασθαι, followed by the adjectives, 'sinful' (ἁμαρτωλός) or 'righteous' (δίκαιος), has its normal sense, amply attested (cf. James 3:5; 4:4), of 'coming into a certain state' or 'becoming actually'" (Paul A. Rainbow, *The Way of Salvation: The Role of Christian Obedience in Justification* [Milton

is *made* or caused to take on a personal attribute, such as *made* to be courageous or bold, the emphasis is still on the state of being and/or the change to that state rather than on the acts of courage or boldness that accompany the attribute.[36] The upshot of all this is that we do not need to back away from the word *made* and make it a synonym for the word *reckon.* Paul's use of καθίστημι is itself the best argument against a transformative interpretation of this text. The confusion over 5:19 stems most likely from the meaning of the English word *made,* rather than to any ambiguity in the Greek text.

The statements in Romans 5:19 refer to statuses. One is either a "sinner" or one is "righteous." It is perhaps the most basic point made in all Scripture, and it is a profound point as well, because each individual person possesses his status because he was "made" a sinner or "made" righteous on the basis of another's action. Again Paul's word selection could hardly be more fitting since he is speaking about being legally placed into one category or the other. The focus in this text is not on the actions of the person receiving the status, nor is it on the instrumentality by which a person acquires the status, but on the status itself with particular emphasis on the actions that resulted in the status. The context leading up to this verse makes it clear that what one is "made" depends upon one's identification with either Adam or Christ. The history and destiny of the human race is determined by the actions of two men.

Keynes, UK: Patersonster/Authentic Media, 2005] n. 16, 130). This book came to my attention just when my manuscript was due so I did not have the opportunity to interact with it sufficiently. I agree that the idea here is to come "into a certain state." It is just that in my view the emphasis here is to come into the moral "state" of being righteous without actually having performed moral righteousness. Paul takes up the discussion of the actions that flow from the status in chapter 6. I do not think my argument in this chapter is an example of "a tendency on the part of many to cling to the tendentious view of the Reformers who would not admit the effective sense here, on purely dogmatic grounds" (ibid). I want to point out, however, that Rainbow does defend the imputation of Christ's righteousness but understands Romans 5:18-19 as a transition. For my part, I think the text is at the brink of a transition and that Paul will argue that the status, "righteous," will be accompanied by a real transformation.
[36] This is an important point to keep in mind. Καθίστημι does not have to be translated outside its domains, or essentially morphed into "reckon," or "count," in order to assert that moral transformation is not in view. It may, and should, be translated within its domain. This does not at all mean that the door is open for it to mean a moral transformation—Paul's word selection, in fact, argues against it.

GETTING BEHIND THE METAPHOR: ROMANS 5:12-19

The seven verses before Romans 5:19 form a dense and complex unit.[37] Chief among the debated issues in this text is the meaning of ἐφ᾽ ᾧ in verse 12. Generally speaking, how one reads verse 12 colors how one reads the following verses. It is therefore necessary to work through some of the main issues, including the leading interpretations that surround this verse, before we make our way back to verse 19.

A Little Phrase and a Big Debate

The long debate over Romans 5:12 stands at a kind of crossroads where grammar and theology intersect. These two subjects are rarely combined these days, but they converge in this text, and any interpretation based solely on theology apart from grammar, or vice versa, will come up short. We must also acknowledge that the meaning of Romans 5:12 is a long-standing debate which will likely continue. As important as it is to this passage, no interpretation of Romans 5:12-21 can hang absolutely on verse 12.

The debate over this one verse revolves chiefly around one phrase: ἐφ᾽ ᾧ. This discussion boils down generally to whether ἐφ᾽ ᾧ functions as a relative clause referring to an antecedent,[38] or whether it is a conjunction typically translated as "because." While this may sound like a purely grammatical debate, there are theological issues at stake. The other grammatical issue surrounds the interpretation of καὶ οὕτως, though this receives less attention. However, at least one interpretation of this verse essentially reads καὶ οὕτως ("and so" or "and in this way") as if it were οὕτως καὶ ("and so") even though it is almost universally recognized that this is not a comparative clause with a completed protasis. Theologically, the main issues or questions surrounding this text are (1) our relation to Adam, that is, are we connected to him primarily on a representational basis, or is the emphasis on our "real" or "seminal" connection to Adam; and (2) are we guilty of Adam's sin, our own sin, or both, and what are the implications for each conclusion.

---

[37] I separate verse 19 from verse 18 simply because the phrase at the center of this discussion comes in verse 19. I take verse 19 as explanatory of verse 18, contra Rainbow who understands verse 18 as dealing with justification while verse 19 is dealing with sanctification (*The Way of Salvation*, 184).
[38] There is also a debate over what serves as the antecedent but that will not play much of a part in this discussion.

Another one of the difficulties in the interpretation of this text is that a particular grammatical reading of Romans 5:12 may be held by people with different theological or conceptual interpretations of the verse. Likewise, interpreters with similar conceptual or theological views may have different understandings of the grammar and syntax of this verse. For instance, interpreters who differ on 5:12 may still agree on 5:19. The goal here is neither to review *all* the possible grammatical interpretations of this verse nor to discuss *all* the various theological issues, but to give a summary of the main points in the debate and finally to argue for a reading of this verse that best fits both Paul's grammar and the theology.

In what follows we will see why it is preferable to read ἐφ᾽ ᾧ as a relative clause, thereby rendering the verse, "Therefore, just as through one man sin came into the world, and death came through sin, *so in this way* death spread to all men *on account of which* condition all sinned." The reasons for this interpretation are both grammatical and theological. This reading maintains a forensic, representational relationship between Adam and humanity while accounting for the structure of the verse. So while disagreeing with those who think ἐφ᾽ ᾧ means "because," this view is in essential agreement with the traditional representational interpretation of the larger text, 5:12-21, particularly in regard to verses 18-19—but more of that later. Though it may seem as though we are going far afield from imputation, Paul's theology of imputation is grounded in the details of this key text.

A Survey of ἐφ᾽ ᾧ in the Bible

In the Septuagint. There are plenty of biblical examples of ἐφ᾽ ᾧ used with an antecedent. In the Septuagint it is consistently used in this way, usually to translate אֲשֶׁר.[39] For example, in Joshua 5:15, Joshua is told to remove his shoes "because [γάρ] the place upon which [ἐφ᾽ ᾧ] you are standing is holy"; Proverbs 21:22 speaks of "the strongholds in which [ἐφ᾽ ᾧ] the ungodly have trusted"; and Isaiah 25:9, "Behold our God, in whom [ἐφ᾽ ᾧ] we have trusted."[40] Other occurrences of ἐφ᾽ ᾧ in the

---

[39] אֲשֶׁר can be used in a causal sense, but in the examples cited here it does not seem to be used in this way. Jeremiah 7:14 is possibly an exception. ἐφ᾽ ᾧ also translates ב, מו, and זה. For זה as a relative, see BDB, 261.

[40] Joshua 5:15 translates preposition מו; Proverbs 21:22 translates אֲשֶׁר; and Isaiah 25:9, זה.

Septuagint are similar.[41] The plural (ἐφ᾿ οἷς) follows the same consistent pattern.[42] Even though ἐφ᾿ ᾧ is not typically used to mean "be-cause" in the Septuagint, these examples alone (particularly the plurals) do not disprove that ἐφ᾿ ᾧ means "because" in Romans 5:12. It simply shows that the Septuagint translators clearly use the phrase in the function of a relative clause. This information, however, simply illustrates how the phrase *can* be read, not how it *must* be read.

In the New Testament. The use of ἐφ᾿ ᾧ in the New Testament, though relatively infrequent, is quite varied. The clearest example of it being used with an antecedent is in Acts 7:33, but this is due to the text (Josh. 5:15) that Stephen quotes. The other examples are found exclusively in Paul's epistles. The meaning of the phrase is debated in Philippians 3:12: "Not that I have already obtained it or have obtained perfection, but I pursue if I might obtain ἐφ᾿ ᾧ I was also obtained by Christ Jesus" (διώκω δὲ εἰ καὶ καταλάβω, ἐφ᾿ ᾧ καὶ κατελήμφθην ὑπὸ Χριστοῦ). Many, if not most, scholars take it to mean "because,"[43] while others understand it as a purpose, "forasmuch as,"[44] or consecutively as "that for which."[45] There are many issues involved in settling this text, but generally scholars recognize that there are good arguments for the various interpretations.[46] It seems, however, that it is not so much a ground for Paul's pursuing as much as he is expressing the purpose for which Christ obtained him. If that is the case, the phrase "that for which" is the best translation in that text.

---

[41] Genesis 38:30; 2 Kings (LXX 4 Kings) 19:10; Isaiah 37:10; 62:8; Jeremiah 7:14; 3 Maccabees 3:28; Epistle of Jeremiah 58.

[42] Deuteronomy 28:52; 32:7 (for כב); Judges 16:26; 2 Chronicles 33:19; Isaiah 20:5; Ezeiel 22:13; Judith 11:16; 2 Maccabees 8:21; 3 Maccabees 2:6 (7-8); 4 Maccabees 4:21; Odes of Solomon 2:37; Wisdom of Solomon 12:11, 27.

[43] G. F. Hawthorne, *Philippians*, WBC, vol. 43 (Waco: Word, 1983), 152; Ralph P. Martin, *Philippians*, New Century Bible (London: Oliphants, 1976), 137; Peter T. O'Brien, *The Epistle to the Philippians: A Commentary on the Greek Text*, NIGTC (Grand Rapids: Eerdmans, 1991), 425; Moises Silva, *Philippians*, The Wycliffe Exegetical Commentary (Chicago: Moody Press, 1988), 201. Silva describes his translation, "after all," as a "mild causal sense" (*Philippians*, 201).

[44] E.g., J. B. Lightfoot, *Commentary on the Epistle of St. Paul to the Philippians* (London: Macmillian, 1913; reprint, Grand Rapids: Zondervan, 1953), 151-52.

[45] E.g., Markus Bockmuehl, *The Epistle to the Philippians*, Black's New Testament Commentaries (London: A&C Black, 1997), 221; Fitzmyer, "The Consecutive Meaning of ΕΦ᾿Ω in Romans 5:12," *NTS* 39, [1993], 330.

[46] The object of καταλαμβάνω, and the antecedent of ἐφ᾿ ᾧ, are two of the central interpretive issues in this text. This verse serves as a good example of how various factors play a role in the interpretation of a word or phrase in any given text.

A little later in Philippians Paul again uses ἐφ' ᾧ: "I rejoiced greatly in the Lord that you have at last revived your concern for me, ἐφ' ᾧ you were concerned but lacked the opportunity" (4:10).[47] Again, there is debate over the meaning. Some commentators render it as a relative clause with the antecedent being Paul's well being.[48] Additionally, there is the common, idiomatic rendering, "of course," or "indeed,"[49] while others choose "for."[50] In this verse a causal sense seems unlikely. The translation "for whom" ("for whom you were concerned" or more loosely, "indeed you were already concerned about me"), in which the phrase refers to Paul, fits well here because it does appear that Paul is rejoicing for the concern the Philippians had for him, concern that went beyond the care they had already expressed.

One further example of ἐφ' ᾧ in the New Testament, and one often taken as causal,[51] is 2 Corinthians 5:4.[52] As in the other examples, the meaning is debated with scholars divided mainly between a causal sense,[53] "because we do not wish to be unclothed," and a condition, "on the condition that/provided that."[54] Is Paul saying that we groan *because* we want to take off our mortal bodies and put on a heavenly body? It is possible, but Paul could be referring back to the groaning in the body as the condition in which we long to be clothed with immortality: "Because we are in this tent we groan, in which condition we do not wish to be unclothed but to be clothed."

Even a brief look at ἐφ' ᾧ outside of Romans 5:12 shows that

---

[47] Ἐχάρην δὲ ἐν κυρίῳ μεγάλως ὅτι ἤδη ποτὲ ἀνεθάλετε τὸ ὑπὲρ ἐμοῦ φρονεῖν, ἐφ' ᾧ καὶ ἐφρονεῖτε, ἠκαιρεῖσθε δέ.

[48] Lightfoot understands the antecedent to be Paul's "wants" and "interests" as expressed generally in τὸ ὑπὲρ ἐμοῦ φρονεῖν (*Philippians*, 163). O'Brien has a similar interpretation and refers specifically to ὑπὲρ ἐμοῦ as the antecedent (*Philippians*, 518). He points out that is different from Paul's typical usage, i.e., "because."

[49] The former is found in Bockmuehl (*Philippians*, 232), with discussion on 233-34), and the latter is translated in NASB, NIV, RSV, NRSV. The AV, "though you surely did care," is quite similar.

[50] Silva appreciates the idiomatic reading, but points out that it adds "a slight concessional force into the phrase" (*Philippians*, 233). See also F. Blass, A. Debrunner, *A Greek Grammar of the New Testament and Other Early Christian Literature* [BDF], trans. Robert W. Funk (Chicago: University of Chicago, 1961), 123 ß235; and BDAG, 365.

[51] As in NKJV; NASB; NRSV.

[52] καὶ γὰρ οἱ ὄντες ἐν τῷ σκήνει στενάζομεν βαρούμενοι, ἐφ' ᾧ οὐ θέλομεν ἐκδύσασθαι ἀλλ' ἐπενδύσασθαι.

[53] C. K. Barrett, *Commentary of the Second Epistle to the Corinthians*, Black's New Testament Commentary (New York: Harper and Row, 1973), 149; Victor P. Furnish, *2 Corinthians*, AB, vol. 32A (New York: Doubleday, 1984), 269.

[54] F. F. Bruce, *1 and 2 Corinthians*, NCB, (London: Oliphants, 1971), 203; Margaret E. Thrall, *Greek Particles in the New Testament: Linguistic and Exegetical Studies*, NTTS (Leiden: Brill, 1962), 94.

there is at least a reason to question the common causal rendering of the phrase.[55] There is, moreover, a possibility that the causal rendering has gained a kind of "default" status beyond what it deserves. If a reader looks up the phrase in a standard lexicon like BDAG, the New Testament texts cited above are all given as examples of the causal meaning of ἐφ' ᾧ. The entry for ἐπί in *LSJ*, however, is more helpful, giving examples of the various nuances of the combination of ἐπί and the dative.[56] Outside the New Testament, Fitzmyer has shown substantial evidence against a causal reading of ἐφ' ᾧ.[57] Reading the phrase as "be-cause" seems rather unlikely; in fact, altogether the evidence from the Septuagint, the New Testament, together with Fitzmyer's extrabiblical examples suggest that the burden of proof rests on the causal reading. Whatever the case, the evidence should be enough to show that "because" cannot simply be the default translation. One thing is clear— we cannot determine the meaning of this verse by grammar alone.

Conceptual views. Cranfield has an extensive and useful discussion of the various interpretations suggested for this phrase over the centuries, including both the grammatical and conceptual rationales behind them.[58] One of the main difficulties in the interpretation of this text is that there are many grammatical possibilities with at least some degree of validity. Without going into all the details surrounding each possibil-

---

[55] I want to express my gratitude to my colleague Duane Garrett for his assistance in regard to thinking through this issue and for his help in translating the above texts without a causal conjunction. His insights into the grammar and syntax of these texts and his broad knowledge of Greek grammar and syntax and Greek literature have been invaluable to me. It was, interestingly enough, Garrett who also influenced Schreiner to question the causal reading of ἐφ' ᾧ (see Schreiner, *Romans*, 272, n. 5).

[56] Henry George Liddell and Robert Scott, *A Greek-English Lexicon*, revised by Henry Stuart Jones, rev. ed., with Supplement (Oxford: Clarendon Press, 1996), 622. Specifically see under the heading "various causal senses."

[57] "The Consecutive Meaning of ΕΦ' Ω," 321-29. Interested readers are encouraged to read this article before jumping to conclusions. Fitzmyer provides many examples to support his argument and a careful consideration of his data will provide a broader perspective on the use of the phrase outside the NT. He divides the meanings of ἐφ' ᾧ into two groups: (1) used as introducing a relative clause; and (2) used as a conjunction. Fitzmyer identifies eleven permutations for the former, and four for the latter (ibid., 322-29).

[58] The six primary interpretations discussed by Cranfield are (1) ᾧ is masculine with ὁ θάνατος as its antecedent; (2) ᾧ is masculine with ἑνὸς ἀνθρωπου as its antecedent; (3) ᾧ is masculine with ἑνὸς ἀνθρώπου as its antecedent, and ἐπί is equal to "because;" (4) ἐφ' ᾧ is equivalent to "because," i.e., it is a conjunction and ἥμαρτον indicates that all humanity had a part in Adam's sin; (5) ἐφ' ᾧ is equivalent to "because," i.e., it is a conjunction and ἥμαρτον indicates the actual sins of individuals, not in participation with Adam's sin, but as following his example; and (6) ἐφ' ᾧ is equivalent to "because," i.e., it is a conjunction and ἥμαρτον indicates the actual sins of individuals, not imitating Adam, but because they inherited a corrupt nature as a result of Adam's sin (*Romans*, 274-79).

ity, the issue boils down to a handful of interpretive options.[59] These groupings do not always follow a particular grammatical interpretation of ἐφ' ᾧ, but represent the conceptual ways in which this verse has been explained. While there is frequently some overlap between one or more of these interpretations, the main ideas are:

1) All humanity was actually "in" Adam, similar to Levi's paying tithes to Melchizedek "while in the loins of his father Abraham (Heb. 7:10). This view is sometimes called the "realist view."

2) "All sinned" because of an inherited, corrupt nature resulting from Adam's sin.[60]

3) "All sinned" *in Adam,* their representative head. The focus here is meant to be on the forensic or legal, rather then the seminal, relationship between Adam and humanity.[61] This view usually interprets ἐφ' ᾧ as "because."[62]

4) "All sinned" because the condemnation that followed Adam's sin, and under which all humanity is born, necessarily results in sin.[63]

---

[59] The following is similar to but not exactly like Cranfield's enumeration. The discussions in Joseph Fitzmyer ("The Consecutive Meaning of ΕΦ'Ω in Romans 5:12," 321-39), and Schreiner (*Romans,* 271-79) for example, are obviously not included in Cranfield's list. In listing the options in the following way, i.e., conceptually, I am not dispensing with grammar. Historically, the issue relies heavily on both grammatical and conceptual factors. There are, moreover, many good grammatical discussions of this text; none of which have won the day, although the causal interpretation is dominant.

[60] Cranfield (*Romans,* 279-81) and others. It should be noted that this view does not exclude a representative understanding of the relationship between humanity and Adam and Christ respectively.

[61] Most people in the Reformed tradition hold this view. Typically the "imputation" of Adam's sin is described as "immediate." That is, there is an "immediate conjunction with the sin of Adam and the death of all." John Murray, *The Imputation of Adam's Sin* (Grand Rapids: Eerdmans, 1953; Phillipsburg, N.J.: Presbyterian and Reformed, n.d.), 65. Murray's defense of immediate imputation is found on 64-70. Dabney, however, recognizing the problems that a hard and fast distinction between "mediate" and "immediate" imputation may cause, particularly in regard to imputation on the Christ-side of the Adam/Christ parallel, states, "The distinction is . . . an attempted overrefinement, which should never have been made, which explained nothing, and whose corollaries increased the difficulties of the subject. . . . [I]t causelessly aggravates the difficulties of the awful doctrine of original sin, exaggerating needlessly the angles of a subject which is, at best, sufficiently mysterious; . . . the arguments by which the immediate imputation must be sustained misrepresent the doctrines of the spiritual union and justification" (R. L. Dabney, *Systematic Theology,* 2ⁿᵈ ed. [Edinburgh; Carlisle, PA: Banner of Truth, 1985], 340-42; first published under the title, *Syllabus and Notes of The Course of Systematic and Polemic Theology* [St. Louis: Presbyterian Publishing, 1871].).

[62] The causal sense is certainly not limited to the Reformed tradition; it is the majority position in the grammars. For instance, see A. T. Robertson, *A Grammar of the Greek New Testament in the Light of Historical Research* (Nashville: Broadman, 1934), 963; BDF, 123, ß235. When taken as causal, ἐφ' ᾧ is basically equivalent to ἐπὶ τούτῳ or ὅτι.

[63] I treat this as a broad category. Various expressions of this view are found in Theodor Zahn, *Der Brief des Paulus an die Römer* (Leipzig: A. Deichert'sche Verlagsbuchhandlung Nachf (George Böhme, 1910), 266-67; Fitzmyer, "The Consecutive Meaning of ΕΦ'Ω in Romans 5:12," 332-39; and Schreiner, *Romans,* 275-77. These views will be taken up below. This category is a sort of catch-all for interpretations that do not take ἐφ' ᾧ as causal, and which do not fit into the other categories. The common denominator here is that they emphasize the consequential nature of the phrase.

Those who fit in this category understand the phrase to refer to an antecedent[64] or as a consecutive clause meaning something like, "with the result that."

5) Adam's sin established the circumstances under which all who followed him "sinned" in imitation of Adam.[65]

6) Paul simply says that "all sinned," and that refers to personal sin but the exact details of how Adam's sin affects humanity are left unexplained.[66]

The "realist" view, that all sinned "in Adam" because all humanity was somehow actually present in the person of Adam, basically maintains a theological rationale for Augustine's interpretation, "in whom." Though Augustine's reading of *in quo* for ἐφ᾽ ᾧ is almost universally rejected, the realist view finds a way to explain how all humanity could be truly "in Adam." This view typically understands ἐφ᾽ ᾧ as a relative clause referring back to Adam. In this view, stress may be laid on either Adam's role as the first man from whom all humanity proceeds seminally, or on the participation of all human nature in the person of Adam.[67]

Fitzmyer, ("The Consecutive Meaning of ΕΦ᾽ Ω) for example, reads the conjunction with a consecutive force. For Schreiner and Zahn (see below), the phrase, as a relative clause, points back to an antecedent.

[64] As do those who hold to a realist view.

[65] This was the interpretation set forth by Pelagius. See Cranfield, *Romans*, 277. Among the problems with this view is that it fails to recognize that the circumstances present in Eden before Adam sinned were destroyed by his sin. The birth of each individual human being does not reconstitute another Eden experience. This view, which does not garner a great deal of support, will not be dealt with individually. As will be seen, however, the fact that there is only one true Eden experience plays a vital role in the interpretation of this text.

[66] Schlatter, *Romans*, 128; Wright, *Romans*, 527. As in the representative view, ἐφ᾽ ᾧ is taken as causal by those who fit under this broad category. This view does not require much discussion because it is fairly straight forward. Some of the criticisms of the other views will easily apply to those holding this view. The views dealt with in more detail here are those that have a more developed conceptual opinion of what is taking place in Rom 5:12ff.

[67] The former was primarily what Augustine had in mind, the latter can be seen in William G. T. Shedd, *Dogmatic Theology*, vol. 2, 2nd ed. (New York: Scribners, 1889), 184, where Shedd speaks of "participation in the first sin itself." A rather thorough defense of an essentially Augustinian view is found in Augustus H. Strong, *Systematic Theology* (Philadelphia: Judson Press, 1953), 622-37. Strong's defense is preceded by a discussion of the other interpretive options. Hughes takes a more or less realist view, though he might also be in his own category. Recognizing the problems that exist in the various views, Hughes concludes that the connection is found in human nature, not in an inherited, corrupt nature but through human nature as some sort of singular entity. "This much is evident from the biblical record, that the totality of human nature was at creation concentrated in Adam, who was the original human being. The original sin of Adam was the sin of the totality of human nature. . . . The sin of Adam and the corruption it introduced were the sin and corruption of our nature, our humanity, for our human nature is one with the human nature of the first man." Philip Edgcumbe Hughes, *The True Image: The Origin and Destiny of Man in Christ* (Grand Rapids: Eerdmans, 1989) 131-32. Analogies from human experience, and oaks and acorns, and a quote from

The problem with this interpretation is that it solves a philosophical and anthropological problem with little support from the text. In the first place, this understanding sets up two distinct ways by which people are connected to the two "heads" in this text.[68] Virtually no one argues that the "real" connection between Adam and humanity is of the same sort that connects Christ with humanity. So the realist interpretation must connect humanity to Christ by some means other than that which connects humanity to Adam since the relationship to Christ cannot be seminal or through human nature. On one hand the link is existential but on the other forensic. Thus people are "sinners" because of their own actual sin, albeit in Adam, but "righteous" because of Christ's obedience—unless it is argued that being "made righteous" refers primarily to a transformation rather than a verdict.[69] One could argue that it is precisely the dissimilarity that Paul is stressing; we are condemned for our own sin, but we are justified by Christ's act of obedience—thus Paul's "how much more" refers to the fundamental contrast between the connection with Adam and Christ.

Without denying the dissimilarities between Adam and Christ in this text, the problem is that this view practically ignores the way Paul argues his case.[70] This kind of argument moves from the lesser ("if *x*") to the greater ("then how much more *y*") and there must be some rec-

---

John Donne, do not support Hughes's claim that this idea "is evident from the biblical record." While Hughes's phrase, "the biblical record," shows that he is interpreting this text in the light of a much larger biblical paradigm, the problem, again, is that Hughes solves a problem, i.e., his interpretation helps explain the difficult doctrine of original sin, but his view requires one to read a great deal of information into Paul's discourse.

[68] In and of itself, it is not wrong to say that we are connected to Adam and Christ in different ways. After all, we become "sinners" on account of condemnation but "righteous" only by faith. However, in both cases the emphasis is on the legal reality of being a sinner or being righteous.

[69] As Murray states: "The analogy instituted in Romans 5:12-19 . . . presents a formidable objection to the realist construction. It is admitted by the realist that there is no 'realistic' union between Christ and the justified. That is to say, there is no human nature, specifically and numerically one, existing in its unity in Christ, which is individualized in those who are the beneficiaries of Christ's righteousness. On realist premises, therefore, a radical disparity must be posited between the character of the union that exists between Adam and his posterity, on the one hand, and the union that exists between Christ and those who are his, on the other. . . . But there is no hint of the kind of discrepancy that would obtain if the distinction between the nature of the union in the two cases were as radical as realism must suppose. . . . But the case is not merely that there is no hint of this kind of difference; the sustained parallelism militates against any such supposition. . . . This sustained emphasis not only upon the one man Adam and the one man Christ but also upon the one trespass and the one righteous act points to a basic identity in respect of *modus operandi*" (Murray, *Imputation*, 33).

[70] The kind of argument here is known as *qal wahomer*. Simply put, it means to argue from the lesser to the greater on the basis that if some minor point is true then a related major point that shares a common premise, must also be true. This is evident in the phrase "how much more."

ognized similarity on both sides. The contrasts in verses 15-17 are based on the connection that exists between Adam and humanity and Christ and humanity. If something is true, such as death reigning through one person (v. 17), and if it's also true that those who receive grace and righteousness will reign (v. 17), there must be a recognized condition that exists for both statements. Otherwise, Paul could not say, "how much more." Therefore, to begin with contrasting ways through which Adam and Christ are connected with humanity or with contrasting ways by which people are either "sinners" or "righteous" (the former through actual sin, the second via another's obedience) undercuts the "how much more" contrasts in verses 15 and 17.[71]

Secondly, a conceptual interpretation such as the realist position may have validity, but even so, the details of the text and context dictate caution. If the antecedent is understood as "one man" (ἑνὸς ἀνθρώπου), then one must account for the distance between the pronoun and its antecedent in the text—by no means an insurmountable obstacle—relying, however, on the aorist tense of ἥμαρτον to establish that the sin in view was clearly in the past fails to convince.[72] Finally, most who hold to a "federal" or "covenant" view (3), or to the view that stresses the consequences or results of Adam's sin for humanity (4), do not deny some sort of real participation in Adam. Adam is the actual father of the human race and every person is thus related to him. As an interpretation of ἐφ' ᾧ, however, the realist position is difficult to maintain. As Blocher points out, no interpretation of this verse and text is immune to criticism, and there is more to consider than simply the meaning of ἐφ' ᾧ.[73] So, while ἐφ' ᾧ may not mean, "in whom," the conceptual idea behind this interpretation is an attempt to make sense of an extremely difficult and continually disputed text.

Some scholars (view 2) interpret the "all sinned" of Romans 5:12 as referring to the actual sins of each individual that are done because

---

[71] In fairness, it could be argued that all that is needed is to say that in spite of different ways of relating to humanity, the actions of both Adam and Christ have universal implications and effects.

[72] Hughes: "The use of the aorist tense in the Greek, when affirming that "all sinned," confirms this conclusion, for the aorist tense is customarily used to designate the commission of a particular deed in the past" (*True Image*, 130).

[73] "The case does not (contrary to a superficial understanding of the issues) rest on the rendering of the connecting words at the end of verse 12 for which Augustine finally settled" (Henri Blocher, *Original Sin: Illuminating the Riddle* [Grand Rapids: Eerdmans, 1997], 71).

of a sinful nature inherited from Adam. This view emphasizes that the easiest way to read "all sinned" (πάντες ἥμαρτον) of 5:12 is to read it as stands in 3:23, "For all sinned (πάντες ἥμαρτον) and have fallen short of the glory of God," which clearly refers to the actual sins of individuals.[74] Another parallel in Romans is 2:12, where ἥμαρτον is also used in reference to the personal sins of both those without and those under the law. As with the realist view, this view finds no problem with proposing a difference between the way Adam's disobedience and Christ's obedience affect humanity. There is "no reason to say that because we are made righteous by Christ apart from anything we do, therefore we must be guilty apart from personal sinning."[75] Unlike the realist view, the operating principle is not a natural relation with Adam, though that relation exists, but a corrupt sin nature inherited from Adam as a result of his sin.[76] The advantage of this view is that there are a myriad of texts that support the principle that all individuals will be punished for their personal sin. Secondly, this view relieves the practical tension that may occur in some formulations of a representational view as a result of humanity being declared guilty and receiving condemnation for another's sin.

Finally, a typically good rule of thumb for interpreting texts is to compare how the same author uses the same words or phrases elsewhere in his writings, and having examples so close at hand is a significant point.[77] This view allows for a consistent reading of πάντες ἥμαρτον with the same phrase in 3:23 and a similar phrase in 2:12. But this view is open to the same criticism as the realist view, in that it must assert a fundamental difference between the way Adam's sin and Christ's righteousness are effective for humanity. In this view, we inherit a sin-nature from Adam with the result that we inevitably sin and are therefore guilty

---

[74] Cranfield says that "there is nothing in the context or in this verse to suggest that ἥμαρτον is being used in an unusual manner and that in every other occurrence of this verb in the Pauline epistles the reference is quite clearly to actual sin" (*Romans,* 279).

[75] Ibid., 278.

[76] "We may understand that the many were made sinners through the disobedience of the one man, in that his transgression gave sin entrance into mankind and meant that the nature passed on by him to his descendents was a nature weak and corrupted" (ibid., 279).

[77] Obviously this is not a fool-proof hermeneutical principle. An author may use the same word or phrase in two or more ways in the same text. It is nevertheless safe to begin with the assumption that an author uses words and phrases in consistent ways unless it is somehow made clear that he intends a different meaning.

for our own sin, but we are "made righteous" on account of Christ's obedience apart from a new nature or any actions of our own. The same criticisms that apply to the realist view apply here.

The more serious problem with this view is that it relies on the addition of a substantial and questionable implication in the text. Though he insists on reading "all sinned" as referring to personal sins (Rom. 3:23), Cranfield nevertheless "wrongly smuggles in the idea of a corrupt nature into the word 'sinned.'"[78] This view is compelling because it addresses and explains our inevitable propensity to sin, while alleviating the tension of guilt apart from personal responsibility, thus taking on difficult biblical-theological problems; but these are not the problems addressed in Romans 5. It is difficult to understand why Paul, or any writer, would rest such an important point on an implicit, rather than explicit, statement.[79]

The view that stresses the representative nature of Adam's and Christ's relationship to humanity, and/or because of this, translates ἐφ᾽ ᾧ as "because" (view 1), is the predominant view in traditional Reformed theology. The second part of the phrase "all sinned" is not understood to refer to personal sins, but to "all sinned" in the person of their representative, or "federal" head, Adam. As the first man, the head of all humanity, Adam's sin counts as the sin of all those who are under his headship. The vital connection with Adam is neither seminal or through human nature, nor through the inheritance of a corrupt nature; it is, rather, a forensic reality.

This view is strengthened by the analogy with Christ, for just as Christ's obedience makes many righteous (v. 19) apart from any good work or personal contribution of any kind on their part, so all are made sinners (v. 19), i.e., they "sinned" and were found legally guilty

---

[78] Schreiner, *Romans*, 275. Moo refers to this, i.e. smuggling in a reference to the "corrupt nature," as adding a "middle term" to the text. In this instance the meaning of the text would be "one man's trespass *resulted in the corruption of human nature, which caused all people to sin, and so* brought condemnation on all men." Moo goes on to say that though "it is possible that Paul would want us to assume these additions, he has given us little basis for doing so" (*Romans*, 326).

[79] Blocher, *Original Sin*, 66. Note Blocher's fitting comment: "Such a reading deserves our consideration, for those who are aware of the elasticity of language, and the conditions under which all exegesis is obliged to labour, may hardly rule it out as impossible. Yet difficulties spring to mind. It is rather strange that the core idea, or the hinge of the apostle's purported logic—that Adam communicated the sinful bent to his posterity—should not be expressed at all in the passage. It *might* be implicit; undoubtedly, Paul did share the opinion; yet how surprising that he should not include something here, of all places, to make it clear!" (*Original Sin*, 66).

"because" they sinned in Adam, apart from personally committing sin.[80] The guilt of Adam's sin spreads to all.[81] This view rightly recognizes the forensic nature of the statements in verse 19 and consistently applies that understanding to the phrase ἐφ᾽ ᾧ πάντες ἥμαρτον.[82] Moreover, this view seeks to understand verse 12 contextually by reading it in light of the following verses that repeatedly emphasize the actions of the one having direct consequences on the many: many died because of one trespass (v. 15); condemnation was the result of one transgression (v. 16); death reigns through the trespass of one (v. 17); condemnation came to all men as a result of one man's transgression (v. 18); and many are "made sinners" through the disobedience of the one (v. 19).[83] The "all sinned" of verse 12 is read consistently as the consequences of the sin or trespass of the one man in verses 15-19 that results in death, judgment, and condemnation for the many. Another contextual argument for this view is the consistent way in which the thought begun in verse 12, broken off through verses 13-17,[84] and taken up again in verse 18 is followed through. The unfinished protasis of verse 12 is not exactly finished in verse 18, but it is essentially restated and completed.[85]

One shortcoming of this view is that it comes very close to reading καὶ οὕτως ("and so," "and in this way") as if it were οὕτως καὶ (so also). It is almost universally recognized that the protasis of verse 12 ("For as sin came into the world through one man and death through sin. . . .")

---

[80] The implications for the Adam-Christ parallel are usually set forth as the strongest reasons for taking this view. See Murray, *Imputation*, 70; and John Piper, *Counted Righteous in Christ: Should We Abandon the Imputation of Christ's Righteousness* (Wheaton: Crossway, 2002) 92-93. In sum, if the meaning is not "because all sinned," i.e., had Adam's sin been imputed to them, then the door is open to say that personal acts of righteousness may contribute to being "made righteous" (v. 19). This conclusion does not necessarily follow. If verse 12 is understood as providing a condition for the condemnation of humanity and the universal spread of sin which does in fact account for personal sins, then there is no lingering concern that the integrity of Christ's obedience as the sole action that leads to being "made righteous" will be injured.

[81] There is disagreement as to whether Adam's sin is imputed to his posterity mediately or immediately. See Murray's extended discussion in *Imputation*, 42-64.

[82] This is not at all to say that the other views miss the forensic nature of this text, at least in regard to how Christ's obedience counts for our righteousness, but the representative view follows the comparison consistently into the relationship between Adam and his posterity as well.

[83] See Murray, *Imputation*, 19-21.

[84] By "broken off," it is not meant that the intervening verses (particularly vv. 15-17) spiral out on a tangent, but that the type of statement in verse 12 is similar to that found in verse 18. Murray points out that verse 18 both *resumes* verse 12 in terms of construction and *recapitulates* the content of vv. 15-17 (*Romans*, 199 n. 30).

[85] Murray, *Imputation*, 20.

is not followed by an apodosis which would typically begin with οὕτως καὶ.[86] If, however, ἐφ᾽ ᾧ is read as "because," then the verse becomes basically a comparative construction—the very thing that is widely denied on the basis of the syntax. If it means "because all sinned," then this makes καὶ οὕτως essentially mean "so also," since the same course of events follows for "all" just as for Adam. The causal reading of ἐφ᾽ ᾧ even without καὶ οὕτως, nearly creates a comparative structure on its own.

In order to avoid this, a qualification must be added to the phrase: "because all sinned *in Adam*." In this way, Augustine's "in whom" returns, not as a rendering of ἐφ᾽ ᾧ but as a qualifier of "because all sinned." There is more here than simply reading ἐφ᾽ ᾧ as "because." A second phrase must be added because of the conceptual or theological difficulty that arises from a causal reading. Only by inserting—conceptually if not in translation—the additional phrase "in Adam," can ἐφ᾽ ᾧ be read as "because," and not refer to personal sin. Taken as a whole, this view has much to commend it, but in spite of all its strengths it is not the only possibility, nor is it required to maintain a theology of representation in Romans 5:12-21.

Some scholars emphasize the consequences and/or results of Adam's sin for the rest of humanity, and this interpretation may include reading ἐφ᾽ ᾧ as either a conjunction meaning "with the result that" or as a relative clause.[87] Fitzmyer argues for a consecutive reading of ἐφ᾽ ᾧ largely on the basis of extra-biblical Greek literature.[88] The examples cited by Fitzmyer are intriguing, but as Schreiner points out, some of them could be read legitimately in other ways.[89] Fitzmyer's view is attractive not only because of the textual evidence, but also because of the philosophical and theological conclusions he draws. The spread of sin into the world is due to a dual causality. Adam is indeed the primary cause of sin and death, but the role of human beings is not merely one of imitation

---

[86] See 5:15, 18-19, 21; 6:4, 11:31; 1 Corinthians 12:12; 15:22; Ephesians 5:24; Colossians 3:13; 2 Timothy 3:8.
[87] Again, though this "view" contains two readings of ἐφ᾽ ᾧ, there is a shared emphasis on the consequences and results of Adam's sin for humanity and both account for the reality of personal sin as it is expressed in the phrase "all sinned." For these reasons they are grouped together.
[88] Fitzmyer, "The Consecutive Meaning of ΕΦ᾽ Ω," 339; idem, *Romans*, 413-16.
[89] Schreiner, *Romans*, 274.

but "a secondary resultant causality."[90] This supposition, however, may be asking too much of the verse.

One clear problem with Fitzmyer's view is that he must, like Cranfield, insert the notion of the sinful nature inherited from Adam as the explanation for human sinfulness.[91] While Fitzmyer would rather refer to "the tainted nature inherited from Adam" than to "corrupt nature," the outcome is the same. The "perverse corruption of humanity" is the result of Adam's sin and serves as the reason why humans themselves sin.[92] Again, even if one agrees with the sentiment, and although it may explain part of the human condition after Eden, this interpretation probably goes beyond whatever Paul establishes in this text.

A truly original sin. As seen above, it is also possible that ἐφ᾽ ᾧ refers to some antecedent, whether it be θάνατος in the immediately preceding clause or in a more general way without reference to a specific word.[93] If there is no specific antecedent, then the emphasis is on accounting for the universality of sin. As such it reads something like, "Death spread to all men, on account of which (condition) all sinned."[94] In this way, the death and sin that came into the world through Adam provides the foundation for the sin that "all" commit.[95] If "death" is understood as the inevitable, existing condition under which everyone *after* Adam lives, and which everyone experiences, then we can understand this text to mean that the condemnation of all on account

---

[90] Fitzmyer, "The Consecutive Meaning of EΦ᾽ Ω," 339.

[91] Fitzmyer himself notes that even though Cranfield reads ἐφ᾽ ᾧ as "because," he (Cranfield) correctly understands the 'result' that comes to humanity as a consequence of Adam's sin (ibid., n. 71).

[92] Ibid.

[93] Zahn understands the antecedent as referring to the entire sentence, but he emphasizes the particular role of death, or "the dominating power of death," ("zur Herrschaft gelangte Macht des Todes") (*Römer*, 266). Zahn's interpretation of this verse has been influential in the present work.

[94] This may seem similar to that of S. Lyonnet, "Le Sens de ἐφ᾽ ᾧ in Rom. 5:12 et l'exÈg'se des P'res Grecs', *Biblica* 36 (1955): 424. Lyonnet, however, renders it "on condition that"—which is not the same thing. In the view taken here, fulfilling the condition, i.e., sin, that leads to death, is only half the story.

[95] Schreiner takes the clause in this way, understanding "death" as referring primarily to spiritual death. As a result of Adam's sin, all are born in a state of spiritual death in which they inevitably sin. "This phrase does not mean that first we commit trespasses and sins and as a consequence die. Rather, the idea is that we are born into the world ('children of wrath by nature,' Eph. 2.3) separated from God, and our sins are a result of the spiritual state of death" (*Romans*, 276). Elsewhere Schreiner says, "The reason all people sin individually is that they enter the world spiritually dead, and they enter the world spiritually dead because they are descendents of Adam" (*Paul: Apostle of God's Glory in Christ* [Downers Grove: InterVarsity, 2001], 148).

of Adam's sin, which "came into the world," is evident because death necessarily "spreads to all men." It is because of this condition—the condition of death—that all sin.[96] There are contextual clues for reading verse 12 in this way.

In verse 15 Paul says "by the transgression of the one, many died," thus forging a link between Adam's transgression and the resultant death for those who followed. In verse 18 he states, "through the transgression of the one there resulted condemnation for all men." Both death and condemnation result from Adam's transgression. The evidence from verse 16 is most compelling because there the judgment upon one results in condemnation. In the context it is clear that the same "one-many" pattern is at work here. So the condemnation flows to "all" from the judgment passed on the one, just as many "died" by the one's trespass (v. 15).

Taken in this way, the condemnation that comes to humanity through Adam is primarily evident in death. All are born under God's condemnation of Adam's sin. In other words, all are born outside of Eden, under the curse that fell upon Adam as the penalty for his sin. God told Adam that if he ate from the tree of the knowledge of good and evil, on that day he would die (Gen. 2:17). The "death" referred to there includes spiritual death, which comes immediately, and also physical death—the ultimate condemnation for Adam's unfaithful disobedience.[97] From that point on, every person is born into a condemned world, separated from God, and all receive the penalty of death.[98] This

---

[96] This is not to assert that Paul is emphasizing an inherited sinful nature—it is a condition in which sin, death, and guilt have become entrenched in the world. Ultimately this includes a sinful nature, and the imitation of Adam's sin, but these are byproducts. It also includes a seminal relationship to Adam, but that merely creates one human family under Adam.

[97] The nature of Adam's sin (i.e., the source of his motivation, his moral capacity as the first man, his "mutability," etc.) is a bit outside the scope of this work. It seems clear, however, that although God gave Adam a command to obey, the heart of the matter was whether Adam would trust God to keep his word. Adam's disobedience signaled unbelief, which is, according to Turretin, "the beginning of sin." (Francis Turretin, *Institutes of Elenctic Theology*, trans. George Musgrave Giger, ed. James T. Denison Jr. [Phillipsburg, N.J.: Presbyterian and Reformed, 1992], 2:605). Turretin is following his predecessor, who said that "disobedience was the beginning of the Fall" and went on to say that "unfaithfulness . . . was the root of the Fall." John Calvin, *Institutes of the Christian Religion*, vol. 1, ed. John T. McNeill, trans. Ford Lewis Battles (Philadelphia: Westminster, 1960), 245.

[98] Regarding "death" as separation from God, Geerhardus Vos thinks that even in the warning "you shall surely die" (Gen. 2:17), "a deeper conception of death seems to be hinted at. It was intimated that death carried with it separation from God, since sin issued both into death and in the exclusion from the garden. If life consisted in communion with God, then, on the principle of opposites, death may have been interpretable as separation from God" (*Biblical Theology* [Grand Rapids: Eerdmans, 1943], 50).

death "that spread to all men" is that which makes Adam's children "sinners" (a status) and is that which accounts for their own, personal sin.

While all people imitate Adam in that they sin and die as a result ("the wages of sin is death"), there is already sin and death in the world prior to birth. The circumstances that originally existed for Adam are not what his children inherit. For Adam, created in innocence, death comes only as result of sin, but for those who follow, born in the world where "death reigns" (vv. 14, 17), death as condemnation for Adam's sin is in the world and gives rise to sin, and sin in turn leads to death; it is a reciprocal relationship. Thus Paul can speak not only of death reigning, but also of sin reigning (5:21).

In sum, no individual repeats the exact experience of Adam. The best analogy for this is found in this same passage. The gift that results in justification did not begin with a clean slate but followed Adam's sin and the condemnation that followed *and* the history of all human sin, i.e., "many transgressions." (5:16). On the other hand, Adam's world was one in which there was no sin, no condemnation, no prior transgressions, no death. When Christ came, he did not "begin where Adam began, he began where Adam left off."[99] He did not merely retrace Adam's steps and succeed where Adam failed. Christ began with the situation as Adam left it. So it is with all who follow Adam—sin and death are the reality they inherit. What is at issue here is not whether Adam's sin brings condemnation—it does—but whether each individual is guilty of Adam's actual sin, or whether condemnation is the universal consequence of that sin. Though there are obvious differences, the role of Adam as the first man whose sin brings God's judgment on the whole world is not in dispute.

The noted drawback of this view, namely, that it reverses the order of sin leading to death and makes death the cause of sin,[100] is answered by the observation that the situation in which humanity finds itself *is not* that which Adam was in prior to his sin. For Adam, neither sin nor death was in the world prior to his disobedience. When Adam disobeyed, sin came into the world and death came through that sin. For every person

---

[99] Wright, *Romans*, 524.
[100] Piper, *Counted Righteous*, 91 n. 37; Wright, *Romans*, 527.

born after Adam, the situation is *already* reversed. This interpretation is supported by the structure of the verse. Verse 12 contains a chiasm that begins with "sin" (12a), then "death" (12b), then "death" again (12c), then finally "sin" (12d). Thus the structure is A, B, B, A, or Sin, Death, Death, Sin. The connection between the original cause—sin—and the direct result—death—neatly existed for Adam only. It was, after all, truly an "original sin," never to be repeated in so far as it was the *first* sin committed before either sin or death was in the world.

After Adam's sin, both sin and death constitute the situation into which every human being is born. Sin still leads to death and each will receive the punishment for his own sin, but death, which Paul will connect with condemnation, is itself the constant presupposition for all humanity after Adam. The structure of the verse argues for this interpretation. As with the traditional view, the interpretation argued for here stresses the solidarity of humanity with Adam. Rather than threatening the "representative" view, this view upholds the headship of Adam as the first man, whose actions affect and bear direct consequences for those "in" him.[101]

Another criticism of this view is that it necessarily creates a tension in the Adam/Christ parallel because if "all sinned" refers to personal sin, then being "made righteous" (v. 19) must entail doing personal acts of righteousness. This is not so. For one, Paul clearly refers to personal sin in verse 14 when he speaks of "those whose sinning was not in the likeness of Adam's transgression," and it is precisely these over whom "death reigns." Even if personal sin is excised from verse 12 there is still an unavoidable reference to it in verse 14. However, in neither place is personal sin given an instrumental emphasis.[102] Read in the way proposed here, verse 12 does not emphasize personal sin but rather accounts for it on the basis of an already existing state of condemnation that resulted from Adam's sin.

There need not be a strict dichotomy drawn between the legal status, "sinner," and the actual committing of sin. Being "made" a

---

[101] Though not explicitly developed in this text, a foundation for the concept of "union" is implicit. One is either "in" Christ or "in" Adam. Here the idea is most closely linked to being "identified" with or "in the sphere of." This does not, however, limit Paul's theology of "union" to either identification or sphere.

[102] Someone holding the realist view may possibly argue this point as well.

sinner, after all, will result in actually fulfilling that role in ways that bear evidence of the reality of the status.[103] This is not less true of the status "righteous."[104] It does not have to be "either/or," and it does not threaten the parallel with Christ by implying that personal righteousness must somehow then be an instrumental cause of the status "righteous."[105] It is the forensic reality that exists because of Adam's sin that Paul emphasizes. Thus all are "made sinners" (v. 19) by Adam's disobedience, and this reality exists logically before the committing of personal sin. Adam's disobedience, therefore, "counts" for the status "sinners," and personal sin and subsequent death derive from that status.[106] Thus the ground for the sinfulness of humanity, outlined in detail in 1:18ff. and summed up in the simple phrase "all sinned," rests upon the situation that resulted from Adam's sin.[107] In the same way, the status that results from Christ's obedience is an established forensic reality *prior* to the personal obedience that must necessarily flow as a consequence (chap. 6).

Finally, this interpretation reads καὶ οὕτως consecutively and as part of the protasis begun with ὥσπερ.[108] The text reads: "Therefore, just as through one man sin came into the world, and death came through sin, *so in this way* death spread to all men, on account of which all sinned." This does not rule out a causal element, but rather places it where it

---

[103] As Dunn notes, Paul has "a very complex notion of sin" which enables him to speak of "sin" in a number of different ways even in this text. From a "personified power" (vv. 12, 21), to something "reckoned" (v. 13), to something that "increases or grows" (v. 20). James D. G. Dunn, *The Theology of the Apostle Paul* (Grand Rapids: Eerdmans, 1998), 96.

[104] This does not at all confuse "status," as a legal reality, with the necessary results that must flow from that status.

[105] Wright, who takes ἐφ' ᾧ as "because," states: "Paul's meaning must in any case be both that an entail of sinfulness has spread throughout the human race from its first beginnings and that each individual has contributed their own share to it" (*Romans*, 527).

[106] On a larger biblical-theological scale this does not, then, threaten what the Bible makes so forcefully clear: each person will be held accountable for his own sins. As Jeremiah puts it, "everyone will die for his own sin; whoever eats sour grapes—his own teeth will be set on edge" (29:30), and commenting on the same popular proverb, Ezekiel declares, "The soul who sins is the one who will die" (18:4). Paul's emphasis in Romans 5:12-21 and judgment for personal sinning can fit quite well together. If each person is *guilty* of Adam's actual sin, then these texts in Jeremiah and Ezekiel hardly make sense, but if Adam's sin establishes the ground upon which all sin, then the reality described in Romans 5:12-21, in which sin and death are the preexisting conditions of all life after Adam, and the reality of judgment for personal sin, are compatible.

[107] Blocher's comments in this regard are instructive. Questioning the need to assert an "either/or" proposition in regard to whether humanity is condemned for Adam's sin, or their own sinfulness: "I submit that the role of Adam and of his sin in Romans 5 is *to make possible the imputation, the judicial treatment, of human sins*. His role thus brings about the condemnation of all, and its sequel, death" (*Original Sin*, 77; his emphasis).

[108] *Pace,* Cranfield, *Romans*, 273.

should be—adhering to the preposition. The translation "because of which condition" retains the causal force of the ἐπί while reading ᾧ as a relative.[109]

This reading also preserves the meaning of πάντες ἥμαρτον as it appears in 3:23 as referring to personal sin. As noted above, rather than making a comparison between the sin of Adam and the sins of his progeny, Paul establishes the original sin of Adam as creating the condition that leads inevitably to, and accounts for, the universal spread of sin to all humanity, bar none. This is, in fact, precisely the point that Paul will clarify in verses 13-14. It is not the case that either people sin and then they die *just like* Adam sinned and died, or Adam sinned and all who followed were immediately guilty of the actual *act* of his sin.[110] All people without exception do sin and die and it is a result of the condemnation that arose from Adam's sin.[111] In this sense, Adam's sin "counts" to make all become "sinners." Only in this qualified sense, should we speak of being "guilty" of Adam's sin.

Clarifying the Scope of "All": Romans 5:13-14

Verses 13 and 14 of Romans 5 have been the cause of much debate due to the inability of scholars to agree upon why Paul seems to break off from verse 12, and what he intends by verses 13 and 14. There is no need to review all the suggestions. For our purposes what is important to note is that Paul is making sure that his readers understand that there is no escaping the reality of what he said in verse 12.

In verses 13-14 Paul shows that the universal dominion of death is

---

[109] The antecedent could be either "death" or the preceding taken as a whole. Ultimately it makes little difference since the point is that sin of Adam brought about the condition for all. This makes it clear that I am not arguing against whether ἐπί can be causal but against reading ἐφ' ᾧ causally. To be clear: the difference is that in my reading the phrase is pointing back to something (e.g., death), not forward, and, therefore, does not need the addition of the phrase (or idea) "in Adam."

[110] Critics of a representative understanding of this text seem to misunderstand this point. As Murray states, "We, the members of his [Adam's] posterity, did not personally and voluntarily as individuals eat of the forbidden fruit" (*Imputation*, 86). Paul never speaks of people being personally "guilty" of Adam's actual sin, any more than he speaks of people being personally responsible for the atonement Christ made on the cross. In *both* cases it is what results from the action that counts for humanity. And in both cases the position taken here is open to Murray's staunch criticism that it only "amounts to judicial liability" (ibid.). In regard to that last sentence, however, I realize that the position taken here is open to Murray's staunch criticism that it only "amounts to judicial liability" (ibid.).

[111] In this way it is legitimate to speak, as Fitzmyer does, of the dual causality of both Adam's sin, and our own sin as the basis for condemnation ("The Consecutive Meaning of ΕΦ' Ω," 339). We can speak of being condemned in regard to the "status" we have from Adam, and being condemned for our own personal sin without making a theological imposition on the text.

a reality quite apart from the presence of the law.[112] The consequences flowing from Adam trump the appearance and role of the law.[113] It is not that sin does not exist without law, but sin is not "counted" (ἐλλογέω, v. 13) as "transgression" (παράβασις, v. 14), as the breaking of a specific command given by God.[114] Elsewhere Paul makes it clear that the law does not create sin; it amplifies it and shows it clearly for what it is—what it already was (5:20; 7:13)—and so it is evident that he is making the point that sin existed before the law, and the evidence is that "death reigned." In reference to the "law written" on the heart (2:14-15), it seems to me that Paul's point here is to account for the reality of death between Adam and Moses before the giving of the law at Sinai and to establish Adam's sin as a specific transgression. While there may be a connection with what Paul says in chapter 2, it is not what he is emphasizing in 5:14, which speaks of those who did not transgress, i.e., break a specific command, like Adam.[115]

The reign of death that flowed to all as the consequence of Adam's sin—manifested in personal sin and actual death—makes it clear that while law may show sin for what it is, there is no one exempt from either sin or death. Paul speaks of both as entities and as personal experiences. These verses prove once and for all what Paul has been saying almost from the very beginning of the letter: all are condemned before God. Whether they are those who sin under the law, or those who sin apart from the law (2:12; 3:23), whether Jew or Gentile, all share the same plight, all are identified with Adam. There can be no more questions regarding Jew *vs.* Gentile or law *vs.* no law, for all are condemned, and this is clear from the fact that sin was in the world and death reigned before the law was ever given.

Two observations are in order. First, Adam was, like Israel later, confronted with a direct command from God, and Adam's disobedience was a direct violation of that command. Thus, Paul refers to Adam's sin specifically as "transgression." Secondly, Adam's role vis-à-vis Christ

---

[112] Moo, *Romans*, 332.
[113] Perhaps answering the Jewish idea that without the law there is no sin. See Dunn, *Romans*, 275.
[114] Schreiner, *Romans*, 279. Obviously there were "commands" before Sinai. God gave commands, for example, to Noah (Gen. 6:14; 7:1-3, 16-17; 9:1, 7) and to Abraham as is made clear in Genesis 26:5. But the point here is that "where there is no law" means where there is no codified law as given at Sinai. It is simply referring to the time before Moses.
[115] Moo, *Romans*, 330.

becomes more explicit. The sin that "came through the one man" (v. 12) is further defined as disobedience to God's command—Adam's transgression brought sin and death. The event that opened a chasm between God and man was disobedience. Regardless of how one describes the relationship between God and Adam in Eden, there must be a similar relationship with presumably similar implications between God and Christ, here described as "the one who was to come."[116] It is not that Paul looks back and finds a helpful analogy from the Scripture, but rather that Adam always prefigured Christ; he was the "type" all along. As such, we can expect his relationship to God, and subsequently to humanity, to be analogous to that of "the one who was to come."

As Schlatter so aptly says, "Adam himself is the promise of Christ because the One determines the relationship to God for all."[117] As is clear in verse 19, the act that will repair the breach created by disobedience between God and man is obedience to God. Thus, rather than "breaking off" the thought of verse 12, verses 13-14 clarify the nature of Adam's sin as disobedience and provide a clue to the "obedience" spoken of in verses 18-19. The sin of the "type" was transgression of a command, and so the obedience of the "one who was to come" must also be obedience to a command.

Finally, these verses clarify the point made in verse 12 that sin spread "to all." There is no need, in my view, to posit either infants, or the mentally challenged, or any other particular group beyond those whom Paul himself mentions: those who lived in the time between Adam and Moses.[118] By far the most troublesome aspect of the idea that Paul is speaking of infants or some other such group is that it means that he is *clarifying* verse 12 with an *implicit* statement. It would be odd for Paul,

---

[116] This phrase prepares the way for what is to follow. The action of the "type" and the results for humanity are clear in verse 12. By referring to Adam as "a type for the one to come," Paul "introduces in the same sentence the agent who is to undo the other's action." Stanley E. Porter, "The Argument of Romans 5: Can a Rhetorical Question Make a Difference?" *JBL* 110/4 (1991): 672.

[117] Schlatter, *Romans*, 129.

[118] Piper, following Murray and Johnson, is quite cautious but nevertheless suggests that "even over" in verse 14 Paul refers to infants (*Counted Righteous*, 95-100). Seeing infants in this verse supports the argument that Paul is emphasizing the legal, not the moral, aspect of grace and sin, respectively. In spite of Piper's concerns, the text seems overwhelmingly "legal," and not "moral," as it is. Whatever the case, the arguments of Murray, Johnson, and Piper do not depend on the presence of "infants" in verse 14. Johnson does not limit the text to "infants" but thinks that the text "seems" to include the mentally challenged as well. S. Lewis Johnson, "Romans 5:12—An Exercise in Exegesis and Theology," in *New Dimensions in New Testament Studies*, ed. Richard N. Longenecker and Merril C. Tenney (Grand Rapids: Zondervan, 1974), 310.

or anyone wishing to make sure he is understood, to clarify a point with an implied statement.[119] The simple point is that there is no distinction between those who came before or those who came after the law. The only difference is that sin under the law is "counted" as transgression; it is, in other words, unveiled as a direct act of disobedience to God.[120] This is no different from saying that "all have sinned and fallen short of the glory of God" (3:23), whether under, or apart from, the law. It is odd that so much of the discussion of this text seems to forget that one of Paul's purposes throughout Romans is to level the playing field in regard to God's justice with respect to *all people*.[121] The reason why all are condemned is because all are identified with Adam.[122]

When verses 13 and 14 are seen in this way, they become an important part of the discussion of imputation in Romans 5:12-21. For the most part, however, they go largely ignored partly because of the trouble readers have over Paul's so-called "break" in the argument, and because of the rather drawn-out, though well intentioned, debate over who Paul has in mind here. But Paul is making a distinction between Adam's sin and sin against a specific, known command. When the Mosaic law came, those who sinned under it did so in the face of the clearly expressed commands of God. Faced with commands, like Adam but now with Adam's condemnation hanging over them, their sinning was just like Adam's. When Christ, the second Adam, came, he too confronted specific commands, but where Adam and Israel failed, he succeeded. He fulfilled the role of the "type," the role of Adam.

---

[119] Some of the motivation (not explicitly in Piper, Johnson, or Murray) for seeing infants in this text is based on the pastoral desire to answer the question of what happens to infants who die. This is a question that needs to be addressed, but addressing it from a text that does not offer more than (at best) a veiled reference will ultimately render little or no hope for those wrestling with the issue—particularly if they decide to weigh the evidence in the text for themselves. The only thing that can be said of infants on the basis of this text is that they are included in Paul's "all."

[120] As Paul says in verse 20, the law comes in order to increase transgressions.

[121] Someone could argue that there is not "explicit" mention of Jews and Gentiles, any more than infants in this text. That would be true if it were not for four preceding chapters overflowing with the topic and numerous and lengthy discussions in the following chapters. It is puzzling that there is not more discussion about this in the commentaries. Many of those scholars associated, to some degree, with the so-called New Perspective have rightly directed our attention to this vital point in the New Testament and in Paul in particular.

[122] These verses are neglected in much of the discussion about the state of both Jews and Gentiles described by Paul in 1:18ff. It seems, however, that these verses sum up his argument in much the same way as 3:23, "for all have sinned and fall short of the glory of God."

Dissimilarity from Similarity: Verses 15–17

In these verses Paul's *qal wahomer* (lesser to greater) argument comes to the foreground. There is a series of contrasts based on one similar and vital element. Whatever the differences, the same operative principle is at work: the actions of one have determining effects on the many. The similarity is essential for proving the dissimilarity, for in these verses the parallel is ultimately overshadowed by the "imbalance."[123] The dissimilarity is in the results or consequences that flow to the many from the one.

From One → To Many		From One → To Many	
v. 15: Trespass	Death	Grace	Abounds
v. 16: Judgment	Condemnation	Free gift	Justification[124]
v. 17: Transgression	Death reigns (over)	Free gift	Will reign

These verses develop the typology of Adam and Christ, and the ἀλλά of verse 15 qualifies the typological comment in verse 14.[125] Adam is the "type," but that need not mean "identical" at every point. The parallel in verse 16 contrasts "one who sinned" with "the gift," but these do not appear to be natural points of comparison. Moo suggests that "condemnation" is the contrast to "the gift" and paraphrases it as "and the gift is not like the condemnation that came through the one who sinned."[126] This rendering fits the context well since the next phrase, "for the judgment from one sin resulted in condemnation," highlights the corporate implication (condemnation) that stems from the one sin. The "judgment" (κρίμα) of Adam's sin resulted in the condemnation (κατάκριμα)

---

[123] Wright, *Romans*, 528.

[124] δικαίωμα (cf. v. 18) is often used for "commandment," or "requirement" (Rom. 1:32; 2:26; 8:4), but here, contrasted with κατάκριμα, it means "justification," with an emphasis on acquittal, as from judgment. The idea of "acquittal" is emphasized in Dunn, *Romans*, 281, and Wright, *Romans*, 228. See BDAG, 249-50. Paul's use of words ending in -μα is well documented in various sources. Otfried Hofius, for instance, puts a great deal of emphasis on the presence of homoioteleuton (a rhetorical device where coordinate clauses contain words with the same endings). He stresses that in defining these words in context "we must certainly take account of the fact that they are selected for rhetorical reasons" (Hofius, "The Adam-Christ Antithesis and the Law," in *Paul and the Mosaic Law*, ed. James D. G. Dunn [Grand Rapids: Eerdmans, 1996] 171. Also, Schreiner, *Romans*, 285). It is worth noting that part of the significance of the -μα words may be owing to the fact that they often signify an emphasis on the results of the action involved; in this case, condemnation, justification, etc. See, BDF 59, ß 109; Moo, *Romans*, 338 n. 108.

[125] Moo, *Romans*, 334.

[126] "The advantage of our rendering is that it provides the most natural basis for the expansion of v. 16b, which focuses on two aspects in which Adam's act differs from Christ's: number of sins taken into account, and outcome" (ibid., 337 n. 104).

of his posterity, and condemnation is primarily stative in this text. This fits with the reading of verse 12 suggested above, and it accounts for the phrase "by the trespass of the one, many died" (v. 15). Adam's single act brings death, the condemnation of God, on all who follow him. This is contrasted with "the gift from many trespasses resulted in justification" (v. 16c). The "imbalance" of Christ's work in comparison with Adam's is made evident here and explained in further detail in verse 17, where the reign of death following the trespass of the one is contrasted with the reign of those who receive the free gift of righteousness.[127]

Again, the unique nature of Adam's sin as the foundation for sin and death is at the forefront. This further strengthens the case that Paul is mainly concerned with the corporate nature of the relationship between Adam and humanity—not foremost with the personal sins people commit. The concept of "personal sin" only appears in this text to further contrast the roles of Adam and Christ. Adam's sin was without precedent, but the free gift that flowed from Christ and results in justification follows on the heels of "many transgressions." While innocence preceded Adam's disobedience, universal guilt is the backdrop against which the free gift of God in Christ shines. After the human race thoroughly establishes itself as the offspring of Adam, and after sin and death are manifestly entrenched in the world, the exceeding grace of God is manifested.

What Obedience? Verses 18-19

Verse 18 both sums up verses 15-17 (Ἄρα οὖν) and completes, or restates and completes, verse 12.[128] The wording is quite dense and elliptical but not too hard to render: "Therefore, just as through the transgression of the one there resulted condemnation for all men, so also through the

---

[127] Not limited to the idea of a "logical future" but pointing toward an eschatological consummation, which includes the present. There is no need to limit this to a "logical future," particularly in light of the eschatological language coming in chapter 6 regarding being "baptized," "buried," and "raised" in Christ, or nearly all of chapter 8 for that matter. Paul's eschatology is inclusive of the present, but not limited to it—even if speaking of individual salvation.

[128] The similarities with verse twelve are evident, note particularly the initial position of the prepositional phrase with διά emphasizing the beginning with one man and leading to the result for "the world" (v. 12) or "the many" (v. 18). Byrne's comments are applicable: "Paul is now [v. 18] in a position . . . to allow the full expression of the comparison/contrast broken off at the end of v. 12 to go ahead. The basis of the similarity remains the fact that in both cases "one" has an influence on 'all.' The contrast lies in the differing effects: 'condemnation' . . . for all in the one instance, 'justification leading to life' . . . in the other. 'Condemnation' here is tantamount to death—so that the first half of v. 18 basically recasts the statement of the 'Adam' side originally given in v 12." Brendan Byrne, *Romans*: Sacra Pagina Series, vol. 6 (Collegeville, Minn.: The Liturgical Press, 1996), 180.

righteous act of the one there resulted the justification that leads to life for all men."[129] There is considerable debate over whether Christ's "righteous act," together with "the obedience of the one" (v. 19), refers to his death on the cross only or whether it includes his obedience during his life.[130] There is little doubt that Paul is referring to the cross as the instrument that brings about justification, as is evident in 5:9 ("justified by his blood"). Some, however, assert that Paul has more in mind here than Christ's death on the cross, understanding "obedience" to mean Christ's total obedience during his life and on the cross.[131] Others assert that Paul's purpose is here restricted to the cross.[132] While Christ's life and death

---

[129] There is some question as to how ἑνὸς δικαιώματος should be rendered, but most understand ἑνὸς to refer to "one" man, i.e., Christ, rather than to "one righteous act," just as they understand ἑνὸς in ἑνὸς παραπτώματος to refer to Adam rather than modifying παραπτώματος. See Cranfield, *Romans*, 289; Dunn, *Romans*, 283; Fitzmyer, *Romans*, 420-21; Käsemann, *Romans*, 156; Moo, *Romans*, 341 n. 125, also, n. 127; Anders Nygren, *Commentary on Romans*, trans. Carl C. Rasmussen (Philadelphia: Muhlenberg Press, 1949), 223; Schreiner, *Romans*, 286 n. 8; Ulrich Wilckens, *Der Brief an die Römer*, teilband 1: *Röm 1–5*, Evangelisch-Katholisch Kommentar zum Neuen Testament 6/1 (Züruch: Benziger/Neukirchen-Vluyn: Neukirchener Verlag, 1978), 326; Wright, *Romans*, 528-29. Examples of scholars who take ἑνὸς as modifying "transgression" and "righteous act" are Murray, *Romans*, 199; W. Sanday and A. C. Headlam, *A Critical and Exegetical Commentary on the Epistle to the Romans*, ICC (Edinburgh: T & T Clark, 1902), 141; Schlatter, *Romans*, 131. As for the phrase εἰς δικαίωσιν ζωῆς, often translated simply, "the justification of life," it is an eschatological phrase that points toward the goal of Christ's representative role as the second Adam. As Adam's life was meant to move forward, so Christ obeys and inaugurates the fulfillment of God's purpose for humanity, i.e., "life," and eternal life at that (v. 21). "Life" is the result of the free gift of justification. As Vos states: "Justification is a δικαίωσιν ζωῆς' (justification of life), and the 'life' thus declared to be its consequent is the endless life, that of which it is promised that the saints 'shall reign' in it, Rom. v. 18-21" (Geerhardus Vos, *The Pauline Eschatology* [Princeton: Princeton University Press, 1930; reprint, Phillipsburg: N.J.: Presbyterian and Reformed, 1994], 57). This does not mean that verse 18 is *only* future oriented; "it certainly includes the eternal life of the consummate state, although it is not necessarily restricted to that" (ibid., 269).

[130] This is often spoken of in terms of "active" and "passive" obedience, the former referring to Jesus' positive acts of obedience during his life and the latter to his sacrificial death on the cross. This distinction is often misunderstood and wrongly characterized. It usually does not mean that Christ's obedience can be neatly portioned off as either active or passive; that dying on the cross did not involve "active" obedience, or that the obedience rendered during his lifetime did not involve passive obedience, e.g., surrendering to his Father's will, etc. It is typically a theological distinction. This distinction is not a concern here, but the conclusions reached here certainly can be applied in working out such distinctions and/or assessing their usefulness.

[131] Cranfield, for instance, says, "Paul means not just His atoning death but the obedience of His life as a whole, His loving God with all His heart and soul and mind and strength, and his neighbor with complete sincerity, which is the righteous conduct which God's law requires" (*Romans*, 289). Piper, though believing Paul has more in mind than Calvary, nevertheless asserts that the more important issue is whether Christ's "righteous act," his "obedience" (v. 19), counts for the justification of the believer, rather than whether Paul has Jesus' whole life in mind (*Counted Righteous*, 110).

[132] Schreiner believes the reference is to the cross, but holds out that "it is possible that his whole life is in view" (*Romans*, 287). Ridderbos sees both the "act of righteousness," and the "obedience," as referring to Christ's death (Herman Ridderbos, *Paul: An Outline of His Theology*, trans. John Richard De Witt [Grand Rapids: Eerdmans, 1975], 167). Further examples of those who understand an exclusive reference to the cross are Dunn, *Romans*, 283; and Schlatter, *Romans*, 131. Wright also thinks the cross is in view here, but it is specifically Jesus' "messianic action," as the Isaianic servant of YHWH (*Romans*, 529).

cannot be separated, it does seem that Paul's main focus is on Christ's death as the supreme act of righteousness, his act of obedience that secures the status of "righteousness" for those identified with him.[133]

As noted above, Adam's disobedience is specifically described as "transgression" (v. 14). Paul himself makes a distinction between the "sinning" of those who lived between Adam and Moses, and the "transgression of Adam" (τῆς παραβάσεως Αδὰμ) which, presumably like the sin of those who had the Mosaic law, was a sin against a specific, known command. Therefore, the "trespass of the one" (v. 18) and the "disobedience of the one" (v. 19) is, according to the text, a transgression against a specific command of God. It follows that there must be some correspondence, some point of similarity, between the disobedience of Adam as disobedience against God's command and the obedience of Christ as obedience to God's command.

One obvious parallel text that speaks of Christ's obedience specifically in terms of his death is Philippians 2:8, where Paul writes of Christ's obedience to death on the cross. There is, however, no explicit command in view. In neither Philippians 2:8 or Romans 5:19 does Paul assert that Christ's obedience is limited to the cross, but he does place particular emphasis upon that event as, in Moo's words, "the ultimate act of obedience."[134] In Galatians 3:13 the cross is linked to the law in that Christ "became a curse for us," specifically a curse derived from the law: "Cursed is everyone who is hanged on a tree." In that sense, Christ did fulfill the law by dying under its curse. This creates a problem if Christ's "active" obedience is conceived as being limited to his active fulfillment of the law's demands. If the distinction is pressed, Galatians 3:13 emphasizes a more "passive" obedience in regard to the law, rather than an active fulfillment of it, since his death was under the curse of the law.

As far as "active" or "passive" obedience is concerned, there is scriptural warrant for viewing the cross as an act of both passive and active obedience.[135] The Gospels in particular show how the cross

---

[133] It is not as if Christ could have merely turned up in Jerusalem at Passover and gone to the cross on Friday. His ministry and mission encompass his life, death, and resurrection. The question is whether the interpretation of this text demands that everything be seen explicitly in verses 18-19.

[134] Moo, *Romans*, 344.

[135] In John 6:38, Jesus says, "For I have come down from heaven, not to do my own will but the will of him who sent me." In Gethsemane Jesus prays that the Father might let "this cup" pass, but nevertheless submits himself to his Father's will (Matt. 26:42; Mark 14:36; Luke 21:42).

exhibits both aspects of obedience. John records Jesus as saying that his death is something that he does willingly, and he does so on the basis of a command from his Father: "No one takes it [life] from me, but I lay it down by my own accord. I have authority to lay it down and authority to raise it up again. This commandment I have from my Father" (10:18). The distinction between active and passive may promote precision in theological discussion, but it should not be pressed to the point where it winds up with two mutually exclusive kinds of obedience. It is difficult, if not impossible, to conceive of an act that is either passive or active.

The theological distinction should not be pressed into service beyond what it intended to do, and that is to make the rather common-sense observation that obedience to God has two sides: (1) a willing submission to his will, and (2) the pursuit to do his will. It is sufficient to say that here Paul has in mind the contrast between Adam's disobedience and Christ's obedience in so far as they affect those identified with them. What God commands is that Christ, as the second Adam and in contrast to Adam, perfectly carries out the will of God. He perfectly obeys his Father's commands, including that he lay down his life. In the historical-redemptive context of Romans 5:12-21, the decisive moment of Christ's faithful obedience is on the cross.[136]

ONE FOR MANY: A BIBLICAL-THEOLOGICAL PERSPECTIVE

It is clear so far that Paul sets up two distinct possibilities for humanity, and each possibility is established by one for many. This is primarily a forensic distinction. Paul divides up all humanity between two representatives, often identified as two *covenantal* heads. Some may object to this description on the basis that the Bible does not refer to a covenant with Adam. That observation is correct, and has led some to reject any notion of a "covenant" with regard to Adam. However, if "covenant" is conceived as simply denoting a particular relationship between two parties based on some sort of agreement containing certain stipulations and promises, etc., then it hardly seems objectionable to describe the relationship between God and

---

[136] Christ's obedience to "the law" as either that which qualified him as a perfect sacrifice and/or as that which is counted for the believer's righteousness is not spelled out in full in this text.

Adam as a covenant.[137] It is at least "covenant-like," in so far as the major redemptive covenants in the Bible reflect or re-establish the relationship between God and Adam.[138] This is the perspective held in the Reformed tradition, as is evident in the phrase "federal theology."[139] On the other hand, "covenant" theology is not limited to the Reformed tradition, and other "covenant" theologies may differ substantially from the Reformed variety.[140] What matters here is that Paul

---

[137] Although this is not the place to pursue the subject at length, Reformed theology, more than any other, is primarily covenant theology. A classic Reformed understanding is provided in Ursinus's definition of a covenant: "A covenant in general is a mutual contract, or agreement between two parties, in which the one party binds itself to the other to accomplish something upon certain conditions, giving or receiving something, which is accompanied with certain outward signs and symbols, for the purpose of ratifying in the most solemn manner the contract entered into, and for the sake of confirming it, that the engagement may be kept inviolate." *The Commentary of Dr. Zacharias Ursinus on the Heidelberg Catechism*, trans. G. W. Willard (Columbus, Ohio: Scott and Bascom, 1851; reprint, Phillipsburg, N.J.: P&R, n.d.), 97 (page citation is for both editions). This definition is given here because the covenant theme in Romans 5:12-21 is developed to the greatest extent in the Reformed tradition, and because it has a "covenant of works" at its foundation, which stresses the unique, representative nature of the relationship that Adam and Christ have with the human race, respectively. There are many aspects of the traditional covenantal view, but chief among them is the dominant theme of a "covenant of works" established by God for Adam, in which Adam had to obey God on the strength of his own innocent integrity (thus, the "covenant of works" may also be called a "covenant of nature" with "nature" referring to Adam's original state of innocence). Adam, of course, failed to obey. But where Adam failed, Christ obeyed on the basis of his own strength and will, and fulfilled the original covenant, and the blessings of that covenant flow to all who are identified with Christ, just as the consequences of Adam's sin flowed to those identified with him. While many object to the phrase "covenant of works," it seems nevertheless clear that there was a principle of "works" in so far as Adam had to obey what God commanded him to do. It also seems clear that Christ's fundamental act as described by Paul was an act of obedience, and this obedience, as Adam's disobedience, is the foundation for the status conferred to those related to him. Regardless of how one works out the details, a covenant relationship provides the best conceptual framework for describing these relationships. For background see, John Murray, "Covenant theology," in *The Collected Writings of John Murray*, vol. 4 (Edinburgh: Banner of Truth, 1977), 4:216-40. Murray provides a helpful, concise discussion of the development of covenant theology and on the "conditional" and "unconditional" nature of the covenant of grace. For a historical study of the development of federal theology by a scholar who sees continuity between Calvin and his successors, see Peter A. Lillback, *The Binding of God* (Grand Rapids: Baker; Carlisle, U. K.: Paternoster, 2001). A helpful discussion of covenant theology as set forth in the Heidelberg Catechism and in Ursinus's commentary, and which interacts with major criticisms aimed at "sub-Protestant contract theology" is found in R. Scott Clark and Joel Beeke, "Ursinus, Oxford and the Westminster Divines," in *The Westminster Confession into the 21ˢᵗ Century: Essays in Remembrance of the 350ᵗʰ Anniversary of the Publication of the Westminster Confession of Faith*, vol. 2, ed. J Ligon Duncan (Christian Focus Publications, 2005), 1-32.

[138] Some have sought to show a covenant in Eden on the basis of Hosea 6:7, "They broke my covenant like Adam." Most modern scholars, however, understand "Adam" as a place name, thus, "like at Adam." This text is too disputed to rest on without more investigation.

[139] Though "federal" may be labeled a "theological" rather than a "biblical" term, it seems often overlooked that "federal" is simply a derivative of *foedus*, Latin for "covenant." I am aware of the debates that surround the use of the terms *foedus, testamentum*, and *pactum* in Reformed theology. That issue, though important for the historical debate, is out of the purview of the present work. It need only be remembered that historically the word "federal" refers to an altogether biblical concept.

[140] A primary example is N. T. Wright. Although covenant plays a fundamental role in Wright's work in general, the piece that relates most clearly to Romans 5:12-21, besides his *Romans*, is "Adam, Israel, and the Messiah" in *Climax of the Covenant: Christ and the Law in Pauline Theology*

establishes the concept of representation as the most basic component of God's plan of creation and redemption.

Representation: A Redemptive-Historical Structure

That Paul has a definite theological understanding of the representative
roles of Adam and Christ in relation to humanity, of the solidarity of
all under one of the two covenant heads, is evident from 1 Corinthians
15:21-22. There Paul argues that "since death came through a man,
also the resurrection of the dead comes through a man" (v. 21). He then
gives the ground for his assertion: "for just as (ὥσπερ) all die in Adam,
so also (οὕτως καὶ) in Christ all shall be made alive." If these verses were
not enough, Gaffin shows convincingly that the context argues for a
corporate relationship. In 15:20, Paul refers to Christ as the "firstfruits"

(Philadelphia: Fortress, 1993), 18-40. With textual support Wright shows that God is "undoing the
sin of Adam" in his dealings with Abraham and subsequently with Israel, and that a "new creation"
is set in process in God's people. "Israel is, or is to become, God's intended true humanity" (ibid.,
21). Adam's disobedience, however, was at work in Israel and when that disobedience met Torah it
magnified the sin in and among God's covenant people. Israel, like Adam, failed in its calling to be
the true people of God. What Jesus did, therefore, was fulfill Israel's role as redeemer of "Adamic
humanity." Adam's sin, made exceedingly manifest by the negative role of Torah (a negative role for
a positive reason) was "drawn onto Israel's representative and so dealt with on the Cross." In fulfilling Israel's role, Jesus fulfills Adam's role (ibid., 38-39). The connection Wright draws from Adam
through Abraham and Israel and through Christ highlights the essential covenantal relationship
between God and his people. It must be pointed out, however, that in spite of points of agreement,
Wright's covenant theology and Reformed covenant theology are similar only in name at many
fundamental points. Wright also develops Jesus' role as Israel's representative in his *Romans.* Jesus'
obedience is that of the servant from Isaiah 53. It is the obedience "to the saving purpose of YHWH,
the plan marked out for Israel from the beginning but that, through Israel's disobedience, only the
servant, as an individual, can now accomplish." Jesus' obedience is his faithfulness as Messiah "to
God's commission (as in 3:22), to the plan to bring salvation to the world" (*Romans,* 529). Two
points deserve comment here. In the first place, Wright chides traditional Reformed theology for the
distinction between "active" and "passive" obedience, but they are not, as mentioned above, always
so neatly separated. Even those who do not make a distinction between active and passive obedience
may still hold to the reckoning of Christ's righteousness. More problematic is Wright's rather pointed
comment that Jesus' role was not "his amassing a treasury of merit through Torah obedience" (ibid.).
On one hand, I could not agree more. However, while some may speak in these kinds of terms, the
idea of a treasury of merit earned by Jesus and meted out to believers is not an accurate description
of Reformed soteriology in general.
    Secondly, Wright seems to create an unwarranted gap between Jesus' role as representative and
the issue of keeping the law. Wright holds that law in this text, rather than being focused on obedience, which "would be beside the point," has a "darker" role. While he is correct to say that the stress
here is on the negative role of the law, is not the primary reason the law has a negative role precisely
because it requires obedience? The negative role becomes clear when the law was not obeyed. I agree
with the "darker" role of the law, but it is precisely the demand for obedience that makes it so. Doing
what Israel (and Adam) failed to do must certainly include obedience to God's commands. Even if the
primary command was to be the true servant of YHWH (the revealed name of God who gave Torah
and commands Israel, his servant, to keep it), how can one be Israel apart from keeping Torah? Israel
was enjoined time and again to "keep" and "obey" Torah. The command to fulfill Israel's role as
the people of God certainly does not seem to exclude keeping Torah, even if keeping Torah is not the
explicit point of this text.

(ἀπαρχή), and the predominately cultic background of this word serves to establish a representative context.[141] The offerings of "firstfruits" represented a greater whole (grain, livestock, etc.), and signified "the notion of organic connection and unity, the inseparability of the initial quantity from the whole."[142] As such, Christ's resurrection is not just an indication of what will happen to believers (though it includes that); "it is the actual beginning of the general event."[143] With this background, verses 21-22 make it clear that the resurrection will take place only as believers are "in Christ"; that is, just as all died "in Adam," so the resurrection will only take place as a corporate event in Christ, who is the "firstfruits."[144] Just as Paul describes the most fundamental level of redemption in terms of the Adam-Christ parallel in Romans 5, so in 1 Corinthians 15 he refers to the same parallel in relation to the consummation of redemptive history. Taken together, 1 Corinthians 15 and Romans 5 suggest that Paul's fundamental theological framework of redemptive history is primarily representational and unfolds around the figures of the first and second Adams.

A biblical current. Returning to Romans 5, recognizing Adam and Christ as covenantal and/or representative heads fits well with the flow of this text. Paul deals with the fundamental issues of the history of redemption. There is nothing more basic to redemption than the unfolding of God's plan to save Adam's race, and this happens in a series of covenant relationships from the Noahic, to the Abrahamic, through the Mosaic, and the Davidic, and coming to fruition in the new covenant.[145] Each of those major covenants works toward the final act of redemption in the cross of Christ, with each reflecting at least some elements of the relationship between God and Adam as recorded in Genesis 1–2 and heading toward the redemption of that relationship broken in Genesis 3.

---

[141] Richard B. Gaffin Jr., *Resurrection and Redemption: A Study in Paul's Soteriology*, 2ⁿᵈ ed. (Phillipsburg, N.J.: Presbyterian and Reformed, 1987), 34. Gaffin cites the following texts, Exodus 23:19; Leviticus 23:10; Numbers 15:20f.; 18:8, 11f.; Deuteronomy 18:4; 26:2, 10, as examples.

[142] Ibid., 34. This is in contrast to understanding "firstfruits" as exclusively temporal, that is, as only the beginning of the harvest, rather than the beginning as representing the entire harvest that was yet to come.

[143] Ibid., 35.

[144] Ibid., 36.

[145] This covenantal schema for understanding the history of redemption from a biblical-theological perspective can be seen in Geerhardus Vos's *Biblical Theology*.

Paul is working at the most basic level showing what had to take place in order for there to be justification, reconciliation, and peace with God (5:1, 11). And the issues that lie behind all other considerations are that humanity is viewed through one of two figures, either Adam or Christ, whose actions determine the status for each individual person, and that Paul is not concerned here to focus on either the personal sin or the righteousness that will flow from each state.[146] It is evident in this text that Paul is working on a large canvas. He begins with the entrance of sin and death (v. 12) and then proves the universality of sin and death (vv. 13-14). From there he develops an idea of the two kingdoms; a kingdom of sin and death over against a kingdom of righteousness and life (vv. 15-17). In both kingdoms the actions of one affects the many, but the results are radically different. One results in condemnation, the other, justification. He then identifies specifically the two actions that determine the status (sinner or righteous) of all people (vv. 18-19). Ridderbos has captured the panoramic vision of this text:

> The presupposition of the whole chain of reasoning lies in the inclusion in the supra-individual situation of sin and death represented by Adam. Here again the basic structures of the Pauline theology are not individualizing, but redemptive-historical, and corporate. It is a matter of two different modes of existence, that of the old and that of the new man, which are determined by two different aeons, and concerning which an all embracing decision has been made in Adam and in Christ. [147]

A positive standing, not a transformation. As stated above, Christ came into a situation caused by Adam; he did not begin with a clean slate but came into a world that was at enmity with God. This point should not be pressed to where Christ's work is viewed as some sort of clean up mission. On the contrary, there is a theme of recapitulation in the parallel. The "obedience" rendered by Christ not only followed Adam's dis-

---

[146] As Wright puts it: "To be a 'sinner' is, to be sure, more than a mere status. It involves committing actual sins. But it is the status that interests Paul here. Likewise, to be 'righteous,' as will be apparent in the next chapter, is more than simply status, but again it is the status that matters here. Justification, rooted in the cross and anticipating the verdict of the last day, gives people a new status, ahead of the performance of appropriate deeds" (*Romans*, 529).

[147] Ridderbos, *Paul*, 99. This emphasis also argues against the claim that traditional views of justification are only concerned with individual salvation and ignore the corporate aspect. The individual is always in the context of being part of the people of God—a corporate body of those "made righteous" through Christ.

obedience, it is also the manifestation of what Adam *should* have done. Christ is truly the Second Adam who succeeds where the first failed. That is why Paul stresses the superior nature of the "free gift" over that which came from Adam (vv. 15-17).[148] The "free gift" flows from the fulfillment of God's purpose in creation, and so "how much more" does that surpass whatever came through the trespass of Adam? The superiority of the "free gift" made available by the obedience of Christ points back to a principle in Genesis 1–2 which illuminates the meaning of "made righteous" as referring to a positive status.

According to Genesis 1:26, God created man in order to exercise dominion over all God's creation. This intention is expressed in the first "command" given to Adam and Eve, when they were told, "Be fruitful and multiply, fill the earth and subdue it. Rule over the fish of the sea and the birds of the sky and over everything that moves on the earth" (1:28).[149] Adam was not born into a static existence, but one that included work—not random work, but work with a goal: the subjugation of God's creation in the context of a perfect relationship with his Creator. In short, though everything in creation was "very good," there was still a sense in which there was movement toward the fulfillment of creation. Geerhardus Vos identifies this as "pre-redemptive eschatology."[150] This end for which God created the world existed without the imposition of sin.[151] This is no mere speculation on "what would have happened," but is the intention made explicit in the narrative. This goal, of course, was not reached because of Adam's disobedience.[152] Christ,

---

[148] Paul also emphasizes a contrast between Adam and Christ in 1 Corinthians 15:45-59. Both the theme of representation and the inferior/superior motif are present. In that text Paul shows that "Christ accomplishes far more than the restoration of what Adam ever lost, he places the two over against each other . . . as the representatives of two successive stages in the carrying out of God's sublime purpose for humanity" (Geerhardus Vos, "The Theology of Paul," in *Redemptive History and Biblical Interpretation: The Shorter Writings of Geerhardus Vos*, ed. Richard B. Gaffin Jr. [Phillipsburg, N.J.: Presbyterian and Reformed, 1980], 259).

[149] NASB.

[150] Geerhardus Vos, *The Eschatology of the Old Testament*, ed. James T. Dennison (Phillipsburg, N.J.: Presbyterian and Reformed, 2001), 73. To support his claim, Vos suggests that the inauguration of the Sabbath (2:3) points to the idea of "consummation" and "an eschatological sign because its meaning lies in the relation of man and God" (ibid., 75).

[151] "There is an absolute end posited for the universe before and apart from sin. The universe as created, was only a beginning, the meaning of which was not perpetuation, but attainment. The principle of God's relation to the world from the outset was a principle of action or eventuation" (ibid., 73).

[152] Note also that this conclusion is not based on a predetermined commitment to the question of whether Adam lived in some kind of probation period. I do believe, however, that Adam was "tested" just as Israel and ultimately Christ were tested. That subject will be discussed in some detail in a forthcoming biblical theology of justification.

however, as the Second Adam, is not only the representative that sets the situation to rights; he ushers in the full eschatological reality for which Adam was intended.[153] The Second Adam did not merely provide a remedy for the first Adam's sin; he also succeeded where the first failed. How else could he really be a Second Adam? What Christ achieved by his obedience was the positive status "righteous" (v. 19) that leads to eschatological life (v. 18), which is the eternal reign of grace through righteousness (v. 21). In other words, Christ's obedience does, in fact, establish a positive status that is part of, and leads to, eschatological consummation—the fulfillment of the intention for Adam.[154]

With this larger biblical framework in mind we return to καθίστημι. It makes sense for Paul to choose this word rather than a more limited word such as λογίζομαι because he is dealing with the foundations of redemption and not with the application or appropriation of redemption. The basic idea of 5:19 as it regards Christ and the many can be seen in the following:

Actor/Subject	Action	Result
Christ	Obedience	Righteous (status)

This pattern is different from Romans 4, where the primary actor is Abraham and the action is faith. The result, however, is similar. Where Abraham's faith was reckoned to him for righteousness, here Jesus' obedience results in many being made "righteous." As argued above, the phrase "made righteous" is surely stative. The discussion of the semantic domain of καθίστημι revealed that the word is not used as a synonym for λογίζομαι, and that it refers usually to an appointment or assignment to a position and that it can also refer to an actual state. It is difficult to separate an appointed position from the "state" of that position. Ultimately the distinction need not be pressed, because it really boils down to a question of emphasis, either on the appointment or the

---

[153] As Vos says elsewhere: "What we inherit in the second Adam is not restricted to what we lost in the first Adam: it is much rather the full realization of what the first Adam would have achieved for us had he remained unfallen and had been confirmed in his state" ("Doctrine of the Covenant in Reformed Theology," in *Redemptive History and Biblical Interpretation: The Shorter Writings of Geerhardus Vos,* ed. Richard B. Gaffin Jr. [Phillipsburg, N.J.: Presbyterian and Reformed, 1980], 243).

[154] Yet this is not God's "plan B" because God's plan for humanity is not fulfilled in the type, but in the "one who was to come" (v. 14).

state. The reason some theologians shy away from a stative meaning here is that they are afraid that if we take Paul as referring to a state, then there might be some sense in which the status "righteous" becomes grounded to some extent in the believer's own acts of righteousness. This fear, however, amounts to "building a hedge around Torah."[155]

Being "made" righteous, even being "appointed" righteous, means that one really is righteous, but it clearly does not mean that Paul is talking about being made righteous on the basis of one's own works, or that he is talking about some sort of transformative righteousness.[156] Interpreters who worry that the translation "made righteous" might sneak in a notion of infused righteousness or open the door for personal acts of righteousness ignore the fact that καθίστημι is not typically used in reference to the actions that characterize the person either "appointed" or "made to be" in whatever position. The word emphasizes *status*, not personal actions.

If the word καθίστημι itself is not enough, there is nothing in the context that argues for a transformative righteousness or for personal righteousness as the ground for the statement made in verse 19. Not even Paul's accounting for the ground and universal nature of sin (v. 12), or his mention of the actual sins committed by those living from Adam to Moses (vv. 13-14), disrupts the parallel between Adam and Christ. There is an inescapable forensic context in the text that builds up to a climax in verse 19. The result of Christ's obedience is that "many will be made righteous."[157] They will be viewed by God as having a right status before him, and the ground of that status is the obedience of Christ.

---

[155] This phrase refers to the practice of making an extra law in order to help protect against breaking an actual law.

[156] This, of course, does not deny that a *transformation* takes place, but that the *transformation* logically follows the declared status. God's word of justification not only declares something; it creates what it declares. The point here is that one aspect can be emphasized and even given logical priority over the other.

[157] The emphasis here is on the future eschatological declaration. Many interpret the word κατασ-ταθήσονται as a "logical future" referring to an action that is ongoing in the present in each generation of believers. For instance see Murray, *Romans*, 206. Dunn, on the other hand, understands it to refer to "the future ratification of the final judgment" (*Romans*, 285). An either/or stance need not be adopted. The end-time declaration is the same as the declaration in the present, but given the vast scope of the history of redemption in this text stretching from the beginning of redemptive history to its fulfillment in Christ the future consummation, the final chapter of redemption, may well receive emphasis.

CONCLUSION

On the textual level Paul does not use the same metaphor he employs in chapter 4. However, there is no need to dispense entirely with the "reckoning" metaphor in regard to Romans 5:12-21. If Christ's obedience has the result that "many will be made righteous," then that necessarily means that there must be a way in which God considers Christ's obedience as the ground upon which he will view "sinners" as "righteous." Theologically we may well describe this by saying that God indeed "counts" Christ's obedience as the ground of the believer's righteousness.[158] To follow the above outline, Christ's obedience "counts" for our righteous status. Taken together with Romans 4, a biblical theology of how a believer is justified begins to take shape. In order for faith to be reckoned for righteousness, a more fundamental redemptive act must take place. Adam's sin, and the resulting spread of sin and death into the world so that "condemnation" became the lot of the world, had to be dealt with. This was accomplished through the second Adam, the second representative head, Jesus Christ.

Romans 5 constitutes, therefore, the very *foundation* of Paul's doctrine of salvation, because the ground for the status "righteous" had to be attained before it could be applied. In this way, Romans 4 sets forth the application of Romans 5. The righteous status, made possible by Christ's obedience, is applied to the believer when he puts his faith in God. Christ's obedience "counts" for the status that is secured at the cross, and appropriated by faith, through which comes the declaration of the actual status, "righteous."

It is important to emphasize what the texts say in their own terms, but separately neither text paints a full picture in regard to the question of "imputation." When read together, however, the various details begin to come into focus. With that in mind we now turn to one more major text in Paul. With the foundation and appropriation of righteousness established, we now consider the way by which Christ has secured our "righteousness," and what it means to "become the righteousness of God."

---

[158] There must be some way by which we conceive of how Christ's obedience is applied to us. Even if Christ's obedience is that of fulfilling the role of the Messiah (i.e., Wright), that obedience still must be applied to people (it must "count" for them in someway) if God is going to consider them righteous.

FOUR

THE PROVISION OF
RIGHTEOUSNESS:
2 CORINTHIANS 5:21

SECOND CORINTHIANS 5:21, like Romans 4:3 and 5:19, is a perpetual centerpiece in the discussion of the imputation of Christ's righteousness. To some readers this may seem curious given that the text does not say explicitly that sins are reckoned to Christ or that Christ's righteousness is reckoned to believers. "God made him who knew no sin, to be sin for us, that we might become the righteousness of God in him." This verse is about what God accomplished in Christ on the cross and what that means for, and how it is applied to, believers. God acts through Christ and the result is righteousness for those "in him."

Even without explicit reference, it is not too difficult to see why 2 Corinthians 5:21 has been among the cardinal texts in this ongoing debate. There are many critical issues in this verse and context, but as with the earlier chapters, the goal here is to isolate those elements that have direct bearing on the issue at hand, relying on the context to serve as a guide for interpretation. The verse will be discussed in terms of what Paul means by "made to be sin," what he means by "become the righteousness of God," and the significance of union with Christ for both this text and the subject of imputation of righteousness in general. Once these elements are investigated, it will be evident why this verse is so crucial to the discussion.

"MADE TO BE SIN":
THE GROUND FOR BECOMING THE RIGHTEOUSNESS OF GOD

There is a great deal of debate over the meaning of the phrase "made to be sin" (ἁμαρτίαν ἐποίησεν). Many readers understand this phrase to mean that Christ was "made to be sin," obviously not in terms of being sinful himself, but that he was in some way "identified with sinful humanity."[1] On the other hand it could mean "sin offering," referring to the Old Testament sacrificial system.[2] The position taken here is that "made to be sin" is sacrificial language and that Paul is speaking of Christ as a sacrifice for sin. This interpretation finds support in the language and concepts related to sacrifices, particularly, but not exactly corresponding to the sin offering in the Old Testament. This interpretation also makes sense in a text that speaks of reconciliation, and it fits the context of the verse.

---

[1] Victor Paul Furnish, *II Corinthians*, AB (New York: Doubleday, 1984), 340. This view is also held, sometimes with modifications or different emphases, by various scholars. Rudolph Bultmann, *The Second Letter to the Corinthians*, trans. Roy A. Harrisville (Minneapolis: Augsburg, 1985), 165. Bultmann follows H. Windisch, *Der zweite Korintherbrief*, MeyerK 6 (Göttingen: Vandenhoeck and Ruprecht, 1924), 197-99. Philip E. Hughes, *The Second Epistle to the Corinthians*, NICNT (Grand Rapids: Eerdmans, 1962), 213-15. Hughes understands Paul to mean that "God the Father made his innocent incarnate Son the object of His wrath and judgment" (ibid., 213). Margaret E. Thrall, *The Second Epistle to the Corinthians*, ICC (Edinburgh: T & T Clark, 1994), 441-42. Thrall concedes that Paul uses "sacrificial language" and the possibility that Paul alludes to Isaiah 53, but she thinks that the phrase should "be understood in terms more personal than that of "sin offering" (ibid., 442). Charles Hodge, *2 Corinthians*, Crossway Classic Commentaries (Wheaton: Crossway, 1995), 120. Hodge denies that "sin offering" is in view because the Septuagint uses ἁμαρτία in the genitive (ἁμαρτίας) when referring to "sin offering," and because Paul uses the same word, ἁμαρτίαν, "in the ordinary sense" in this verse. He does say that whether it means "sin" or "sin offering," the result is similar: "The meaning in either case is the same, for the only sense in which Christ was made to be sin is that he bore the guilt of sin; in this sense every sin-offering was made sin" (ibid., 120). Hodge emphasizes the substitutionary element in this verse. Paul Barnett, *The Second Epistle to the Corinthians*, NICNT (Grand Rapids: Eerdmans, 1997), 313-14. Barnett does not come down forcefully on the issue. He does, however, reject the rendering "sin offering," and states that "Paul's words summarize without explaining Isaiah 52:13–53:12" (ibid., 314 n. 65). Jan Lambrecht, *Second Corinthians*, Sacra Pagina Series, vol. 8 (Collegeville, Minn.: The Liturgical Press, 1999), 101.

[2] Linda Belleville, "Gospel and Kerygma in 2 Corinthians," in *Gospel in Paul: Studies on Corinthians, Galatians, and Romans*, Festschrift for Richard Longenecker, ed. L. A. Jervis and P. Richardson (Sheffield: Sheffield Academic, 1995), 151-52; idem, *2 Corinthians*, InterVarsity New Testament Commentaries Series (Downers Grove: InterVarsity, 1996), 159; James M. Scott, *2 Corinthians*, New International Biblical Commentary (Peabody, Mass.: Hendrickson, 1998), 142; Scott J. Hafemann, *Second Corinthians*, NIV Application Commentary (Grand Rapids: Zondervan, 2001), 247. Belleville, Scott, and Hafemann all connect "sin offering" with the "Suffering Servant" of Isaiah 52–53. It should be noted, however, that the link with Isaiah's servant is not limited to those who interpret ἁμαρτίαν ἐποίησεν as "sin offering." It should also be noted that the "identification" theme is not at all absent in the "sin offering" view.

"Made to Be Sin": Old Testament Background

The Septuagint translators sometimes render חַטָּאת ("sin," "sin offering") with ἁμαρτία. Typically the phrases the translator employs are περὶ τῆς ἁμαρτίας; περὶ ἁμαρτίας; and τὸ περὶ τῆς ἁμαρτίας. Leviticus 4:3 is a good example of how ἁμαρτία can be used for both "sin" and "sin offering":

> If the anointed priest sins, bringing guilt on the people, let him offer to the LORD a bull without defect as a *sin offering* [חַטָּאת, περὶ τῆς ἁμαρτίας] for the *sin* [לְחַטָּאת, περὶ τῆς ἁμαρτίας] he has committed (emphasis mine).

Similarly, Leviticus 5:6 shows that the phrase can be used both ways:

> He [the one bringing the sacrifice] shall bring his guilt offering to the LORD for his *sin* [עַל חַטָּאתוֹ, περὶ τῆς ἁμαρτίας] which he has committed [sinned], a female from the flock, a lamb or a goat as a *sin offering* [לְחַטָּאת, περὶ ἁμαρτίας], and the priest shall make atonement for him for his sin [מֵחַטָּאתוֹ, περὶ τῆς ἁμαρτίας] (emphasis mine).[3]

In addition to these texts, there is evidence that ἁμαρτία, at least with περὶ τῆς or with περὶ alone, can refer to "sin offering."[4]

---

[3] Both 4:3 and 5:6 are also cited by Richard E. Averbeck, "Sacrifices and Offerings," in *Dictionary of the Old Testament: Pentateuch*, ed. T. Desmond Alexander and David W. Baker (Downers Grove: InterVarsity), 717. Averbeck points out that while the translation "'sin offering' is problematic," it nevertheless "makes a lot of sense." Citing Jacob Milgrom (*Leviticus*, AB [New York: Doubleday, 1991], 253-54), and J. E. Hartley (*Leviticus*, WBC [Dallas: Word, 1992], 55-57), Averbeck comments that חַטָּאת may also be rendered "purification offering" (Sacrifices and Offerings, 717). Wenham opts for the translation "purification offering" in both Leviticus 4:3 and 5:6. He does this in order to show that "it [the sin offering] was not the one and only atoning sacrifice, as some commentators seem to suggest" (Gordon J. Wenham, *The Book of Leviticus*, NICOT [Grand Rapids: Eerdmans, 1979], 88). The point is well taken, but for the purposes of this study it is only important to see that חַטָּאת may be translated by ἁμαρτία in reference to "sin offering."

[4] E.g., Leviticus 5:7, 11; 7:37; 9:2-3; 12:6, 8; 14:13, 22, 31; 15:15, 30; 16:3, 5, 9; 23:19; Numbers 6:11, 16; 7:16, 22; 28, 34, 40, 46, 52, 58, 64, 70, 76, 82, 87; 8:8, 12; 15:24, 27; 28:15, 22, 30; 29:5, 11, 16, 19, 22, 25, 28, 31, 34, 38; 4 Kings (2 Kings) 12:17; 2 Chronicles 29:21, 23-24; 2 Esdras (Ezra) 6:17; 8:35; 20:34 (Neh. 10:34); Psalm 39:7 (40:7); Job 1:5; Isaiah 53:10; Ezekiel 42:13; 43:19, 21; 2 Maccabees 12:43; Baruch 1:10. These citations correspond roughly to those cited by N. T. Wright, "The Meaning of περὶ ἁμαρτίας in Romans 8:3," in *Climax of the Covenant: Christ and the Law in Pauline Theology* (Minneapolis: Fortress, 1993), 220-25. Wright explores the background of the phrase in Romans 8 and concludes that "sin offering" is the correct meaning in that text. Even with the absence of περὶ, Wright's study is suggestive for 2 Corinthians 5:21. At the very least, he makes a good case for ἁμαρτία being used for "sin offering" in the Septuagint. On the other hand, McLean takes strong exception to any idea of "sin offering" in 2 Corinthians 5:21 (Bradley H. McLean, "Absence of Atoning Sacrifice in Paul's Soteriology," *NTS* 38 [1992]: 540). McLean's study is not limited to 2 Corinthians, but as his title suggests, he challenges the entire concept of sacrificial atonement in Paul.

The link between "made to be sin" and "sin offering" is stronger if one does not try to limit Paul's meaning to a particular sacrifice or aspect of a sacrifice. That is to say, perhaps there is a more general idea of Christ's being a sacrifice for sin in this verse, rather than a one-to-one correspondence with the Old Testament "sin offering." It is what the sacrifice accomplished, not the particular sacrifice itself, that comes into focus. There are many particular aspects of the sin offering itself. For instance, the sin offering was employed for unintentional sins; it differed in procedure depending on whether the offering was for a priest, a leader, a regular worshiper, or everyone; and it was closely connected to the purification of both worshiper and the temple.[5] But regardless of whether the sin was involuntary[6] or for whom the sacrifice was performed, the point of the sacrifice and what it effected is basically the same. The general and more important idea is that sins, whether involuntary or not, were atoned for by the offering of an animal "without defect" (e.g., Lev. 5:15, 18, 25 [Eng. 6:6]; 9:2-3), with the result that the one who brought the sacrifice was forgiven (e.g., Lev. 4:20, 26, 31, 35; 5:10, 13, 16, 18, 26 [Eng. 6:7]). The blood of the sacrifice, in the various ways it was applied, made atonement for sin.[7] In this sense it seems legitimate to understand "made to be sin" in a sacrificial context.[8]

---

[5] Averbeck gives a concise review of the various participants and procedures of the sin offering ("Sacrifices and Offering," 717-20).

[6] As Averbeck shows, בִּשְׁגָגָה does not necessarily mean "unintentional," but also simply "in error," though he does cite texts where the word refers to "unintentional sins," e.g., Numbers 35:11, 15, 22-23; Joshua 20:3, 9 (ibid., 719). Leviticus 4:27-35 also deals with "unintentional sins." See Gerhard von Rad, *Old Testament Theology*, vol. 1, trans. D. M. G. Stalker (New York: Harper and Row, 1962), 258. In regard to 2 Corinthians 5:21, it does not make a difference if the "sin offering" was mostly for "unintentional sins." It is the sacrifice itself, not the particular kind of sin for which it was prescribed, that is in view.

[7] This is not to say that the rather complex rules and regulations surrounding the sin offering are unimportant. The point is, however, that the rules and regulations guided the priests and people in bringing a sacrifice that was pleasing and acceptable to God. The end result, i.e., forgiveness, is the end that the rules and regulations serve to bring about.

[8] The suggestion here in regard to a sacrificial background for "made "sin" is based on reasoning similar to that of Beale in regard to the Old Testament background of reconciliation. "That such a background has not been looked into more is perhaps due to a too narrow view of establishing parallels on a semantic basis, often to the exclusion of conceptual considerations." Greg. K. Beale, "The Old Testament Background of Reconciliation in 2 Corinthians 5–7 and Its Bearing on the Literary Problem of 2 Corinthians 6:14-7:1," *NTS* 35 (1989): 551. The contention here is that although exact parallelism may not exist between Paul's language in 2 Corinthians 5:21 and that found in the Old Testament sacrificial texts, there is nevertheless enough semantic and conceptual similarity to warrant investigation. Beale's understanding of the New Testament use of the Old Testament, like my own, is antithetical to that of McLean ("Absence of Atoning Sacrifice").

Reconciliation and sacrifice. Another reason to understand "made to be sin" as referring to a sacrifice for sin is that verse 21 is set in the context of a larger discussion of reconciliation. Paul's doctrine of reconciliation has received a great deal of attention, particularly in regard to the background of Paul's idea. The discussion centers on the appropriate background of the words *reconcile* and *reconciliation* (καταλλάσσω and καταλλαγή). The fact that the "reconciliation" word group is not common in the Septuagint has led to multiple suggestions from scholars on both semantic and/or conceptual grounds.

Because there seems to be a lack of Jewish background for "reconciliation," Breytenbach concludes that the primary background is found in Hellenistic military and political settings.[9] On the other hand, Hofius sees Isaiah 53 and its surrounding context as the background for Paul's understanding of reconciliation.[10] Kim argues that Paul's doc-

---

[9] Cilliers Breytenbach, *Versöhnung: eine Studie zur paulinischen Soteriologie* (Neukirchen: Neukirchener, 1989), 73-76. Danker sees a Greco-Roman militaristic background: "It is evident from what Paul said about God in earlier chapters of his letter that his image of God as Supreme Benefactor here finds its ultimate expression. . . . All humanity is reconciled. . . . Pronouncement of amnesty is one of the marks of a benevolent head of state." Frederick W. Danker, *II Corinthians*, Augsburg Commentary on the New Testament (Minneapolis: Augsburg, 1989), 82-83. Danker cites Caesar Augustus' *Res Gestae* as a parallel example. This Greco-Roman background also explains Paul's language: "Much of his apparently fanatic and reproving language receives elucidation from the Greco-Roman social and cultural context in which the Corinthians lived, for they were accustomed to stories about generals and heads of state who tried to win laurels for upstaging predecessors" (ibid). On the other hand, I. Howard Marshall, writing before Breytenbach, discusses the Jewish background of "reconciliation" primarily on the basis of Josephus, Philo, and 2 and 4 Maccabees. He makes a case for an Old Testament rather than a Hellenistic background, with Paul's specific idea perhaps arising from the martyr tradition in 2 and 4 Maccabees. Marshall admits that "evidence . . . is admittedly very thin," but sees Paul's emphasis on reconciliation as an act of God rather than man, in which God himself provides "an atonement for sin and so reconciled them to himself," as an indication that the Maccabean background is a "catalyst" for Paul's doctrine. As Marshall himself says, "The point is beyond proof" (Marshall, "The Meaning of 'Reconciliation,'" in *Unity and Diversity in New Testament Theology: Essays in Honor of George E. Ladd*, ed. Robert A. Guelich [Grand Rapids: Eerdmans, 1978], 118-21). One issue that comes up often in studies of reconciliation in 2 Corinthians 5:18-21, and which cannot be dealt with here, is the assertion that the text contains some amount of pre-Pauline material that Paul employs for his argument. This presupposition has obvious effects on one's conclusions about Paul's language in this text. The discussion takes on a "Q"-like character. For instance, Ernst Käsemann views 5:18-21 as originating from a pre-Pauline hymn. Käsemann, "Erwägungen zum Stichwort 'Versöhnungslehre im NT,'" in *Zeit und Geschichte*, ed. E. Dinkler (Tübingen: Mohr-Siebeck, 1964), 48-49. Ralph Martin sees evidence for "a specimen of confessional statement expressing in summary form what the first Christians believed about God's redemptive work in Christ" (Martin, *Reconciliation: A Study of Paul's Theology* [Atlanta: John Knox, 1981], 94). Likewise, Peter Stuhlmacher understands verse 19 to contain pre-Pauline material (*Gerechtigkeit Gottes bei Paulus* [Göttingen: Vandenhoeck, 1966], 77). Stuhlmacher sees Paul drawing on, rather than simply quoting an earlier tradition. Likewise, Furnish, *II Corinthians*, 351. One might wonder if the difficulty of determining the background for Paul's teaching does not have some influence on the desire to identify a pre-Pauline tradition in this text. This study proceeds on the assumption that the text should be dealt with as a thoroughly Pauline construction.

[10] O. Hofius, "Erwägungen zur Gestalt und Herkunft des Paulinischen Versöhnungs-gedankens," *ZThK* 77 (1980): 188. Also cited in Seyoon Kim, "2 Cor. 5:11-21 and the Origin of Paul's Concept of 'Reconciliation,'" *NovT* 39 (1997): 366.

trine arises from his experience on the Damascus Road, and also finds the background in Isaiah.[11] This Isaianic background for reconciliation has been developed more precisely by Beale.[12] Before discussing that idea further, there is another aspect of the Old Testament background of reconciliation that ties the idea still closer to the sacrificial concept discussed above.

That "reconcile" and "reconciliation" and cognates are uncommon in the Septuagint is undisputed. There is, nevertheless, evidence that the concept of reconciliation can be found in sacrificial contexts. While καταλλάσσω and καταλλαγή may not appear, words that share their same semantic domain appear frequently in sacrificial texts; specifically the words ἀφίημι and ἐξιλάσκομαι.[13] These words occupy the same semantic domain as καταλλάσσω and καταλλαγή and cognates[14] and are found clustered around the same texts discussed above regarding "sin offering" and "sacrifice for sin."

In Leviticus, ἀφίημι is used consistently to render סלח, "forgive, pardon." In each verse in Leviticus or at least in each context in which ἁμαρτία means "for sin" or "for a sin offering," ἀφίημι appears.[15] As noted above, the theme of forgiveness is shared by both the sacrificial texts in the Old Testament and 2 Corinthians 5. The presence of one word from the same semantic domain as καταλλάσσω and καταλλαγή does not, however, establish a clear link between a sacrificial backdrop for "made to be sin" and Paul's discussion of reconciliation. The link

---

[11] Kim builds on both the theme of his earlier work, *The Origin of Paul's Gospel*, WUNT, 2/4 (Tübingen: Mohr-Siebeck, 1984), and the work of both Hofius and Beale, noting that both understand the Damascus road as the "catalyst" for the development of Paul's doctrine of reconciliation along the lines of Isaiah 40–66. Kim, "2 Cor. 5:11-21," 366, and n. 22.

[12] Beale argues persuasively for links between Isaiah's Suffering Servant and Paul's discourse in 2 Corinthians 5–7. He emphasizes that the theme of "new creation" (2 Cor. 5:17; Isa. 43:18-19; 65:17) arises from Isaiah, notes the close association with the theme of sacrificial atonement (53:4-12) and restoration (e.g., 40:3-11; 41:17-20; 51:1-13; 52:7-10), and sees these themes coalescing to provide a basis for understanding Paul's doctrine of reconciliation. "In light of the thematic overview of Isaiah 40–66 it is plausible to suggest that 'reconciliation' in Christ is Paul's way of explaining that Isaiah's promises of 'restoration' from the alienation of exile have begun to be fulfilled by the atonement and forgiveness of sins in Christ" (Beale, "The Old Testament Background of Reconciliation," 556; see also, 550-59). This discussion will be taken up below.

[13] ἄφεσις, ἱλασμός, and ἱλαστήριον also share the same domain.

[14] In Louw and Nida, these words are in Domain 40 "Reconciliation and Forgiveness." Johannes P. Louw and Eugene A. Nida, *Greek-English Lexicon of the New Testament Based on Semantic Domains*, 2nd ed. (New York: United Bible Societies, 1989), 502-4. Note that ἐξιλάσκομαι does not appear in Louw and Nida. It is not a New Testament word, and thus not covered by Louw and Nida, but it clearly belongs in the same domain as ἱλασμός and ἱλαστήριον.

[15] Leviticus 4:20, 26, 31, 35; 5:6, 10, 13, 16, 18, 26; 16:10; 19:22.

does, however, become stronger when one notes that yet another word from the same semantic domain appears in these texts. In the texts cited for ἄ^ημι, the word ἐξιλάσκομαι appears either in the same verses or in the immediate contexts. Thus, the words for "forgive" and "make atonement,"[16] which share the same semantic domain as the word for "reconcile," appear together when the "sin offering" is in view. Leviticus 4:20 is a good example:

> And he will do with the bull what he did with the bull of *the sin offering* [τῆς ·ἁμαρτίας], so it will be done, and the priest *shall make atonement* [ἐξιλάσεται] for them, and their sins *will be forgiven* [ἀφεθήσεται] (emphasis mine).[17]

In Leviticus 5:6-13 these same words are grouped together, with ἁμαρτία, ἀφίημι, and ἐξιλάσκομαι appearing together in verse 6 and verses 11-13,[18] and ἀφίημι and ἐξιλάσκομαι together in verse 10. Throughout chapters 4 and 5, where "sin offering" is highlighted, ἀφίημι and ἐξιλάσκομαι appear together in several verses.[19]

When one considers how the sacrifices functioned in these contexts, there are clear links with the concept of "reconciliation." Broadly speaking, the sacrifices for sin served to make atonement (ἐξιλάσκομαι) for the sin(s) of the one bringing the sacrifice, and in this sense stood as a substitute for the one who sinned. The worshiper was forgiven (ἀφίημι) for his sins, which ultimately were sins against God who gave the commandments. The result was that a breach in a relationship with God, namely between an individual, a priest, or the community, was healed, and the party in view was restored with and before God. The end result

---

[16] ἐξιλάσκομαι is the typical translation of כפר, which appears numerous times in the Old Testament for "cover over; atone for sin; make propitiation" etc. In the texts cited in this section, the basic meaning is to "make atonement" for sin. The various debates concerning the meaning of כפר and its cognate כפרת in particular need not concern us here. The point is simply to show that the Greek word which often means "atone," and shares the same semantic domain as "reconcile, reconciliation," frequently appears in sacrificial settings with "sin offering."

[17] Septuagint: καὶ ποιήσει τὸν μόσχον ὃν τρόπον ἐποίησεν τὸν μόσχον τὸν τῆς ἁμαρτίας, οὕτως ποιηθήσεται, καὶ ἐξιλάσεται περὶ αὐτῶν ὁ ἱερεύς, καὶ ἀφεθήσεται αὐτοῖς ἡ ἁμαρτία.
MT: וְעָשָׂה לַפָּר כַּאֲשֶׁר עָשָׂה לְפַר הַחַטָּאת כֵּן יַעֲשֶׂה־לּוֹ וְכִפֶּר עֲלֵהֶם הַכֹּהֵן וְנִסְלַח לָהֶם׃
The translation of the Septuagint is my own.

[18] In 5:6 the Septuagint has the phrase καὶ ἀφεθήσεται αὐτῷ ἡ ἁμαρτία, "and his sin will be forgiven him," but there is no corresponding phrase in the MT. Note that at the end of 5:12 ἁμαρτία likely refers to "sin offering" and appears without either an article or a preposition.

[19] Leviticus 4:26, 31, 35; 5:16, 18, 26.

of this whole process might be summed up in a word: "reconciliation." The collocation of these words that share the same semantic domain with καταλλάσσω and καταλλαγή suggests that "made to be sin" in 2 Corinthians 5:21 refers to Christ's being made a sacrifice for sin. Even if one is not convinced that "made to be sin" refers to Christ's being a sacrifice for sin, the concepts of atonement, substitution, and forgiveness are all tied into Paul's view of how reconciliation takes place.[20] These same concepts, along with the results (a mended relationship with God), are present in the Old Testament texts in which the Septuagint uses ἁμαρτία for "sin offering."[21]

The surrounding context of 2 Corinthians 5:21 also bears evidence

---

[20] Murray, for instance, does not discuss "sacrifice" but in his comments on reconciliation in this text, he stresses these same elements. "It (reconciliation) presupposes a relation of alienation and it effects a relation of favour and peace. This new relation is constituted by the removal of the ground for the alienation. The ground is sin and guilt. The removal is wrought in the vicarious work of Christ, when he was made to be sin for us that we might become the righteousness of God in him. Christ took upon himself the sin and guilt, the condemnation and the curse of those on whose behalf he died." John Murray, *Redemption Accomplished and Applied* (Grand Rapids: Eerdmans, 1955; reprint, 1987), 42. These words could easily be applied to a sacrificial context. See also the comments by Hodge quoted above in this chapter (n. 1). Owen denies that Paul speaks of a sacrifice for sins. He nevertheless finds the meaning of "made to be sin" in Isaiah 53:6, "laying all our iniquities on him" (Owen's translation), and in the very next sentence says, "this was by the imputation of our sins unto him, as the sins of the people were put on the head of the goat, that they should be no more theirs, but his, so as that he was to carry them away from them." John Owen, "The Doctrine of Justification by Faith," in *The Works of John Owen* (n.p.: Johnstone and Hunter, 1850; Edinburgh: Banner of Truth, 1965), 5:349. This is, however, a sacrificial context. Owen is obviously alluding to Leviticus 16:20-22 and the "scapegoat" that symbolically bears the sins of the Israelites into the wilderness on the Day of Atonement. It should be noted, in Owen's favor, that the scapegoat was not sacrificed. There is a close similarity between the views of Murray, Hodge, and Owen and the view that "made to be sin" does refer to a sacrifice for sin. In either case, what is in view is Christ's vicarious bearing of sin. "Take sin in either sense before mentioned, either of a sacrifice for sin, or a sinner, and the imputation of the guilt of sin antecedently unto the punishment for it, and in order thereunto, must be understood." Owen himself seems to allow for a sacrificial concept but not the translation of ἁμαρτία as "sin offering." As he puts it, "I shall not contend about this exposition ["made to be sin" = sacrifice for sin], because that signified in it is according unto the truth" ("The Doctrine of Justification by Faith," 348).

[21] David Garland holds that "interpreting the word as 'sin offering' destroys the parallel structure of the sentence." Garland, *2 Corinthians*, NAC (Nashville: Broadman and Holman, 1999), 300. Yet, shortly after this he refers explicitly to a sacrificial background for understanding Christ's sinless death on the cross (ibid., 301). Garland understands the text to mean that Christ was made a sinner, and he argues for a substitutionary interpretation. He employs sacrificial language but rules out the idea that "made sin" refers to a sin offering. Garland, and others, argue that if "made sin" means a sacrifice for sin then Paul uses ἁμαρτία in two different ways. He uses it for "sin offering" and he uses it to refer to Christ's sinlessness ("knew no sin"). Yet if Paul means that Jesus, who did not know sin, was nevertheless made "a sinner"—is that not also using ἁμαρτία in at least slightly different ways? Moreover, ἁμαρτία is used in the sacrificial texts in Leviticus in two different ways: in reference to sin and in reference to a sin offering. I am unclear on why taking "made sin" as a sacrifice for sin means that the parallel between "sin" and "righteousness" is ruined. The first phrase is the action of God, the second the result. God made Christ a sacrifice for sin and the result is that we "become the righteousness of God in him." As with the scholars cited above, Garland's basic interpretation of the verse as a whole and the one set forth here share a majority of things in common. The substitutionary nature of Christ's death, including the results, is the main thing. Perhaps it is simply that Garland and others recognize the sacrificial language in this text but balk at a specific reference to the sin offering.

for understanding "made to be sin" as a sacrifice for sin. In verse 14 Paul asserts that Christ's death was representative, saying, "one died for all" (εἷς ὑπὲρ πάντων ἀπέθανεν), thus stressing the vicarious nature of the cross—that Christ died "for all," i.e., in their place.[22] In verse 19 Paul describes God's work of reconciliation through Christ as the non-imputation of sin ("not reckoning their sins to them"), which again implies a vicarious act.[23] And finally, Christ is described in verse 21 as one "who knew no sin" (μὴ γνόντα ἁμαρτίαν), recalling the description that occurs frequently in regard to the sacrificial offerings, "without defect" (תָּמִים, ἄμωμον).[24] If this is correct, the phrase "who knew no sin" is in accord with other New Testament texts that describe Christ as an "unblemished" or "undefiled" sacrifice.[25] Taken together, the Old Testament sacrificial backdrop, the link between reconciliation and what the sacrifices accomplished, and the context of 2 Corinthians 5:21 suggest that Paul is referring to Christ as a sacrifice for sin with the phrase "made to be sin."[26]

---

[22] The death of Jesus was both representational and substitutionary. See below, n. 28.

[23] Furnish, favorably citing Hughes, Second Corinthians, 209, says "This presupposes a substitutionary view of Christ's death. The trespasses of others have been charged to him, and he has died in their place paying the penalty for those sins." Furnish, II Corinthians, 335.

[24] E.g., Leviticus 1:3, 10; 3:1, 6; 4:3, 23, 28, 32; 5:15, 18, 25 (Eng. 6:6); 9:2-3; 14:10; 22:19; 23:12, 18; Num. 6:14; 28:3, 9, 11, 19, 31; 29:8, 13, 17, 20, 23, 26, 29, 32, 36.

[25] First Peter 1:19, "a lamb spotless and undefiled." Hebrews 7:26 describes Christ as "a high priest, holy, innocent and undefiled," and goes on to tie Christ's priesthood to his sacrificial death as one "who does not need daily, like those high priests, to offer up sacrifices, first for His own sins, and then for the sins of the people, because this He did once for all when He offered up Himself" (v. 27, NASB). The great high priest is also the perfect sacrifice. This text is instructive for the way the New Testament interprets Christ as the fulfillment of various Old Testament offices and functions (it is also a presupposition of this dissertation). The New Testament writers do not conform Christ to the Old Testament type (e.g., high priest, sacrifice), but rather conform the Old Testament figures to their fulfillment in Christ. It goes without saying that in the Old Testament high priests and sacrifices were not the same thing, and served different functions. No Old Testament priest flung himself on the altar as a sacrifice. For the New Testament writers this is hardly the point. They see Old Testament figures and practices serving as pointers to Christ and, moreover, fulfilling this function all along—whether or not those living in Old Testament times would have understood these things fully, or in some cases, even at all. So, as stated above, a sacrificial background for 2 Corinthians 5:21 cannot be dismissed on the grounds that certain elements of the "sin offering" do not match exactly with Paul's teaching. Christ fulfills the sacrificial system in toto. This is why the New Testament writers can allude to so many different sacrifices. Moreover, as George B. Caird points out, Paul can also speak generally in sacrificial language as when "he uses the phrase 'the blood of Christ' (Rom. 3:25; 5:9; 1 Cor. 10:16; 11:25, 27; Eph. 1:7; 2:13; Col. 1:20)." Caird, New Testament Theology, completed and ed. L. D. Hurst (Oxford: Clarendon, 1994; reprint, 1995), 152. This is not to say that the Old Testament context should be dismissed; on the contrary, it is only by understanding the Old Testament contexts that we can rightly understand the ways in which the New Testament teaches Christ as the fulfillment of the OT. This is, after all, the way Christ himself taught the disciples to understand the entire OT—as pointing to him (Luke 24:27; cf., Acts 7:2-53; 13:16-41; 17:2-3).

[26] Furnish disagrees, saying, "Sin here cannot mean 'sin offering' . . . for that would import an idea foreign to this context" (2 Corinthians, 340). It is unclear why Furnish thinks "sin offering" is a foreign idea.

Sacrifice and the Suffering Servant. Isaiah speaks of one upon whom the Lord "caused the iniquity" of others to fall, who will become "a guilt offering" (אשם), and "justify many" and "bear their sins" (53:6, 10-11). Furthermore, this one who bears the sins of others is innocent of any wrongdoing (53:9). There can be little doubt that the Servant of Isaiah 52:13–53:12 fulfills a vicarious role as a substitute punished for the sins of others. The key phrase for this study is "guilt offering" (v. 10), which the translator of Isaiah rendered with περὶ ἁμαρτίας. Though the "guilt offering" is distinguished from the "sin offering" (חטאת), they are "regarded as the primary expiatory offerings in the levitical system of offerings"[27] and closely associated.[28] The concepts involved, particularly substitutionary atonement and forgiveness, are similar if not identical.[29] The Servant's role, in part, is that of a sacrifice.

That Paul had Isaiah in mind in 2 Corinthians 5:21 is also suggested by the larger context, since Isaiah provides much of the backdrop for what Paul is saying. As noted above, Beale views Paul's doctrine of reconciliation as an expression of Paul's understanding of the fulfillment of Isaiah's prophecy of the Suffering Servant, who brings about a new creation and restoration by his "vicarious suffering."[30] The "new creation" (v. 17) is brought about by Christ's "death for all" (v. 15), which

---

[27] Averbeck, "Sacrifices and Offerings," 720.

[28] In Leviticus, the "guilt offering" and the "sin offering" appear in context together. E.g., Leviticus 5:6-7, 15, 16, 18-19, 24 (Eng. 6:5), 24 (6:6); 7:7. Following Milgrom, Averbeck points out "that the primary purpose of the guilt offering was to make atonement for *desecration* of 'sancta,' the mishandling of holy (sacred) things, as opposed to the sin offering, which made atonement for *contamination* of sancta" (ibid.). Whatever the case, the sanctuary and its furnishings were desecrated and contaminated by the sins of the Israelites; therefore while the temple may have been cleansed by the offerings, it is through the atonement for sins that the cleansing took place. It is the atoning for sin and forgiveness that is of interest here, and these are precisely what both the sin and guilt offerings accomplished. As with the sin offering, "forgiveness" (ἀφίημι) and "atonement" (ἐξιλάσκομαι) are in view of the guilt offering.

[29] Dunn takes exception to substitution language in this verse, seeing substitution as "only half the story." James D. G. Dunn, *The Theology of Paul the Apostle* (Grand Rapids: Eerdmans, 1998), 223. Dunn seems to think that substitution is not an accurate description of Christ's death because it somehow obscures the idea of believers being identified with Christ or participating in his death. These are not, however, mutually exclusive concepts. Paul speaks in both substitutionary (v. 21) and representative (v. 14) terms in this text. Dunn himself points out that "representation" (like "participation") "is not an adequate single-word description" (ibid.). Nevertheless, these words "help convey the sense of a continuing identification with Christ in, through, and beyond his death." If "participation," like representation, is not "adequate" as a definition of atonement, could we not say that it is "only half the story" as well? Even if substitution is relegated to "half the story" (I am not taking "half" as absolutely literal), it is, nevertheless, still *half*. These concepts work together as part of a greater whole. Note that Dunn's comments are made in the context of several Pauline texts and not limited to 2 Corinthians 5.

[30] Beale, "The Old Testament Background of Reconciliation," 556.

corresponds to the "something new" (Isa. 43:18-19) that is made possible "by the sacrificial death of the Servant, who becomes the `āshām for the people (53:4-12)."[31] In addition, these themes are tied together by the theme of restoration in Isaiah, a time when the rift between God and his exiled people would be healed and the relationship restored.[32] One might say that through the Servant, God reconciles his people to himself.

More contextual support is found in 6:1-2. In further defending his apostleship and continuing his appeal for the Corinthians to be reconciled to God (5:20), Paul urges the Corinthians "not to receive the grace of God in vain," and then he quotes Isaiah 49:8, aligning himself with the prophet who prophesied a message of hope to the exiles.[33] Isaiah's message, like Paul's, centers on an innocent One who sacrificially bears the sins of others and brings them into a right relationship with God. The general context of 2 Corinthians 5:21 is rife with themes and quotes from the Servant songs of Isaiah 40-65.[34] This lends support to the idea that Paul had the Servant in mind when he said that "God made him sin, who knew no sin."

In the reconciliation that Paul speaks of in 5:18-20, God initiates and

---

[31] Ibid., 556-57.

[32] Beale cites many "restoration" and "creation" texts in Isaiah for support, including 40:28-31; 41:17-20; 42:5-6; 44:21-23; 24-48; 45:1-8; 9-13; 18–20; 49:8-13; 51:1-3; 9-11; 54:1-10; 55:6-13. Ibid., 557. "The primary text to which Paul alludes in v. 17 is Isa. 43:18-19. The context of these two verses refers to God's promise that a time will come when He will cause the Israelites to return from the Babylonian exile and to be *restored* to their land in Israel. . . . Furthermore, Israel's promised restoration is referred to both as an imminent 'redemption' (43:1; cf. v. 14) and creation (43:6-7). In this context Yahweh's role as Israel's 'creator' (43:1) is portrayed as the one who 'created,' 'formed' and 'made' the nation for His 'glory' (43:7). The point of this emphasis upon God as creator is not to focus on the first creation nor primarily the first Exodus when the nation was initially created, but the recreation of the nation through restoring it from exile to its homeland, as Isa 43:3-7 makes clear" (ibid., 554-55). In at least one of these verses Beale cites, there is yet another link to 2 Corinthians. Just as Isaiah 43:7 speaks of these things happening for God's glory, Paul is confident that "the grace which is abounding to more and more people may cause the giving of thanks to abound to the glory of God" (2 Cor. 4:15). The ultimate purpose of the restoration that God effects for his people through the suffering of the Servant and the spread of grace through the gospel which God effected by the suffering of Christ is one and the same thing: God's glory.

[33] Scott J. Hafemann, 2 *Corinthians*, The NIV Application Commentary (Grand Rapids: Zondervan, 2000), 249.

[34] Further quotes and/or allusions to Isaiah follow in the next section. Isaiah 49:8 (6:2), 52:11 (6:17), 43:6 (6:18). There are a number of Old Testament texts alluded to in this section as well as a number of conflations, specifically in verses 16-18. Scholars are not in total agreement as to which exact texts are quoted and/or alluded to. Beale's discussion of the possibilities is helpful ("The Old Testament Background of Reconciliation, 570-72). His comment about the original contexts of the quotes is insightful for tying this section together with 5:11-21: "*Almost without exception, the six generally agreed upon Old Testament references refer in their respective contexts to God's promise to restore exiled Israel to their land*" (ibid.; Beale's emphasis). The six agreed upon references are, apparently, Leviticus 26:11-12; Ezekiel 37:27; Isaiah 52:11; Ezekiel 20:34; 2 Samuel 7:14; and Isaiah 43:6 (ibid).

accomplishes a restored relationship with humanity through the death of Christ, who fulfills the prophecy about the innocent Servant of God. The Servant becomes a vicarious sacrifice bearing the sins of God's people, and thus Paul can speak of God "not reckoning sins" to people because their sins are reckoned to Christ, the sacrificial Servant.[35] This thought is summed up in the phrase "for us." This is how God was reconciling the world to himself. The essential background is the sacrifice for sin through which atonement and forgiveness were made possible. "Accordingly, this portrayal of Christ's death as a sacrifice for sin indicates that the death/ blood of Christ is the means by which God fulfills the need for atonement prefigured in the sacrifices of the Sinai covenant."[36] Thus two themes run together through this text and coalesce in 5:21. The Levitical sacrifices are connected to the death of Christ via the Servant described in Isaiah.[37] The Old Testament background of Paul's language, the concept of recon-ciliation, and the context all point to a sacrificial interpretation of "God made him who had no sin *to be sin*" in 2 Corinthians 5:21.

BECOMING THE RIGHTEOUSNESS OF GOD

The meaning of the phrase "the righteousness of God" in 2 Corinthians 5:21 is perhaps the most debated issue in this text. For some, the "righ-teousness of God" refers mainly to God's saving power that is at work reordering the creation through Christ who overcame the power of sin.[38]

---

[35] While Paul does not say that sins are reckoned to Christ but only that God, in Christ, did not reckon trespasses (v. 19), the "exchange" is unavoidable. Carson's comments are instructive: "True, the text does not explicitly *say* that God imputes our sins to Christ, but as long as we perceive that Jesus dies in our place, and bears our curse, and was made "sin" for us, it is extraordinarily dif-ficult to avoid the notion of the imputation of our sins to him." D. A. Carson, "The Vindication of Imputation: On Fields of Discourse and, of Course, Semantic Fields" (from a collection of essays from the Wheaton Theology Conference, April, 2003, InterVarsity).

[36] Hafemann, *2 Corinthians*, 247.

[37] As Hafemann puts it: "The explicit link between the Old Testament sacrificial system and the death of Christ is found in the fact that Jesus, as the suffering servant of Isaiah 52:13–53:12, bears the sins of God's people as their ransom. . . . Paul's reference to Christ as the One who "had no sin" . . . whom God nevertheless 'made . . . to be sin,' thus recalls the death of the 'righteous servant' who did not sin in Isaiah 53:1-9. . . . In his sacrificial death as the sinless Son of God, Jesus pays the penalty for our sin." Ibid., 247-48.

[38] Stuhlmacher, *Gerechtigkeit Gottes*, 76-77. Thus, for Stuhlmacher, God's power (righteousness) is set over against sin (ibid., 75). Similarly, Karl Kertelge, "*Rechtfertigung*" *bei Paulus: Studien zur Struktur und zum Bedeutungsgehalt des paulinischen Rechtfertigungsbegriffs* (Münster: Aschendorff, 1967), 103. Stuhlmacher develops the phrase "righteousness of God" generally along the lines of Jewish apocalyptic literature, e.g., 1QS 10:25ff; 11:12; 1QM 4:6; and with minor differences in Enoch (Eth.) 71:14; 99:10; 101:3; 4 Ezra 8:36 (*Gerechtigkeit Gottes*, 175). The apocalyptic background, and the idea of God's righteousness as his creation power, traces back to Käsemann, e.g., "'The Righteousness of God' in Paul," in *New Testament Questions of Today*, trans. W. J. Montague (Philadelphia: Fortress, 1969), 168-82.

Another idea is that "the righteousness of God" here, as in other places, refers to God's faithfulness to his covenant.[39] These are but two views that gained popularity in recent decades, but there are a variety of views set forth by other modern scholars.[40] Finally, there is the traditional view that understands this phrase to refer to justification through the imputation of Christ's righteousness.[41] Through interaction with these various

---

[39] J. A. Ziesler, *The Meaning of Righteousness in Paul: A Linguistic and Theological Enquiry*, Society for New Testament Studies Monograph Series, vol. 20, ed. Matthew Black (Cambridge: Cambridge University Press, 1972), 160. N. T. Wright, *What Saint Paul Really Said* (Grand Rapids: Eerdmans, 2000), 104-5; idem, "On Becoming the Righteousness of God," in *Pauline Theology*, vol. 1, ed. David M. Hay (Minneapolis: Fortress, 1993), 205-6. Wright argues that ἡμεῖς refers to Paul and his fellow workers (or to Paul only). The context of Paul's apostolic defense is the key to Wright's interpretation. As God's "covenant ambassador," Paul "*becomes* the embodiment of his sovereign" ("On Becoming the Righteousness of God," 206). In other words, Paul himself, as an apostle of the new covenant, is a manifestation of God's covenantal faithfulness. Wright, therefore, translates the verse as, "so that in him we might become God's covenantal faithfulness." More attention is given to Wright's view below.

[40] E.g., Thrall thinks that δικαιοσύνη stands in "literary symmetry" with ἁμαρτίαν, which explains the "strange form," but adopts what she calls a "traditional understanding," i.e., justified, having the status of righteousness, acquittal in God's court (Margaret E. Thrall, *The Second Epistle to the Corinthians*, ICC [Edinburgh: T & T Clark, 1994], 1:442-43). In support of her "traditional understanding," she cites H. A. W. Meyer, *Kritisch exegetischer Handbuch über den zweiten Brief an die Korinther*, MeyerK 6 (Göttingen: Vandenhoeck & Ruprecht, 1840), 279; P. Bachmann, *Der zweite Brief des Paulus an die Korinther*, Kommentar zum Neuen Testament VIII (Leipzig: Verlagsbuchhandlung Verner Scholl, 1922); F. F. Bruce, *1 and 2 Corinthians*, New Century Bible (London: Marshall, Morgan, & Scott, 1971), 221; and C. K. Barrett, *A Commentary on the Second Epistle to the Corinthians*, Black's New Testament Commentary (London: A & C Black, 1973), 180. Thrall, as those she cites, does not hold to the other part of the "traditional" understanding of this verse, that is, a concept of "imputation." For Thrall, but not necessarily for the others, the phrase ἐν αὐτῷ, which indicates an identification of the believer with Christ in his death *and* resurrection, rules out "any notion of an imputed 'alien righteousness'" (Thrall, *Second Corinthians*, 1:444; her emphasis). Christ was vindicated as righteous at his resurrection, a righteousness which believers receive by way of being "united with his personal being" (ibid.). Rudolph Bultmann understands the phrase to refer to the righteousness that God gives, and becoming righteous is "the possibility of being righteous, a possibility realized by faith" (*Second Corinthians*, 165). Martin, following the lead of J. F. Collange (*Enigmes de la deuxième épître à la de Paul aux Corinthiens*, Society for New Testament Studies Monograph Series 18 [Cambridge: University Press, 1972], 278-80) and Kertelge, (*Rechtfertigung*, 304), sees a combination of the individual (Bultmann) and cosmic (Käsemann and Stuhlmacher) aspects coming together in this text in the phrase "in Christ." This does not, of course, deny that the two ideas are combined in some sense in Käsemann and Stuhlmacher. Käsemann, for instance, while strongly de-emphasizing the individual nature of justification (arguing against Bultmann) does not discount it altogether ("*Righteousness of God*," 175-76). Belleville is somewhat vague on the conclusion: "In identifying with our sin, Christ paved the way for us to become identified with *the righteousness of God*. The genitive can be subjective . . . objective . . . or possessive. In Paul's writings the noun *dikaiosynē* typically is used of character. It is not merely that we acquire a right standing or do good works; we actually *become* righteous—although the latter may well presume the former" (*2 Corinthians*, 160-61; her emphasis). James M. Scott's comments are similar at points to a more (truly) traditional view of this verse: "It is clear that the righteousness of God comes from him and is conferred on believers who are in Christ. Godless sinners, who previously possessed no righteousness of their own, receive righteousness in sinless Christ who, by a process of substitution, became a sin offering for them" (*2 Corinthians*, 142).

[41] John Calvin, *Institutes of the Christian Religion*, 3.6.4, 21-23, trans. Ford Lewis Battles, ed. John T. McNeill, The Library of Christian Classics, vol. 20 (Philadelphia: Westminster, 1960), 751-54. Calvin views reconciliation and justification synonymously, and emphasizes the primary place of forgiveness in justification. Being reckoned righteous in Christ is to have one's sins forgiven. In 3.11.21

views, particularly with the views of God's righteousness as power and as covenantal faithfulness, the interpretation of the phrase argued in this study will become evident.[42]

"Righteousness of God" as Power

Stuhlmacher understands the phrase, "the righteousness of God" to refer to God's cosmic power, which in the proclamation of Paul both creates and judges.[43] In this interpretation there is no tension between an alien righteousness imputed to the believer and an actual righteousness possessed by the believer because both ideas are tied together through Paul's doctrine of the Spirit.[44] "The righteousness of God," therefore, means not only God's loyalty to his covenant, but also his loyalty to his creation that is being recreated through the eschatological event of the cross that ushers in the kingdom of God. Believers do not receive God's righteousness as a mere gift; they have it through participation in the kingdom through Christ, and thus the creating and saving power of God is a reality in the life of believers now.[45]

While Stuhlmacher's emphasis on creation is fitting in a text that aligns becoming "the righteous of God" in Christ (v. 21) with being a

---

Calvin says, "The righteousness of faith is reconciliation with God, which consists solely in the forgiveness of sins." Shortly after he states: "It is obvious, therefore, that those whom God embraces are made righteous solely by the fact that they are purified when their spots are washed away by forgiveness of sins. Consequently, such righteousness can be called, in a word, "remission of sins" (ibid., 751). In the next section (3.6.22), the first text he cites to prove the connection between justification and forgiveness is 2 Corinthians 5:19, 21 (ibid., 751-52). Under the topic of "Justification," Turretin cites this text, saying that Christ's "righteousness and all his benefits" are given to us. "Hence it happens that as he was made of God sin for us by the imputation of our sins, so in turn we are made the righteousness of God in him by the imputation of his obedience." Francis Turretin, *Institutes of Elenctic Theology*, trans. George Musgrave Giger, ed. James T. Dennison, Jr. (Phillipsburg, NJ: Presbyterian and Reformed, 1994), 2:647. Following in this tradition, see James Buchanan, *The Doctrine of Justification* (Edinburgh: T & T Clark, 1867; Grand Rapids: Baker, 1954), 326-27 (2 Cor. 5:21 cited among other texts); Hodge, *2 Corinthians*, 122; idem, *Systematic Theology* (Grand Rapids: Eerdmans, 1965), 3:157; Louis Berkhof, *Systematic Theology*, 4th ed. (Grand Rapids: Eerdmans, 1972), 523; John Murray, "Justification," in *The Collected Writings of John Murray* (Edinburgh: Banner of Truth, 1977), 2:214; John Piper, *Counted Righteous in Christ: Should We Abandon the Imputation of Christ's Righteousness?* (Wheaton: Crossway, 2002), 81-83.

[42] It must be emphasized that the point here is to determine what this phrase means in this text. What it means here is suggestive to what it means elsewhere and vice versa, but a full investigation of the phrase, including the history of interpretation, is not possible here.

[43] Stuhlmacher, *Gerechtigkeit Gottes*, 77. Stuhlmacher sees "the righteousness of God" as not limited to this text. To the contrary, Stuhlmacher sees "the righteousness of God" as the foundational core of Pauline theology.

[44] Ibid., 76. I was directed to this discussion in Stuhlmacher by Scott J. Hafemann in his introduction to Stuhlmacher, *How to do Biblical Theology*, Princeton Theological Monograph Series (Allison Park, PA: Pickwick, 1995), xxiii.

[45] Ibid., xxii-xxiii.

"new creation" in Christ (v. 17), his blurring of the line between forensic and effective righteousness is difficult to maintain in this text. For one, the emphasis in the text is on the sacrificial death of Christ because of which God did not "reckon transgressions" to the world (v. 19). The non-reckoning of sin is surely a reference to a forensic act. Just as being made a sacrifice for sin does not imply that Christ become effectively "sinful," so "becoming the righteousness of God in him" does not imply that Paul is including, *a priori*, the concept of effective or transformative righteousness.[46] It is precisely the forensic element that is emphasized in this text in both directions. On one hand, Christ bore the punishment for trespasses that he did not commit, but on the other, those trespasses are not reckoned to those who do commit them, and these people "become the righteousness of God" by something accomplished outside of them on their behalf. The sacrifice of Christ is the instrumental means by which sin is atoned, and from it flows the forgiveness of sins (again, v. 19). For Paul then to speak of "becoming the righteousness of God" indicates that the barrier between God and man, namely sin, has been removed, but this does not involve a transformation (though transformation certainly follows)—it involves a legal decision based on just grounds.[47]

A second objection is based on Paul's emphasis on reconciliation, an emphasis that points away from a transformative or effective righteousness in verse 21. There is a breach between God and the world (and with some of the Corinthians too), which God himself set out to repair. Verse 19 says that "God was in Christ reconciling the world to himself," which is explained as the non-reckoning of sins and as the heart of Paul's ministry. Paul's ministry includes proclaiming what God has done in Christ to bring about the forgiveness of sins: Paul proclaims the end of the division between God and man, initiated and accomplished by God through Christ. Sin divided man from God, and God overcame that divide through the sacrifice of Christ. So when Paul pleads with the Corinthians in verse 20, "be reconciled to God," he is proclaiming an

---

[46] Note that this objection does not require that one see "sacrifice for sin" in verse 21. If one understands "made to be sin" in the sense that the punishment of God for our sins was laid upon Christ, the objection to Stuhlmacher would be the same.

[47] "Believers are declared to be righteous before God as the divine judge because Jesus, as the sinless one, bore their sins." Thomas R. Schreiner, *Paul: Apostle of God's Glory in Christ* (Downers Grove: InterVarsity, 2001), 201.

end to the hostilities brought about by sin, including the *legal* means by which this was accomplished. He urges them to accept his message as an ambassador of Christ and as one speaking for God.

The message of reconciliation is not about taking part in an effective righteousness but about being identified with one who died in the place of others as their substitute (vv. 14, 21); it is the message of forgiveness, a restored relationship, and as such is proclaimed as a forensic reality.[48] As will become clearer below, the qualification "in him" does not shift the emphasis from a forensic to an effective righteousness. Undoubtedly, becoming the righteousness of God refers to a status accompanied with power, and that power is the Holy Spirit, but it does not follow that God's righteousness *is* his saving and creating power.[49]

"The Righteousness of God" as Covenant Faithfulness

Some scholars argue that "the righteousness of God" refers to his covenantal faithfulness.[50] Arguing from an Old Testament background, Wright asserts that the phrase "righteousness of God" (δικαιοσύνη θεοῦ), unlike the phrase "a righteousness from God," (τὴν ἐκ θεοῦ δικαιοσύνην [Phil 3:9]), does not refer to a status conferred upon people but to "God's own righteousness," which is his loyalty to his covenant.[51] Specific to

---

[48] I do not mean that the forgiveness of sins does not result in a Spirit-transformed life. It certainly does. The comment has to do with the nature of God's act of reconciliation in Christ. The sacrifice was forensic and the forgiveness that resulted is forensic.

[49] Stuhlmacher's view appears somewhat similar to that of Lombard and others, and refuted by Calvin. Calvin, defending justification on the basis of Christ's righteousness alone, says that "man is not righteous in himself but because the righteousness of Christ is communicated to him by imputation." He contrasts that with the view "that man is justified by faith because by Christ's righteousness he shares the Spirit of God, by whom he is rendered righteous" (*Institutes*, 3.6.23, 753). This is merely an observation—further work would be necessary to establish definite links.

[50] Though Wright is most closely associated with this view, others make a similar argument. Dunn, for instance, speaking of God's obligation to his people based on both creation and election, states: "It should be equally evident why God's *righteousness* could be understood as God's *faithfulness* to his people. For his righteousness was simply the fulfillment of his covenant obligation as Israel's God in delivering, saving, and vindicating Israel, despite Israel's own failure" (*The Theology of Paul*, 342). At issue for Dunn is that *righteousness* connotes primarily a *relational* concept. Much of the discussion centers on the phrase in Romans 1:17; 3:21-22, 26, etc., and the Old Testament background for the phrase. See also, Sam K. Williams, "'The Righteousness of God' in Romans," *JBL* 49 (1980): 241-90.

[51] N. T. Wright, *Romans*, The New Interpreter's Bible, vol. 10 (Nashville: Abingdon, 2002), 403-4. Wright cites an array of texts in support of his view: Deuteronomy 33:21; Judges 5:11; 1 Samuel 12:7; Nehemiah 9:8; Psalm 45:4; 72:1-4; 103:6; Isaiah 40-55; Daniel 9:7-9, 14, 16; Micah 6:5; Wisdom of Solomon 5:18; Psalms of Solomon 1:10-15; 2 Baruch 44:4; 78:5; 4 Ezra 7:17-25; 8:36; 10:16; 14:32; Testament of Dan 6:10; 1QS 10:25-6; 11:12; 1QM 4:6. While these texts cannot be examined here, it can be stated that these texts do indeed support a connection between God's righteousness and his covenant faithfulness. Wright's *Romans* is cited here because his treatment of 2 Corinthians 5:21 rests on the same presupposition.

2 Corinthians 5:21, Wright holds that ἡμῶν ("us") and ἡμεῖς ("we") in 2 Corinthians 5:21 refer to Paul as the embodiment of God's covenantal faithfulness. In this text there are, therefore, two related issues to address. Before discussing "the righteousness of God," a brief investigation in regard to whom "we" refers is in order since it constitutes a unique interpretation of this text, and because it is a key component of Wright's exegesis of the verse in its context.

Paul as "the righteousness of God." The casual reader might miss why a discussion of the pronouns in verse 21 is vital for understanding the meaning of "the righteousness of God." The pronouns, or the personal referents, are in fact the linchpin in Wright's argument for "covenantal faithfulness" in this verse. It is necessary, therefore, to summarize his argument. Wright says that 2 Corinthians 5:21 "offers *an apparently* clear exception" to the idea that "the righteousness of God" is a technical term in Paul that means "the covenant-faithfulness of [Israel's] God."[52] In the traditional reading, Wright points out, the phrase in this verse means a righteous status that God credits to an individual. If that reading is true, Wright conjectures, it could at least raise a question mark over the meaning "covenant faithfulness" in Romans as well (Wright himself admits that he would not press for "a spurious harmony"). With all this in mind there is, however, another reason in Wright's view to reject the traditional view of "the righteousness of God," and it is found in the broader context.[53] Because this is such an important aspect of the argument against a traditional reading of this text, it is worth taking time to explore it in more detail. If Wright's interpretation is wrong, it weakens the concept of covenant faithfulness in this text.

---

[52] Wright, "On Becoming the Righteousness of God," 203; my emphasis.

[53] Wright clearly finds the traditional view troubling. It is worth quoting him at length, because this is probably similar to the criticism he would level at the interpretation argued for here: "The verse has traditionally been read as a somewhat detached statement of atonement theology: we are sinners; God is righteous, but in Christ what Luther called a 'wondrous exchange' takes place, in which Christ takes our sin and we his 'righteousness.' And the difficulty with this, despite its being enshrined in a good many hymns and liturgies, as well as in popular devotion, is (a) that once again Paul never actually says this anywhere else; (b) that here it is *God's* righteousness, not Christ's, that 'we' apparently 'become;' (c) that there seems to be no good reason why he suddenly inserts this statement into a discussion whose actual thrust is quite different, namely, a consideration of the paradoxical apostolic ministry in which Christ is portrayed in and through the humiliating weakness of the apostle (4:7–6:13); and (d) the verse, read in this way, seems to fall off the end of the preceding argument, so much so that some commentators have suggested that the real break in the thought comes not between 5:21 and 6:1 but between 5:19 and 5:20" (Wright, "On Becoming the Righteousness of God," 203-4).

Wright correctly notes that Paul's defense of his apostleship is in the foreground of the context. Tracing Paul's argument from 3:6 and his new covenant ministry, which is, contrary to the opinion of his opponents, shown to be valid by his suffering (4:7-18), Wright points out that Paul's defense of his "covenantal ministry" proceeds through chapter 5, where Paul is "explaining what it is that his apostleship involves."[54] Rather than being "mere snippets of traditional soteriology," verses 14-15 and 16-17 pave the way for verses 18-19, in which Paul's argument reaches a climax:

> Here, then, is the focal point to which the long argument has been building up. Paul, having himself been reconciled to God by the death of Christ, has now been entrusted by God with the task of ministering to others that which he has himself received, in other words, reconciliation.[55]

Coupled with verse 20, where Paul makes the bold assertion that when he speaks, he does so as the very mouthpiece of God, these statements lead up to verse 21, in which it becomes clear that as a minister of the new covenant (3:6) Paul himself has "become the righteousness of God"; that is, his ministry "is the covenantal faithfulness of the one true God, now active through the paradoxical Christ-shaped ministry of Paul, reaching out with the offer of reconciliation for all who hear his bold preaching."[56]

It is evident that verse 21 is situated in the larger context of Paul's defense of his apostolic ministry. And while it is true that some theologians disregard the context, simply identifying the context does not mean that a correct interpretation of a particular paragraph, verse, phrase, etc., will follow. Throughout the section primarily cited by Wright (3:6ff), there are important places where the "we" (apostles) and "you" (readers) division that is sustained for a majority of the time is replaced with a collective reference.

In 3:18 Paul uses the phrase "we all" (ἡμεῖς πάντες): "And we all, with unveiled face, who are looking at the glory of the Lord, are being transformed into the same image." Here ἡμεῖς is a collective including Paul and the Corinthians, in contrast to those whose eyes are still

---

[54] Ibid., 104.
[55] Ibid., 105.
[56] Ibid., 106.

veiled "whenever Moses is read" (v. 15). Verse 3:18 can be extended to include all believers, as well, due to πάντας.

After 3:18, the distinction between the apostles and the Corinthians extends through chapter 4 and up to 5:10, where Paul declares: "For we must all (πάντας ἡμᾶς) appear before the judgment seat of Christ, so that each one (ἕκαστος) may receive what is due for what he has done in the body, whether good or evil."[57] The referent in this passage is not as clear as 3:18, and one could argue that the connections in the text argue for a restricted meaning of "we."[58] The "for" (γάρ) in 5:10 grounds Paul's previous statements that refer to the life of faith that aims to please God regardless of circumstances (vv. 6-9). The "therefore" (οὖν) of verse six links verses 6-10 together as an inference drawn from verses 1 to 5. That is, their certainty of the future, which is guaranteed by the down payment of the Spirit (vv. 1-5), is the reason they have courage and faith in the present (vv. 6-9). Moreover, the "for" (γάρ) in verse 1 gives the reason why they are not discouraged in the face of temporary affliction (4:16-18). Paul's declaration that they "do not lose heart" (v. 16), is itself an inference ("therefore" [διό]) from the preceding verses probably all the way back to 4:1 where he also declares, "we do not lose heart."[59]

In other words, through a series of logical connections (γάρ, οὖν, γάρ, διό,) the statement in 5:10 connects back to the heart of Paul's apostolic defense.[60] Nevertheless, the "all" (πάντας) of 5:10, as in 3:18, would seem to indicate a general reference.[61] The carefully organized argument in 4:1–5:9 leads up to a kind of climactic, leveling statement.

---

[57] ESV.

[58] Wright does not argue for this, but seems to assume the same referents throughout. The argument for "we" in 5:10 is offered in order to try and find evidence in the text that might support Wright's view.

[59] As Hafemann points out, in 4:1 "the parallel was between not losing heart and ministering with integrity in spite of his suffering (cf. 4:1-2). Here the corresponding parallel is between not losing heart and the daily renewal of Paul's inner self" (2 Corinthians, 189).

[60] I found that Barnett traces a similar path through Paul's discourse back as far as 4:16 (Second Corinthians, 273).

[61] Ibid., 216. There may well be a reference here to Paul's opponents who must also stand before Christ and give an account of their actions. Other interpreters also take "we . . . all" as a general reference. See Thrall, II Corinthians, 1:394, who restricts the referent to believers only; Furnish, 2 Corinthians, 305; Martin, 2 Corinthians, 114; Barnett, Second Corinthians, 273-74; Lambrecht, who sees Paul as speaking of his own apostleship up through 4:16, comments: "It would be rather unwise to hold that this change ["we" is Paul, to "we" is all] took place no earlier than v. 10. One has the impression that Paul has been broadening his horizon, perhaps beginning already in 4:16b. This is due partly to the density or importance of the reflection. Considerations about the eschatological future concern all Christians" (2 Corinthians, 86).

The nature of the subject, judgment, argues conceptually for an inclusive meaning of "we all." The extended defense of Paul's apostleship is grounded in the fact that all people must one day stand before the judgment seat of Christ. No one, neither Paul, nor his opponents and those who follow them, nor anyone else is excluded. Like everyone else, Paul must stand ultimately before Christ who will judge his work. The validity of Paul's ministry will be manifested at the very same hour that the works of all men will be judged publicly by Christ. In this way, 5:10 stands not only as a basic fact but also as a warning.

The referent in verses 14c-15 is clearly all believers. Paul shifts from a self-referent in verse 14a (which was sustained from verse 11), "For the love of Christ controls *us* (ἡμᾶς)," to a general referent in verse 14c, "one died for all, therefore all (πάντες) died," and continues through verse 15. It seems difficult to dispute that Paul includes all believers here, especially considering the purpose clause, "so that those who live might no longer live for themselves but for the one who died and rose for them."[62] Likewise, verse 17, "If *anyone* is in Christ, he is a new creation," is inclusive of "all" believers.[63] The content of these verses demands a general referent. These verses are instructive because it is not so much an issue of pronouns, but evidence that throughout a text largely devoted to Paul's apostolic defense, he continually, and increasingly as he nears 5:21, makes general statements that declare the content of his apostolic ministry, not just a defense of it. Better still, Paul's defense of his apostolic ministry *includes* his proclamation of God's redemptive action in Christ.

This last point should be born in mind when reading 5:21. In 5:18 Paul speaks of himself (and probably his coworkers) as those whom God has reconciled to himself through Christ and to whom he gave "the ministry of reconciliation." This is restated and further explained in verse

---

[62] Verse 16, "Therefore, from now on we no longer know anyone according to the flesh" can be applied generally, but the phrase "even if we knew Christ according to the flesh," seems to indicate that Paul is referring to the radical change in his perspective as a result of his experience on the Damascus road. Given the general referents in the surrounding verses and the easy application of this verse to believers in general (though "knew Christ" obviously would not apply strictly to everyone), a universal Christian principle seems to be in view. The main thrust of my argument, however, survives either way.

[63] Barnett holds that when Paul says "anyone" in verse 17, he "is speaking in the first instance of himself" just as he does in 14-16. Paul's personal experience is at the forefront but even so, "Paul is also speaking representatively for all" (*Second Corinthians*, 298-99).

19, which is introduced by the phrase "that is" (ὡς ὅτι).[64] Paul says, "God was in Christ reconciling the world to himself, not counting their trespasses against them, and entrusting to us the message of reconciliation."[65] Even though the "us" of verse 19c refers to Paul, as it does in verse 18, there is of course a general referent in the phrase "the world." The redemptive event (the non-reckoning of sin) is given an inclusive reference, while the proclamation of that event, as central as it is to the event itself, is narrowed down to Paul—the minister of the gospel message of reconciliation.

There is a pattern here that holds throughout this section. Whenever Paul generalizes a historical-redemptive event, or the result of it, he does so with an inclusive reference. In 3:18, the "we all" refers to those who have the Spirit, who "are being transformed into the same image." The judgment is an event in which "all" will participate (5:10). Christ's representative death and his resurrection were "for all," and "all" are identified with this event (5:14-15). The "new creation," which comes about through the representative death of Christ, is a designation or status for "anyone" identified with Christ (5:17).[66] God's action in Christ, which made the non-reckoning of trespasses possible, was for "the world" (5:19). And "reconciliation" is ultimately an act that includes all those

---

[64] See Porter, Καταλλάσσω in Ancient Greek Literature, with Reference to the Pauline Writings, Estudios De Filologia Neo Testamentaria 5 (Cordoba, Spain: Ediciones El Almendro, 1994), 132. He has a brief and helpful discussion of this phrase.

[65] There are a host of grammatical problems in this verse. One that seems to give interpreters a great deal of trouble is the difference in the tenses of καταλλάσσων and θέμενος. See Thrall, for example, who states: "The aorist tense of the participle, strictly interpreted, gives an illogical sense, and the θέμενος should be regarded therefore as the equivalent of the finite verb ἔθετο, lit. 'he placed'" (II Corinthians, 1:435). This is an unnecessary suggestion based on over-interpreting the temporal significance of the tenses of the participles. The participle θέμενος matches the tense of the corresponding participle in verse 18, δόντος. Both refer to the act of God in terms of making Paul's gospel an inextricable part of reconciliation. God both gives (v. 18) and entrusts (v. 19) Paul with the ministry of reconciliation. The aorist tenses may well serve to put this action in the background while God's act in Christ, καταλλάσσων, is emphasized and brought more to the foreground, as indicated by the present tense. Here I am clearly influenced by Porter, Καταλλάσσω in Ancient Greek Literature, 133. Idem, Verbal Aspect in the Greek New Testament: with Reference to Tense and Mood (New York: Lang, 1989; particularly Chapter 2, "A Systematic Analysis of Greek Verbal Aspect," 75-109). Even if one is not convinced by Porter's arguments at every point, the extended grammatical discussions in the commentaries, which try to come up with solutions for interpreting the past-time of the aorist participles, hardly offer alternatives.

[66] The "anyone" of verse 17 defines and limits the "all" of verses 14-15. This self-evident fact is a difficult obstacle for anyone interested in arguing for an unrestrained universalism in 14 and 15. It is also a text that should be brought into service to argue against the continually erupting assertion that Romans 5:18 teaches universalism.

who do not have their trespasses reckoned to them, though Paul can apply it personally as in verse 18.

When Paul comes to 5:21, therefore, we have no reason to wonder why he would include such a sweeping, general, soteriological statement in the midst of his apostolic defense. His defense, as already noted, includes the proclamation of the historical-redemptive act of God in Christ. Thus, when Paul urges the Corinthians to "be reconciled to God" (v. 20; cf. 6:1-2), he does so in the context of defending his own ministry, which is itself part and parcel of God's redemptive action (being the God-ordained means by which God's act in Christ is made known). He also spells out exactly what God's act entailed: "God made him who did not know sin, to be sin for us, so that we might become the righteousness of God in him." Taken in this way, 5:21 does not at all stand awkwardly at the end of the paragraph as a disconnected, timeless truth of salvation, but as a powerful summary of the ultimate historical-redemptive event that lies at the heart of Paul's ministry of reconciliation.[67] It is precisely the truth of salvation that Paul is pressing as he makes clear in 6:1-2. There is no compelling reason, after all, to understand 5:21 as referring exclusively to Paul, a minister of the new covenant, as "an incarnation of the covenant faithfulness of God."[68]

Covenantal faithfulness. If the argument above is right, the evidence points away from the apostolic ministry being the manifestation of God's covenantal faithfulness, and therefore casts doubt over the idea that God's covenantal faithfulness is the meaning of "the righteousness of God" in 5:21. There is nevertheless still a need to address why "covenantal faithfulness" should not be equated with the righteous-

---

[67] Contrary to Wright's comment that someone trying to read this text with a traditional interpretation "will find, as many commentators have, that it detaches itself from the rest of the chapter and context, as though it were a little floating saying which Paul threw in for good measure" (*What St. Paul Really Said*, 105). I do, though, agree with the statement he makes next: "The proof of the theory is in the sense it makes when we bring it back to the actual letter" (ibid.).

[68] Ibid., 104-5. There is another general reference in the larger context that further argues for the position taken here. After rehearsing a litany of the suffering he endures as a servant of God (6:4-10), Paul addresses the Corinthians directly in 6:11-13, then admonishes them not to be "unequally yoked with unbelievers" (vv. 14-16) which he further expands with a series of Old Testament quotes and allusions (vv. 16c-18). This section is then brought to a conclusion with a reference that clearly includes Paul and the Corinthians together: "Therefore having these promises, beloved, let us cleanse ourselves of every defilement of the flesh and spirit, by bringing holiness to its fulfillment in the fear of God" (7:1).

ness of God apart from the question of whether Paul is the referent in this verse. If the idea that "God's righteousness" and "God's covenant faithfulness" were not already presumed to be synonymous, it is highly unlikely that it would be the topic of discussion in 2 Corinthians 5:21. A full study of the idea is not possible here, but a few comments are in order since the covenant-faithfulness view continues to gain popularity.

First, and this is vitally important, it is right to assert that God's covenant faithfulness is inseparably linked to God's righteousness.[69] The Old Testament texts cited by Wright and others argue conclusively that the theme of God's righteousness is most often, if not usually, in a covenantal context. After all, one need only consider two general observations to prove this point. The first is that the Old Testament revelation unfolds through a series of covenants, beginning explicitly with Noah, then with Abraham, then with the nation of Israel, with David, etc.[70] "Covenant," broadly speaking, is the biblical structure and the *modus operandi* of the unfolding of the history of redemption. In a real sense the entire Old Testament is a covenantal context. More specifically, covenant faithfulness, by both God and people, is among the most prominent themes in the Old Testament.

Secondly, the language of the Old Testament regarding God's relationship with his people is covenantal language almost by definition. The best example of this is God's special covenant name, YHWH (Ex. 3:13-17). God's revelation of this covenantal name, moreover, is prefaced by his remembrance of "his covenant with Abraham, with Isaac, and with Jacob" (Ex. 2:24). Thus, in most places where the Old Testament speaks, for example, of YHWH's "loving kindness," his law, his blessings and curses, his mercy, salvation, protection of his people, *and his "righ-*

---

[69] I am afraid that "covenant faithfulness," besides being a technical term for those who think it means God's righteousness, could become so vilified by some who oppose whatever notion of "the new perspective on Paul" they happen to have, that the legitimate and biblically necessary use of the phrase will be nearly lost.

[70] An Adamic covenant is purposely left out because one must agree that there is a covenant between God and Adam before accepting that the language in the early chapters of Genesis is in a historically covenantal context. At the textual level, however, the story of Adam was meant for and read in a covenantal context, i.e., the nation of Israel. I think a strong case can be made that a covenant relationship does exist in Eden and that it coheres with the whole scope of historical redemption. However, many people from many traditions would disagree. That there is an explicit covenant context(s) beginning after the flood is surely recognized by most Bible readers.

teousness," it does so in a covenantal context.[71] Therefore it is entirely correct to connect God's covenant faithfulness *with* his righteousness.

A problem, however, arises when someone says that God's righteousness *is* his covenant faithfulness.[72] It is more accurate to say that God's covenant faithfulness is an expression of this righteousness,[73] or that it manifests his righteousness, rather than being his righteousness.[74] While debate may rage over texts such as Romans 3:5 and 3:21-22, it is difficult to see how God's covenantal faithfulness is in view in 2 Corinthians 5:21.[75] How does one *become* God's faithfulness to his covenant? Even if one argues that believers are living proof of such faithfulness, it is still not the same thing as *being God's* covenant faithfulness. The forensic element of 2 Corinthians 5:21 argues forcefully against the covenant faithfulness view. The righteousness of God in judging the sin of the world is clearly evident in this text. "God was in Christ reconciling the world to himself, not reckoning to them their trespasses," which, as seen above, took place through the sacrificial atoning death of Christ. Thus, on the cross God's saving righteousness and judging righteousness converge on Christ who vicariously bears the judgment for sin, provid-

---

[71] The argument against God's righteousness being his covenant faithfulness based on the observation that ברית and the צדק word group rarely occur together helps establish that the concepts should not be equated, but it does not follow from this observation that covenant faithfulness and righteousness are not connected. The most developed work on this topic is found in Mark A. Seifrid, "Righteousness Language in the Hebrew Scriptures and Early Judaism," in *Justification and Variegated Nomism*, vol. 1, ed. D. A. Carson, Peter T. O'Brien, and Mark A. Seifrid (Grand Rapids: Baker, 2001), 415-42.

[72] I suspect that in some cases the problem is semantic. One could say that God's righteousness *is* his covenant faithfulness but not mean that categorically. For instance, I could comment on a text that speaks of God's righteousness and say something like, "What is in view here is God's faithfulness to his covenant." That would not mean that I defined God's righteousness but that I had simply, without qualification, spoken about what a given text says. If every statement made in every place were fully qualified we would end up saying nothing at all. Sometimes, after all, it really does depend on what we mean by "is."

[73] "Surely, God's righteousness expresses his faithfulness to his covenant, and yet this is not the same thing as saying that God's righteousness *is his faithfulness to the covenant*." Schreiner, *Paul*, 199.

[74] John Piper, *The Justification of God: An Exegetical and Theological Study of Romans 9:1-23*, 2nd ed. (Grand Rapids: Baker, 1996), 112. After surveying the arguments, Piper prefaces his investigation of Old Testament texts with the following comment: "But the most important evidence for an alternate interpretation is the array of texts in the Old Testament in which we find men appealing to God's righteousness as something basic to, rather than equivalent to covenant faithfulness." Rather than being God's covenant faithfulness, "God's allegiance to the covenant is a real manifestation of God's righteousness" (ibid.).

[75] Though if it is shown that covenant faithfulness is not in view in 2 Corinthians 5:21, it does weaken the argument for "the righteousness of God" as basically a technical term for "covenant faithfulness." It does not by itself, as Wright points out, discredit the notion in Romans, but it does call it into question.

ing the objective basis for the justification of sinners and the reconciliation of man to God.[76]

When one recognizes the sacrificial background for 2 Corinthians 5:21, the substitutionary atonement that background entails supported by the theme of representation in verses 14-15, and the non-reckoning of sin in verse 19 that takes place by Christ's vicarious bearing of sin—this text begins to look and sound similar to Romans 3:21-26.[77] The vicarious death of Christ as an atoning sacrifice for sin, which takes place according to the initiative and judging action of God, is the shared theme of 2 Corinthians 5:21a and Romans 3:25-26—two texts that highlight the righteousness of God. The idea that 2 Corinthians 5:21 refers to God's covenantal faithfulness is not finally convincing.

The Righteousness of God in Christ

The meaning of "become the righteousness of God" is qualified by the short but powerful phrase "in him." This is not an abstract notion of righteousness conceived as a mere transaction, but a declaration that whoever is "in Christ" has a right standing before God owing to the fact that he is in union with Christ.[78] This designation is not a subjective

---

[76] As Schreiner says in regard to this text: "Believers are declared to be righteous before God as the divine judge because Jesus, as the sinless one, bore their sins. God's righteousness, therefore, consists both of this judgment and salvation . . . both the saving righteousness of God (by which he declares sinners to be in the right in his sight) and the judging work of God (by which he pours out his wrath on Christ) meet in the cross of Christ" (*Paul*, 201-2). Although the parallel with Romans 5:11 is not explored in this discussion, Garland's observation is worth noting: "In Rom. 5:1-11 Paul starts with justification and ends with reconciliation. Here he begins with reconciliation and ends with justification" (*2 Corinthians*, 302 n. 840).

[77] " . . . whom God put forth as a propitiation in his blood by faith, so as to show his righteousness through passing over sins committed beforehand, in the forbearance of God, in order to show his righteousness at the present time, so that he might be just and the justifier of the one having faith in Jesus." This does not at all mean that these texts are identical, but that they are complementary.

[78] Union with Christ is too large a topic to cover here. Paul's various uses of the phrases like "in," "with," and "through" Christ point to the highly fluid character of this biblical theme. For instance, here are some examples taken just from Ephesians in which Paul can speak of having blessings "in Christ . . . in the heavenly places" (1:3); having "in him . . . an inheritance" (1:11); being "sealed with the promised Holy Spirit" in him (1:13); of being "made alive together with Christ" (2:5); being "raised . . . and seated in the heavenly places in Christ Jesus" (2:6); being "created in Christ Jesus" (2:10); of the Gentiles being "brought near" in Christ; (2:12); of Jews and Gentiles being "one new man" in Christ (2:15); that "through him" Jews and Gentiles have equal "access in one Spirit to the Father" (2:18; cf. 3:12); being "built" as a temple in Christ (2:21-22); and, as believers as the body of Christ (4:15-16). In these and other Pauline texts union with Christ may have local, corporate, salvific, and representational references or may refer to a legal status or a state of being, etc. It is clear that Paul employs a wide range of metaphors to describe how believers are united with Christ. Failure to appreciate the multi-dimensional nature of union has led many scholars to attempt to reduce the idea down to one main theme. For a good survey of Paul's various expressions, as well an overview of modern scholarship, see Mark A. Seifrid, "In Christ," in *Dictionary of Paul and his Letters*, ed. Gerald F. Hawthorne and Ralph P. Martin (Downers Grove: InterVarsity, 1993), 433-36. Seifrid divides Paul's usage in five general categories.

or mystical experience but refers to "an abiding reality determinative to the whole Christian life."[79] A believer has a share in that righteousness that comes from God because he is incorporated into Christ who is himself the supreme manifestation of God's righteousness. Here is the cornerstone of justification and also the thing that rules out any notion of a "legal fiction."[80]

The significance of "in Christ" in 5:21 is made clearer by considering the preceding verses. There is a clear progression as each verse gives further focus to each successive verse. In the immediate context, the union theme develops as Paul expounds the representative nature of both the death and resurrection of Christ. When Paul says that Christ "died for all, therefore all died," he indicates that there is an element of participation in the death of Christ. This is not primarily an existential participation but a representational participation, as is made clear in the phrase "for all" ($\dot{\upsilon}\pi\grave{\epsilon}\rho\ \pi\acute{\alpha}\nu\tau\omega\nu$).[81]

Though not explicitly stated as in Romans 5 or 1 Corinthians 15, Christ's role as the second Adam is in view. Support for this interpretation exists not only in the similarity with Paul's more explicit Adam/Christ texts, it is found in the context as well. Just as Adam was head of the original creation and his act affected the status of those who

---

[79] Herman Ridderbos, *Paul: An Outline of his Theology*, trans. John Richard De Witt (Grand Rapids: Eerdmans, 1975), 59.

[80] Because of Paul's emphasis on union with Christ, "one may not speak," says Ridderbos, "of an 'as if'" (ibid., 175). It has long been recognized that union with Christ is a foundational element of justification. This emphasis is often forgotten and/or neglected. When the importance of union is missed, then justification, and imputation for that matter, begins to resemble a mathematical formula or the simple matter of a transaction similar to something in business or law. On the relationship between justification and union, Calvin remarks: "But the best passage of all on this matter [acceptance and forgiveness] is the one in which he teaches that the sum of the gospel embassy is to reconcile us to God, since God is willing to receive us into grace through Christ, not counting our sins against us. . . . Let my readers carefully ponder the whole passage. For a little later Paul adds by way of explanation: 'Christ, who was without sin was made sin for us' . . . to designate the means of reconciliation [cf. vv. 18-19]. Doubtless, he means by the word 'reconciled' nothing but 'justified.' And surely, what he teaches elsewhere—that 'we are made righteous by Christ's obedience' [Rom. 5:19]—could not stand *unless we are reckoned righteous before God in Christ* and apart from ourselves." *Institutes*, 3.6.4, 728-29 (my emphasis). See book III of the *Institutes* in general for the importance Calvin puts on union. In Calvin's tradition, John Murray writes: "Union with Christ is really the central truth of the whole doctrine of salvation not only in its application but also in its once-for-all accomplishment in the finished work of Christ" (*Redemption Accomplished and Applied*, 161). Murray sees union as the key to understanding election, redemption, new creation, life and conduct, death, and resurrection. "It embraces the wide span of salvation from its ultimate source in the eternal election of God to its final fruition in the glorification of the elect" (ibid., 165). It is because Murray understood the central role of union with Christ in salvation that he placed it near the end of his book.

[81] The representational nature of this verse is further confirmed by the sacrificial themes present in vv. 19-21.

followed, so the act of Christ (i.e., death for sin [vv. 14, 19, 21]) affects the status of those who follow him.[82] His death "for all" leads to their becoming a "new creation" in him. Christ's representative death, moreover, has real results for those for whom he died. The purpose (ἵνα) of his death "for all" was to bring about a new life that is lived for Christ rather than living, as previously, for themselves (v. 15, "they who live might no longer live for themselves"). Just as Adam's act of sin led to a life of sin and death for those who followed, so Christ's death for sin brings about a new life for those who follow him. As in Romans 5:17 (cf. v. 21), the life in view is ultimately life in its eschatological fulfillment, when all things become fully new.

This idea of a new existence is still clearer in the result clause found in verse 16. The result of Christ's representative death (v. 14), which entails a new life characterized by a Christ-centered perspective and way (v. 15), is that nothing, including Christ, is now known "according to the flesh" (v. 16). There is a debate over the meaning of κατὰ σάρκα, but based on his discussion in 2 Corinthians 3, the clearest explanation is that Paul is contrasting knowing "according to the flesh" with knowing "according to the Spirit."[83] Thus, knowing according to the flesh refers to knowing apart from the Spirit. There is a general emphasis on the Spirit in 2 Corinthians, particularly in chapter 3, where the Spirit is declared to be the sign that the new covenant era, in contrast to the old covenant, has dawned in Christ (3:3, 6 [2x], 8, 17 [2x]).[84] This "new" era becomes more explicit in verse 17 when Paul says, "So then, if anyone is in Christ, he is a new creation. The old things have passed away, Behold the new has come."[85] A new order, centered in Christ and

---

[82] "Paul's connection of Christ to Adam derives from his understanding of the universal scope of Christ's atoning work on the cross: 'One died for all therefore all died.'" Seifrid, "In Christ," 435.

[83] Hafemann, 2 Corinthians, 242. Also, Barnett, Second Corinthians, 294.

[84] Other references include 1:22; 4:13; 5:5; 6:6; 11:14; 13:14. "Spirit" is often spelled with a lower case "s" in 4:13 and 11:4, but a good argument can be made for a capital letter. Even if those two verses are omitted, Paul's emphasis on the historical-redemptive role of the Spirit is not significantly diminished.

[85] Many scholars discuss the background of Paul's "new creation" language in terms of parallels found in Jewish literature, such as 2 Baruch 32:6; 44:12; 57:2, 4 Ezra 7:75; Jubilees 4:26; 1QS 4.25; 1QH 13:11-12, 1QH 3:19-22; 11:10-14, as well as in rabbinic sources. See especially Peter Stuhlmacher, "Erwägungen zum ontologischen Charakter der kainē ktisis bei Paulus," Evangelische Theologie 27 (1967): 12-16. Stuhlmacher, and others (for instance, Furnish, II Corinthians, 314-15; and Thrall, II Corinthians, 421-22) note that there are both individual and cosmic elements in the various parallel texts. This background has some relevance in that it shows that when Paul speaks of a new creation (cf. Gal. 6:15), he is not inventing an entirely new vocabulary unfamiliar to all his hearers. But it is not clear how deep the parallel runs, particularly in terms of Paul's eschatological perspective. As

evidenced by the presence of the Spirit, is the result of Christ's death and resurrection and explains the "no longer" of verse 15, and the "no longer according to the flesh" of verse 16. These verses are crucial for understanding what it means to "become the righteousness of God in him," because they provide the key for understanding Paul's meaning of "in Christ" in this text. The phrase "new creation" emphasizes that which comes about through God's saving act in Christ as the one who "died for all."[86]

Thus, when verse 17 is read in the context of verses 14-15, the two basic elements of what Paul means by the righteousness of God are manifest. God's righteousness in judging and punishing sin and God's righteousness in salvation are revealed in Christ's representative death and his resurrection.[87] God is not only faithful to his covenant—he is faithful to himself, to his own character. God saves but not without punishing the offenses against him. There is pardon, but only through sacrifice. God makes a "new creation," secured in and by Christ's resurrection, through the death of Christ. Those "in Christ" are *counted* to have both "died and risen" (v. 15) in him. His death is their death, and his resurrection is their life. God's righteousness is revealed in both, and God himself, who brought all this to pass, is the one who recognizes or identifies people as being "in Christ." In this text, "in Christ" has primarily a representative, or corporate, connotation.

When, therefore, Paul speaks of "becoming the righteousness of God in him," he is speaking of becoming a "new creation," and

---

Thrall points out, "It seems that the belief in a new act of creation or cosmic renewal at the end of history is adequately attested for the Judaism of Paul's day. But it is rather less certain that, when similes of new birth or new creation are applied to individuals, there is any real idea of present anticipation of this strictly eschatological event in the future" (Thrall, *II Corinthians*, 422).

[86] After quoting 5:14-17 Ridderbos states the following: "From this it is to be concluded that 'having died,' 'being in Christ,' 'being [a] new creation,' the fact that his own are no longer judged and 'known according to the flesh' (namely, according to the worldly mode of existence), has been given and effected with the death of Christ himself" (*Paul*, 60).

[87] This is not to say that God's righteousness can be separated neatly into component parts, but that Christ's death and resurrection understood as essentially one event shows God's righteousness in both judgment and salvation. Seeing both elements in God's righteousness is not a theological imposition on the text. God's "saving righteousness" is inseparable, and in fact incomprehensible, apart from his judgment and punishment of sin. Christ's death and resurrection both announce that God is just. But God's righteousness cannot be limited to his "saving righteousness" *unless* one presupposes that this includes the punishment for sin and the vindication of God's own righteousness. The emphasis on God's saving righteousness, so prevalent in recent decades, is often taken out of the context of the necessity for God to uphold his righteousness in the judgment of sin. (See quote from Schreiner above, n. 76). Christ's death for sin (v. 14) makes the "new creation" pronouncement possible.

becoming a new creation means that one has been united to Christ in his death and resurrection, which manifested God's judging and saving righteousness. One has been taken from the old age marked by sin and death and graciously brought into the age of the new covenant.[88] By becoming united with Christ, identified and incorporated in him, people are identified with God's righteousness as supremely revealed in Christ's death and resurrection. They "become" God's righteousness, and are declared to be righteous, just as they are united with Christ who is the embodiment and revelation of God's righteousness.[89] In this way it is fair to say that Christ himself became the righteousness of God in his death and resurrection "so that we might become the righteousness of God in him."

The justification for this reading of the text is seen in verse 19 where it is God acting "in Christ" to reconcile the world to himself by not counting their trespasses, which, as seen above, entails that those trespasses are counted to Christ in his sacrificial death. Christ's death for those trespasses is, in corollary fashion, counted to those who committed them. If Christ's death and resurrection manifest the righteousness of God in saving through judgment, and if God was thus working in Christ to bring about the reconciliation of the world to himself, then it is entirely legitimate to say that the righteousness of God and the righteousness of Christ are inseparable. Becoming the righteousness of God, therefore, means taking on Christ's righteousness through union with him.[90]

The upshot of all this is that becoming the righteousness of God in Christ puts the emphasis on an event and an act that takes place outside the believer, in which the believer becomes a participant in Christ (cf. Rom. 6:3-7).[91] It is God who supplies the means of believers becoming

---

[88] Beale shows the link between "new creation" and the fulfillment of God's promises through Isaiah to restore his people, citing 43:18-19; 65:17; 66:22 in support of his argument ("The Old Testament Background of Reconciliation," 556). Similarly, Kim, "2 Cor. 5:11-21," 380; and Hafemann, *2 Corinthians*, 243-44 (who cites both Beale and Kim). Many others have cited these texts in Isaiah, but Beale's argument is the most thorough treatment of the influence of Isaiah on this text.

[89] This should not be confused with Osiander's error, in which the believer becomes righteous by the impartation of Christ's "essential righteousness" which derives from his divinity. The sacrificial basis and forensic nature of justification are excluded in favor of participation in Christ's divine, eternal essence. See Calvin's refutation of Osiander in 3.11.5-12 of the *Institutes*.

[90] "As a result of Christ's death, not only does Christ take on our sin, we take on his righteousness. When God sees us in Christ, he sees the perfection of Christ having already been granted to us as a gift" (Hafemann, *2 Corinthians*, 248).

[91] The term "believer" is used here, as elsewhere, as a convenient designation for those "in Christ." The text itself does not emphasize the role of faith in salvation.

"a new creation," and it is God who both incorporates and recognizes them in Christ and ultimately *counts* them righteous in him. This does not at all diminish the fact that being a new creation means a transformation brought about by the Spirit; to the contrary, it provides the only sure foundation for understanding that transformation has a definite, objective beginning in union with Christ. Becoming God's righteousness is not an attribute but a declaration that God counts individuals as having a right standing before him, because he sees them with respect to their union with Christ their representative rather than as part of the old age of sin and death.[92] This objective reality precedes, establishes, and provides assurance for the Spirit-driven eschatological completion of the work that begins with becoming a new creation, becoming the righteousness of God in Christ. "It is God who establishes us with you in Christ, and has anointed us, and who has also put his seal on us and given us his Spirit in our hearts as a guarantee" (1:21-22).[93]

GOD, THE CROSS, AND RIGHTEOUSNESS

Second Corinthians 5:21 is yet another example of the richness of Paul's presentation of the various aspects of justification. Here God is the actor, the action is Christ's sacrificial death on the cross, and the result is, again, righteousness:

Subject/Actor	Action	Result
God	Cross	Righteousness

Notice that although the result is similar, both the one acting and, at least to some extent, the action are different from that in Romans 4 or 5. Yet, the texts are obviously similar in their general content. Again it is important to realize that although 2 Corinthians 5:21 is often and justifiably discussed in regard to imputation, Paul's emphasis here is different from either of the two texts. In other words, Paul is not saying the same thing here as in either Romans 4 or 5. Here the emphasis is not primarily on the appropriation of righteousness (faith), or the foundation for

---

[92] Union with Christ is not opposed to, antithetical to, or an alternative to an emphasis on the forensic nature of justification. It establishes the ground for a legitimate, legal declaration and standing.
[93] ESV.

righteousness (Christ's obedience), but on the means by which it is possible for God to count people as righteous, i.e., Christ's sacrificial death
on the cross. When these texts are read together, then a fuller picture
develops, but in order to see that picture rightly, we must first recognize
the various details and the richness of its various components.

While some may balk at the mention of the imputation of Christ's
righteousness in regard to this text, the basic idea of something "counting" for righteousness is again unavoidable. As shown above, by its
very nature a sacrificial death implies that the death of the sacrifice in
some way "counts" for those for whom it is intended. In 5:19, the non-
reckoning of sins is clear: because of the cross of Christ God does not
reckon trespasses to those who committed them. In his death "for all"
Christ takes on the penalty of those trespasses. Surely there is reason to
say that those trespasses, i.e., our sin, were reckoned to Christ.

Another more explicit emphasis in this text is union with Christ, and
this theme, perhaps more than any other, provides the conceptual basis
for a biblical conception of the reckoning of Christ's righteousness. What
is implied in Romans 4,[94] and made clearer in Romans 5,[95] comes to the
forefront in 2 Corinthians 5. It is here, as seen above, that the discussion
of whether Christ's righteousness is reckoned to believers must proceed,
and it is here that the question is answered. The biblical doctrine of union
with Christ lies at the heart of the assertion that Christ's righteousness
"counts" for believers. The very idea that God recognizes people as "righteous" argues for God's counting Christ's righteousness to them. If there
were some other ground for the declaration "righteous," there would
be no need to be "in Christ." In other words God sees his people only
"in Christ," and only in Christ are they counted righteous. It is essential
to understand that whatever else we might say about union with Christ
(and there is a great deal to say) it is a union that exists essentially from
God's perspective. One does not first identify oneself "in Christ"; one is
identified by God as being "in Christ."[96] This explains why Paul makes
the point that being a "new creation" and "becoming the righteousness of

---

[94] That is, faith as that which unites us to Christ, its object.

[95] United with Christ as our representative head.

[96] As Calvin says: "We do not, therefore, contemplate him outside ourselves from a far in order that
his righteousness may be imputed to us but because we put on Christ and are engrafted into his
body" (Institutes, 3.11.10, 737).

God" take place only "in Christ." God both creates and declares a person righteous because he now sees that person in union with his Son and so covered with the Son's righteousness.[97]

Here the emphasis is centered particularly on Christ's death for the forgiveness of sins. His death, however, is not neatly separated from his life. He "knew no sin," that is, he was a perfect sacrifice, a lamb without spot or blemish. His perfect life led in obedience to God is undoubtedly in view here, although it is not the focus of Paul's discussion. As in Romans 5, Christ's life and death are inherently connected. Again, there is no need to assert that every aspect of Paul's doctrine of justification is fully present in this text. A proper synthetic reading of Paul must first deal with the individual characteristics of each text under investigation.

CONCLUSION

In the context of 2 Corinthians 5:21 Paul teaches that Christ's sacrificial, atoning death counts to those "in him." The themes of representation, reconciliation, and the forgiveness of sins, here spoken of as the non-reckoning of sin (v. 19), all point to a sacrificial meaning for the phrase "made sin." From first to last this is an act of God, who made Christ a sacrifice for sin by causing the sins of others to be counted to him. The twin statements, "a new creation" and "become the righteousness of God," both centered in the phrase "in Christ" and dependent on his representative death, indicate that just as sin was reckoned to Christ, so too is Christ's sacrificial death counted for righteousness to those "in him." God counts them righteous because they have Christ's righteousness, they have Christ himself, and he has them.

With these three texts discussed in terms of how each relates to the theme of the reckoning of Christ's righteousness, attention now turns to how these texts work together for the development of a Pauline synthesis.

---

[97] Taken this way it is entirely valid to speak of an "alien righteousness." While the phrase may be obscure to modern ears given the connotations of "alien" in popular usage, historically it refers simply to a righteousness that has its origin outside the individual. It is not the phrase but the meaning that is important.

FIVE

THE IMPUTATION OF
CHRIST'S RIGHTEOUSNESS:
A PAULINE SYNTHESIS

AFTER CONSIDERING EACH key text individually, it is now time to see what it looks like when we view them all together:

	Actor	Action	Result
Romans 4:3	Abraham	Faith	Reckoned Righteous
Romans 5:19	Christ	Obedience	Made Righteous
2 Corinthians 5:21	God	Made Christ Sin	Became Righteousness

In each case the actor and the explicit action changes, but the results are quite similar. It is clear that Paul is not simply saying the same thing in different ways. Yet in each text Paul is dealing with the same basic subject: what it means to be right with God. It is also true that Paul never says explicitly, word-for-word, that the righteousness of Christ counts for, is reckoned to, or is imputed to believers. As we have seen, however, in each text—even taken separately—there is a sense in which something may be said to "count" to believers. Romans 4 contains obvious imputation language, i.e., faith reckoned as righteousness, but this is most closely associated with forgiveness. It was, nevertheless, argued that contextual evidence prior and subsequent to Romans 4 points to justifying faith as instrumental (Rom. 3:25; 5:1), and as that which unites the believer with faith's object, rather than faith itself being the object. This helps make the case for an external righteousness counting to the believer.

Romans 5 contains language different from Romans 4. In 5:19 many "are made righteous" rather than "reckoned righteous." However, in Romans 5 it is difficult to avoid saying that Christ's obedience does indeed "count" for those identified with him, just as Adam's disobedience "counted" for his progeny. Two acts, disobedience and obedience, affect the standing of many before God. The "counting" metaphor certainly is not far off. In 2 Corinthians 5 Paul mentions explicitly the non-imputation of sins (v. 19), but again the imputation of Christ's righteousness is not explicit in the text. It was, however, argued that it is legitimate to say that Christ's sacrificial death "counts" for those in union with him. As pointed out several times along the way, none of these texts hold all the pieces of the puzzle. Rather, each text itself is a piece of the puzzle. What remains is to see what the puzzle looks like when all the pieces are put together.

On the basis of the language and the various common themes that recur with consistent frequency in those texts most closely associated with the doctrine of imputation, it is legitimate and necessary to say that the believer stands in a right relationship with God on the basis of Christ's righteousness. This conclusion is the theme of this chapter and, indeed, of the entire book.

READING "SYNOPTICALLY"

Read individually, none of the three texts analyzed above presents the whole story of how a person may be right with God. When read together, however, these texts give a fuller perspective on God's gift of salvation through Christ. A fitting analogy may be borrowed from Gospel studies. Taken individually, none of the Gospels gives us a complete picture of Jesus. That is not to say that any one of the Gospels is deficient or lacks the authority or reliability of the others. Nor does it mean that each Gospel gives us wildly different stories about Jesus, or that any one or more of the Gospels is lacking in some way. Each Gospel contains, for instance, teaching, accounts of healing and miracles, sayings, and historical narrative, but each Gospel contains the specific emphases of its particular author that differs in various ways from the emphases of the others. Taken together, the emphases and purpose of each author combines with that of the other writers to give us a fuller understanding of the person and work of Jesus Christ. We have many perspectives and angles by which we can look at the same person and gain a far richer and fuller view than if we had but one or two Gospels, or if they were identical.

So it is with these three "key texts." When read together, or "synoptically," we have a fuller understanding of how we come to have a right standing before God. Of course, this idea can and should be expanded to include other Pauline texts. The first thing to do, however, is to identify themes common to the "key" texts.

Common Threads in the "Key" Texts

When one considers Romans 4:3, Romans 5:18-19, and 2 Corinthians 5:21 together, many common links emerge from the diversity of metaphors and emphases Paul employs in each text.[1] The most noticeable of these links is the role of some person, God or Christ, and/or some action operating externally to the believer. In Romans 4:3, though Abraham believes, it is God who reckons righteousness. That is not to downplay the role of faith, but only to note that faith is not the only action central to that text. In Romans 5:19 it is the obedience of Christ that results in many being made righteous. Faith is taken for granted, having already been established before 5:12, but there the emphasis shifts from faith to Christ's obedience. Similarly, it is God's action through the sacrifice of Christ on the cross that results in becoming "the righteousness of God" (2 Cor. 5:21). In each of these texts, then,

---

[1] The underlying presupposition here, and the justification for this chapter, is the conviction that in spite of the occasional nature of Paul's letters, they are all written from a foundational, unified, theological perspective. The common, modern assertion that "Paul was not a systematic theologian" has led some scholars to believe that any attempt to link the various themes in the Epistles is an imposition that Paul himself would neither support nor understand. To say that Paul was not a systematic theologian is, at best, a relative statement. Compared to, say, high-scholasticism, or to any theological method that organizes biblical teaching under synthetic categories that are not derived from Scripture, Paul was not a systematic theologian. Unfortunately, "not a systematic theologian" means for some scholars that Paul had no interest in how biblical teaching functions together as a whole. Paul was, as Geerhardus Vos (and Richard Gaffin after him) points out, a theologian. He read Scripture in light of the whole, and interpreted Scripture with Scripture. The various circumstances Paul faced in the churches to which he wrote were addressed from a coherent theology. In support, many of Vos's works could be cited. For a short but representative example, see "The Theology of Paul," in *Redemptive History and Biblical Interpretation: The Shorter Writings of Geerhardus Vos*, ed. Richard Gaffin (Phillipsburg, NJ: Presbyterian and Reformed, 1980), 355-60. See also, Richard B. Gaffin Jr., *Resurrection and Redemption: A Study in Paul's Soteriology*, 2nd ed. (Phillipsburg, N. J.: Presbyterian and Reformed, 1987), particularly 19-30. While some will disagree with this notion, it is nevertheless the hermeneutical framework that guides this work.

the unavoidable conclusion is that one cannot be righteous before God on the basis of one's own actions, accomplishments, or moral standing. Thus, when "faith is reckoned as righteousness,"[2] when one is "made righteous" or when one "becomes the righteousness of God," it is only because something has taken place externally and is subsequently appropriated by and applied to the individual.

There is a common contextual feature in these texts as well. In the context of each text, a right standing before God depends specifically on God doing something in or through Christ that applies to the believer. This is closely related to the observation made above about the external nature of the actions, but the specific divine acts are in view here. First, in the larger context of Romans 4 the object of faith is Jesus, through whom God demonstrated "his righteousness that he might be just and the justifier of the one who has faith in Jesus" (Rom. 3:26), "who was delivered up [by God] on account of our transgressions, and was raised for our justification" (Rom. 4:25). God's action in Christ results in justification by faith and peace with God (Rom. 5:1). Second, Christ's "righteous act" (Rom. 5:18), his death on the cross, is the means by which God's enemies are reconciled to him ("reconciled to God through the death of his Son" (5:10)). The similarity with the message of 2 Corinthians 5 is unmistakable. Through the death of his son, God brings about a righteous standing for those united to Christ. Moreover, the discussion of reconciliation in 2 Corinthians 5 is all about what God has done through Christ.

A distinct absence of any sort of personal contribution toward a righteous standing before God is another common feature. Consider the ways Paul describes those receiving the righteousness. In terms of personal status, he refers to the justification of "the ungodly" (Rom. 4:5), "sinners" being made righteous (Rom. 5:19),[3] and those to whom God has not counted their transgressions (i.e., "sinners") becoming God's righteousness (2 Cor. 5:19-21). The principle at work in each text is that people, who not only bring nothing but, more importantly, deserve

---

[2] Note that "faith reckoned as righteousness" is parallel with the justification of the ungodly (Rom. 4:5) and a person being reckoned righteous (Rom. 4:6).

[3] Another descriptive term, "weak" (ἀσθενής), appears with "ungodly" and sinners" in Romans 5:6, 8.

nothing (except to be justly punished for their sin), are nevertheless the beneficiaries of God's grace.

God's grace is itself another common theme in these key texts. It is not justification by works that simply receives its due compensation, but justification by faith that, implicitly, is "reckoned according to grace" (Rom. 4:4). Unlike the transgression of Adam that resulted in death, "much more did the grace of God and the gift by the grace of the one man, Jesus Christ, abound to the many" (Rom. 5:15). And while "sin increased, grace abounded all the more" (Rom. 5:20). God's grace is not mentioned explicitly in 2 Corinthians 5, but it is implied in his unilateral act of reconciliation of the world with himself through Christ and by the non-reckoning of sin (5:19). God's grace is also evident in that he himself makes an appeal through Paul, his minister of reconciliation: "be reconciled to God" (v. 20). God takes the initiative, God acts, and humans receive the results as a gift.

Finally it is clear that being righteous before God is intrinsically related to union with Christ. In these texts it is primarily a representative union, with the believer being incorporated into Christ and identified as such by God and so partaking of all Christ's benefits. This is not as clear perhaps in Romans 4, but even without that text, the union of Christ and the believer is clearer in Romans 5 and even more so in 2 Corinthians 5. And again, in both texts the focus is on a representative union.

None of these texts deals with abstract ideas, events, or results. For all the rich diversity in Paul's language, in each text it is God acting in and through Christ on behalf of sinners undeserving of God's grace, who by faith in Jesus have their sins forgiven, are reconciled to God, and declared righteous. Therefore, though the texts speak of different actions, i.e., "reckoned," "made," and "become," there are common threads that run through each text. We might also connect them in a way so that each flows to the next: (1) an external act, which is specifically (2) God acting in Christ, (3) on behalf of sinners, and is, thus (4) an act of grace, and is affected or applied in (5) union with Christ. Taken together, these common themes do not prove imputation, but they do argue forcibly against any conception of justifying righteousness apart from Christ. We will see shortly that these same themes appear in other supporting texts.

The Obedience of Christ, the Second Adam

A second major point in this synthesis results from reading Romans 5 with 2 Corinthians 5. This will again reveal how different emphases in different texts may be brought together to form a greater whole. First of all, reading these texts together can shed some light on one of the more debated aspects of imputation; namely, the so-called "active" and "passive" elements of Christ's obedience.

It was noted earlier that there is not a strict division in these texts between the ideas of Christ's "active" obedience, sometimes thought primarily to consist in the obedience he rendered to the Father in terms of obeying his will or keeping the law, and Christ's "passive" obedience, referring primarily though not exclusively to his dying on the cross. Yet the designations "active" and "passive" are not necessarily theological abstractions. It was noted that the obedience Paul speaks of in Romans 5:19 most likely refers to Christ's death, even though his death ultimately cannot be detached from his life. At the same time, the clear emphasis in that text is on Christ's obedience to God in contrast to Adam's disobedience. At the cross, Christ obeyed the will and command of the Father. Even if Christ's obedience cannot be divided absolutely between passive and active, we may still say with certainty that his obedience is a central element in what happened at the cross. There is yet more to say.

Along with Christ's obedience, the cross manifests an explicit act on the part of God the Father. It was God who "made him to be sin" (2 Cor. 5:21).[4] Thus, a second essential element of the cross is that God made Christ a sacrificial offering for sin (Rom. 3:25; cf. 5:9). At the cross God's own just wrath against sin was met (Rom. 3:26), and sin was thereby forgiven. Thus, the sacrifice of Christ on the cross brings about both the justification of God and the justification of the ungodly. Sins are forgiven because of the sacrificial death of Christ on the cross. This is what makes it possible for God not to reckon sin without violating his own righteousness. Paul spells this out just as clearly as he states that Christ's death on the cross was an act of obedience. It is not,

---

[4] Compare the role of God in the substitutionary work of the Servant in Isaiah 53:4-6, 10. If Isaiah provides Paul's background, and it seems certain it does, than it reinforces the active role of God in bringing about his promised salvation through Christ—as promised.

therefore, going astray from Paul to describe the cross itself as display-ing both active and passive obedience. Now, however, instead of merely parsing out Christ's obedience, the distinction is applied to two aspects of what took place at the cross. God made Christ a sacrifice for sin *and* Christ fully obeyed God and became that sacrifice for sin. He willingly accepted God's wrath against sin as it was placed upon him (passive) and he willingly bore that penalty for sin on the cross (active).

What this shows us is that in two texts where Paul discusses Christ's role as the second Adam *in explicit relation to the cross*, he emphasizes two things about the same event. First, Christ as the rep-resentative second Adam in 2 Corinthians 5:14-15 dies "for all" so that they might live. This representative death is described in terms of a sacrificial death for sin in 5:21. In Romans 5:12-21, Paul emphasizes Christ's representative death (for "all" and "many") as a positive act of obedience that counters and overturns the disobedience of the first man Adam. This is not the same emphasis found in 2 Corinthians 5, just as the sacrificial nature of the cross is not emphasized in Romans 5:12-21, though it is certainly not absent from the larger context.[5] In one text the positive nature of Christ's obedience is emphasized while his negative obedience is emphasized in the other.[6] This leads to the conclusion that Christ's role as the second Adam does, in fact, include the provision for the forgiveness of sins *and* a positive standing before God on the basis of Christ's obedience. It is true that Paul can speak of forgiveness as a positive standing before God, and he can make forgiveness essentially synonymous with justification (Romans 4), but at the same time, Paul can speak of more than forgiveness because more than forgiveness is involved in recapitulating and overturning the actions of the first Adam.

The preceding conclusion argues against understanding Christ's obedience as limited to that which made him a perfect sacrifice for sin. His obedience to the Father did render him a spotless and undefiled

---

[5] Even though Paul says we are "justified by his blood" (5:9), the emphasis in 5:12-21 is not on Christ as a sacrifice for sin. The key word here is "emphasis." It has been noted several times that Paul makes it extremely clear in 3:21-27 that Christ died a sacrificial death on the cross. The point here is that Paul is able to speak of one event (the cross) and emphasize different elements of that event while keeping sight of the greater whole.

[6] Again, for clarity, "positive" and "negative" are not value statements. Note also that this discussion of positive and negative obedience/righteousness is not a mere defense of the traditional arguments even though the terms are employed. It is an attempt to show that there is a legitimate way to speak biblically about this distinction.

sacrifice, but it is difficult to say that Christ's obedience only manifested that he qualified as a perfect sacrifice for sin. Christ's obedience, even if Romans 5:19 is limited to the cross, was an assertive, freely taken, act of will. Thus at the cross, as the climax of his incarnation, Christ fulfills his mission as the second Adam—to obey where the first disobeyed, to be faithful where the first was faithless. Thus even if limited to the cross, we may say that Christ's obedience includes both negative and positive aspects.

Someone may object that this conclusion conveniently leaves off the text in favor of a theological assumption, an underlying presupposition, about the nature of the relationship between Adam and Christ, as well as the nature of Adam's disobedience. At issue is whether Christ's obedience as the second Adam brings about a positive standing before God in addition to, or along with, forgiveness. The role of Adam leaves the interpreter few choices. If one thinks that Adam was moving to some sort of confirmed state of existence, i.e., that the creation itself was moving forward to a state of perfection or blessedness (and what that entails is not important here), then the "positive" element of imputation is nearly a given. When Adam sinned, he disbelieved and disobeyed God, and he therefore failed to accomplish what God commanded. What humanity needs as a result of this is forgiveness for Adam's sin and its consequences, *and* a positive standing before God—that which Adam would have achieved.[7] This idea is heartily rejected by many interpreters.

Some may assert that Adam was already in a confirmed state before God, and that rather than moving toward a perfect existence (or however one chooses to say it) his job was to keep on subduing the earth, stretching Eden's boundaries to include the whole world, all the while continuing to live in fellowship and communion with God. Adam was not moving up; he was moving out. Yet if this second option is correct, one is not left with a greatly different situation after the fall from that described in the first option. Adam still failed to believe and obey God, and creation was still not subdued. More importantly, the commandment not to eat from the Tree of the Knowledge of Good and Evil was

---

[7] As noted in several places, this is, more or less, the traditional Reformed view. Adam's existence was not static. Recall that Vos describes a "pre-redemptive eschatology" (Vos, *The Eschatology of the Old Testament*, ed. James T. Dennison Jr. [Phillipsburg, N.J.: P&R, 2001], 73-76).

still disobeyed. Adam, as the representative man, still did not do what God commanded. Even if Adam had been forgiven on the spot, there would still be the need for positive obedience.[8] This result is not substantially different from the former option.[9]

There is a sense, then, in which we can speak legitimately of needing a "positive standing," and mean by that, something besides forgiveness when speaking of Christ's fulfilling the role of second Adam. This makes sense in the flow of Romans where Paul works his way back to the explicit fountainhead of sin. There is a point at which sin entered the world, and what is needed is forgiveness for sin *and* a new beginning that not only takes up where the first left off but also recapitulates the first. It must be remembered that Christ did not go back to the beginning but fulfilled his role as the second Adam in the world as it was left by the first Adam—filled with sin and death. In place of the first creation, there is now a "new creation in Christ" (2 Cor. 5:17), the second Adam whose actions are applied to those united with him. Thus, taken together Romans 5:12-21 and 2 Corinthians 5:14-21 bring us a view of the cross that emphasizes two essential aspects related to one event. In both cases, human beings acquire a right standing before God solely on the basis of what Christ has done for them. It is right to say that what Christ did as the second Adam, both securing forgiveness and positively obeying the Father, *counts* for that standing.

These are the main themes common to the three texts discussed in the preceding chapters. Clearly, as in much traditional Protestant theology, Christ's role as the second Adam plays a foundational role in this discussion. It is not an exaggeration to say that the imputation of Christ's righteousness hangs on the interpretation of Romans 5:12-21. Yet even such a central biblical text, in which Paul addresses the most foundational issues, does not itself establish the imputation of Christ's righteousness. The same can be said of Romans 4 and 2 Corinthians 5. One must read these texts together in order to get a broader perspective. With that in

---

[8] This statement is for the sake of argument. I am fully aware of the problems of Adam just simply being "forgiven" as if on a whim or without God's justice being vindicated.

[9] Another option is to say that we do not know what "might have happened," and that what happened was according to God's plan (not everyone would say "God's plan," but every objection cannot be considered) and that questions of "what if" are irrelevant. While I am on the whole sympathetic with this idea, this does not relieve us of the task of trying to understand what all is entailed in Paul's teaching about Christ as the second Adam.

mind, we now turn to other texts in Paul that typically enter into the discussion of imputation and thereby broaden our "synoptic" reading.

THE TIES THAT BIND: THE WITNESS OF OTHER TEXTS

The imputation of Christ's righteousness in the Pauline literature does not stand solely on the three texts discussed above. While many texts may play a role in the overall discussion, the texts in this section are historically and exegetically important to this topic. We will consider the following texts with a narrow focus on how they apply to a study of imputation. Particular emphasis will be laid on the conceptual parallels common to these texts and also to their connections with the "key" texts.

1 Corinthians 1:30

The common elements listed above are evident, to different degrees, in other texts related to the historical discussion of imputation. These texts further fill out the picture. One such text is 1 Corinthians 1:30: "By him [God] you are in Christ Jesus, who has become wisdom to us from God, righteousness and also sanctification and redemption." In this text Paul speaks of the holistic nature of the believer's union with Christ. The four things mentioned here (wisdom, righteousness, sanctification, and redemption) belong to the believer only as the believer belongs to Christ. This verse is a summary verse, similar to 6:11,[10] and Paul leaves out many details in regard to how these elements are applied to believers and how Christ has become all these things for believers. Nevertheless, it is clear that (1) these elements originate externally to the believer, since they are "by God," "in Christ," and "for us"; (2) these same phrases also indicate that God was at work in Christ to bring about these things; (3) in the context, Paul describes the beneficiaries of God's act in Christ as undeserving, i.e., not wise, mighty, or noble (v. 26), but as foolish and weak (v. 27), base, and despised, and as "things that are not" (v. 28);[11] (4) God's grace is the operating principle, i.e., "by him"; and, (5) these elements apply to believers only in union with Christ, i.e., "in Christ Jesus."

---

[10] "And such some of you were [fornicators, idolaters, adulterers, etc.], but you were washed, but you were sanctified, but you were justified in the name of the Lord Jesus Christ, and in the Spirit of our God."
[11] Granted that these descriptions are based on the world's perception of those God has called, it still seems clear that the Corinthians are not set forth as eminently deserving of God's grace. If 1:18-28 is not enough evidence to support this claim, then the content of 1 and 2 Corinthians should suffice.

While Paul does not state how these aspects of being in Christ are applied to believers, there is no reason to assume that they must all apply or be appropriated in the same way.[12] One can argue that righteousness is reckoned to believers without asserting that wisdom, sanctification, and redemption must be reckoned as well. For instance, it is clear from the context what Paul means by "wisdom," and it is not something reckoned to believers.[13] The "wisdom" that Christ has become is manifested in the cross, a message that is foolishness to the world, "but to us who are being saved, it is the power of God" (v. 18). Christ is the wisdom of God manifested in "the foolishness of the message preached," that is, the gospel (v. 21). Wisdom from God is "Christ crucified, a stumbling block to the Jews and foolishness to the Greeks" (v. 23). "Christ" is, "to those who are called . . . the power of God, and the wisdom of God" (v. 24). The "wisdom," therefore, that Christ has become for us is our very salvation, because "wisdom" here is God's saving act in the cross of Christ. It is thus another way of saying that salvation is wholly in Christ, and thereby he has become our righteousness.

There is, then, no reason to assert that if righteousness is reckoned, then wisdom must be reckoned.[14] It is neither a communicable attribute

---

[12] N. T. Wright comments that 1 Corinthians 1:30 "is the only passage I know where something called 'the imputed righteousness of Christ' . . . finds any basis in the text." However, he goes on to say that "if we are to claim it as such, we must also be prepared to talk of the imputed wisdom of Christ; the imputed sanctification of Christ; and the imputed redemption of Christ; and that, though no doubt they are all true in some overall general sense, will make nonsense of the very specialized and technical senses so frequently given to the phrase 'the righteousness of Christ' in the history of theology." N. T. Wright, *What St. Paul Really Said: Was Paul of Tarsus the Real Founder of Christianity?* (Grand Rapids: Eerdmans, 1997), 123.

[13] Some of the problem in the interpretation of this text comes from reading the ἡμῖν before σο'α. In this way, "wisdom" is most naturally understood as functioning like the other three nouns, δικαιοσύνη, ἁγιασμός, and ἀπολύτρωσις. This is the way the AV reads the text. As Godet notes, there is good support from the manuscripts to read ἡμῖν after σοφία, thus separating "wisdom" from the other three (Louis Godet, *Commentary on First Corinthians* [Grand Rapids: Kregel, 1977], 117-21).

[14] Gundry's criticism of imputation in this text is similar to Wright's: "One could I suppose, imagine that Christ's sanctification is imputed to us in that God counts the sanctification of Christ as ours too (cf. John 17:19). But it is harder to imagine that Christ's wisdom is imputed to us in that God counts the wisdom of Christ as ours." Robert H. Gundry, "Why I Didn't Endorse 'The Gospel of Jesus Christ: An Evangelical Celebration' . . . Even though I Wasn't Asked To," *Books & Culture*, January/February (2001): 7. Gundry's article does not include exegesis of 1 Corinthians 1:30, so it is difficult to know what he thinks this text means, since his goal is to say what he thinks it does not mean. Gundry's objection, like Wright's, raises a simple question: What indication is there that Christ "became for us . . . wisdom, righteousness, sanctification, and redemption" in all the same way? For instance, why "imagine that Christ's sanctification is imputed?" There is no real reason to think that because Christ's righteousness is imputed, Christ's sanctification must also be imputed. How Christ "became" any of these things to us must be answered one concept at a time and in concert with other texts. When we recognize that terms and themes very similar to those discussed above in regard to

in this text nor a christological statement.[15] It is not, therefore, a matter of how we become wise, for Paul describes true wisdom simply in terms of knowing "nothing other than Christ and him crucified" (2:2). It is God's wisdom manifested in saving those who are not wise, mighty, noble, but who are foolish, weak, despised, etc. In so doing, God brings the things "that are" to nothing. It is in the context of this wisdom from God that the terms righteousness, sanctification, and redemption appear. Each is descriptive of a state of being, a status that one has from God as a result of believing in God's wisdom, the cross of Christ (v. 18). These are components of salvation.

There is no order of salvation in view at this point, but "three different metaphors for the same event (our salvation that was effected in Christ), each taken from a different sphere and each emphasizing a different aspect of the one reality."[16] And the purpose is clear: "that no flesh might boast

being righteous before God, (i.e., grace, union, external righteousness, etc.) also appear in this text, then we have an indication of how Christ "became" righteousness to us. The same mode (by imputation) need not apply to redemption, sanctification, and wisdom. Piper asks, and answers, a similar question in a similar way: "[W]hy should we assume that Christ's becoming righteousness for us refers to an imputed righteousness? In answer, I don't *assume* it. Instead I note that the other passages that connect righteousness with being 'in Christ' have to do with justification (Galatians 2:17) and speak of a righteousness that is 'not our own' (Philippians 3:9) and that 'we become the righteousness of God' in the same way Christ became sin, that is, by imputation (2 Corinthians 5:21). Then I observe that there is no reason to think that Christ must 'become' for us righteousness exactly the same way he becomes wisdom and sanctification and redemption" (John Piper, *Counted Righteous in Christ: Should We Abandon the Imputation of Christ's Righteousness?* [Wheaton: Crossway, 2002], 86).

[15] Fee thinks the AV reading causes the verse to make a christological assertion that Paul never intended. Gordon Fee, *First Epistle to the Corinthians*, NICNT (Grand Rapids: Eerdmans, 1987), 85. In this reading, similar to Colossians 2:2-3 and James 1:5, Christ "is the source of wisdom for Christians, whereby they either come to know God or are enlightened about his ways; in other words, Christ became wisdom for us so that we might thereby become wise" (ibid.). Conzelmann argues against any idea of "wisdom Christology" in this text, observing that "the expression that Christ is 'our' wisdom prohibits any interpretation which would here regard him as the hypostatized creation Wisdom." Hans Conzelmann, *1 Corinthians*, Hermeneia (Philadelphia: Fortress, 1975), 51 n. 25.

[16] Fee, *First Corinthians*, 86. Fee also references 6:11 in this regard: "You were washed you were sanctified you were justified in the name of the Lord Jesus Christ, and in the Spirit of our God" (ibid.). He states: "The metaphors themselves lack what we might ordinarily consider logical sequence. . . . There are not three different steps in the saving process; they are rather three different metaphors for the same event (our salvation that was effected in Christ), each taken from a different sphere and each emphasizing a different aspect of the one reality" (ibid.). The multiple metaphors recognized by Conzelmann and Fee argue against the idea that if one element is applied by imputation, then all must be applied by imputation. There is no reason to assert that different aspects and/or benefits of salvation must be applied to the believer in the same way. There is no single, monolithic term that captures the fullness of salvation in Christ. Ironically, those who argue against imputation in this text on the basis that if one element is imputed they must all be imputed, read the text more narrowly than those who argue for the imputation of righteousness. By way of observation, I do not think that because there is no "order" here, logical or otherwise, in the way of a process of salvation, this text rules out speaking, as in traditional Protestant theology, of an *ordo salutis*, as long as temporal and logical orders are not confused, and as long as it is realized that Paul does not always speak in terms of strict order. While discussions of "order" may digress to levels that stretch absurdly beyond the bounds of anything taught in Scripture, there is nevertheless a place for making distinctions in

before God" (v. 29; cf. Rom. 4:2).[17] The purpose is restated after verse 30 in a quotation from Jeremiah 9:23: "Let him who boasts, boast in the Lord" (v. 31).[18] The words of Jeremiah are fulfilled in the message of the gospel. There is no room for human boasting—not in wisdom, might, or riches, but only in the Lord.[19] This reality is made manifest in the Corinthians, for they had no grounds by any standards to boast in themselves, but in the wisdom of God they came to be sharers in Christ. Now they could boast in God alone for all they had was from God in Christ, the wisdom and power of God. This same idea is repeated in 3:21-23 after the wisdom of God and the foolishness of the world are again contrasted:

> So then let no one boast in men. For all things belong to you, whether Paul or Apollos or Cephas or the world or life or death or things present or things to come; all things belong to you, and you belong to Christ; and Christ belongs to God.[20]

Similarly, Paul reminds them that they have nothing that they "did not receive," and therefore he asks them, "why do you boast as if you had not received it?" (4:7). That each substantive—righteousness, sanctification, and redemption—refers to a status believers have in Christ is seen in the definitive or positional nature of the terms as used here.[21] As many have noted, sanctification in Paul is frequently definitive.[22] Such is the

---

theological discussion. The point here, however, is neither to argue for or against an "order of salvation." I mention it here because texts like 1 Corinthians 1:30 and 6:14 are often cited as "proof" that Paul never thought of an "order of salvation." Romans 8:29-30, on the other hand, may indeed argue for some notion of an *ordo salutis*.

[17] The purpose clause is marked by ὅπως.

[18] The quote is joined to verse 30 by ἵνα καθὼς γέγραπται ("so that, just as it is written").

[19] Jeremiah 9:23-24: "Thus says the LORD, 'Let not a wise man boast of his wisdom, and let not the mighty man boast of his might, let not a rich man boast of his riches; but let him who boasts boast of this, that he understands and knows Me, that I am the LORD who exercises lovingkindness, justice, and righteousness on earth; for I delight in these things,' declares the LORD."

[20] NASB.

[21] Although Thiselton refers to all four terms as "qualities" that "both characterize Christ and are imparted by Christ," he nevertheless understands the last three (righteousness, sanctification, and redemption) as a redefinition of what comprises wisdom. "As against the obsession with status seeking and success at Corinth, wisdom is redefined and explicated as receiving the *gifts* of righteousness, sanctification, and redemption *freely bestowed through Christ and derivative from him*" (his emphasis). Anthony C. Thiselton, *First Corinthians*, NIGTC (Grand Rapids: Eerdmans, 2000), 191-92.

[22] As Murray says: "It is a fact too frequently overlooked that in the New Testament the most characteristic terms that refer to sanctification are used not of a process, but of a once-for-all definitive act" (John Murray, "Definitive Sanctification," in *Collected Works of John Murray* [Edinburgh/ Carlisle, Pa.: Banner of Truth, 1977], 2:277). See also Thistleton, *First Corinthians*, 193-94. This, of course, does not deny progressive sanctification.

case here. Paul has already addressed the Corinthians in the following manner: "To the church of God which is at Corinth, to those who have been sanctified (ἡγιασμένοις) in Christ Jesus, holy ones (ἁγίοις) by calling." In chapter one Paul uses the verb ἁγιάζω, the adjective ἅγιος, and the noun ἁγιασμός in reference to the Corinthians—not referring to a state to which they are progressing, but as a position they already hold. That Paul addresses them in this way is all the more remarkable given the myriad of troubles at Corinth. Yet that observation itself helps explain how Paul can refer to the Corinthians as "holy ones" who have been sanctified. They are sanctified not because of anything they can boast in, but because they are sanctified in Christ.[23]

"Redemption" too is frequently used by Paul in reference to a status, particularly the position believers have in union with Christ as a result of the cross.[24] For instance, believers are "justified freely by grace through the *redemption* which is in Christ" (Rom. 3:24, emphasis mine); "In him; [Christ] we have *redemption* in his blood" (Eph. 1:7, emphasis mine); and, "in whom [Christ] we have *redemption*, the forgiveness of sin (Col. 1:14, emphasis mine).[25]

Thus, it makes sense to read δικαιοσύνη as referring to a status that believers have from God, in Christ.[26] The wisdom of God in the gospel brings a new standing of righteousness because one is now in Christ—incorporated and recognized by God in the person of Christ and there-

---

[23] Their sanctified status vis-à-vis Christ provides the foundation for Paul's argument against their various vices, scandals, divisions, etc. Rather than leading to antinomianism, or false assurance, Paul argues that the Corinthians' behavior should match their profession.

[24] As Conzelmann points out, ἀπολύτρωσις is a word Paul uses "in few passages, but emphatic ones" (*1 Corinthians*, 52 n. 31).

[25] Paul also speaks of "redemption" with a strong emphasis on the redemption that is still to come (Rom. 8:23; Eph. 1:14; 4:30). As will be seen shortly, eschatology is an important argument against the charge that imputation amounts to a "legal fiction." Note also the prominence of forgiveness.

[26] In his argument against any idea of imputation in this text, Gundry does not deal with the issue of union with Christ. He makes a distinction between God's righteousness and Christ's righteousness arguing that "The death is Christ's; but the righteousness is God's. It comes from God, not from Christ, and does not consist in an imputed righteousness of Christ any more than God imputes to believers a wisdom of Christ, a sanctification of Christ, or a redemption of Christ." Robert H. Gundry, "The Nonimputation of Christ's Righteousness," in *Justification: What's at Stake in the Current Debates*" ed. Mark Husbands and Daniel J. Trier (Downers Grove: InterVarsity, 2004), 41. As seen above, there is no question here of wisdom, sanctification, or redemption being imputed, nor is there any reason to say that if one thing, namely righteousness, is imputed than the other three must be imputed as well. We *become the righteousness of God in him*, there is no substitution of God's righteousness for Christ's righteousness, as Gundry says happens "time after time after time" by those who defend a traditional view of imputation. Christ himself has become God's righteousness *for us* and we have that righteousness in union with Christ.

fore sharing in all his benefits, chief among them a right relationship with God.[27] Is this righteousness, therefore, *counted* to the believer? An indication that Christ's righteousness is counted toward the believer is found in the phrases "to us, from God." This does not mean that everything is spelled out in detail, but it is evident that the righteousness we have from God in Christ is a righteousness that originated outside us, comes as a result of God's action through Christ, is undeserved, comes as a gift from God, and is possessed in union with Christ. This fits the profile for a righteousness that counts before God, a righteousness that is reckoned to those who believe the gospel of God's wisdom and power manifested in Christ crucified. In this way, 1 Corinthians 1:30 supports the idea that Christ's righteousness is counted to believers.

Philippians 3:9

In Philippians chapter 3 Paul contrasts his former way of life as a seemingly faithful Jew in terms of birth, lineage, and observance of the law, with his new life as a believer in Christ. Paul has given up on "whatever was gain" (v. 7), and now considers it all "dung" (v. 8). The contrast is summed up as a difference between "a righteousness of my own derived from law" and "that which is by faith in Christ, the righteousness which comes from God on the basis of faith" (v. 9). A central issue here is whether Paul's "own righteousness" is an actual status that counts before God but is done away with now that faith in Christ is the focal point of righteousness. Is Paul's former righteousness an effective, true righteousness? There is good reason based on the text to conclude that the answer to these questions is no. There is only one kind of righteousness that counts before God.

In verse 6 Paul gives the ultimate illustration of his former zeal: "a persecutor of the church." This is followed by "as to the righteousness which is in the law, found blameless."[28] In this verse Paul shows

---

[27] I agree with the following statement from Wright: "The point Paul is making is the large one, that all the things of which human beings are proud are as nothing before the gospel of the cross of Christ. All that we have that is worth having comes from God and is found in Christ" (*What St. Paul Really Said*, 123). Paul's statement is global in scope and is not a precise commentary on *how* we have righteousness, sanctification, or redemption in Christ. Nevertheless, I think there is more to say about this text in regard to imputation than Wright believes.

[28] My interpretation of this text turned on the realization of what Paul's persecution of the church meant in terms of his "blamelessness" and about his description of himself before the Damascus Road

that although he had a certain kind of righteousness, he actually failed to comprehend or attain true righteousness—"the righteousness that comes from God and is by faith" (3:9). Paul's persecution of the church is proof that his former "blamelessness" amounted to nothing more than "confidence in the flesh" (vv. 3-4).[29] The one who considered himself "blameless," is the same one who persecuted the church, which is equal to persecuting Jesus himself (Acts 9:4-5).[30] In effect, by persecuting the church, the lawkeeper (Paul) was persecuting the Lawgiver (Christ).

It is illustrative to compare Paul's reception of Christ (whom he clearly heard preached by Stephen [Acts 7, see Luke's remark in 8:1]), with that of Simeon, who upon seeing the baby Jesus declared, "For my eyes have seen your salvation, which you prepared in the presence of all peoples, 'a light for revelation to the Gentiles, and the glory of your people Israel'" (Luke 2:30-32). Simeon saw all the promises of God to Israel and to the world as reaching their fulfillment in the baby he held in his arms. Likewise, when Anna saw the child she immediately began telling "all those who were looking for the redemption of Jerusalem" (Luke 2:38).[31] If Paul's confidence had not been in his own flesh, and if

---

in general. It may seem that this point is not central to the topic of imputed righteousness, or that I am going on a tangent, but to my mind this is vital for understanding the whole passage. It was this "insight" (if I may call it so) that radically changed my mind on how I read Philippians 3.

[29] I am not arguing that Paul was merely fooling himself by thinking he was blameless. As far as his credentials (his circumcision, tribe, sect, his behavior, etc.) were concerned, there is no reason to doubt that Paul was in a sense "blameless." Nor am I arguing, as Stendahl, that there is any sort of psychological import attached to Paul's comment about being a persecutor of the church. Krister Stendahl, "The Apostle Paul and the Introspective Conscience of the West," in *Paul among Jews and Gentiles* (Philadelphia: Fortress, 1976), 13. Stendahl understands Paul's comments as indicating a "robust conscience" (ibid., 14). But if these comments are from Paul's "subjective conscience," and if his opponents understood them that way, they would be of little or no effect in Paul's argument. Paul's boasting-in-the-flesh-list is, as Silva notes, a counter measure against "the Judaizers' claims by showing his *credentials*; all of the items listed are accessible, objectively verifiable claims" (Moises Silva, *Philippians*, Wycliffe Exegetical Commentary [Chicago: Moody Press, 1988], 175). Silva rightly adds, "It would be almost pointless to introduce a subjective, and therefore greatly biased, judgment at the very end" (ibid.). Espy insightfully points out that Stendahl, and others after him, in an effort to expose the "Western conscience" that has been perniciously at work in the reading of Paul since Luther, has simply managed to "perpetuate it." John M. Espy, "Paul's 'Robust Conscience' Re-examined," *NTS* 31 (1985): 164. Espy rightly says that "[t]he true alternative to any overemphasis on the introspective would be to take the letters, not as passively revelatory of 'something human', but as careful and didactic workmanship formed in accordance with definite beliefs" (ibid., 165). One of Espy's best criticisms of Stendahl is that he reads Paul's auto-biographical comments as "self-indulgent" rather than interpreting them as "purposeful," i.e., as vital parts of Paul's arguments (ibid., 164).

[30] I do not equate "blameless" with "sinless." See Thomas R. Schreiner, "Paul and Perfect Obedience to the Law: An Evaluation of the View of E. P. Sanders," *WTJ* 42 (1985): 261.

[31] After considering this contrast of "blameless" Paul with Simeon and Anna, I was glad to see Thielman cite the similar examples of Zechariah and Elizabeth. Thielman, *Paul and the Law*, 285 n. 39. Another example, and in some ways the best, is John the Baptist.

he had understood the promises of God, he would not have persecuted the church but would have responded as Simeon and Anna did to Christ.[32] As opposed to Simeon and Anna, Saul missed the very One to whom the law pointed and in whom the law was fulfilled (Rom. 10:4).

Compare also Saul the observant Pharisee, well versed in Scripture, who opposed the message of the gospel—that Jesus Christ was the Messiah—with Paul the missionary, who entered synagogues, towns, houses, and court rooms teaching that Jesus was the fulfillment of everything written in the Law and the Prophets (Acts 13:16-47; 17:2-3; 18:4; 22:14; 24:14; 26:22; 28:23; 1 Cor. 15:3-4). Saul, like the Jews who crucified Jesus and the rulers and authorities who persecuted and killed the prophets in the Old Testament, did not see that the God he thought he served was working right before his eyes. This is the grid through which we must interpret Paul's description of his former life. Paul came to understand that because he formerly failed to see that the old covenant was christocentric (that is, "everything in the Law and Prophets"), his zeal, blamelessness, lineage, and practice were of no avail to him.[33] Apart from Christ, blamelessness before the law means nothing other than having confidence in the flesh. The following could easily have been spoken to Saul of Tarsus: "[T]he one who accuses you is Moses, in whom you have set your hope. For if you believed Moses, you would believe me, for he wrote about me" (John 5:45b-46).[34]

---

[32] I realize that on one level the issue of revelation comes into play. Christ was revealed to Simeon (Luke 2:26), and later to Paul himself (Acts 9:3-4; Gal. 1:15-16). Paul, though, never excuses his former actions because Christ was not yet revealed to him.

[33] Again, Paul's pre-Christian experience was not simply trying to gain righteousness only on the basis of works. As Seifrid points out, "Paul's 'blamelessness according to the righteousness in the Law' consisted not merely in his own obedience, but in the heritage into which he was born" (Mark A. Seifrid, "Justification by Faith: The Origin and Development of a Central Pauline Theme" [Ph.D. diss., Princeton University, 1992], 228). The issue seems to be that missing Christ in the law resulted in Paul's entire background, both practiced and inherited, to count for nothing before God.

[34] Another example from John's Gospel illustrates the same point. As a persecutor of the church (i.e., a persecutor of Christ), Paul missed what was right in front of him, much like the Pharisees, who, questioning the blind man just healed by Jesus "reviled him and said, 'You are His [Jesus'] disciple, but we are disciples of Moses. We know that God has spoken to Moses, but as for this man, we do not know where He is from'" (John 9:28-29 NASB). The irony is that they see themselves as Moses' disciples, yet they are out to kill the very one about whom Moses wrote. Could it be said of them that they were "blameless" before the law? Perhaps they were "blameless" in the sense that they did what was required, including participating in the sacrifices. Yet their blamelessness before the law counts for nothing before God. Unless, of course, God awards them for persecuting and crucifying Christ. Time and again Jesus admonishes them for keeping the law and thinking they were righteous on the basis of their heritage, ethnicity, and, yes, their works. The true nature of their righteousness was on public display when they persecuted and ultimately crucified Jesus. That Paul was precisely like those who continually opposed Jesus during his ministry is supported unequivocally by Luke's report in Acts 7–9.

Paul's problem was not a simple case of self-deception; it was the object in which he was placing his confidence. "Paul's 'own righteousness' was not a self-righteous attitude but his inadequate righteousness."[35] What makes Paul's former righteousness inadequate is not that it was merely a legalistic accumulation of merit that he thought would count before God, but that he was trusting in himself (i.e., his ethnicity, ancestral heritage, actions, and lawkeeping), rather than trusting in God.[36] This is the issue. Whatever Paul thought was to his benefit was in reality his stumbling block. Whatever he thought of himself in the past, he now knows that he is of "the true circumcision, who worship in the Spirit of God, and boast in Christ, and put no confidence in the flesh" (v. 3).[37] Therefore, righteousness that comes only from law, thereby missing the true purpose of the law and the God who gave it (v. 9), is a "false righteousness, an illusory righteousness"[38] that was never intended or even able to make someone righteous in the sight of God. All it does is provoke a false sense of security, a misguided sense of assurance. True righteousness, in any age, is only the righteousness that comes by faith (3:9; cf., Rom. 4:3; Gal. 3:6; Gen. 15:6).[39]

---

[35] Thielman, *Paul and the Law*, 155.

[36] In this sense, contra Dunn, it was a matter of what Paul had attained. Paul's confidence was in *himself* and that would include any "practice . . . within the covenant" (James D. G. Dunn, *The Theology of the Apostle Paul* [Grand Rapids: Eerdmans, 1998], 369). Dunn's point is to argue against any notion that Paul speaks of his "own" righteousness in terms of something he has achieved through his own effort. His "own" righteousness, rather, was his loyalty to the covenant. As such, being a Pharisee, a persecutor of the church, and being "blameless" in regard to the law were all "self-chosen" rather than "self-attained" (ibid., 370). Even if Paul was aware of the "essentially gracious character" (ibid.) of the things he included under his "own" righteousness, one cannot get around the fact that in these verses Paul describes a shift from trusting in himself, to trusting something "outside himself for the righteousness that only God, the righteous judge, can grant" (Silva, *Philippians*), 187.

[37] It is interesting to note that "the circumcision" (or "the *true* circumcision") are contrasted with "the mutilators" (τὴν κατατομήν), along with the contrast between "no confidence in the flesh" (v. 3) and Paul's "confidence in the flesh" that he had in his former life. So, there are the "*true* circumcision" who have "no confidence in the flesh," and then there are the Judaizing opponents, "the mutilators," who, like the one-time Saul of Tarsus, have "confidence in the flesh." The phrase, "and have no confidence in the flesh" is, as O'Brien, points out, "a negative restatement of the preceding (rather than a separate and third assertion), and signifies that we as Christians, who do have grounds for boasting, 'have no confidence in the flesh.'" Peter T. O'Brien, *Commentary on Philippians*, NIGTC (Grand Rapids: Eerdmans, 1991), 362. In this way, it is not simply a contrast between having confidence in the flesh and not having confidence in the flesh, but a contrast between putting confidence in the flesh or putting confidence in Christ.

[38] Schreiner, "Paul and Perfect Obedience," 262.

[39] As opposed to Sanders, who views the era of law and the era of Christ as "two dispensations. There is a righteousness which comes by law, but it is now worth nothing." E. P. Sanders, *Paul the Law and the Jewish People* (Philadelphia: Fortress, 1983), 140. Sanders seems to miss that Paul is not at all saying that his "blamelessness" was in fact some sort of righteousness until Christ came. Paul himself calls it "having confidence in the flesh." Having confidence in the flesh can never, in any age, coincide with a righteous status before God. Furthermore, and again contrary to Sanders, Paul's "own

Instead of a self-confident righteousness, which ultimately is no righteousness at all but merely "having confidence in the flesh, "Paul now values the righteousness that originates outside himself and comes as a gift ("from God"), is appropriated only by faith in Christ, and is had in union with Christ ("found in him"). The theme of undeserved, not simply unearned, grace is also prevalent. It is Paul, the former persecutor of the church (v. 6), who has received this gift from God. In this text we find the same basic elements discussed above in the "key" texts and in 1 Corinthians 1:30.

Two of the common themes, namely, external righteousness and union, are of particular interest. In verse 9 Paul emphasizes the external nature of true righteousness.[40] Not only is it "from God" (ἐκ θεοῦ), it is explicitly contrasted with a righteousness that is his own and derived from the law (ἐκ νόμου). Likewise, the theme of union plays an important and related role in this text. Paul wants to "be found in him," and presumably this means he desires to "be found" by God in Christ. This is vital for understanding what Paul is saying. Paul does not want to be found having his own righteousness (which will avail him nothing); he wants to be found *in Christ*.[41] If being found in Christ is directly linked

---

righteousness" as he describes it here, is a form of "self-righteousness" (ibid., 44-45). I found that some of the same references in Sanders and this same point about "self-righteousness" are recognized in Peter T. O'Brien, "Justification in Paul and Some Critical Issues of the Last Two Decades," in *Right with God: Justification in the Bible and the World*, ed. D. A. Carson (London: Paternoster; Grand Rapids: Baker for World Evangelical Fellowship, 1992), 87-88. There was never a righteousness that came merely from law—this is precisely Paul's point. How, for instance, can Paul the persecutor of the church, and Simeon who recognized the fulfillment of God's entire history of salvation in Christ, be equally "righteous" in the same "dispensation"? Was Paul "blameless" even after the incarnation of Christ? If for the sake of argument we grant "two dispensations," the first one ended with the incarnation of Christ. Sanders, however, accords to the "pre-Christian Paul" the same status as those living in the "dispensation" before Christ. There was not a dispensation of law and a dispensation of faith, both with their associate forms of legitimate righteousness. There is only faith, the object of which, after the incarnation, was personified in Christ. Only in that way is it legitimate to speak of a change in dispensations. What was always implicit in the OT, as it directly adhered to God's promises, was made explicit in Christ. Paul's real plight was that like many of his ancestors and contemporaries he failed to see the God of Israel at work right before his eyes. Paul's keeping of the law was useless in terms of righteousness because he did not understand that to which it pointed. It was useless also because that kind of law-keeping was never able to make one righteous. Until the Damascus road, Paul missed Christ in the law. Said another way, Paul missed the law. Sanders, as Dunn after him (see above, n. 35), misses the paradigm shift that took place when Paul ceased to trust in himself (and that would include anything he had by way of being *in* the covenant) and began to trust in what lies externally to himself, namely, the righteousness from God by faith in Jesus Christ.

[40] Again, "external" does not mean "unreal" or "fictional." It simply means a righteousness that derives from a source outside oneself. At the same time, it does not mean an external righteousness that is somehow infused into the believer. Thus Paul can speak of being "found" with a righteousness that is "not my own." It is had by the instrument of faith.

[41] O'Brien concludes that ἵνα Χριστὸν κερδήσω ("so that I might gain Christ") and εὑρεθῶ ἐν αὐτῷ ("be found in him") are "essentially the same" (*Philippians*, 392). But it seems that to "gain Christ"

to the righteousness that comes from God by faith, then the righteousness that Paul wants can only be Christ's righteousness. Thus, being "found in Christ" means to be found with Christ's righteousness—the righteousness that is not Paul's own. There are no other possibilities in view.[42] This is why Paul cannot put confidence in his own life and actions (i.e., "in the flesh"), but boasts only in Christ (v. 3; cf., 1 Cor. 1:31), for it is only in Christ that he can have the righteousness that counts before God.

Returning to our synoptic reading, this conclusion is supported by the way Paul speaks of the instrumentality of faith. Like Romans 4:3-8, one of the main elements of Philippians 3:8-9 is faith, but unlike Romans 4:3-8, Paul refers explicitly to faith as an instrument. The clear reference to the instrumentality of faith, however, argues that in this text the righteousness of the object of Paul's faith counts to him as a right standing before God. Just as the instrumentality of faith is implicit in Romans 4:1-8, so the reckoning of righteousness is implicit in Philippians 3:8-9. Read together, we see that faith is the instrument by which righteousness is reckoned.

Romans 4 is about faith rather than works counting for righteousness, and Philippians 3 is about having a righteousness that is by faith rather than derived from law. Yet the difference is a matter of emphasis, for central to both texts is the contrast Paul draws between righteousness by faith and righteousness by works.[43] While Paul says simply "law" in Philippians 3:9, because he speaks of a righteousness that

---

stands in contrast with "whatever was to my gain (κέρδη)" (v. 7). All those things that gave Paul "confidence in the flesh," all his achievements, are now nothing. All he hoped in, worked for, and boasted in stands in stark contrast to that which is gained not through ethnic or social privilege, or through working, and which is the only ground for human boasting: Christ. It is true that Christ is "gained" through union with him, but it seems to me that Paul is making two separate, though related, statements. O'Brien may be right in asserting that εὑρεθῶ ("I might be found") does not here, contrary to some Old Testament usage, refer to "persons 'found' by God to be such and such" (ibid., 393). Following Ernest De Witt Burton, *The Epistle to the Galatians*, ICC (Edinburgh: T & T Clark, 1921), 125, O'Brien understands "be found" to mean something like "prove to be, be shown to be, turn out to be." Although O'Brien directs readers to Burton for evidence concerning the passive form of εὑρίσκω, Burton himself does not include this text in his citations—though Burton does not claim to give an exhaustive list of New Testament citations. Even if the O'Brien/Burton assertion is correct, it does not greatly affect the argument here. The union with Christ theme stands either way.

[42] I suppose one could simply argue that while there is perhaps no other identified righteousness in this text, since Paul does not *say explicitly* that the righteousness that is not is own is indeed Christ's then we should not say it either.

[43] "Works of the law" is a subset of "works" in general. Thus Paul can deny that "works," without qualification, serve any basis for justification, e.g., Ephesians 2:9; Titus 3:5.

[44] Again, even if "the faithfulness of Christ" was a better reading of Romans 3:22 than the phrase

comes from law, he is therefore speaking of "law" in terms of what the law commands, i.e., the works of the law. Paul specifically speaks of righteousness on the basis of doing the works of the law. If this is so, then it is similar to "works of the law" in Romans 3:28. There faith, in contrast to "works of the law," is the instrumental means of justification: "For we reckon a man to be justified by faith, apart from the works of the law."

As seen earlier, the phrases "by faith" in Romans 3:28 and "through faith" in 3:25 (cf. v. 30), establish the instrumentality of faith in regard to justification, so that when "faith" appears in 4:3 and following, Paul's readers have a ready guide for understanding the specific nature of faith in relation to the reckoning of righteousness—it is that which unites the believer with the object of faith, Jesus Christ. [44] We have already seen that the righteousness of which Paul speaks in Philippians 3:9 is an external righteousness and that it is Christ's righteousness ("not my own"; "from God"; "found in him") because it comes from God, and is contrasted with having a personal righteousness that comes from law. One appropriates that righteousness by faith.

There is one other important similarity to notice, and it is that righteousness in both texts is a gift from God.[45] There is nothing earned, only righteousness received. There are, therefore, several crucial parallels between Romans 4:1-8 and Philippians 3:8-9: (1) a righteousness that is by faith and not by works (of law), (2) faith that is instrumental, (3) righteousness that originates outside the believer, and (4) righteousness that is a gift from God. When compared in the context of a discussion about imputation, the most substantial difference between Philippians 3:8-9 and Romans 4:1-8 is simply that the word λογίζομαι does not appear in Philippians.[46] The parallels between them, however, argue that Philippians 3 supports the idea that Christ's righteousness is indeed reckoned to believers.

"by faith," (i.e., subjective rather than objective genitive), the instrumentality of faith is securely established in the context.

[45] Contrary to the reckoning of "what is owed" (Rom. 4:4). In Philippians the righteousness is ἐκ θεοῦ.

[46] I am not at all arguing that the two texts are identical. Romans and Philippians were written to two different churches and for different circumstances. For the purposes here the focus is not on the occasional nature of the letters, but the parallels in two Pauline texts that share similar themes. Again, the conviction behind this dissertation is that Paul addressed various issues in the churches from a unified, theological framework.

[47] Wright interprets "their own" as a special covenant status that the Jews had tried to establish that

Romans 9:30–10:4

Romans 9:30–10:4 is another text that does not speak explicitly about the imputation of righteousness. Yet there are themes present in this text that are important to notice, particularly on the heels of the discussion of Philippians 3. Chief among them is Paul's distinction between a righteousness that is by faith and a righteousness that is self-established. The former is the righteousness that is attained by the Gentiles in spite of the fact that they did not pursue it (9:30). This righteousness is described as the righteousness that is by faith (9:30), and it stands in contrast to a righteousness that is "their own" (i.e., unbelieving Jews). The latter is the righteousness that the unbelieving Jews pursued, but to which they did not arrive (9:31-32). The law was pursued "as if it were by works" (9:32), and in distinction from God's righteousness, results in a righteousness of "their own" (10:3). Though disputed in the last couple of decades, this is commonly called "works righteousness"—any attempt to be right before God on the basis of one's own achievements, personal attributes, background, or anything else besides trusting only in God.[47]

The contrast between these two kinds of righteousness, if I may borrow from Luther, is quite similar to that of Philippians 3. Paul's righ-

---

would be "for all Jews, and only for Jews" in exclusion of the Gentiles. N. T. Wright, *Romans*, New Interpreters Bible Commentary, vol. 10, ed. Leander Keck (Nashville: Abingdon, 2002), 655. Thus "righteousness" has nothing to do with earning God's favor through works. Granting for the sake of discussion that Wright's conclusion is correct, the status of the main question, i.e., faith in God *vs.* faith in oneself, does not seem greatly altered. What is unclear is how seeking to establish a special covenant status contrary to the covenantal plan and purpose of God is really that much different from trying to establish one's own righteousness on the basis of works. Either way, the issue comes down to whether people are putting their trust in God or in themselves. Granted, on the one hand works are being done to earn favor, while on the other hand there is the establishment of a "covenant-status" as the chosen people of God that is contrary to God's own covenant. Even if the Jews Paul addresses were not "proto-Pelagians, trying to pull themselves up by their own moral bootstraps" (ibid.), is this not every bit as much an effort to call God a liar, just like trying to earn salvation through works? Even if it was the case that the Jews did not submit to God's covenant faithfulness, i.e., "God's decisive action in Jesus the Messiah," in favor of a self-established "covenant membership" (ibid.), it is still akin to saying that they sought to be righteous by their own efforts. Establishing one's own covenant membership is not, practically speaking, greatly different from establishing one's own righteousness on the basis of one's own works. We either trust God, or we trust ourselves. These same observations and questions apply to Dunn's comment that "Paul's criticism in effect is that in seeking to 'establish' covenant righteousness as 'theirs' they failed to appreciate the full significance of the fact that only God's righteousness can 'establish' the covenant" (James D. G. Dunn, *Romans 9–16*, WBC, vol. 38b [Dallas: Word, 1988], 588). Are they not still trying to achieve something on the basis of their own merit? Surely Schreiner is correct to say that "the fault of Israel is that they were attempting to gain righteousness via works" (*Romans*, 539). While I do not agree that works of the law are boundary markers, even if they were, the sin would still be attempting to establish oneself apart from God; it is still reliance on self rather than faith in God. It is, in other words, works righteousness.

[48] Moo is right to cite Deuteronomy 9:4-6, in which God declares that Israel will enter the land

teousness that came from law (Phil. 3:9) is parallel to the law of righteousness pursued, but not arrived at, by the Jews (Rom. 9:31-32), and the righteousness that comes from God and is by faith (Phil. 3:9) parallels the righteousness attained by the Gentiles (Rom. 9:30). Both texts make the same point. There are only two choices: the righteousness that comes from God, or one's own.

When Paul says the Jews tried to "establish their own" righteousness, it was a righteousness pursued by "works," that is, by relying on their own actions, rather than by total reliance on God.[48] In the debates that swirl around this text about the nature of first-century Judaism, it seems that one fundamental point is often obscured: only one kind of righteousness is deemed acceptable by God at all times and in all places—the righteousness that is by faith.[49] Paul implies in 10:3 that the righteousness of God was always by faith, even if the Jews did not realize it. So the issue comes down to trusting in oneself (or *themselves*) or trusting in God. Thus, he can say that the Jews "did not subject themselves to the righteousness of God" because they did not know of God's righteousness and tried to establish their own. It becomes increasingly difficult to extract all notions of "works righteousness" from this text.[50] Even if it is granted that the Jews understood the grace of God in election, redemption, and whatever else, it is hard to avoid the idea that when Paul speaks of "trying to establish" their own righteousness (10:3), and pursuing the law "as if it were by works," rather than "by faith" (9:32), he is speaking to a basic failure to grasp the fact that righteousness is altogether a matter of faith in a merciful God.[51] This last idea is supported by Paul's citation of Isaiah 8:14 and 28:16.

---

because of his electing grace, and not because of "their own" righteousness, Douglas Moo, *The Epistle to the Romans*, NICNT (Grand Rapids: Eerdmans, 1996), 635.

[49] Again, contra Sanders (*Paul, the Law and the Jewish People*, 44); see above, n. 38.

[50] As Moo points out, Sanders (*Paul, the Law, and the Jewish People*, 42) and others are right to observe that Paul is "condemning Israel for failing to recognize the shift in salvation history that has come with Christ" but are wrong in seeing this as Paul's only problem with their theology (Moo, *Romans*, 627 n. 47). Paul is also concerned to show that "the righteousness to which the law pointed had never been available through works done in obedience to the law" (ibid.). As seen in many occasions in the course of this study, arguments against one perceived extreme may often proceed to replace it with the another extreme.

[51] Contra D. P. Fuller (*Gospel and Law: Contrast or Continuum? The Hermeneutics of Dispensationalism and Covenant theology* [Grand Rapids: Eerdmans, 1980], 71-79), Moo argues that Paul is not saying that "Israel should have believed the law. Rather, he is claiming that their pursuit of the law with respect to the righteousness that it promised should have been carried out on the basis of faith" (*Romans*, 626 n. 44).

Isaiah's Cornerstone: Righteousness in Christ Alone

Romans 9:33 is a combination of two texts from Isaiah. In Isaiah 8:14 the Lord himself "shall become a sanctuary; but to both the houses of Israel, a stone to strike and a rock to stumble over." Then in 28:16, the Lord says through Isaiah, "Behold I am laying in Zion a stone, a tested stone, a costly cornerstone for the foundation, firmly placed. He who believes in it will not be disturbed" (NASB). In the context surrounding 8:14, a promise to a believing remnant is coupled with the threat of imminent judgment. In the second text, 28:16, the Lord acts in the face of Jerusalem's faithlessness.[52] Though judgment is strongly emphasized in this text, there is also the theme of God's grace to the undeserving. Regardless of what Jerusalem had done, the Lord is still setting a cornerstone which will be for the benefit of whoever believes, but to some it will be a stumbling stone.

In Romans 9–10 it is evident the "stone of stumbling" is none other than the righteousness of God in Christ and is attained by faith, not pursued by works (cf. Phil. 3:8-9). This is what God had promised centuries earlier though Isaiah, and it was precisely this message that many Jews failed to understand. The Jews of whom Paul speaks did not fully recognize that attaining righteousness before God was purely an act of God's mercy (Isa. 28:16; Rom. 9:16, 23; cf. "from God" 1 Cor. 1:30; Phil. 3:9). The law pointed to the righteousness of which Paul speaks, and it also commanded works,[53] but the Jews had missed the point; they did not see that righteousness was by faith (alone), so they pursued the law "as though by works" (9:32). Thus God's act is a stumbling stone to the Jews because they do not believe, but "he who believes in him will not be put to shame" (cf. 1 Cor. 1:18; 2 Cor. 2 15-16).

What, then, is this act of God, this cornerstone? It is nothing other than the righteousness that comes from God that is set over against a self-established righteousness that generates confidence in the flesh; it is Christ himself. Christ, and the righteousness from God that is by faith,

---

[52] לָכֵן כֹּה אָמַר אֲדֹנָי יְהוִה ("Therefore, thus says the Lord God"). The faithlessness of Jerusalem is answered by an act of redemption from the Lord. In context, the "therefore" may come as a surprise.

[53] Andrew A. Das, *Paul, the Law and the Covenant* (Peabody, Mass.: Hendrickson, 2001), 244-45. "The Jews are pursuing a law that witnesses to righteousness as if it were based on their active pursuit and performance of its works. The Jews do not perceive the law in its inner connection to righteousness: righteousness is based on faith and not the doing of what the law prescribes" (ibid.).

is what the law pointed to all along. Apart from this christocentric perspective that righteousness is by faith, the law really is a matter of keeping commands through which one can never attain righteousness.[54] Ultimately Paul condemns the Jews for a lack of faith that resulted in their stumbling over the stone of stumbling. There is no righteousness apart from faith, i.e., apart from Christ. For the one who gains this perspective, attempts to establish one's own righteousness by the law come utterly to an end.[55] Only the righteousness that comes from God and is by faith counts before God.

Where Else Could We Go?

A synthesis of Paul's teaching warrants the assertion that no other grounds for a right status before God can be found other than Christ's righteousness. The options seem quite limited otherwise. In regard to righteousness as a status, Paul consistently speaks of the source of that righteousness as external to the believer.[56] That righteousness comes

---

[54] By "christocentric perspective" I mean simply faith in God, which in the Old Testament meant specifically faith in God's promises to be who he says he is and to save and redeem his people, and which comes to fulfillment in Christ. In this sense, all who *believed* God and his promises had a "christocentric" perspective (at least as described on the cross-side of salvation history). The "faith" that justified Abraham (Gal. 3:15-18; cf. Rom. 4:3; Gal. 3:6) in terms of believing God's promises is the same faith that after the incarnation becomes explicit belief in Christ (Rom. 4:23-24). I am not saying, therefore, as does Wilckens (*Der Brief an die Römer*, Teilband 2: *Röm. 6–11*, Evangelisch-Katholischer Kommentar zum Neuen testament 6/2 [Zürich: Benziger/Neukirchen-Vluyn], 215-16), that Paul is critiquing the Jews only because they do not believe in Christ. Paul's criticism is that they are characterized by a lack of faith, just like their ancestors, and that this condition is manifested in their stumbling over the stone.

[55] I am quite aware that I am taking the "both/and" view of what Paul means by τέλος. See Das, *Paul the Law and the Covenant*, 250-51. The secondary literature on this text is overwhelming, and there is no time to review it here. Thielman, for instance, understanding a continuation of the race metaphor from 9:30-32, reads τέλος exclusively as "goal." Frank J. Thielman, *Paul and the Law: A Contextual Approach* (Downers Grove, Ill.: InterVarsity, 1994), 206, n. 45, 299. On the other side, Schreiner, noting that the race metaphor ends in 9:32, supplies a proposition and reads the verse as, "Christ is the end of using the law for righteousness for everyone who believes." Thomas R. Schreiner, *Romans*, BECNT 8 (Grand Rapids: Baker, 1998), 547. For the mediating position taken here (and influenced by Das), consider Paul's own experience. As a zealous Jew, Paul, by his own admission, tried to establish his own righteousness, which amounted to "confidence in the flesh" (Phil. 3:4). The means of this is through works, specifically the works required by the law. Though this is not a matter of sheer salvation by works it is nevertheless the way a "faithful" Jew described his life before Christ. Yet Paul, after being confronted with the revelation of God's righteousness in Christ, now counts all that went before as dung in comparison to knowing Christ (Philippians 3:7–8). Now consider that this same Paul is the one who said that faith in Christ does not abolish the law, but to the contrary, faith in Christ "establishes the law." (Rom. 3:31). On the one hand, Paul is done with establishing his own righteousness (i.e., pursuing righteousness "as if by works" and stumbling "over the stumbling stone" [Rom. 9:32]), and on the other he is convinced that "faith in Christ" is the very thing that confirms the law. This seems very much like saying that when Paul met Christ he realized that his (Paul's) efforts at establishing his own righteousness were finished, and that Christ was the one to whom the law always pointed. Paul's personal experience mirrors that of the Jews he describes in Romans 9–10.

[56] Traditionally referred to as "alien righteousness."

to believers exclusively by God's grace, as a gift. The evidence points to that righteousness as a legal standing before God on the basis of what Christ has accomplished. The forensic status of "just" is a reality because of what Christ has done. It is also evident that human beings contribute nothing to this status. It is, in fact, just the opposite—the human objects of God's grace are consistently presented as in no way earning God's favor, and moreover, as undeserving of God's favor.

Finally, Paul speaks of being justified only insofar as the believers are identified in Christ. There is nothing the believer has that he does not have in Christ. In regard to justification, we saw that union primarily refers to being incorporated into Christ as the covenantal head of God's promised new creation. As the second Adam, Christ's obedience in life and in death establishes the standing of all those united with him. It is extraordinarily difficult to locate the believer's standing before God anywhere else than on the basis of Christ's righteousness. All these considerations argue for the imputation of Christ's righteousness.

OBJECTIONS CONSIDERED

The doctrine of the imputation of Christ's righteousness is an idea that has never lacked opposition. In what follows, a few of the more common and recurring objections are considered. Dealing with objections will also help clarify the argument for imputation.

A Legal Fiction?

It is often said that the Protestant doctrine of justification by faith in general,[57] and the subsidiary doctrine of the imputation of Christ's righteousness in particular, amounts to a legal fiction. This righteousness is "fictitious" because its ground lies wholly outside the believer in the righteousness of Christ. The status "righteous" is simply counted, not actual. It is a mere transaction. The believer does not possess it, nor can he, properly speaking, call it his own. That the criticism is long-standing is made evident by the fact that the charge

---

[57] Specifically in the Lutheran and Calvinist traditions.

of "legal fiction" has been addressed on a relatively frequent basis for nearly five-hundred years.[58]

Chemnitz, writing in the third quarter of the sixteenth century, noted that the Jesuits made this very claim against imputed righteousness, claiming that it is "an inane fantasy and illusion" because it "does not have an inherent basis in us."[59] In the seventeenth century, Turretin, argued against any kind of inherent righteousness, infused or otherwise, as a basis for justification, and he defended against the "legal fiction" charge, saying that "the judicial act of God does not lack truth because he does not pronounce us righteous in ourselves."[60] The fact that Buchanan devotes a section of his book on justification to argue against the legal fiction charge is a good indication that criticism was commonplace in the nineteenth century as well. The following question from Wright is therefore not a new inquiry: "If the righteousness is something humans have 'from God,' is it 'imputed' to them . . . that is, 'reckoned' to be theirs, almost as a legal fiction?"[61] Just because it is an old question that has been addressed numerous times in the past few centuries does not make it less valid. On the contrary, one could argue that the persistence of the question argues for the validity of the question.

Also, and in all fairness, the charge is sometimes legitimate, not because imputation is inherently fictitious, but because some presentations of it often reduce it down to a cold formula. It may indeed sometimes appear as a mere "transfer *apart* from being included in Christ,"[62] a cut-and-dry transaction in which Christ's righteousness is doled out

---

[58] The following are cited simply as examples. Because of the scope of this work, the historical arguments cannot be unpacked and analyzed. It is sufficient to note that the question of a "legal fiction" is not new. A work that thoroughly compared the historical arguments both for and against the traditional formulation with the arguments set forth by scholars today would be a valuable resource.

[59] Martin Chemnitz, *Justification: The Chief Article of Christian Doctrine as Expounded in "Loci Theologici,"* trans. J. A. O. Preus (St. Louis: Concordia, 1985), 151.

[60] Francis Turretin, *Institutes of Elenctic Theology*, trans. George Musgrave Giger, ed., James T. Dennison Jr. (Phillipsburg, N.J.: P&R, 1994), 2:648. He devotes a substantial amount of space to argue for the imputation of Christ's righteousness as the only grounds of justification. In this section he also argues against both Roman Catholic and Socinian claims (ibid., 633-56). Being righteous only in Christ is a central theme in Turretin's discussion.

[61] Wright, *What St. Paul Really Said*, 102.

[62] As Carson points out in "The Vindication of Imputation: On Fields of Discourse and, of Course, Semantic Fields," in *Justification: What's at Stake in the Current Debates*, eds. Mark Husbands and Daniel J. Treier (Downers Grove: InterVarsity, 2004), 72.

as if it were some sort of legal entitlement.[63] With that admission aside, there are three considerations that argue against the legal fiction charge. By now at least three of these are familiar themes: (1) union with Christ, (2) substitution, and (3) eschatology. These three themes work in conjunction, all appear in the major "imputation" texts, and all three themes coalesce in Christ as the second (or last) Adam.

Union with Christ. Union with Christ, among other things, argues against imputation being a legal fiction. When Paul speaks of union with Christ in direct connection with salvation and justification, he emphasizes the identification of the believer in Christ by God. Thus, while we may speak of "vital" or even "mystical" union with Christ, Paul's focus, when dealing with the forensic nature of justification, is on the idea that God now views the believer not as he is in himself but in Christ.[64] That is, the believer holds the status of "righteous" before God because God only views the believer in light of Christ's atoning death and resurrection. Believers are identified with the second Adam who lived in obedience to the Father and died a sacrificial death in their place (2 Cor. 5:14-15, 21; 1 Cor. 15:20-22). In Romans 6:3-5, Paul makes it clear that the representative death of Christ (5:18-19) is effective only because the believer is "united with him in the likeness of his death." Likewise, a believer has redemption, the forgiveness of sin, only because he has it "in Christ." (Rom. 3:24; Eph. 1:7). The phrase "redemption in his blood" (Eph. 1:7; cf. Rom. 5:9) is indicative of the operative principle in these union texts: believers are united with Christ, their legal, sacrificial substitute.

Substitution. There is a corollary consideration to the believer's union with Christ, as seen most clearly in 2 Corinthians 5:14-21 and Romans 3:21-26, which is Christ's representative death on behalf of

---

[63] I am thinking more in terms of popular defenses of imputation, such as some I have heard in a few sermons. In an effort to defend the doctrine, zealous advocates sometimes end up saying things that sound every bit like the characterizations made by those who object to imputation.

[64] Many union texts speak in general terms referring to the life that is now lived in Christ and/or as a member of his body, and of the continuing presence of Christ with the believer, e.g., Galatians 2:20; Ephesians 3:17; 4:12, 15-16; Colossians 3:3. It is widely recognized that union with Christ is a multi-faceted designation in the New Testament. The point being made here is that the concept of union as seen in texts such as Romans 5 and 2 Corinthians 5 is primarily about the connection between the believer and Christ as the one who secured their right status before God. The emphasis is on representative union. This neither defines nor exhausts the topic of union with Christ.

believers. The benefits of Christ's sacrificial death flowing to the believer are no more a legal fiction than Christ's dying for sinners is a legal fiction. In other words, the "legal fiction" argument must logically conclude that Christ's sacrifice was also a legal fiction, a transaction that took place only in the mind of God.[65] So, one would have to say that it was an effective, substitutionary sacrifice only because God deemed to acknowledge it as such, but not because it was that in reality. If this were true, then we would no longer be talking about substitution but about some form of a moral government idea of atonement. If all ideas of imputation are lost, substitutionary atonement, if not lost, is seriously jeopardized. Substitutionary atonement demands some concept of imputation, even if imputation is restricted only to forgiveness of sins.

Eschatology. Eschatology also argues against the legal fiction charge. The legal fiction idea comes about in part when justification is viewed "*only* from the historical frame of reference, from which it appears that the believer is 'counted' righteous but is 'really' a sinner."[66] Paul's assertion that "if anyone is in Christ he is a new creation" (2 Cor. 5:17) refers to "a totally new environment, or, more accurately speaking, a totally new world."[67] This "new world" is that which was

---

[65] This is essentially the way Green and Baker conceive of substitutionary atonement, a "legal transaction within the Godhead." Joel B. Green and Mark D. Baker, *Recovering the Scandal of the Cross: Atonement in New Testament and Contemporary Contexts* (Downers Grove: InterVarsity, 2001), 149. Green and Baker, however, present a straw man in their assessment of substitutionary atonement. In their discussion of Hodge's formulation, they comment that in the substitutionary model "the only aspect of Jesus' life that is presented concretely is his physical suffering, which helps to validate that the penalty was sufficient" (ibid.). They have missed the fact that for Hodge, writing in the Reformed tradition, there is *far* more to consider about Jesus' life than just his suffering. Green and Baker apparently did not put Hodge's discussion of penal substitution in the context of his covenant theology. More to the point, Green and Baker seem completely to miss the centrality of union with Christ to understanding justification by faith, and as a result misconstrue the relationship between justification and substitution. Contrary to Green and Baker, substitutionary atonement (which, they assert, is what makes the traditional formulation of justification by faith "all the more palatable or inviting") is not simply a matter of "the manifestly guilty person stands before the divine judge for sentencing and hears the verdict, 'Not Guilty!'" (ibid., 25). God is not reacting to some abstract notion of justice, but is acting in accordance with his own divine character and justice. Justification and substitution are thus *extremely* personal matters, beginning with God; his Son, after all, bore his wrath in place of sinners. I include this rather long note because arguments against substitution often parallel arguments against imputation. Note how similar the last citation from Green and Baker is to saying that substitution is a "legal fiction."

[66] Anthony C. Thiselton, *The Two Horizons: New Testament Hermeneutics and Philosophical Description* (Grand Rapids: Baker; Carlisle, UK: Paternoster, 1980), 421. Thiselton is not arguing against Luther. He is actually defending the notion of "simultaneously a saint and a sinner" on the grounds of eschatology (ibid.).

[67] Geerhardus Vos, *The Pauline Eschatology* (Princeton: University Press, 1930; Phillipsburg, NJ: P&R, 1994), 47.

promised through Isaiah (43:18-21; 65:16-23; 66:22-23) and which has dawned in Christ.[68] As such, the designation "new creation in Christ" is an announcement of the inauguration of the "the new heavens and a new earth" that God promised to create (Isa. 65:17; 66:22). And the entrance into God's inaugurated kingdom is through becoming "the righteousness of God" in Christ on the basis of his sacrificial death (2 Cor. 5:21). Being a "new creation" means first of all gaining a right standing before God. There are connections that run back through some familiar texts.

Paul's comment in 2 Corinthians 5:16, that he now knows "no one according to the flesh," contrasts his old way of thinking with the knowledge that has come in the new covenant era of the Spirit (3:3 ff.).[69] He says, "If we once knew Christ according to the flesh, now we no longer know him in that way" (5:16). Paul's past perception of Christ is well known to us. Paul once expended every effort to persecute the followers of Jesus, and later came to find out that persecuting Jesus' followers is the same thing as persecuting Jesus himself (Acts 9:4-5). When Paul knew "Christ according to the flesh," he knew him as an enemy of the Jewish religion and of the old ways and traditions. Paul's "fleshly" perception of Christ was part and parcel of his having "confidence in the flesh" (Phil. 3:4), and just as he describes his countrymen, Paul was trying "to establish [his] own righteousness" (Rom. 10:3).

The righteousness associated with the new creation is by faith, originates outside the believer, and is purely of God's grace. In this new era of salvation history, however, the folly of trying to establish one's own righteousness has been exposed by the fulfillment of God's promise. The eschatological fulfillment of that promise has taken place in Christ, who has, among other things, become for us righteousness from God (1 Cor. 1:30). In this way, partaking of Christ's righteousness is how one participates in the new creation promised by God (Isa. 65:17) as it is now manifested "in Christ" (2 Cor. 5:17). One is part of the new creation in so far as one is in Christ. Even though the full experience of the new creation union, and all it entails, is still to come and must be pursued

[68] Scott J. Hafemann, *2 Corinthians*, The NIV Application Commentary (Grand Rapids: Zondervan, 2000), 244.
[69] Ibid., 242.

by faith (Phil. 3:10-17), it is the righteousness of Christ that gives us the status of "righteous," thus making us "a new creation." Union and eschatology are thus inter-related themes.

These themes merge most clearly in Paul's theology of Christ as the second, or last, Adam (Rom. 5:12-21; 1 Cor. 15:20-22; 2 Cor. 5:14-15). As the second Adam, Christ is the covenantal head of those identified with him. As the covenantal head, Christ's obedient act of righteousness, his death on the cross, brings about a righteous, legal status for his people (Rom. 5:18-19; cf. 5:9). This comes about through a transfer from one kingdom (the realm of sin and death from Adam) to another kingdom marked by grace, righteousness, and life. The ground for one's status (either "sinner" or "righteous") is determined by the actions of another, whether Adam or Christ. The actions of the two heads *count* for their people. Paul, speaking in eschatological terms, says that the recipients of God's free gift in Christ will "reign in life" (Rom. 5:17), and that through Christ's "one act of righteousness there resulted justification leading to life" (5:18). Moreover, "grace will reign through righteousness to eternal life through Jesus Christ" (5:21). The results for those incorporated into Christ as their covenant head are couched in highly eschatological language, but at the same time Paul speaks of the reality of this status in the present time (5:1). Paul does not speak in terms of any sort of "fiction" but of a present and future reality, or to be more precise, an eschatological reality that is declared and experienced already in the present.[70] We may, therefore, say that those "made" righteous are in fact righteous because those in Christ have been declared to be so on the grounds of his obedience and his death.[71] On this basis, referring to the declaration as "a fiction" is excluded.

Likewise, in 1 Corinthians 15 Paul grounds his whole discussion on the basis of Christ as the "first fruits" (v. 20). He is the first portion of

---

[70] Ridderbos is worth citing again regarding the conjunction between union and eschatology. After citing, among other texts, Romans 5:18-19, 2 Corinthians 5:21, and 1 Corinthians 1:30, Ridderbos states: "The significance of this abundant testimony is unmistakable: In Christ's death God has sat in judgment, has judged sin, and in this way he has caused *the eschatological judgment to be revealed in the present time*. But for those who are *in Christ*, he has therefore become righteousness, and the content of the gospel of the death and resurrection of Christ can be defined as the revelation of the righteousness of God for everyone who believes." Herman Ridderbos, *Paul: An Outline of His Theology*, trans. John Richard De Witt (Grand Rapids: Eerdmans, 1975), 168 (my emphasis). See also, George Eldon Ladd, *New Testament Theology*, rev. ed., ed. Donald A. Hagner (Grand Rapids: Eerdmans, 1993), 488.

[71] Ladd, *New Testament Theology*, 489.

the harvest, and as such, he represents the portion yet to be harvested. Just as death came down to humanity through the past action of the first Adam, so the future resurrection of believers is guaranteed by the past resurrection of the second Adam with whom they are united: "For since through a man death came, the resurrection of the dead also comes through a man" (v. 21). How death and resurrection come "through a man" is by covenant representation (v. 22). It is not "as if" one is identified with either Adam or Christ; one *is* identified with either Adam or Christ. There is simply no room for claiming this as a "fiction." Only if Christ's resurrection is a fiction, can the believer's hope be a fiction. The reality of Christ's resurrection is the very thing Paul is at pains to establish as the absolute guarantee for hope for the future. Paul's argument depends on the validity of representative headship, and representative headship depends on the idea that the actions of the head *count* for the body. This is precisely the way Paul argues in this chapter.

This same theme appears again in 2 Corinthians 5:14-15, where the representative death of Christ causes many to live. The present reality is clear in the radical change in their perspective, turning from those who "live for themselves" to those who live "for the one who was dead and raised for them" (v. 15).[72] This is the result of being "a new creation in Christ," which, again, indicates the eschatological fulfillment of God's promise. Christ's representative death, as a sacrifice for sin, brings about the eschatological reality of a "new creation."

It is also apparent that the theme of substitution is never far from Paul's argument regarding Christ as the second Adam. This is readily seen in the fact that in each of the texts in which the Adam/Christ parallel appears, Paul makes mention of Christ's representative death.[73] The three themes of union, substitution, and eschatology, which ultimately join together in Christ as the second Adam, our covenant head, make it difficult for the "legal fiction" charge to stick.

---

[72] There is a connection between this truly "new perspective" (living for Christ instead of living for oneself) and the contrast between knowing "Christ according to the flesh" and Paul's new knowledge of Christ (v. 16). This is quite similar, therefore, with the contrast between a desire to establish one's own righteousness, i.e., "having confidence in the flesh" (Rom. 10:3; Phil. 3:4), and having the righteousness that comes from God (Rom. 10:4; Phil. 3:9).

[73] Whatever one concludes about the scope of Christ's "one righteous act," his death on the cross cannot be excluded. Some may exclude Christ's obedience during his life, but a reference at least to his death is clear. In this way it seems fair to call this an explicit mention of Christ's death. Moreover, the resulting "righteousness" argues for a reference to his death as well (cf. 3:25; 4:25; 5:9).

Other Objections

Although the legal fiction objection is the oldest and most common, there are other objections to address. Most can be boiled down into three main points. The following, therefore, are general, or possible, objections to imputation.[74] Addressing these objections will also afford an opportunity to speak to other issues related to this topic as well as the method employed in the present work.

1) "A systematic, not a biblical idea." This is a common objection based on the observation that Paul does not use imputation language (i.e., λογίζομαι) in any "imputation" text except Romans 4. And if that is the only true "imputation text," then it should further be noted, so the argument goes, that Paul does not emphasize positive imputation but only the non-reckoning of sin. Paul, in fact, seems nearly to equate forgiveness with justification. One may easily prove this point, for Paul cites Genesis 15:6, "and Abraham believed God and it was reckoned to him as righteousness." He then goes on to clarify and explain this with another Old Testament quote (this time from Ps. 32:1), using the quotation formula "just as David also says," which equates those whose lawless deeds are forgiven and whose sins are covered with "the man to whom the Lord will not reckon sin." Clearly, forgiveness is central to Paul's argument. So even in the text that speaks most explicitly about imputation, the question concerning the imputation of righteousness appears as yet unanswered. The language of Reformed theology, so the objection goes, is not the language of Paul.[75] To

---

[74] I have made an effort to distill various objections into a few main objections. Much of the debate over imputation has taken place in public, and sometimes private, meetings rather than on paper. One major exception is the criticism of imputation lodged by Robert H. Gundry ("Why I Didn't Endorse 'The Gospel of Jesus Christ,'" and "The Nonimputation of Christ's Righteousness"). Gundry's objections have been addressed nearly point by point by Piper (*Counted Righteous*), and also by Carson ("The Vindication of Imputation"), though it should be noted that Piper and Carson take different tacks. Piper answers more or less text by text, while Carson's treatment (which is shorter and written for a different format) moves forward on the distinction between biblical and theological discourse (the method in this work lies somewhere between the two), and while he discusses several texts, the bulk of the essay is on Romans 4. The criticisms of N. T. Wright are also well known and appear in more than one source. Throughout the course of this work I have dealt to some extent with criticisms that come up in regard to specific texts, particularly those from Wright, and to a lesser extent from Gundry, so those will not be re-addressed here. For these reasons I will address objections that comprise something of an amalgamation of the general objections.

[75] This objection, it appears to me, is the essence of Gundry's critique of imputation. His article briefly considers various texts, including the ones discussed in this work, with a view to show that none of the texts speak explicitly of the imputation of Christ's righteousness, "Why I Didn't Endorse 'The Gospel of Jesus Christ.'" This holds true also in Gundry's response to Thomas Oden, "On Oden's 'Answer,'" *Books & Culture*, March/April (2001): 14-15, 39.

answer this question, as seen in the entire discussion prior to this section, we must turn to other texts.

When we turn to Romans 5:18-19, we see that Paul does not use imputation language but speaks of being "made righteous" (δίκαιοι κατασταθήσονται). As noted in chapter 3 of this work, καθίστημι does not share semantic fields with λογίζομαι, and is not used in the Septuagint or in the New Testament to mean "reckon." Likewise, in 2 Corinthians 5:21, Paul does not speak of being reckoned righteous, much less of Christ's righteousness being imputed to the believer, but says that we "become the righteousness of God" (γενώμεθα δικαιοσύνη θεοῦ). Similar comments could be made about texts such as 1 Corinthians 1:30 and Philippians 3:9. None of them say that Christ's righteousness is imputed the believer. The objection, therefore, is that for one to believe in imputation is essentially like saying that even though the Bible does not teach it, one can still hold to imputation *theologically*.

In answer to this objection, it is helpful to consider the distinction Carson makes regarding "domains of discourse, viz. exegesis and theology."[76] This distinction does not mean that the two are hermetically sealed off from each other, as though theological discourse can legitimately be bereft of exegetical support or that exegetical discourse has no connection to theology.[77] Carson, rather, refers to the fact that we may speak legitimately of some biblical idea or doctrine, even if the texts claimed to support it do not refer "*explicitly*" to it.[78] Obviously this can be somewhat tricky ground, and it is a concept that opens almost effortlessly to abuse. Yet the point is not to say, "Well, even though it is not in the Bible, this is nonetheless true." The point is that if biblical teaching can be shown, on the basis of exegesis, to support a concept that is expressed in "theological discourse" (to use Carson's phrase), then there is room to discuss that concept even if it does not derive explicitly from

---

[76] Carson, "The Vindication of Imputation," 47.

[77] Though both of these extremes are far more frequent than one could wish.

[78] Ibid., 50 (I have borrowed Carson's emphasis). Carson cites the compelling examples of progressive sanctification and the idea of God's being reconciled to us. While Paul's use of ἁγιάζω and cognates is overwhelmingly "positional" or "definitive," it is nevertheless valid to speak of sanctification in a progressive sense when one takes a broader look, for example, at Paul's statements about "spiritual growth" where ἁγιάζω is not used. Likewise, while Paul does not speak of God's being reconciled to us, the "biblical treatments of God's wrath, and the nature of the peculiarly Christian (as opposed to pagan) understanding of propitiation," provide for a discussion that is "convincingly Pauline," even though Paul speaks exclusively in terms of us being reconciled to God (ibid., 3-5).

a text.[79] The operative phrase, of course, is "on the basis of exegesis."[80] Maintaining these realms of discourse and allowing both to play a role in the course of the argument is the goal of this dissertation.

The present work relies on a mixture of exegesis and synthesis to argue for imputation. Hopefully, this synthesis is *based on* exegesis, because the goal has never been to argue for imputation on purely "theological" or traditional grounds, though the question derives from traditional Protestant, particularly Lutheran and Reformed, categories.[81] For example, taken by itself, it seems legitimate to say that Romans 5:18-19 speaks of Christ's obedience "counting" for others just as Adam's disobedience "counted" for others. The concept of covenantal headship argues for some idea of imputation. Yet that is not the only reason to argue for it from Romans 5:18-19. It is just as essential to see that it shares common themes associated with Romans 4:1-8, 2 Corinthians 5:14-21, 1 Corinthians 1:30, Philippians 3:1-9, Romans 9:30–10:4, etc. When the various elements of the texts discussed in this work are compared, there is legitimate ground to argue for the imputation of Christ's righteousness, even though the texts do not use that precise language.[82] These common elements and concepts in the texts (e.g., undeserved grace, substitution, etc.) are essential to the argument for imputation given here. Thus, one may hold to the imputation of Christ's righteousness, not in spite of the fact that Paul does not teach it, but because even though he does not say it explicitly, it expresses something valid, even vital, in Paul's teaching.

One must be careful to note that this does not mean that the distinctions between λογίζομαι, καθίστημι, and γίνομαι should be ignored—far from it. It is only to say that imputation does not depend solely on the meanings of these words. As a metaphor it may be bor-

---

[79] This was also one of John Wesley's objections. See quote in Williams, *John Wesley's Theology Today* (Nashville: Abingdon, 1960), 71.

[80] Some scholars, no doubt, will not accept Carson's distinctions in discourse, or at least not to merging them, opting instead to limit their discourse only to that which appears explicitly in the text. Many, if not most, scholars in biblical studies see this as their task, i.e., descriptive biblical theology. Yet this desire is no less open to extremes than "theological discourse."

[81] I want to echo Carson's comment: "I should add that informed Protestants would not want to say that the Reformation invented their understanding of justification," "The Vindication of Imputation," 46, n. 1.

[82] This is essentially, it seems to me, the way Piper argues for imputation in, say, 1 Corinthians 1:30 (and in other texts as well), (*Counted Righteous*, 86). See above, n. 14.

rowed from λογίζομαι, but that does not mean that λογίζομαι must appear in every text traditionally associated with imputation. Paul's emphases in Romans 4, Romans 5, and 2 Corinthians 5 should be maintained in our exegesis, teaching, and preaching. One need not come to Romans 4 and preach a sermon that would be identical to Romans 5. Paul's emphasis on free forgiveness, on the justification of the ungodly by faith apart from works, should be *our* emphasis. There would be no compelling reason to expound on Christ's role as covenant head of his people (Romans 5) in Romans 4. Certainly connections can be drawn between texts with similar themes, but the integrity of each text must be maintained or else we have jettisoned biblical authority for the authority of the interpreter.

We must never allow our zeal for theological truth to overwhelm our adherence to the text. Exegeting and preaching a valid synthesis of biblical teaching, however, is not an abandonment of biblical theology for systematic theology. On the one hand we can say that the term "imputation" is, technically, borrowed from systematic theology. On the other hand, "imputation" is simply another way of saying "reckoning" (a thoroughly biblical term), and whatever one calls it, whether imputation, reckoning, or counting, it cannot be dismissed as "theological" rather than "biblical." A discussion of "imputation" is, rather, a biblical-theological subject.

2) **"Christ's positive obedience does not count."** A long-standing objection to imputation is that while the Bible teaches forgiveness on the basis of Christ's death (his passive obedience), it nowhere speaks of Christ's active obedience, whether one is referring specifically to a vicarious fulfillment of the Mosaic law or to his obedience to the Father in general.[83] Christ's perfect obedience, it is argued, is not imputed to

---

[83] The imputation of Christ's righteousness can, in my opinion, be *established* without recourse to a discussion of Christ's perfect obedience to the Mosaic law when the discussion focuses on Paul's letters. I am not arguing that Christ did not obey the law or that his obedience to it is not part of his positive righteousness. He succeeded where both Adam and Israel failed. Succeeding where Israel failed means keeping the law. While Christ's fulfillment of the Mosaic law has been a major component in the historical discussion of imputation, the issue lies at a more fundamental level of obedience and disobedience that springs from Eden. Sin and death were already in the world before the law (Rom. 5:14), and the law served to manifest, magnify, and exacerbate the dilemma in which human beings lived as a result of Adam's sin and as a result of being his children (Rom. 3:20; 5:20; 7:7-13; Gal. 3:19). For certain, the law had to be obeyed and Christ did obey it, but the issue of humanity's plight, living under the just wrath of God, is at a level more basic than the law and existed

believers but is that which guaranteed the perfection of his sacrifice. That is, Christ obeyed perfectly in order to be a perfect sacrifice.[84] This matter was addressed above, but a few more general comments are in order.[85]

The argument from Paul's teaching on the Adam/Christ parallel and antithesis again provides the best ground for asserting that Christ's righteousness, his positive obedience, is imputed to believers. Historically, the discussion of imputation often includes the assertion that Christ had to secure not only the forgiveness of Adam's sin, but also that positive standing Adam would have achieved had he not sinned. Thus, there is the need for both a negative (forgiveness) and a positive (obedience) righteousness. Regardless of what one thinks of that idea, agreeing that Christ's righteousness is imputed to believers does not require one to consent to the idea based on what "would have" happened.

The argument for imputation simply emphasizes that Adam not only sinned, but that his sin was, as all sin is inevitably, a *failure* to obey God.[86] There is, therefore, a need to overturn not only Adam's sin (forgiveness is needed) but also his *failure to obey*. That is, in a nutshell, the basis for saying that Christ, as the second Adam, had to obey the Father in all things, including "obedience to the point of death" (Phil. 2:8), and that his righteousness, including his obedience, must be imputed to believers in order for them to have a right status before

---

prior to the law. The law shined a floodlight on it. In this sense, Christ's obedience of the Mosaic law was a kind of subset, or necessary component, of his obedience in general. A study of the Mosaic law, including a thorough consideration of the Old Testament and the nature of the obedience required in the law, with a specific view of Christ's role/obedience in regard to imputation, would be another valuable contribution to the larger discussion. Such a study would have to include thorough evidence outside the purview of this work.

[84] This was, apparently, the view held by Johann Piscator. See Alistair McGrath, *Iustitia Dei: A History of the Christian Doctrine of Justification*, 2nd ed. (Cambridge: University Press, 1989), 233. I am grateful to Mark A. Seifrid, who brought Piscator to my attention. See also Carson's comment, "The Vindication of Imputation," 54, n. 21. This is the other fundamental idea in Gundry's critique of imputation. After quoting the paragraph in "The Gospel of Christ: an Evangelical Celebration" that affirms the imputation of Christ's perfect obedience, Gundry comments: "Certainly evangelicals affirm that Jesus had to live a life of perfect righteousness if he was to qualify as the bearer of our sins. But the demand that Jesus' life of perfect righteousness prior to his death constitutes an indispensable part of the righteousness that 'Celebration' presents as imputed to sinners who believe in him puts on "Celebration" a Reformed stamp that many evangelicals cannot knowingly endorse. For they believe that reconciliation and justification derive from Jesus' 'one act of righteousness,' which contrasts with Adam's 'one transgression' and therefore refers solely to Jesus' propitiatory death on the cross" ("Why I Didn't Endorse 'The Gospel of Jesus Christ'," 6).

[85] See pp. 198-203.

[86] The root sin is unbelief which is manifested in disobedience. Nevertheless, "sin is lawlessness" (1 John 3:4).

God. As pointed out numerous times, Christ's obedience need not be sharply divided between "active" and "passive"; Christ's obedience (as all obedience) was active *and* passive. Ironically, those who oppose the imputation of Christ's righteousness are often the ones who make the most explicit distinction between "active" and "passive" obedience. The "active obedience" only counts to make Jesus a perfect sacrifice (passive) on the cross.[87] As seen earlier, however, there is no separating one kind of obedience from another in a practical sense; in traditional Protestant theology the distinction has always been a matter of precision and clarity in discussion, not a creation of two distinct or disconnected categories of obedience.

Finally in this regard, the imputation of Christ's righteousness is not simply a by-product of traditional covenant theology. It is a matter of recognizing a similarity between the relationship of Adam to humanity and Christ to humanity. Romans 5:12-21 is the issue, not a presupposition about whether the relationship between Adam and God was a covenant.[88]

3) **"Imputation leads to antinomianism."** This is easily the most anecdotal objection to the imputation of righteousness.[89] Someone might

---

[87] E.g., Gundry. See above, n. 84. This is not to deny that the two may be separated for the purpose of discussion. But in actual relation to Christ's life and death, and in regard to what is imputed to believers, the distinction can be an abstraction.

[88] I will work out these issues in more detail in an upcoming work.

[89] One of the better known critics of imputation on the grounds that it leads to antinomianism is John Wesley. "I have had abundant proof that the frequent use of this unnecessary phrase [Christ's imputed righteousness], instead of 'furthering men's progress in vital holiness,' has made them satisfied without any holiness at all." (Cited in Colin W. Williams, *John Wesley's Theology Today* [Nashville: Abingdon, 1960], 71; and in Woodrow W. Whidden, "Wesley on Imputation: A Truly Reckoned Reality or Antinomian Wreckage," *Asbury Theological Journal* 52/2 [1997]: 65). In 1765, however, Wesley preached a sermon in which he states that "[t]he first thing then which admits of no dispute among reasonable men is this: to all believers the righteousness of Christ is imputed," "The Lord our Righteousness," in *The Bicentennial Edition of the Works of John Wesley*, ed. Albert C. Outler, vol. 1 *Sermons, I, 1-33* (Nashville: Abingdon, 1984), 454. Wesley's view of imputation, however, seems to have been restricted to forgiveness. Wesley's desire was to maintain the necessity of ongoing sanctification, the importance of which, he feared, was weakened by the doctrine of the imputation of Christ's positive righteousness. As Oden remarks, "Wesley affirmed that Christ is 'our substitute as to penal sufferings' but not as a substitute for our personal acts of obedience. That we are 'complete in him' refers also to our sanctification by cooperating grace, not merely justification by grace operating. . . . Hence we should never talk an easy game of imputation without taking seriously the process of behavioral sanctification" (Thomas C. Oden, *John Wesley's Scriptural Christianity: A Plain Exposition of his Teaching on Christian Doctrine* [Grand Rapids: Zondervan, 1994], 210). This is obviously not the place to open a discussion of Wesley's view of justification, sanctification, etc. It is sufficient to note that he was critical of imputation, in the traditional sense, because he thought it would lead to lawlessness.

say that the belief in Christ's imputed righteousness will lead to the presumption that faith *and* obedience are not necessary for the believer. If one believes that saving righteousness is Christ's righteousness, then we may well excuse any sort of sinful behavior on the basis that it is not our own righteousness, but Christ's, that makes us right before God. While the latter idea, that believers are righteous before God on the basis of Christ's righteousness, is true, it does not mean that sinful behavior is excusable, or safe, or that anyone should or could feel secure in their sinning.

This is precisely the question Paul addresses in Romans 6:1: "What then shall we say? Should we go on sinning so that grace will abound? May it never be!" Paul's theology of justification drew the criticism, or the misunderstanding, that obedience to God no longer matters. Similarly, in verse 15 Paul asks, again rhetorically, "Therefore what? Should we sin because we are not under law but under grace? May it never be!" In other words, Paul's theology of justification by faith was interpreted by some people as antinomianism.[90] There are two issues to address. First, it is possible that an erroneous view of Christian obedience may lead to the idea that imputation will lead to lawlessness. By addressing this issue we will also have opportunity to observe the true basis for obedience. Secondly, there is a sense in which the charge of antinomianism may be legitimate, but not because of anything inherent to the doctrine of imputation.

The first issue that needs addressing is that the charge of antinomianism itself is often based on a false presupposition, namely, that a right standing before God depends, somehow, on works that either earn something, or are done because one "has" to do them. Simply put, the antinomian charge may simply be saying: "If you believe imputation, you will not do what you are supposed to do." The charge is leveled before considering why it is that a Christian should do good works, what the foundation for them is, and what the motivation should be for doing them. Paul's argument, on the other hand, in Romans 6 establishes both the "why"

---

[90] I realize that I am implicitly begging the question and engaging in a bit of circular argumentation. "Paul teaches imputation; imputation draws the charge of antinomianism; Paul's theology of justification drew the charge of antinomianism; Paul, therefore, held to imputation, which can be proved from Paul's teaching." Yet I am assuming the conclusion, for better or worse, because up to this point the goal has been to show this very thing—that Paul does teach the imputation of Christ's righteousness.

and the "what" of Christian obedience. The "why," or the foundation for good works, is the death, burial, and resurrection of Christ, all of which the believer shares in through union with Christ (6:3-11).

The Christian does not pursue obedience merely because he "must" do it, but because he *can* do it. If it is all a matter of simply what we *must* do, then practically speaking we may think that wages, not faith, are reckoned as righteousness. Being motivated only by *must* is similar to saying: "I must do my job in order to collect my wages."[91] This attitude could also manifest itself when so-called "rewards" become *the* motivation for obedience;[92] i.e., a Christian should obey *because* God will reward him.[93] Thus, belief in a wrong view of Christian obedience can itself be the cause of someone's objecting to imputation. Christian obedience, however, is "from the heart" (v. 17), i.e., has a different motivation than simply what "must" be done. What makes Christian obedience "from the heart" is the knowledge of the free grace of God in Jesus Christ that has set the Christian free to obey, again, "from the heart," not out of compulsion.[94]

Secondly, what motivates a Christian to do good works is not a sense of "this must be done," but an understanding of what has been done on his behalf (e.g., Rom. 3:25; 4:25; 5:1, 19). In other words, not only does the imperative follow the indicative, but the imperative is *grounded* in the indicative. Paul's teaching is often treated as if it is of two kinds: doctrine and practical commands. While it is true that "doctrine" may be stressed to the point of ignoring what comes after (thus signifying that the doctrine is not understood), it is also true that

---

[91] Contra Romans 4:4.

[92] Calvin remarks: "For if it is only a matter of men looking for reward when they serve God, and hiring or selling their labor to him, it is of little profit. God wills to be freely worshipped, freely loved. That worshipper, I say, he approves who, when all hope of receiving reward has been cut off, still ceases not to serve him." John Calvin, *The Institutes of the Christian Religion*, 3.16.2, ed. John T. McNeill, trans. Ford Lewis Battles, *Library of Christian Classics*, vol. 10 (Philadelphia: Westminster, 1960), 799. Note that Calvin is not discrediting all ideas of rewards, but rewards as a primary motivation for serving God. Calvin comments, it seems to me, on those times, "when," in the words of Screwtape, "a human, no longer desiring, but still intending, to do our Enemy's will, looks round upon a universe from which every trace of Him seems to have vanished, and asks why he has been forsaken, and still obeys." C. S. Lewis, *The Screwtape Letters* (New York: Macmillan, 1962), 39.

[93] The point here is not whether there are rewards (that is another discussion), but simply to assert that rewards cannot be the sole ground or motivation for obedience.

[94] There is, of course, still a sense of "must" for the Christian. All I am addressing is the possibility that underneath the charge of antinomianism is a view that understands biblical parenesis as simply more "law" apart from the new allegiance to Christ. Thus from a certain perspective, criticism of imputation may be based on a view of Christian works-righteousness.

the commands may be thought of as simply bits and pieces of the law that made their way from the Old Testament, apart from the fact that the entire motivation for obeying is set forth in terms of what God has done in Christ. In other words, having begun with grace, believers often attempt to continue with works. Only the acts of God in Christ are motivation for the actions of Christians.

A good example of the idea that Christian acts are motivated solely by God's acts in Christ is found in Romans 12:1: "Therefore I urge you brethren, because of the mercy of God, to present your bodies as living sacrifices, holy and pleasing to God, your spiritual act of worship." Regardless of whether οὖν ("therefore") refers to the entire epistle, chapters 9–11, or even 11:33-36, the ground for Paul's exhortation is crystal clear: "God's mercy."[95] In other words, Paul sees that the only proper response to what God has done is to live one's entire life in service to God. Paul's call for the erring Corinthians to repent (2 Cor. 6:1-2) is set in the context of Christ's sacrifice on behalf of believers (5:21). Likewise, the exhortation to "cleanse ourselves from all defilement of flesh and spirit, perfecting holiness in the fear of God" (2 Cor. 7:1) is grounded in God's promises from the Old Testament (6:16-18), which were fulfilled through the cross (5:21). In Philippians 3 the goal of striving to win the prize (v. 14) is firmly set in the reality of "the righteousness that comes from God and is by faith" (v. 9).[96] Justification by faith, redemption from the sphere of sin and death, and participation in the new kingdom of righteousness and life through the obedience of Christ (Romans 4–5) lay the groundwork for the new obedience of Romans 6.

Finally, there is no denying that there are cases where the doctrine of imputation (or any context where justification is generally conceived as forensic) has led to presumption or a sense of lethargy regarding the necessity of obedience and faith. At one point this tendency caused Wesley to exclaim: "We swarm with Antinomians on every side!"[97] It is, however, invalid to indict a doctrine on the basis of wrong conceptions

---

[95] Calvin cites this text in the same regard, saying, "Paul, when he devoted an entire letter to showing that we have no hope of life save in Christ's righteousness, when he gets down to exhortations, implores us by that mercy of God which He has deigned to give us" (*Institutes*, 3.13.3, 800).

[96] This text illustrates the eschatological nature of God's grace to us in Christ as a motivation for obedience. Not only is the past act emphasized (v. 10, resurrection and suffering of Christ), but the future action in which the work begun in the believer (1:6) will be completed (vv. 20-21).

[97] Quoted in Oden, *John Wesley's Scriptural Christianity,"* 211.

or practices. It is not the idea in and of itself that is wrong; the problem is with faulty teaching and ultimately with people. The doctrine of imputation cannot be judged on the basis of what it *might* lead to, or what it *has led* to in the experience of some who hold to it. One may as well say that obedience should not be stressed because it *might*, and indeed sometimes *has*, led to legalism. In other words, extremes or misconceptions, whether antinomian or legalistic (and both may exist at once in human beings), are not valid grounds for condemning a doctrine. Imputation cannot be denied by saying it will lead to lawlessness. Some people may fall into lawlessness and use imputation as their excuse, but imputation biblically conceived will not lead to antinomianism unless the desire for antinomianism is already present. The desire, not the doctrine, is at fault.

CONCLUSION

A synthesis of Paul's teaching leads to the conclusion that Christ's righteousness is, after all, imputed to believers. A variety of themes merge in such a way as to establish that the righteousness that counts before God and is by faith can be nothing other than Christ's righteousness.[98] From various texts it is evident that when discussing justification Paul speaks of, among other things, God's actions through Christ on behalf of sinners, who though undeserving are forgiven and declared righteous as a free gift from God on the basis of Christ's substitutionary death. Christ as the second Adam, the covenant head of his people, and the first fruits of the harvest, obeys the will and command of God, and his obedience results in a right standing before God for those identified in union with him. This righteousness is appropriated by faith, which, as the instrumental means of justification, effects their union with Christ.

---

[98] "It is an unavoidable logical conclusion that people of faith are justified because Christ's righteousness is imputed to them" (Ladd, *New Testament Theology*, 491).

SIX

CONCLUSION:
"NO HOPE WITHOUT IT"?

ALTHOUGH NOT EVERY scholar mentioned in chapter 1 is mentioned in later discussion, each nevertheless helped provide a historical context within which to place the question of imputation. The debate over imputation is not new. What is different today, however, is that many modern scholars rarely mention imputation, except perhaps to disprove it. There are a variety of reasons for this phenomenon, the primary reason being different theological presuppositions about justification. At the same time, there are scholars who use the term "imputation" but without all the nuance and detail with which the doctrine is often associated. Historically, both Luther and Calvin often lay special emphasis on the comprehensive nature of forgiveness, sometimes speaking of it synonymously with justification. This does not at all mean that either one made a one-to-one correspondence between forgiveness and justification, much less that that there is no notion of positive righteousness, but merely that their own writings attest to the comprehensive way Paul can speak of forgiveness. In Luther and Calvin there is also an emphasis on the importance of union with Christ for understanding justification. This proved to be an important point in the subsequent chapters. Taken as a whole, the scope of the first chapter hints at the sheer breadth of the topic of imputation.

Much of the discussion in chapter 2 revolved around λογίζομαι. We saw that Abraham's faith was reckoned to him as righteousness; however, the faith itself was not the righteousness, but was the thing that united him to the object of his faith, namely, God. Paul picks up the story of Abraham to prove that righteousness before God depends, and always has depended, on faith and not on works. Righteousness is something granted to Abraham solely by faith, as a gift, and not as earned wages. Paul further explains what he means by quoting Psalm 32. The reckoning of Abraham as righteous is just like the blessing spoken by David: "Blessed is the one whose lawless deeds are forgiven, whose sins are covered. Blessed is the man whom God does not reckon sin" (Rom. 4:7-8). Paul thus emphasizes forgiveness in this text. This is entirely in keeping with his argument up to this point in Romans. There is not explicit mention of the imputation of Christ's righteousness, but given the antecedents in Romans 3:21-26 and the subsequent statements in 4:23-25, the focus, or object of faith, is clearly Christ. The object of faith is the source of righteousness. The righteousness that is reckoned flows from his death on the cross, a death through which we were "justified freely" and took place "on account of our transgression."

It is when we move on to Romans 5:12-21 that the aspect of Christ's positive obedience comes to the fore. The phrase "made righteous" is not synonymous with "reckoned righteous," but given the range of meaning for the word καθίστημι, and especially given the context of Romans 5, Paul is referring to a state of being (that is, "righteous") that one has as a result of Christ's obedience. In other words, Christ obeys and that obedience has direct consequences for many. The issue in this text is not the obedience of believers—it is not even their faith—but rather the obedience of Christ that secures forgiveness of Adam's sin, and the sin and death that flowed from it as condemnation. As the second Adam, the "type of the one to come," Jesus did what Adam was created to do—he lived in obedience to his heavenly Father. Adam disobeyed with the result that many were made sinners; Christ obeys and many are made righteous. His obedience, dare we say, *counts* to make them righteous.

God's action through the sacrificial death of Christ results in believers' "becoming the righteousness of God in him" (2 Cor. 5:21). Once again we see Paul emphasizing the theme of representation, as Christ's death is described as a death "for all" (v. 14). Christ's representative death is captured in the phrase ("made to be sin"), which points to a sacrificial background associated with but not limited to the Old Testament "sin offering." This is linked to another Old Testament background, namely Isaiah's servant, who as an offering will "bear sins" and "justify many" (Isa. 53:6, 10-11). Christ, whom God "made to be sin," dies a representative, substitutionary death, and thus God reconciles "the world to himself" and does not count "their trespasses to them" (2 Cor. 5:19). "Becoming the righteousness of God in him" means being "a new creation" in Christ (v. 17), and therefore locates "becoming the righteousness of God" solely in union with Christ. Believers are not righteous apart from Christ, and it is only through their identification with him that his substitutionary death is effective for them.

In other words, it is only in union with Christ that God's act of reconciliation in Christ "counts" for believers. While some may balk at using the word "count," it is a valid way of describing this exchange of sin for righteousness between Christ and the believer. Christ takes our sin, we receive all his benefits, chiefly righteousness, which in context refers primarily to a status before God on the basis of Christ's death on the cross.

Taken alone, not one of the "key" texts that have played such an integral role in the historical discussion argues decisively, or explicitly, for a full-orbed doctrine of imputation. But when read together certain parallels become evident that point toward a synthesis of Pauline teaching. When read in their respective contexts, five common themes run through these texts: (1) An action takes place outside the believer, and (2) that action is specifically God acting in Christ (3) on behalf of sinners, and is, therefore, (4) an act of grace that is affected or applied (5) in union with Christ. These common themes make it difficult to locate justifying righteousness apart from Christ and his righteousness. Combinations of these themes were noted also in 1 Corinthians 1:30, Philippians 3:3-9, and Romans 9:30–10:4. In addition, in both Philippians 3 and Romans 9–10 Paul draws a distinction between a self-generated righteousness and a righteousness that comes from God: "seeking to establish their own [righteousness] they did not subject themselves to the righteousness of God" (Rom. 10:3); and "not having a righteousness of my own from the law but that which is through faith in Christ, the righteousness from God by faith" (Phil. 3:9). God's righteousness, the righteousness that is from God, is Christ—he is the believer's righteousness. This is another way of saying that the righteousness of Christ is imputed to believers.

CONCLUSION: ". . . *AND* RIGHTEOUSNESS"

Imputation has suffered from a fairly modern disease: the conception that biblical studies and theology are absolutely distinct disciplines and never the two shall meet. A fully developed view of imputation does indeed fall under the domain of theological discourse, and it is theological discourse based on the exegesis of texts.[1] While traditionally imputation is closely associated with systematic theology, it is not somehow then off limits for a biblical-theological study such as this one.[2] Just the opposite is true: where else better to study and evaluate such a theme? We must pursue theological synthesis without allowing ourselves to import unnecessarily the entirety of a doctrine into one text. We must pursue exegesis with respect for the integrity of each text, while keeping an eye focused on how various texts that share common themes and concepts relate to one another. In other words, we should ask, what does this particular text say, and how does it all fit together? The doctrine of imputation requires that we ask both questions.

One of the goals of this book is, hopefully, to spark others to ask these questions about related themes such as the connection between imputation and the atonement or the relationship between imputation and necessity of obedience. Perhaps the book will even lead others to a comprehensive biblical study of imputation itself, reaching out beyond Paul. Such a study would require far more than tracking the use of particular words.

Imputation is clearly linked to two central, biblical, Pauline themes, namely, forgiveness and justification. Regardless of the close connection between these concepts, they are not finally synonymous. For instance, although Paul can equate the reckoning of Abraham's *faith* as righteousness with "the *man* whom God reckons righteous apart from works" (Rom. 4:6), this does not mean that imputation *is* justification.

---

[1] D. A. Carson, "The Vindication of Imputation: On Fields of Discourse and, of Course, Semantic Fields," in *Justification: What's at Stake in the Current Debates* (Downers Grove: InterVarsity, 2004), 47. Carson's distinction between theological and exegetical discourse is vital for the integration of exegesis and systematic theology.

[2] As stated at the outset, this book is in the stream of work modeled by biblical theologians such as Geerhardus Vos. The method employed here is in keeping with the parameters and distinctions discussed by Vos in "The Idea of Biblical Theology as a Science and as a Theological Discipline," in *Redemptive History and Biblical Interpretation: The Shorter Writings of Geerhardus Vos*, ed. Richard B. Gaffin (Phillipsburg, N.J.: Presbyterian and Reformed, 1980): 3-24. See also, Richard B. Gaffin, "Systematic Theology and Biblical Theology," *WTJ* 38 (1976): 281-99.

Imputation is integral to Paul's theology of justification but it is not the whole of justification. Similarly, though Paul closely associates the reckoning of righteousness with forgiveness (Rom. 4:6-8; cf. 2 Cor. 5:19), imputation is not forgiveness any more than justification *is* forgiveness. These concepts are complementary, and each is necessary for understanding how the ungodly can stand before God and be declared right with him. Being justified by faith means we are forgiven *and* we stand before God as those who have fulfilled his righteous standards—even though we were previously "dead in our trespasses and sins."[3] The forgiveness we have in Christ is inseparable from the positive standing we have before God in Christ. It is little wonder that these words can appear at times as synonyms. The historic doctrine of imputation reflects an appreciation for the richness and breadth of Paul's language.

It is difficult to overemphasize that the imputation of Christ's righteousness takes place in union with Christ. Only as a person is identified with Christ is Christ's righteousness imputed to that person.[4] Another way of saying this is that Christ's righteousness is counted to the believer because God now sees the believer only in relation to Christ and his accomplished work. Union with Christ, so prominent in Luther and Calvin and in many of their successors, needs, and I think is getting, renewed appreciation in our day.

Do I then agree with Machen?[5] Is there no hope without the active obedience of Christ? Without driving a wedge between "active" and "passive" obedience, I agree—"there is no hope without it."[6] A right standing before God depends on Jesus' blood *and* righteousness. By this I mean that Christ's fulfilling of all righteousness—his obedience to the Father's will and commands in his role as the second Adam, his sacrificial death, and his resurrection that vindicates the cross and ushers in a new eschatological era—becomes ours by faith in union with him. It is on this basis that a believer is reckoned righteous. "Christ's righteousness becomes our righteousness and all that he has becomes ours, rather

---

[3] Ephesians 2:1.

[4] The title of Piper's book, *Counted Righteous in Christ*, points to the centrality of union with Christ and away from imputation as an abstract doctrine.

[5] J. Gresham Machen, *God Transcendent*, ed. Ned B. Stonehouse (Edinburgh; Carlisle, PA: Banner of Truth) 14; see above, Introduction, n. 1.

[6] As noted in several places above, Christ's obedience to the Father, in his life and in his death, is both active and passive in nature.

he himself becomes ours."[7] Simply put, Christ fulfills Jeremiah 23:5-6 (cf. 33:14-16):

> Behold, the days are coming, declares the LORD, when I will raise up for David a righteous Branch, and he shall reign as king and deal wisely, and shall execute justice and righteousness in the land. In his days Judah will be saved, and Israel will dwell securely. And this is the name by which he will be called: *The LORD is our Righteousness.*[8]

---

[7] Martin Luther, *Sermo de duplici iustitia*, WA 2 (1884): 146; trans. Lowell J. Satre under the title *Two Kinds of Righteousness*, in LW 31, *The Career of the Reformer: I*, ed. Harold J. Grimm (Philadelphia: Mulenberg, 1957), 298.

[8] ESV; my emphasis.

BIBLIOGRAPHY

COMMENTARIES

Achtemeier, Paul. *Romans.* Interpretation. Louisville: John Knox, 1985.

Barrett, C. K. *Commentary on the Second Epistle to the Corinthians.* Black's New Testament Commentary. New York: Harper and Row, 1958.

_____. *The Epistle to the Romans.* Rev. ed. Black's New Testament Commentary. London: A & C Black, 1991.

Barth, Karl. *The Epistle to the Romans.* Translated by Edwyn C. Hoskyns. New York: Oxford University Press, 1933.

Belleville, Linda L. *2 Corinthians.* InterVarsity New Testament Commentary Series. Edited by Grant R. Osborne. Downers Grove, InterVarsity, 1996.

Best, Ernest. *Second Corinthians.* Interpretation. Atlanta: John Knox, 1987.

Black, Matthew. *Romans.* 2nd ed. New Century Bible. Grand Rapids: Eerdmans, 1989.

Bockmuehl, Markus. *The Epistle to the Philippians.* Black's New Testament Commentaries. London: A & C Black, 1997.

Bruce. F. F. *1 and 2 Corinthians.* New Century Bible. London: Oliphants, 1971.

Bultmann, Rudolph. *The Second Letter to the Corinthians.* Translated by Roy A. Harrisville. Minneapolis: Augsburg, 1985.

Byrne, Brendan. *Romans.* Sacra Pagina 6. Collegeville, MN: Liturgical, 1996.

Calvin, John. *Calvin's Commentaries.* Edited by David W. Torrance and Thomas F. Torrance. 12 vols. Grand Rapids: Eerdmans, 1959–1979.

Conzelmann, Hans. *1 Corinthians.* Hermeneia. Philadelphia: Fortress, 1975.

Cranfield, Charles E. B. *A Critical and Exegetical Commentary on the Epistle to the Romans.* 2 vols. International Critical Commentary, Edinburgh: T.& T. Clark, 1977, 1979.

Denny, James. *St. Paul's Epistle to the Romans.* The Expositor's Greek Testament, vol. 2. Edited by W. Robertson Nicholl, 555-725. Grand Rapids: Eerdmans, 1979.

Dodd, C. H. *The Epistle of Paul to the Romans.* Moffatt New Testament Commentary. London: Hodder and Stoughton, 1932.

Dunn, James D. G. *Romans.* 2 vols. Word Biblical Commentary 38A, 38B. Dallas: Word, 1988.

Edwards, James R. *Romans.* New International Biblical Commentary. Peabody, MA: Hendrickson, 1992.

Fitzmyer, Joseph A. *Romans.* Anchor Bible, vol. 33. New York: Doubleday, 1993.

Furnish, Victor P. *II Corinthians.* Anchor Bible, vol. 32A. New York: Doubleday, 1973.

Garland, David E. *2 Corinthians.* The New American Commentary. Nashville: Broadman & Holman, 1999.

Hafemann, Scott J. *2 Corinthians.* The NIV Application Commentary. Grand Rapids: Zondervan, 2000.

Hawthorne, Gerald F. *Philippians.* Word Biblical Commentary, vol. 43. Waco: Word, 1983.

Hughes, Philip E. *The Second Epistle to the Corinthians.* The New International Commentary on the New Testament. Grand Rapids: Eerdmans, 1962.

Johnson, Luke Timothy. *Reading Romans: A Literary and Theological Commentary.* Reading the New Testament Series. New York: Crossroad, 1997.

Käsemann, Ernst. *Commentary on Romans*. Translated by G. W. Bromiley. Grand Rapids: Eerdmans/London: SCM, 1980.

Leenhardt, Franz J. *The Epistle to the Romans*. Translated by Harold Knight. London: Lutterworth, 1961.

Lightfoot, J. B. *Commentary on the Epistle of St. Paul to the Philippians*. London: Macmillian, 1913. Reprint, Grand Rapids: Zondervan, 1953.

Luther, Martin. *Lectures on Romans*. Edited by Hilton C. Oswald. In *Luther's Works*, vol. 25. St. Louis: Concordia, 1972.

Martin, Ralph P. *2 Corinthians*. Word Biblical Commentary, vol. 40. Dallas: Word, 1986.

_____. *Philippians*. New Century Bible. London: Oliphants, 1976.

Melanchthon, Philip. *Commentary on Romans*. Translated by Fred Kramer. St. Louis: Concordia, 1992.

Moo, Douglas J. *The Epistle to the Romans*. New International Commentary on the New Testament. Grand Rapids: Eerdmans, 1996.

Morris, Leon. *The Epistle to the Romans*. Grand Rapids: Eerdmans, 1988.

Murray, John. *The Epistle to the Romans*. New International Commentary on the New Testament. Grand Rapids: Eerdmans, 1968.

Nygren, Anders. *Commentary on Romans*. Translated by Carl C. Rasmussen. Philadelphia: Muhlengerg, 1949.

O'Brien, Peter T. *The Epistle to the Philippians: A Commentary on the Greek Text*. New International Greek Text Commentary. Grand Rapids: Eerdmans, 1991.

Sanday, William, and Arthur C. Headlam. *A Critical and Exegetical Commentary on the Epistle to the Romans*. International Critical Commentary. Edinburgh: T & T Clark, 1902.

Schlatter, Adolf. *Romans: The Righteousness of God*. Translated by Siegfried S. Schatzmann. Peabody, Mass.: Hendrickson, 1995.

Schlier, Heinrich. *Der Römerbrief Kommentar*. Herders theologischer Kommentar zum Neuen Testament. Freiburg: Herder, 1977.

Schreiner, Thomas R. *Romans*. Baker Exegetical Commentary on the New Testament. Grand Rapids: Baker, 1998.

Scott, James M. *2 Corinthians*. New International Biblical Commentary. Edited by W. Ward Gasque. Peabody, Mass.: Hendrickson, 1998.

Silva, Moisés. *Philippians*. The Wycliffe Exegetical Commentary. Chicago: Moody Press, 1988.

Stuhlmacher, Peter. *Paul's Letter to the Romans*. Translated by Scott J. Hafemann. Louisville: Westminster/John Knox, 1994.

Thiselton, Anthony, C. *First Corinthians*. New International Greek Testament Commentary. Grand Rapids: Eerdmans, 2000.

Thrall, Margaret E. *A Critical and Exegetical Commentary on the Epistle*. Vol. 1. The International Critical Commentary. Edited by J. A. Emerton, C. E. B. Cranfield, and G. N. Stanton. Edinburgh: T & T Clark, 1994.

Vermigli, Peter Martyr. *Most Learned and Fruitful Commentaries of Doctor Peter Martir Vermilius*. Translated by H. B. Bolton. London: John Daye, 1568.

Wenham, Gordon. *Genesis*. 2 vols. Word Biblical Commentary 1A, 1B. Waco: Word, 1987, 1994.

Westermann, Claus. *Genesis 12–36*. Translated by John J. Scullion. Minneapolis: Augsburg, 1985.

Wilckens, Ulrich. *Der Brief an die Römer*. Evangelisch-Katholischer Kommentar zum

Neuen Testament. 3 vols. Neukirchen/Vluyn: Neukirchener Verlag/Zürich: Benziger: 1978–1981.

Wright, N. T. *Romans*. In vol. 10 of *The New Interpreters Bible*. Edited by Leander Keck. Nashville: Abingdon, 2002.

Zahn, Theodor. *Der Brief des Paulus an die Römer*. 1 und 2 Auflage. Leipzig: A. Deichert'sche Verlagsbuchhandlung Nachf. 1910.

Ziesler, John. *Paul's Letter to the Romans*. Trinity Press International New Testament Commentaries. Philadelphia: Trinity Press International, 1989.

BOOKS

Badenas, Robert. *Christ the End of the Law: Romans 10.4 in Pauline Perspective*. Journal for the Study of the New Testament Supplement Series 10. Sheffield: JSOT Press, 1988.

Barth, Karl. *Church Dogmatics*. Edited by G. W. Bromiley and T. F. Torrance. 4 vols in 14 parts. Edinburgh: T. & T. Clark, 1956–1975.

Beker, J. Christian. *Paul the Apostle: The Triumph of God in Life and Thought*. 2nd ed. Philadelphia: Fortress, 1984.

Berkhof, L. *Systematic Theology*. 4th ed. Grand Rapids: Eerdmans, 1941.

Berkouwer, G. C. *Faith and Justification*. Studies in Dogmatics. Grand Rapids: Eerdmans, 1954.

Blocher, Henri. *Original Sin: Illuminating the Riddle*. Grand Rapids: Eerdmans, 1997.

de Boer, M. *The Defeat of Death: Apocalyptic Eschatology in 1 Corinthians 15 and Romans 5*. Journal for the Study of the New Testament Supplement Series 22. Sheffield: JSOT Press, 1988.

Braaten, Carl, and Philip Jenson. *Union with Christ: The New Finnish Interpretation of Luther*. Grand Rapids: Eerdmans, 1998.

Bruce, F. F. *Paul: Apostle of the Heart Set Free*. London: Paternoster, 1977; Grand Rapids: Eerdmans, 1980.

Buchanan, James. *The Doctrine of Justification: An Outline of Its History in the Church and of Its Exposition from Scripture*. Edinburgh: T. & T. Clark, 1867. Reprint, Grand Rapids, Baker, 1955.

Bultmann, Rudolph. *Theology of the New Testament*. 2 vols. Translated by Kendrick Grobel. New York: Charles Scribner's Sons, 1954.

Caird, George B. *The Language and Imagery of the Bible*. 2nd ed. Grand Rapids: Eerdmans, 1997.

————. *New Testament Theology*. Completed and edited by L. D. Hurst. Oxford: Clarendon Press, 1994.

Calvin, John. *Institutes of the Christian Religion*. 2 vols. Translated by Ford Lewis Battles. Edited by John T. McNeill. Library of Christian Classics, vols. 20-21. Philadelphia: Westminster, 1960.

Carson, D. A. ed. *Right with God: Justification in the Bible and the World*. Grand Rapids: Baker; Carlisle, UK: Paternoster (published on behalf of the World Evangelical Fellowship), 1992.

Carson, D. A., Peter T. O'Brien, and Mark Seifrid, eds. *Justification and Variegated Nomism*. Vol. 1., *The Complexities of Second Temple Judaism*. Tübingen: Mohr Siebeck/Grand Rapids: Baker, 2001.

————. *Justification and Variegated Nomism*. Vol. 2, The Paradoxes of Paul Tübingen: Mohr/Grand Rapids: Baker, 2004.

Childs, Brevard S. *Biblical Theology of the Old and New Testaments: Theological Reflection on the Christian Bible.* Minneapolis: Fortress, 1993.

_____. *The New Testament as Canon: An Introduction.* Valley Forge, Pa.: Trinity Press International, 1994

Cranfield, Charles E. B. "St. Paul and the Law." In *New Testament Issues,* edited by R. Batey, 148-72. New York: Harper and Row, 1970.

Das, A. Andrew. *Paul, the Law, and the Covenant.* Peabody, MA: Hendrickson, 2001.

Davies, Glenn N. *Faith and Obedience in Romans: A Study of Romans 1-4.* Journal for the Study of the New Testament Supplement Series 39. Sheffield: JSOT Press, 1990.

Davies, W. D. *Paul and Rabbinic Judaism: Some Rabbinic Elements in Pauline Theology.* 4th rev. ed. Philadelphia: Fortress, 1980.

Donfried, Karl P., ed. *The Romans Debate.* 2nd ed. Peabody, Mass.: Hendrickson, 1991.

Dumbrell, William J. *Covenant and Creation.* Carlisle, UK: Paternoster, 1997.

Duncan, Ligon J. ed. *The Westminster Confession into the 21st Century: Essays in Remembrance of the 350th Anniversary of the Publication of the Westminster Confession of Faith.* Vol. 2. Fearn, Rosshire, Scotland: Christian Focus Publications, 2004.

Dunn, James D. G. *The Theology of Paul the Apostle.* Grand Rapids: Eedrmans, 1998.

_____, ed. *Paul and the Mosaic Law.* Wissenschaftliche Untersuchungen sum Neuen Testament 89. Tübingen: Mohr Siebeck, 1996/Grand Rapids: Eerdmans, 2001.

Edwards, Jonathan. *The Works of Jonathan Edwards.* 2 vols. Edinburgh: Banner of Truth, 1974.

_____. *Sermons and Discourses 1723-1729.* Edited by Kenneth P. Minkema. *Works of Jonathan Edwards.* Vol. 14. Edited by Harry S. Stout. New Haven, Conn.: Yale University Press, 1997.

Eichrodt, Walter. *Theology of the Old Testament.* 2 vols. Translated by J. A. Barker. Philadelphia: Westminster, 1967.

Elliott, Mark Adam. *The Survivors of Israel: A Reconsideration of the Theology of Pre-Christian Judaism.* Grand Rapids: Eerdmans, 2000.

Ellis, E. Earle. *Paul's Use of the Old Testament.* Grand Rapids: Eerdmans, 1957. Reprint, Grand Rapids: Baker, 1981.

Fitzmyer, Joseph A. *According to Paul: Studies in the Theology of the Apostle.* New York: Paulist Press, 1993.

_____. *Pauline Theology: A Brief Sketch.* Englewood Cliffs, NJ: Prentice-Hall, 1967.

Fuller, Daniel P. The Unity of the Bible: Unfolding God's Plan for Humanity. Grand Rapids: Zondervan, 1992.

Gaffin, Richard B. *Resurrection and Redemption: A Study in Paul's Soteriology.* 2nd ed. Phillipsburg, NJ: Presbyterian and Reformed, 1987.

Garlington, Don. *Faith, Obedience, and Perseverance: Aspects of Paul's Letter to the Romans.* Wissenschaftliche Untersuchungen sum Neuen Testament 79. Tübingen: Mohr Siebeck, 1994.

Gaston, Lloyd. *Paul and the Torah.* Vancouver: University of British Columbia Press, 1987.

Gathercole, Simon J. *Where Is Boasting? Early Jewish Soteriology and Paul's Response in Romans 1-5.* Grand Rapids: Eerdmans, 2002.

Gloer, Hulitt W. *An Exegetical and Theological Study of Paul's Understanding of New*

Creation and Reconciliation in 2 Cor. 5:14-21. Mellen Biblical Press Series. Vol. 32. Lewiston, NY: Mellen Biblical Press, 1996.

Goodwin, Thomas. *The Object and Acts of Justifying Faith.* Vol. 8 of *The Works of Thomas Goodwin.* Edinburgh: James Nichol. Reprint, Carlisle, Pa.: Banner of Truth. 1985.

Hafemann, Scott J. *The God of Promise and the Life of Faith: Understanding the Heart of the Bible.* Wheaton: Crossway, 2001

_____. *Paul, Moses and the History of Israel: The Letter/Spirit Contrast and the Argument from Scripture in 2 Corinthians 3.* Wissenschaftliche Untersuchugen zum Neuen Testament 81. Tübingen: Mohr Siebeck, 1995.

Hanson, Anthony Tyrell. Studies in Paul's Technique and Theology. London: SPCK, 1974.

Hay, David M. ed. *Pauline Theology.* Vol. 2, *1 & 2 Corinthians.* Minneapolis: Fortress,1993.

Hay, David M, and E. Elizabeth Johnson, eds. *Pauline Theology.* Vol. 3, *Romans.* Minneapolis, Fortress, 1995.

Hays, Richard B. *Echoes of Scripture in the Letters of Paul.* New Haven: Yale University Press, 1989.

Hodge, Charles. *Systematic Theology.* 3 vols. New York: Scribner's, 1872-73. Reprint, Grand Rapids, Eerdmans, 1973.

Hübner, Hans. *Law in Paul's Thought.* Translated by J. Greig. Edinburgh: T & T Clark, 1984.

Hughes, Philip Edgcumbe. *The True Image: The Origin and Destiny of Man in Christ.* Grand Rapids: Eerdmans, 1989.

Husbands, Mark, and Daniel J. Trier, eds. *Justification: What's at Stake in the Current Debates* (Downers Grove: InterVarsity, 2004).

Jervis, L. Ann, and Peter Richardson, eds. *Gospel in Paul: Studies on Corinthians, Galatians, and Romans for Richard N. Longenecker.* Journal for the Study of the New Testament Supplement Series 108. Sheffield: JSOT Press, 1994.

Joüon, Paul. *A Grammar of Biblical Hebrew.* 2 vols. Translated and Revised by T. Muraoka. Subsidia Biblica 14/1, 2. Rome: Editrice Pontificio Istituto Biblico, 1996.

Käsemann, Ernst. *New Testament Questions of Today.* Translated by W. J. Montague. Philadelphia: Fortress, 1969.

Kautzsch, E. *Über die Derivate des Stammes* צדק *im Alttestamentlichen Sprachgebrauch.* Tübingen: N.p., 1881.

_____, ed. *Gesenius' Hebrew Grammar.* 2nd English ed. Translated by A. E. Cowley. Oxford: Clarendon Press, 1910.

Kim, Seyoon. *The Origin of Paul's Gospel.* Grand Rapids: Eerdmans, 1982.

_____. *Paul and the New Perspective: Second Thoughts on the Origins of Paul's Gospel.* Grand Rapids: Eerdmans, 2001.

Kruse, Colin. *Paul, the Law and Justification.* Leicester: Apollos, 1996.

Ladd, George Eldon. *A Theology of the New Testament.* Rev. ed. Edited by Donald A. Hagner. Grand Rapids: Eerdmans, 1993.

Lillback, Peter A. *The Binding of God.* Grand Rapids: Baker; Carlisle, UK: Paternoster, 2001.

Lohse, Bernhard. *Martin Luther's Theology: Its Historical and Systematic Developments.* Minneapolis: Fortress, 1999.

Louw, Johannes P. *A Semantic Discourse Analysis of Romans.* 2 vols. Pretoria: University of Pretoria, 1997.

Louw, Johannes, and Eugene A. Nida. *Greek-English Lexicon of the New Testament Based on Semantic Domains.* 2nd ed. New York: United Bible Societies, 1989.

Luther, Martin. D. *Martin Luthers Werke: Kritische Gesamtausgabe.* 67 vols. to date. Weimar: Hermann Böhlaus Nachfolger, 1883–.

_____. *Luther's Epistle Sermons: Advent and Christmas Season.* Vol. 1. *Luther's Complete Works,* vol. 7. Translated by John Nicholas Lenker. Minneapolis: Luther Press, 1908.

_____. *Luther's Works.* Edited by Jeroslav Pelikan (vols. 1-30) and Helmut T. Lehmann (vols. 31-55). Philadelphia: Muhlenberg; St. Louis: Concordia, 1955–1986.

Machen, J. Gresham. *God Transcendent.* Edited by Ned B. Stonehouse. Grand Rapids: Eerdmans, 1949. Reprint, Edinburgh; Carlisle, Pa.: Banner of Truth, 1982.

_____. *The Origin of Paul's Religion.* Grand Rapids: Eerdmans, 1947.

Martin, Brice. *Christ and the Law in Paul.* Supplements to *Novum Testamentum* 62. Leiden: Brill, 1989.

Martin, Ralph P. *Reconciliation: A Study of Paul's Theology.* Atlanta: John Knox, 1981.

Melanchthon, Philip. *Melanchthon on Christian Doctrine: Loci Communes 1555.* Translated by Clyde L. Manschreck. New York: Oxford, 1965.

_____. *Melanchthons Werke in Auswahl.* Edited by Robert Stupperich. 7 vols. in 9 parts. Gütersloh: C. Bertelsmann Verlag, 1951-75.

McGrath, Alistair. *Iustitia Dei: A History of the Christian Doctrine of Justification.* 2nd ed. Cambridge: Cambridge University Press, 1998.

Minear, Paul S. *The Obedience of Faith: The Purpose of Paul in the Epistle of Romans.* Studies in Biblical Theology 2/19. London: SCM, 1971.

Moberly, R. W. L. *The Bible, Theology, and Faith: A Study of Abraham and Jesus.* Cambridge: Cambridge University Press, 2000.

Morris, Leon. *The Apostolic Preaching of the Cross.* 3rd rev. ed. Grand Rapids: Eerdmans, 1965.

Murphy-O'Connor, Jerome. *Paul the Writer: His World, His Options, His Skills.* Collegeville, MN: Liturgical Press, 1995.

Murray, John. *Collected Writings of John Murray.* 4 vols. Edinburgh; Carlisle, Pa.: Banner of Truth, 1977.

_____. *The Imputation of Adam's Sin.* Grand Rapids: Eerdmans, 1959. Reprint, Phillipsburg, NJ: Presbyterian and Reformed, n.d.

_____. *Redemption Accomplished and Applied.* Grand Rapids: Eerdmans, 1955.

Oberman, Heiko. *The Harvest of Medieval Theology: Gabriel Biel and Late Medieval Nominalism.* Durham, NC: The Labyrinth Press, 1983.

Oden, Thomas C. *John Wesley's Scriptural Christianity: A Plain Exposition of His Teaching on Christian Doctrine.* Grand Rapids: Zondervan, 1994.

Outler, Albert C, ed. *The Bicentennial Edition of the Works of John Wesley.* Nashville: Abingdon, 1984.

Owen, John. *The Works of John Owen.* Edited by William H. Gould. 17 vols. in 16. London: Johnstone & Hunter, 1850-53; reprint, Edinburgh and Carlisle, PA: Banner of Truth Trust, 1965–1968.

Pate, Marvin, C. *Adam Christology as the Exegetical and Theological Substructure of 2 Corinthians 4:7-5:21.* Lanham, MD: University Press of America, 1991.

Pelikan, Jaroslav. *The Christian Tradition: A History of the Development of Doctrine.* 4 vols. Chicago: University of Chicago Press, 1983.

Piper, John. *Counted Righteous in Christ: Should We Abandon the Imputed Righteousness of Christ?* Wheaton: Crossway, 2002.

_____. *The Justification of God: An Exegetical and Theological Study of Romans 9:1-23.* 2nd ed. Grand Rapids: Baker, 1993.

Polhill, John B. *Paul and His Letters.* Nashville: Broadman and Holman, 1999.

Porter, Stanley E. *Idioms of Biblical Greek.* Sheffield: JSOT Press, 1994.

_____. *Καταλλάσσω in Ancient Greek Literature, with Reference to the Pauline Writings.* Vol. 5 of Estudios de Filologia Neotestamentaria. Edited by Juan Mateos. Cordoba, Spain: Ediciones El Almendro, 1994.

_____. *Verbal Aspect in the Greek of the New Testament with Reference to Tense and Mood.* Vol. 1 of Studies in Biblical Greek. Edited by D. A. Carson. New York: Peter Lang, 1989.

Rainbow, Paul R. *The Way of Salvation: The Role of Christian Obedience in Justification.* Paternoster: Milton Keynes, 2005.

Räisänen, Hekki. *Jesus, Paul and Torah: Collected Essays.* Journal for the Study of the New Testament: Supplement Series 43. Sheffield: JSOT Press, 1992.

_____. *Paul and the Law.* Wissenschaftliche Untersuchungen sum Neuen Testament 29. Tübingen: Mohr (Siebeck), 1983/Philadelphia: Fortress, 1986.

Reed, Jeffrey T. *A Discourse Analysis of Philippians: Method and Rhetoric in the Debate Over Literary Integrity.* Journal for the Study of the New Testament: Supplement Series 136. Sheffield: Sheffield Academic Press, 1997.

Reumann, John H. P. "Christology in Phillipians, Especially Chapter 3." In *Anfänge der Christologie,* 131-40. Göttingen: Vandenhoeck & Ruprecht, 1991.

_____. *Righteousness in the New Testament: "Justification" in the United States Lutheran-Roman Catholic Dialogue.* Philadelphia: Fortress; New York: Paulist Press, 1982.

Reymond, Robert. *A New Systematic Theology of the Christian Faith.* Nashville: Thomas Nelson, 1998.

_____. *Paul: Missionary Theologian.* Fearn, Rosshire, Scotland: Christian Focus Publications, 2000.

Ridderbos, Herman. *Paul: An Outline of his Theology.* Translated by John T. de Witt. Grand Rapids: Eerdmans, 1975.

Ritschl, Albrecht. *The Christian Doctrine of Justification and Reconciliation.* Edited by H. R. Mackintosh and A. B. Macaulay. Clifton, NJ: Reference Book Publishers, 1966.

Sanders, E. P. *Paul, the Law, and the Jewish People.* Philadelphia: Fortress, 1983.

_____. *Paul and Palestinian Judaism: A Comparison of Patterns of Religion.* Philadelphia: Fortress, 1977.

Schaff, Philip. *The Creeds of Christendom: With a History and Critical Notes.* 3 vols. 6th ed. New York: Harper and Row; reprint, Grand Rapids: Baker, 1993.

Schlatter, Adolph. *The Theology of the Apostles: The Development of New Testament Theology.* Translated by Andreas Köstenberger. Grand Rapids: Baker, 1999.

Schmid, H. *Gerechitigkeit als Weltordnung.* Beiträge zur evangelischen Theologie 40. Munich: Kaiser, 1968.

Schoeps, H. J. *Paul: The Theology of the Apostle in the Light of Jewish Religious History.* Translated by Harold Knight. Philadelphia: Westminster Press, 1961.

Schreiner, Thomas R. *The Law and Its Fulfillment: A Pauline Theology of the Law.* Grand Rapids: Baker, 1993.

_____. *Paul, Apostle of God's Glory in Christ: A Pauline Theology.* Downers Grove: InterVarsity, 2001.

Seifrid, Mark A. *Christ Our Righteousness: Paul's Theology of Justification.* Downers Grove: InterVarsity, 2001.

Shedd, William G. T. *Dogmatic Theology.* Vol. 2. 2nd ed. New York: Scribners, 1989.

Soderlund, S. K., and N. T. Wright, eds. *Romans and the People of God: Essays in Honor of Gordon D. Fee on the Occasion of His 65th Birthday.* Grand Rapids: Eerdmans, 1999.

Stendahl, Krister. *Paul among Jews and Gentiles and Other Essays.* London: SCM, 1977.

Strong, Augustus. *Systematic Theology.* Philadelphia: Judson Press, 1907.

Stuhlmacher, Peter. *Biblische Theologie des Neuen Testament. Band 1. Grundlegung vom Jesus zu Paulus.* Göttingen: Vanderhoeck & Ruprecht, 1997.

_____. *How to Do Biblical Theology.* Allison Park, Pa.: Pickwick, 1995.

_____. *Reconciliation, Law, and Righteousness.* Translated by Everett Kalin. Philadelphia: Fortress, 1986.

_____. *Revisiting Paul's Doctrine of Justification: A Challenge to the New Perspective.* Downers Grove; Leicester: InterVarsity, 2001.

Thielman, Frank. *The Law and the New Testament: Questions of Continuity.* Companions to the New Testament. New York: Herder & Herder, 1999.

_____. *Paul and the Law: A Contextual Approach.* Downers Grove: InterVarsity, 1994.

Thiselton, Anthony, C. *The Two Horizons: New Testament Hermeneutics and Philosophical Description.* Grand Rapids: Baker; Carlisle, UK: Paternoster, 1980.

Thrall, Margaret E. *Greek Particles in the New Testament: Linguistic and Exegetical Studies.* New Testament Tools and Studies. Leiden: Brill, 1962).

Thucydides. *History of the Peloponneisian War.* Translated by Foster Smith. Loeb Classical Library, vol. 108. New York: G. P. Putnam's Sons, 1919.

Turretin, Francis. *Institutes of Elenctic Theology.* 3 vols. Translated by George Musgrave Giger. Edited by James T. Denison Jr. Phillipsburg, NJ: Presbyterian and Reformed, 1992.

Ursinus, Zacharias. *The Commentary of Dr. Zacharias Ursinus on the Heidelberg Catechism.* Translated by G. W. Willard. Columbus, OH: Scott and Bascom, 1851. Reprint, Phillipsburg, NJ: Presbyterian and Reformed, n.d.

von Rad, Gerhard, *Old Testament Theology.* 2 vols. Translated by D. M. G. Stalker. New York: Harper and Row, 1962.

Vos, Geerhardus. *Biblical Theology Old and New Testaments.* Grand Rapids: Eerdmans, 1948.

_____. *The Eschatology of the Old Testament.* Edited by James T. Dennison Jr. Phillipsburg, NJ: Presbyterian and Reformed, 2001.

_____. *The Pauline Eschatology.* Princeton: Princeton University Press, 1930. Reprint, Phillipsburg, NJ: Presbyterian and Reformed, 1994.

_____. *Redemptive History and Biblical Interpretation: The Shorter Writings of Geerhardus Vos.* Edited by Richard B. Gaffin. Phillipsburg, NJ: Presbyterian and Reformed, 1980.

Waters, Guy Prentiss. *Justification and the New Perspectives on Paul: A Review and Response.* Phillipsburg, NJ: Presbyterian and Reformed, 2004.

Weavers, John William. *Notes on the Greek Text of Genesis.* Society of Biblical Literature Septuagint and Cognate Studies Series 35. Atlanta: Scholars Press, 1993.

Wedderburn, A. J. M. *The Reasons for Romans.* Philadelphia: Fortress, 1991.

Wesley, John. *The Works of John Wesley.* Vol. 5, *Sermons on Several Occasions.* London: Wesleyan Methodist Book Room. Reprint, Grand Rapids: Baker, 1996.

Westerholm, Stephen. *Israel's Law and the Church's Faith: Paul and His Recent Interpreters.* Grand Rapids: Eerdmans, 1988.

_____. *Perspectives Old and New on Paul: The "Lutheran" Paul and his Critics.* Grand Rapids: Eerdmans, 2004.

Williams, Colin W. *John Wesley's Theology Today.* Nashville: Abingdon, 1960.

Witsius, Herman. *The Economy of the Covenants Between God and Man.* Translated by William Crookshank. London: R. Baynes, 1822. Reprint den Dulk Christian Foundation: Kingsburg, Calif., 1990.

Wright, N. T. *The Climax of the Covenant: Christ and the Law in Pauline Theology.* Edinburgh: T & T Clark, 1991; Minneapolis: Fortress, 1993.

_____. *The New Testament and the People of God.* Vol. 1 of *Christian Origins and the Question of God.* Minneapolis: Fortress, 1992.

_____. *The Resurrection of the Son of God.* Vol. 3 of *Christian Origins and the Question of God.* Minneapolis: Fortress, 2003.

_____. *What Saint Paul Really Said: Was Saul of Tarsus the Real Founder of Christianity?* Grand Rapids: Eerdmans, 1997.

Zeisler, J. A. *The Meaning of Righteousness in Paul: A Linguistic and Theological Enquiry.* Cambridge: Cambridge University Press, 1972.

ARTICLES

Baird, William. "Abraham in the New Testament: Tradition and the New Identity." *Interpretation* 42 (1988): 367-79.

Beale, G. K. "The Old Testament Background of Reconciliation in 2 Corinthians 5–7 and Its Bearing on the Literary Problem of 2 Corinthians 6:14–7:1." *New Testament Studies* 35 (1989): 550-81.

Black, Matthew. "The Pauline Doctrine of the Second Adam." *Scottish Journal of Theology* 7 (1954): 170-79.

Byrne, Brendan. "'The Type of the One to Come' (Rom. 5:14): Fate and Responsibility in Romans 5:12-21." *Australian Biblical Review* 36 (1988): 19-30.

Cosgrove, Charles H. "Justification in Paul: A Linguistic and Theological Reflection." *Journal of Biblical Literature* 106 (1987): 653-70.

Cranfield, C. E. B. "Paul's Rhetorical Vision and the Purpose of Romans: Toward a New Understanding." *Novum Testamentum* 32.4 (1990): 317-39.

_____. "St. Paul and the Law." *Scottish Journal of Theology* 17 (1964): 43-68.

_____. "'The Works of the Law' in the Epistle to the Romans." *Journal for the Study of the The New Testament,* 43 (1991): 89-101.

Cranford, Michael. "Abraham in Romans 4: The Father of All Who Believe." *New Testament Studies* 41 (1995): 71-88.

Davies, W. D. "Paul and the Law: Reflections on Pitfalls in Interpretation." In *Paul and Paulinism: Essays in Honour of C. K. Barrett.* Edited by Morna Hooker and S. G. Wilson, 4-16. London: SPCK, 1982.

De Bruyn, Theodore S. "Pelagius' Interpretation of Rom. 5:12-21: Exegesis within the Limits of Polemic." *Toronto Journal of Theology* 4 (1988): 30-43.

DeSilva, David A. "No Confidence in the Flesh: The Meaning and Function of Philippians 3:2-21." *Trinity Journal* 15 (1994): 27-54.

Doughty, Darnell J. "Citizens of Heaven: Philippians 3:2-21." *New Testament Studies* 41 (1995): 102-22.

Dunn, James D. G. "The New Perspective on Paul." *Bulletin of the John Ryland's Library* 65 (1983): 95-122.

Erickson, Richard J. "The Damned and the Justified in Romans 5:12-21: An Analysis of Semantic Structure." In *Discourse Analysis and the New Testament*, ed. Stanley E. Porter and D. A. Carson, 282-307. Sheffield: Sheffield Academic Press, 1999.

Fitzmyer, Joseph A. "The Consecutive Meaning of Εφ' Ω in Romans 5:12." *New Testament Studies* 39 (1993): 321-39.

Garlington, Don B. "The Obedience of Faith in the Letter to the Romans: [Part 3]: The Obedience of Christ and the Obedience of the Christian." *Westminster Theological Journal* 55 (1993): 87-112.

Gaston, Lloyd. "Abraham and the Righteousness of God." *Horizons in Biblical Theology* 2 (1980): 39-68.

Gentry, Peter J. "The System of the Finite Verb in Classical Biblical Hebrew." *Hebrew Studies* 39 (1998): 7-39.

Godet, F. "The Logical Arrangement of Romans V. 15-17." *Expositor* 4.1 (1890): 285-95.

Gundry, Robert. "Grace, Works, and Staying Saved in Paul." *Biblica* 66 (1985): 1-38.

_____. "On Oden's Answer." *Books and Culture* 7 (March/April 2001): 14-15, 39.

_____. "Why I Didn't Endorse 'The Gospel of Jesus Christ: An Evangelical Celebration' . . . even though I wasn't asked to." *Books and Culture* 7 (January/February 2001): 6-9.

Hays, Richard B. "Adam, Israel, Christ." In Romans. Vol. 3 of *Pauline Theology*. ed. by D. M. Hay and E. E. Johnson. Minneapolis: Fortress, 1995.

_____. "Have We Found Abraham to be Our Forefather According to the Flesh? A Reconsideration of Rom 4:1." *Novum Testamentum* 27 (1985): 76-98.

Hofius, Otfried. "Die Adam-Christus-Antithese und das Gesetz: ErwUagungen zu Röm 5:12-21." In *Paul and the Mosaic Law*, 165-206. The Third Durham-Tübingen Research Symposium on Earliest Christianity and Judaism. Tübingen: J. C. B. Mohr (Paul Siebeck): 1996.

Hooker, Morna D. "Adam in Romans 1." In *From Adam to Christ: Essays on Paul*, 73-84. Cambridge: Cambridge University Press, 1990.

_____. "Paul and Covenantal Nomism." In *Paul and Paulinism: Essays in Honour of C. K. Barrett*, ed. Morna Hooker and S. G. Wilson, 47-56. London: SPCK, 1982.

Howard, G. E. "Romans 3:21-31 and the Inclusion of the Gentiles." *Harvard Theological Review* 63 (1970): 223-33.

Kaiser, Otto. "Die Ersten und die Letzten Dinge." *Neue Zeitschrift für systematische Theologie und Religionsphilosophie* 36 (1994): 75-91.

Kertelge, Karl. "The Sin of Adam in the Light of Christ's Redemptive Act According to Romans 5:12-21. *Communio* 18 (1991): 502-13.

Kirby, J. T. "The Syntax of Romans 5:12: A Rhetorical Approach." *New Testament Studies* 33 (1987): 283-86.

Kline, Meredith. "Abraham's Amen." *Westminster Theological Journal*. 31 (1968): 1-11.

_____. "Gospel until the Law: Romans 5:13-14 and the Old Covenant." *Journal of the Evangelical Theological Society* 34 (1991): 433-46.

Johnson, Bo. "Who Reckoned Righteousness to Whom?" *Svensk Exegetisk Årsbok* 51-52 (1986): 108-15.

Johnson, S. Lewis. "Romans 5:12—An Exercise in Exegesis and Theology." In *New Dimensions in New Testament Studies*, ed. Edited by Richard N. Longenecker and Merril C. Tenney, 298-316. Grand Rapids: Zondervan, 1974.

Lyonnet, S. "Le Sens de ἐφ' ᾧ in Rom 5:12 et l'exégèse des Pères Grecs.' *Biblica*, 36 (1955): 436-56.

Mayer, Günter. "Aspekte des Abrahamibildes in der Hellenistisch-Jüdischen Literatur." *Evangelische Theologie* 32 (1972): 118-27.

McLean, Bradley H. "The Absence of Atoning Sacrifice in Paul's Soteriology." *New Testament Studies* 38 (1992): 531-53.

Moberly, R. W. L. "Abraham's Righteousness." In *Studies in the Pentateuch*, 103-30. Supplements to Vetus Testamentum. Vol. 41. Edited by J. A. Emerton. Leiden: Brill, 1990.

Morris, Leon. "The Theme of Romans." *In Apostolic History and the Gospel: Biblical and Historical Essays Presented to F. F. Bruce on His 60th Birthday*. Edited by W. W. Gasque and R. P. Martin, 249-63. Grand Rapids: Eerdmans, 1970.

Moo, Douglas J. "Law, 'Works of the Law,' and Legalism in Paul." *Westminster Theological Journal* 45 (1983): 73-100.

_____. "Paul and the Law in the Last Ten Years." *Scottish Journal of Theology* 40 (1987): 287-307.

Muddiman, J. "Adam, the Type of the One to Come." *Theology* 87 (1984): 101-10.

Oeming, Manfred. "Ist Genesis 15:6 ein für die Anrechnung des Glaubens zur Gerechtigkeit?" *Zeitschrift für altestamentliche Wissenschaft* 95 (1983): 182-97.

Porter, Stanley E. "The Argument of Romans 5: Can a Rhetorical Question Make a Difference?" *Journal of Biblical Literature* 110 (1991): 655-77.

_____. "The Pauline Concept of Original Sin in Light of Rabbinic Background." *Tyndale Bulletin* 41 (1990): 3-30.

Rapinchuk, Mark. "Universal Sin and Salvation in Romans 5:12-21." *Journal of the Evangelical Theological Society* 42 (1999): 427-41.

Reid, Marty L. "A Rhetorical Analysis of Romans 1:1-5:21 with Special Attention Given to the Rhetorical Function of 5:1-21." *Perspectives in Religious Studies* 19 (1992): 255-72.

Robertson, O. Palmer. "Genesis 15:6: New Covenant Expositions of an Old Covenant Text." *Westminster Theological Journal* 42, no 2 (1980): 259-90.

Silva, Moisés. "The Law and Christianity: Dunn's New Synthesis. *Westminster Theological Journal* 53 (1991): 339-53.

_____. "Old Testament in Paul." In *Dictionary of Paul and His Letters*, 630-42. Downers Grove: InterVarsity, 1993.

Soards, Marion L. "The Righteousness of God in the Writings of the Apostle Paul." *Biblical Theology Bulletin* 15 (1985): 104-9.

Strehle, Stephen. "Imputatio Iustitiae: Its Origin in Melanchthon, Its Opposition in Osiander." *Theologische Zeitschrift* 50 (1994): 201-19.

Stuhlmacher, Peter. "Erwägungen zum ontologischen Charakter der kainē ktisis bei Paulus." *Evangelische Theologie* 27 (1967): 1-35.

Weaver, David. "Exegesis of Romans 5:12 among the Greek Fathers and its Implications for the Doctrine of Original Sin: 5th-12th Centuries." *Saint Vladimir's Theological Quarterly* 29 (1985): 231-57.

Wedderburn, A. J. M. "The Theological Structure of Romans 5:12." *New Testament Studies* 19 (1972-73): 339-54.

Williamson, Paul R. "Covenant." In *Dictionary of the Old Testament: Pentateuch*. Edited by T. Desmond Alexander and David W. Baker. Downers Grove: InterVarsity: 139-55.

Whidden, Woodrow H. "Wesley on Imputation: A Truly Reckoned Reality or Antinomian Wreckage?" *Asbury Theological Journal* 52/2 (1997): 63-70.

Wright, N. T. "The Paul of History and the Apostle of Faith." *Tyndale Bulletin* 29 (1978): 61-88.

Youngblood, Ronald. "The Abrahamic Covenant: Conditional or Unconditional?" In *The Living and Active Word of God: Studies in Honor of Samuel J. Schultz*. ed. Morris Inch and Ronald Youngblood, 31-46. Winona Lake, IN: Eisenbrauns, 1983.

DISSERTATIONS AND UNPUBLISHED WRITINGS

Karlberg, Mark Walter. "The Mosaic Covenant and the Concept of Works in Reformed Hermeneutics: A Historical Critical Analysis with Particular Attention to Early Covenant Eschatology." Ph.D. diss., Westminster Theological Seminary, 1980.

Seifrid, Mark A. "Justification by Faith: The Origin and Development of a Central Pauline Theme." Ph.D. diss., Princeton University, 1990.

Person Index